Social Studies
Innovative Approaches for Teachers

Nancy Maynes

Nipissing University

Jennifer Straub

Nipissing University

Pearson Canada
Toronto

Library and Archives Canada Cataloguing in Publication

Maynes, Nancy A.
    Social studies : innovative approaches for teachers / Nancy A.
Maynes, Jennifer M. Straub.

Includes bibliographical references and index.
ISBN 978-0-13-800610-5

    1. Social sciences—Study and teaching (Elementary).   I. Straub, Jennifer M., 1975–
II. Title.

LB1584.M39 2011   372.83'044   C2010-904315-4

ISBN 978-0-13-800610-5

Vice-President, Editorial Director: Gary Bennett
Editor-in-Chief: Ky Pruesse
Editor, Humanities and Social Sciences: Joel Gladstone
Marketing Manager: Loula March
Developmental Editor: Rema Celio
Project Manager: Marissa Lok
Production Editor: Melissa Churchill
Copy Editor: Melissa Churchill
Proofreader: Nancy Mucklow
Compositor: Integra
Photo and Permissions Researcher: Karen Hunter
Art Director: Julia Hall
Cover and Interior Designer: Miriam Blier
Cover Image: Simon Jarratt/Corbis

Photo Credits: p. 2, AP Photo/Anja Niedringhaus/Canadian Press; p. 15,
iStock/Thinkstock; p. 24, Gabe Palmer/Alamy; p. 155, Used by permission of Lori Henry;
p. 306, Toronto Star Archives/GetStock.com; p. 327, Lana/Shutterstock.com; p. 330,
Micheal de Adder/Artizans Entertainment Inc.; p. 337 and p. 345 (all), Kartographie
Huber, Munich, Germany; p. 346 (top), Science Photo Library; p. 346 (bottom), Plantery
Visions Ltd./ Photo Researchers Inc.; p. 359, Mark Holleron/Courtesy of the Canadian
War Museum; p. 378, Rick Eglinton/GetStock.com; p. 431, Stockbyte/Thinkstock.com.

1 2 3 4 5   14 13 12 11 10

Printed and bound in USA.

For John.
—N.M.

For Kristan, Mackenzie, Eriksen, and Ruby.
—J.S.

Brief Contents

Contents

6 The Study of Controversial Issues in Social Studies 129

7 Aboriginal Education within a Canadian Context 155

8 The Methodology of Social Studies: Unit Design 178

Preface

We have designed this book in much the same way that we would want teachers of social studies to approach the design of their courses. We have kept the big ideas that are essential to a strong social studies program at the centre of the curriculum planning process. We have tried to show teachers ways to align the required curriculum (that which is mandated through provincial or territorial guidelines) with the planned or intended curriculum (that which the teacher develops at the classroom level), the actual curriculum (that which is learned by students because of the influence of students' interests, readiness, and developing skills both academically and socially), and the assessed curriculum (that which is given value through marks assigned via many forms of assessment).

This book provides direction for teacher candidates about the use, development, evolution, instruction, and special supports needed as they select resources for the classroom. Each type of resource, both those in the classroom and in the community, requires special consideration by the teacher before students are provided with these resources for learning. Special direction about the use of in-school resources includes the provision of ideas for the effective use of artifacts, fictional text, informational text, photographs, tables, and charts. Specific direction is provided for the use of print resources in both traditional and electronic form.

We have provided many suggestions for teachers who intend to use the community as a resource to enrich the classroom learning experience for students. Ideas for the use of museums, archeological strategies and simulations, cemetery studies, and the people of the community are presented in detail in this book.

All of these strategies that characterize rich and effective instruction in social studies are further supported by a clear conception of strong teaching through both direct and indirect instructional methods. A graphic framework for conceptualizing the elements of instruction, and their most effective interaction, is presented to help teacher candidates understand the instructional options available to support learning.

An extensive development of information about the assessment of social studies is provided in the closing chapters of this book and is referenced throughout the book in relation to learning strategies. Our treatment of assessment owes much to the many researchers, teachers, and writers who have discussed the nature of traditional and authentic assessment in many worthwhile resources. We present assessment as an integral and non-intrusive aspect of the learning that takes place in effective classrooms. Assessment is a function of the teacher's clearly articulated learning goals, along with the students' developing social skills, their strengthening inquiry understanding, and the social justice values that are essential to young learners in our democratic society.

Finally, we maintain a consistent message throughout the book about the value and flexibility of social studies as a medium for teaching. The subject area has the power to support strong student interest if the story aspects of the subject are optimized in teaching it.

Social studies has humanity at its centre. When we teach the subject with that in mind, we choose to highlight the aspects of the program that relate to people and their activities, challenges, choices, hardships, and successes. We have highlighted ways to construct a program of social studies that focuses on the social and supports the evolution of students' values, skills, and knowledge that position them to contribute to, and improve, the global society in which they live.

SUPPLEMENTS

The following supplements are available for downloading on a password-protected section of Pearson Education Canada's online catalogue (vig.pearsoned.ca). Navigate your book's catalogue page to view the list of supplements that are available. Contact your local sales representative for details and access.

Instructor's Manual: This manual is available in PDF format and includes lesson plans for each chapter.

PowerPoint Presentation: The slide presentations complement the material found in the text, highlighting key topics in the chapters.

COURSESMART FOR INSTRUCTORS

CourseSmart goes beyond traditional expectations–providing instant, online access to the textbooks and course materials you need at a lower cost for students. And even as students save money, you can save time and hassle with a digital eTextbook that allows you to search for the most relevant content at the very moment you need it. Whether it's evaluating textbooks or creating lecture notes to help students with difficult concepts, CourseSmart can make life a little easier. See how when you visit **www.coursesmart.com/instructors**.

COURSESMART FOR STUDENTS

CourseSmart goes beyond traditional expectations–providing instant, online access to the textbooks and course materials you need at an average savings of 50%. With instant access from any computer and the ability to search your text, you'll find the content you need quickly, no matter where you are. And with online tools like highlighting and note-taking, you can save time and study efficiently. See all the benefits at **www.coursesmart.com/students**.

PEARSON
mysearchlab

MySearchLab offers extensive help to students with their writing and research project and provides round-the-clock access to credible and reliable source material.

Research Content on MySearchLab includes immediate access to thousands of full-text articles from leading Canadian and international academic journals, and daily news feeds from The Associated Prss. Articles contain the full downloadable text—including abstract and citation information—and can be cut, pasted, emailed, or saved for later use.

Writing MySearchLab also includes a step-by-step tutorial on writing a research paper. Included are sections on planning a research assignment, finding a topic, creating effective notes, and finding source material. Our exclusive online handbook provides grammar and usage support. Pearson SourceCheck™ offers an easy way to detect accidental plagiarism issues, and our exclusive tutorials teach how to avoid them in the future. And MySearchLab also contains AutoCite, which helps to correctly cite sources using MLA, APA, CMS, and CBE documentation styles for both endnotes and bibliographies.

To order this book with MySearchLab access at no extra charge, use ISBN 978-0-13-265688-7.

Take a tour at **www.mysearchlab.com**.

Acknowledgments

We want to thank everyone who went out of their way to answer our questions and provide us with material to write this book. To all those who shared their stories with us and gave us feedback, we offer our most sincerest appreciation and thanks.

We would also like to thank those who reviewed the manuscript at various stages and offered valuable suggestions: Marion Austin, University of Western Ontario; Fred Israels, University of Western Ontario; Lorna McLean, University of Ottawa; and Jim Parsons, University of Alberta.

We would also like to thank Pearson Education for all the support provided us during each stage of the process, particularly, Joel Gladstone, Rema Celio, Marissa Lok, Melissa Churchill, and Nancy Mucklow.

Chapter 1
Social Studies as a Transformative Discipline

Learning Topics

EXAMINING THE ROLE OF SOCIAL STUDIES IN OUR SCHOOLS

The nature of social studies reflects the complexities of what it means to be Canadian, and social studies is a product of that very dialogue and debate.

—*Shields and Ramsay, 2004*

The study of social studies as a school subject in Canada is relatively new. First introduced as an American secondary school subject, the early social studies program in Canada followed the evolution of American education, incorporating much of the American school curriculum in our texts and reference materials (Clark, 2004). However, in the late 1930s, provincial sharing of curriculum ideas, approaches, and professional growth strategies started

Developing a sense of national pride enables students to value what it means to be a Canadian citizen.

evolving in an effort to preserve our Canadian culture and to develop recognizably Canadian processes and products. Curriculum documents for social studies that appeared in various jurisdictions in the late 1930s often reflected similar ideological and pedagogical frameworks, which allowed Canadian social studies to develop a distinct Canadian "flavour."

WHAT IS SOCIAL STUDIES?

Within our school curriculum, social studies is unique in its combination of the perspectives, approaches, and values that permeate the many disciplines that combine to form this area of study. Social studies provides a coordinated vision that draws from the disciplines of anthropology, archeology, economics, geography, environmental studies, history, law, philosophy, political science, psychology, religion, and sociology (see Figure 1.1). Social studies as a discipline is also evolving to include new aspects of space studies, including the study of space geography. Each of these disciplines may be taught by varying the level of sophistication depending on the grade. The impact of each of these disciplines on the development of approaches in social studies as a coordinated discipline is evident in the breadth of curriculum approaches in Canadian classrooms today.

It is through the judicious and informed blend of the perspectives and investigation techniques of these areas of study that we develop a viable and vibrant social studies program.

DEFINING THE STRANDS OR THEMES IN A SOCIAL STUDIES PROGRAM

As teachers of social studies, it is important for us to remember the debt and the limitations of the American influence on the development of this area of study in a Canadian context. While social studies as a multifaceted discipline is an American concept, the application of this framework for study in Canadian schools is a responsibility of Canadian teachers.

Figure 1.1 The Disciplines of Social Studies

Discipline	Is a Study of . . .
Anthropology	Cultural and physical influences on human interaction; the evolution of humans and their culture
Archeology	The culture of the human past examined and interpreted; cultural, environmental, and developmental evidence providing materials for interpretation of the past
Economics	An understanding, explanation, and prediction of patterns of production, acquisition, exchange, and utilization of goods and services
Geography	Environmental and cultural situations and interactions; examination of physical and cultural interactions
Environmental studies	Examination of environmental issues and actions
History	Examination and analysis of events, people, and data to inform interpretations of the past for relevance, accuracy, and predictive value
Law	Examination of the enforced rules of conduct among citizens as informed by the laws, constitutions, legislation, relationships (internally and internationally), and court processes
Philosophy	Aesthetics, knowledge, ethics, and reality examined as they combine to form belief systems and govern behaviour
Political science	Power relationships and their development, use, and influences; observations and analysis of power in operation within political systems
Psychology	Thought and behaviour in humans and animals in various structures and circumstances
Religion	Beliefs and practices relative to supernatural, spiritual, or divine concepts; rituals, roles, and conventions as they influence beliefs and morality of a society
Sociology	The examination of social institutions and their impacts on the individual and the society
Space sciences	The exploration, theories, and technology that enable research beyond planet Earth

While the National Council for Social Studies (NCSS) has developed common curriculum strands for social studies in the United States, efforts to standardize such strands across Canada have yet to gain consensus (Shields and Ramsay, 2004).

It is common, however, for individual provinces and territories to identify focal strands within provincial guidelines. See Figure 1.2 for examples.

Figure 1.2 Sample Guideline Strands in Canadian Provincial and Territorial Social Studies

Ontario	New Brunswick	British Columbia
The Ontario Curriculum Social Studies Grades 1 to 6 (2004)	Foundation for the Atlantic Canada Social Studies Curriculum	Western Canadian Protocol for Collaboration Social Studies
Power and Governance	Citizenship, Power, and Governance	Citizenship and Governance
Interactions and Interdependence	Interdependence People, Place, and Environment	Global Connections
Environment		Global Connections: The Land, People, and Places
Change and Continuity	Time, Continuity, and Change	Time, Continuity, and Change
Culture	Culture and Diversity	Identity, Culture, and Community

Note: This figure clearly identifies the commonalities of the strands across samples of provincial curriculum guidelines. We will provide another view of what an updated version of these strands might be in Chapter 5.

Since issues and concerns in society always reflect the evolution of the society, these strands for social studies programs are changing and need to remain responsive to the cultural context of Canadian education in a complex global environment. As teachers of social studies, one of our roles is to remain current about the issues related to curriculum development and its evolution, so that our students may be the beneficiaries of our ongoing commitment to our own professional learning.

> More recently developed social studies curricula have been influenced by renewed interest in the nature of effective, participatory citizenship, increased recognition that such citizenship is multifaceted, the teaching of history and, to a lesser degree, geography as distinct subjects, and a more explicit focus on human rights and globalization (Shields and Ramsay, 2004, p. 52).

THE EXPANDING ENVIRONMENTS APPROACH TO SOCIAL STUDIES CURRICULUM DEVELOPMENT

The "expanding environments" approach to social studies has been common in both Canada and the United States (McKay & Gibson, 1999). As reflected in the strands of curriculum themes (see Figure 1.2), the student is led to understand the global context by gradually expanding their view of reality and their role in the world by looking first at self, then, in ever widening spheres, their family, their community, province or territory,

Figure 1.3 Expanding Environments Approach to Social Studies

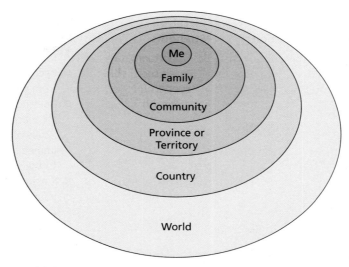

country, then world (see Figure 1.3). This approach allows students to develop deeper understandings of each strand as contexts broaden and issues become more complex.

APPROACHES TO THE STRANDS OF SOCIAL STUDIES

There are four approaches to the strands of social studies (Horton, 1999). Figure 1.4 identifies these and the perceived strengths and weaknesses of each approach. These approaches should not be seen as exclusive of each other, and a combination of these approaches can often be detected in guidelines.

Figure 1.4 Approaches to the Strands of Social Studies

Strands of Social Studies	Explanation	Perceived Strengths	Perceived Limitations
Expanding horizons/ environments	Studies centre on the child, beginning with the child's immediate environment and expanding through space/location and time	■ Moves from concrete to abstract ■ Evolving vision; early experiences are building blocks for later ones ■ Learning is approached through experience as well as intellect	■ New technology challenges the basic assumption that children are unfamiliar with remote environments ■ The sequencing of the expansion of environments can create a grade-bound curriculum

(Continued)

Figure 1.4 (*Continued*)

Strands of Social Studies	Explanation	Perceived Strengths	Perceived Limitations
		■ Opportunities to teach social skills support the approach	■ Topics can become isolated from each other ■ Does not allow for teaching about issues of the most immediate concern to the students ■ It assumes that young children cannot understand abstract concepts related to time and space (e.g., provinces, nations, world, etc.)
Social roles	Studies centre on society organized around common roles that people occupy in their lives; seven common roles are considered (citizen, worker, consumer, family member, friend, member of a social group, and self); roles are considered at each grade	■ Based on the rationale that social studies can contribute to our concept of society by focusing on who we are, what we do, and how these interrelate ■ Roles are relevant to students because they are taught within the context of students' experiences ■ Tries to prepare students for political participation, the economic and social	■ Does not clarify the role of the citizen sufficiently ■ Does not address the importance of the role of citizenship adequately ■ Too focused on the individual rather than on the individual in the role of citizen ■ The seven social roles is a western view that may not apply globally or in the future ■ Tedious repetition may result if examining seven social roles in every grade

Figure 1.4 *(Continued)*

Strands of Social Studies	Explanation	Perceived Strengths	Perceived Limitations
		realities of work, the family, and the marketplace ■ Blends approaches from different curriculum orientations	
Developmental studies	Studies centre on society by tracing common phenomena through time (e.g., democracy, technology, energy, etc.)	■ Provides opportunities for multidisciplinary approaches ■ Broader understandings emerge through the various disciplines ■ Allows us to trace ideas, practices, and inventions through time to understand their interconnected impact ■ Focuses on the idea of continuous flow of change running through time rather than on isolated events and trivia ■ Starts with a familiar contemporary experience and examines changes over time and space	■ Tendency to examine issues over long periods of time causes a loss of perspective ■ Deep understanding is lost when context is not studied closely ■ People are often not given enough prominence in favour of the easier focus on things ■ Program lacks breadth because of too strong a focus on trivial details

(Continued)

Figure 1.4 (*Continued*)

Strands of Social Studies	Explanation	Perceived Strengths	Perceived Limitations
Regional or area studies	Studies centre on society organized around geo-political regions (e.g., North America, Pacific Rim, Middle East, etc.)	■ Can be readily incorporated into the expanding horizons/environments model ■ Manageable geographic chunking is possible ■ Similar geographic spaces are grouped so program approach has cohesiveness ■ Multidisciplinary approach allows for in-depth study of a region ■ Helps students understand that grouped regions have common features historically, geographically, politically, economically, or culturally ■ Helps students understand that regions are made up of both people and place ■ It is simple to organize for study	■ Relationships among people and places are not clearly understood when studies divide the world into small chunks ■ The constant interaction and reciprocal influence of regions on each other is not understood by students ■ Certain global areas of the world may not be treated in their full context ■ Can lead to selective study of dominant portions of the world

Source: Adapted from Horton, T. (2004). Forms of dimension-based strands. In Case and Clark (Eds.), *The Canadian anthology of social studies*. Vancouver, BC: Pacific Educational Press.

PUTTING THE "SOCIAL" INTO SOCIAL STUDIES

Many educators will agree that social studies instruction must go beyond teaching students *what* to be and also provide instruction about *how* to be. Intrapersonal qualities are skills that can be taught and developed in many school contexts but have a particularly applicable role in social studies. Teachers can use stories of historical events to exemplify various desirable qualities. Educators often think of these skills as learning skills or learning-to-learn skills. Among them are skills such as

- active listening;
- active participation;
- conflict resolution;
- cooperation;
- goal setting;
- independence;

- initiative;
- organization;
- problem solving;
- study skills;
- task completion; and
- use of information.

A 2001 Alberta School Boards Association online poll (see www.asba.ab.ca) compiled responses from the public about what they envisioned as the characteristics of a good citizen in Canada. Responses included many of the skills and attitudes listed above, as well as

- compassionate;
- gets along with others;
- goal directed;
- hard working;
- humble;
- kind;

- optimistic;
- patient;
- respectful;
- responsible;
- self-reliant; and
- tolerant.

As educators, we must remember that these skills, regardless of which ones we choose as our foci within our social studies program, must be taught explicitly. We need to teach these social skills as we concurrently address the learning of the content in our subject area. Teaching these learning skills becomes part of how we teach and must define our process of instruction so that students have many opportunities to practise being their best selves as they investigate the social studies content.

SELECTING INSTRUCTIONAL APPROACHES FOR SOCIAL STUDIES

The social studies teacher is faced with many choices when designing instruction for the classroom. In the early primary grades, students' literacy levels will influence the choices made about resources. Their social literacy levels (sometimes referred to as *emotional intelligence*), how they interact with others, will determine the structures, social skills, groupings, and amount of open-endedness of learning tasks.

The effective social studies teacher will recognize that the social literacy skills for productive learning must be taught, in the same way language literacy must be taught, to broaden students' access to resources.

It will also be important to consider the range of approaches that are available. Social studies is interdisciplinary in nature; so too are the strategies available for instruction. The social studies teacher can use the forms of inquiry and the resources that characterize learning in anthropology, archeology, geography, environmental studies, history, law, sociology, and the other disciplines that contribute to the structure of this subject.

The most effective teachers of social studies will recognize the need to adapt approaches to meet the needs of each group of students they teach. It is important to acknowledge the value of sound and reflective teaching practices on the impact and success of your social studies program. By ensuring that we are aware of who the students are and their prior knowledge, we can make effective use of the learning time available in our social studies classrooms.

Instruction in social studies is always evolving. This evolution reflects many social, environmental, political, and economic changes that put pressure on governments and curriculum developers alike to adjust the curriculum and to update it so that what we teach our young social studies learners is reflective of the issues of the day. Updates in our programs ensure that we are current and responsive to a variety of factors that influence this multidisciplinary subject. Factors that can be expected to have a significant impact on our social studies programs in the future include

- science and technology;
- space and ocean explorations;
- cultural interactions;
- communication and transportation improvements worldwide;
- peace initiatives;
- treaty rights;
- genetic research, aging, and evolving concepts of privacy and human dignity;
- sustainability concepts; and
- global stewardship.

In Canada, provincial and territorial authority over education, as defined by the 1867 Constitution Act, creates program differences across provinces and territories. There is no federally mandated social studies program; provinces have autonomy over what is taught and how it should be approached. Much of our history of social studies instruction in Canada is reactionary, responding to studies that challenge approaches based on perceived weaknesses in students' ability to respond to some aspect of their knowledge about their heritage or country. These pressures to develop responsive, inclusive, and wide-reaching curriculum are not likely to disappear. We can address these influences by ensuring that our social studies curricula are designed with clarity of purpose, breadth of approaches, richness

Figure 1.5 Stating Learning Objectives

Objective Stated in Terms of What Teachers Will Teach	Objective Stated in Terms of What Students Will Learn
Have students explore the structure and construction of a medieval castle.	Have students name the materials used to construct a medieval castle and demonstrate through a model how each material was used.

of resources, and attentiveness to the need to differentiate to meet students' needs. By defining our program objectives so that they are stated in terms of what students will learn, rather than in terms of what teachers will teach, we can also ensure that we create programs with internal consistency, reflective of well-understood curriculum orientations (see Figure 1.5).

Some curriculum guidelines refer to objectives as goals, outcomes, or expectations.

THE EXPLICIT AND IMPLICIT CURRICULUM

Specific curriculum goals will help keep the social studies program on track. When goals are specifically stated, they are referred to as explicit goals for instruction. However, teachers also need to be aware of the unwanted intrusion of implicit values that may affect how *our teaching* is received by students. Consider the situation outlined below:

> Grade 4 students are being given their first social studies test. Some of these young students have never written a test before. The teacher hands out the test then tells students they may not talk, must complete all of the work in 30 minutes, and that marks will be deducted for spelling mistakes.

In this scenario, students are learning that the test is a trap, designed to test what they don't know and can't explain quickly. The implicit curriculum, the valuing of speed and correct spelling, has taken precedence over the students' ability to demonstrate what they have learned. Test-taking strategies have not been taught, so students have been set up to produce something less than their best work. Contrast this situation to the following one:

> Grade 4 students have been learning about Canada's provinces and territories. They have interactively developed maps, PowerPoint presentations, and weblinks, to demonstrate their knowledge of the names, locations, capitals cities, and transportation routes within each jurisdiction. Now each group will present their products to the remaining students. Students have been trained to evaluate each group's presentation using a rubric that focuses on the clarity of information provided under the required categories for the knowledge they were to learn.

In this second scenario, there is a match between the explicit and the implicit curriculum. The teacher is evaluating and modelling what the goals for the past lessons have been and has not introduced unexpected or unfamiliar situations or criteria. Consistency between the implicit and explicit expectations in the classroom is a necessary condition for ensuring that students feel they can trust the teacher, and are safe to take learning risks in the classroom.

VALUE SYSTEMS AND THE "EVOLVING" SOCIAL STUDIES CURRICULA

Each province or territory in Canada defines its expected curriculum for each grade level through its curriculum guidelines. It is the role of the teacher to implement each guideline at the classroom level with integrity and respect for the overall focus and intent of the guideline.

A dynamic social studies program will include the examination of values. Social studies educators will address instruction about values in three instances:

1. When we examine an historical or geographic situation that requires a value-laden perspective (e.g., considering a government policy to address homelessness)

2. When we require students to be involved in a simulated experience and take a perspective of another individual (e.g., examining unequal resource distribution that affects the wealth distribution in an area)

3. When we include direct instruction in a value that is commonly held to be of interest in local education (e.g., we promote initiative among our students)

Teaching is not about applying pressure to students to have them adopt our values. Rather, it is about creating inherently value-laden learning environments and supporting students' exploration of their developing values.

Students come to us with attitudes about many issues. These are the products of their earliest experiences and reflect the level of involvement they have had in situations that expose them to controversy or issues. Attitudes are the least stable form of valuing and are easily influenced. As students experience more situations that relate to an issue, their attitudes will evolve and become more solidified, forming beliefs. As beliefs are confirmed by further experience, and students are able to articulate those experiences and what they believe as a result, their core values will become clearer. As social studies teachers, it is our role to create opportunities for students to experience a range of situations, and to provide opportunities for reflection on those experiences, so that students develop positive values that are consistent with a productive, democratic society.

To do this effectively, teachers will benefit from having a structure to support their analysis of the guidelines. Joseph M. Kirman (2008) provides a valuable structure that allows teachers to examine any guideline in social studies and determine how it is treating the main topics that are consistent with this area of study. By adding some aspects to this valuable outline, we offer Figure 1.6 Examining the Guidelines for Values, to direct the inclusion of topics that promote values exploration and instruction in social studies.

There are many online and print resources that provide further direction for strategies to include character and values education in the social studies classroom.

Figure 1.6 Examining the Guidelines for Values

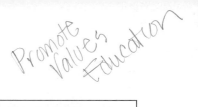

Promote Values Education

Focus Area	Description	Values That May Be Addressed through Study of This Focus Area
Character education and citizenship studies	■ The rights and responsibilities of democratic citizenship	■ Responsibilities ■ Inclusiveness ■ Sharing ■ Fairness
Communication skills	■ Use and application of local and global communication skills through electronic sources	■ Sensitivity ■ Inclusiveness ■ Fairness
Complex skill instruction	■ Data gathering and analysis ■ Comparison ■ Correlation	■ Active listening ■ Inclusiveness ■ Respect for diversity
Critical thinking	■ Data gathering and analysis ■ Problem solving ■ Data-based decision making	■ Sensitivity ■ Impartiality
Economic education	■ Knowledge of, and participation in, the economic structures in our democracy and globally	■ Fairness ■ Frugality ■ Resourcefulness
Environmental and resource management	■ Wise use and stewardship of natural and human resources for the common good	■ Wisdom ■ Resourcefulness ■ Foresight ■ Fairness
Future studies	■ Imaginative and inventive exploration of possibilities	■ Risk-taking ■ Sensitivity ■ Inclusiveness
Global education	■ Awareness of issues outside the sphere of self and the local context	■ Other-awareness ■ Sensitivity ■ Kindness ■ Generosity
Human rights education	■ Balancing personal rights and responsibilities to others	■ Responsible action

(Continued)

Figure 1.6 (*Continued*)

Focus Area	Description	Values That May Be Addressed through Study of This Focus Area
Inclusiveness	■ Respect for human differences ■ Understanding of democratic processes	■ Sensitivity ■ Kindness ■ Responsiveness
Peace education	■ Respect for all life	■ Empathy ■ Trust ■ Integrity
Space studies	■ Exploration of space and potential colonization or resource acquisition	■ Fairness ■ Responsibility
Sustainability and global stewardship	■ Awareness of the limitations of resources ■ Awareness of the impact of resource development on other peoples	■ Responsibility ■ Sharing ■ Fairness
Technological skills	■ Responsible and informed consumer use of technological advances	■ Sensitivity ■ Inclusiveness
Treaty rights education	■ Knowledge of the legal basis for ongoing treaty rights actions by Native peoples	■ Fairness ■ Sensitivity ■ Inclusiveness
Valuing and conflict resolution	■ Ethical behaviour ■ Situational problem solving ■ Criterion-based decision making	■ Ethics ■ Appreciation for diversity ■ Non-violent conflict resolution

PROGRAMMING CHOICES IN SOCIAL STUDIES

When considering how to plan for the most effective primary and junior social studies programs, teachers will make choices that affect how students learn. To do this most effectively, it would benefit both teachers and students to have a clear view of who the learners are, including their strengths and interests. Through early and careful observation, teachers can gather data that will help them design the most effective social studies programs.

By keeping a clear view of what they want students to know and be able to do and value at the end of their unit of study, teachers can ensure that their social studies program achieves the intended outcomes and avoid having the program deteriorate into a series of disconnected activities. Keeping the end goals in sight is often referred to as *backwards design* or *design down* approaches (Wiggins and McTighe, 1998).

Some curriculum literature sets up a false contrast between teacher-directed learning and teacher-guided learning, promoting one approach over the other as the *preferred* approach. Both approaches have value and should be selected for the circumstances and the goals of each learning opportunity. Sometimes modelling a strategy will be the most efficient and effective way for students to learn. At other times, independent or small-group investigation will be the most effective approach. By being aware of how to use both approaches well, transformative teachers have options that allow them to be responsive to students' needs and changing requirements as learning progresses.

Establishing a strong learning environment also requires that teachers consider their options for organizing learning. Students can be taught

- in large groups;
- individually;
- in small, homogeneous groups; or
- in small, heterogeneous groups.

By knowing the goal of each learning experience, teachers can be sure to select the most appropriate grouping arrangement for the goals they have in mind.

Resources in the social studies classroom should be rich and varied. Inquiry approaches require that up-to-date resources are readily available and accessible at many reading levels so they can be used to promote easy comprehension by students with a range of reading abilities. Figure 1.7 outlines potential resources for social studies.

Teachers need to be aware of how to use various strategies in different environments. Small-group instruction is an excellent option for organizing learning.

Figure 1.7 Resources for Social Studies

- Age-appropriate diagramming, graphing, spreadsheet, and word processing software
- Artifacts
- Calculators
- Collections
- Computers
- Costumes and culturally accurate dress samples
- Designated space for ongoing work
- Display boards
- Disposable or digital cameras
- Field trips
- Globes
- GPS units
- Literature
- Local officials (for interviews)
- Magazines
- Maps
- Newspapers
- Photographs
- Reference texts
- Samples
- Scanners
- Storage containers
- Summaries of conflicting opinions
- Telephone access
- Volunteers

While this list is extensive, it may not be exhaustive. It provides a guide to stress the importance of enriching the program by providing students with easy and unencumbered access to the resources that will facilitate their learning.

Volunteers represent a resource that is often underutilized. Volunteers can come to the classroom from many avenues; parents, grandparents, high school students, community members, and other adults can be an invaluable source of support in a busy classroom. When they have clearly defined roles and respectful tasks while they are with students, volunteers feel fulfilled and inclined to return to share their particular expertise. Consider the use of volunteers in the classroom to supervise individual or small-group excursions related to an inquiry that engages the individual or group. All field trips don't need to be class field trips. Junior level students can be taught to organize their own field trips to benefit an area of study that differs from that of the rest of the class. Chapter 15 will address planning field trips in more detail.

REFLECTIVE PRACTICE FOR PROFESSIONAL LEARNERS IN THE TEACHING PROFESSION

Follow effective action with quiet reflection. From the quiet reflection will come even more effective action.

—*James Levin*

Teaching effectively is about continuously learning how to improve instruction. Improving instruction means changing what you do so that student success is increased.

Changing so that the student success is increased.

Respectful tasks — appropriate to cognitive constructivism & social constructivism [handwritten annotation]

By being challenged with respectful tasks that increase students' understanding of central concepts, students' engagement, interest, and effort all become part of the investment they will make in their own learning. Respectful tasks are those that consider the approaches appropriate to cognitive constructivism and social constructivism. Such tasks are sometimes referred to as authentic assessment tasks or "messy" real-world tasks (Wiggins, 1990). Such tasks have many characteristics that make them distinct from other types of assessment. Authentic assessment will be addressed in more detail in Chapters 17 and 18.

Not everything that counts can be counted, and not everything that can be counted, counts.

—*Albert Einstein*

Discussions about reflective practice and concerns about learning standards are parallel discussions. As we address our own learning about the profession of teaching, we focus on the standards of performance we expect from our students. By engaging the practice of examining students' work in detail and determining whether it meets, exceeds, or far exceeds our expectations for what students produce, we are also forced to examine how we get students to improve so that their success in achieving our standards is constantly growing.

By creating a classroom where social studies teaching is responsive to students' needs, well founded in our clearly defined vision of the learner, and reflective of how students learn, we can ensure that our students are well supported in the move toward responsible citizenship in a democratic context.

INNOVATIVE APPROACHES IN YOUR SOCIAL STUDIES CLASSROOM

Every topic has a story line. That story line can be examined by asking a sequence of questions specific to the topic. Students can also be taught to remember this sequence of questions, which would support increasingly sophisticated levels of inquiry through many forms. This sequence of questions is called *topic elaboration* and was the idea of a study group that worked together to develop and refine several forms of inquiry in the 1980s. The group was called the Thinking Skills Consortium and included several university professors from the Ontario Institute for Studies in Education (O.I.S.E.) and Brock University, school board consultants and superintendents, and classroom teachers.

The generic sequence of questions for topic elaboration includes the following:

- What is it?   *"TOPIC ELABORATION"* [handwritten annotation]
- How does it work?
- What are its interesting characteristics?
- How do those characteristics change over time, place, etc.?

w/ series of skills Inquiry skills

- What are those changes related to?
- What would happen if . . . ?
- What could/should/can/will be done about it?

This sequence of questions leads the student from an initial introduction to a topic through several investigations through to informed action. Teachers could teach topic elaboration at a relatively low level, by just having students memorize the series of questions. However, to maximize the ability to undertake sustained inquiry, students could also be taught a series of inquiry skills that relate to each question. We will demonstrate how to teach each inquiry skill in the Innovative Approaches in Your Social Studies Classroom sections found throughout this book.

Each inquiry question elicits one or more inquiry skill that students can be taught to use in many contexts to investigate a topic. The appropriate inquiry skills to match each question are outlined in Figure 1.8.

If we examine the scheme of topic elaboration applied to a social studies topic, such as democratic government, we get a sense of the power of this scheme to guide students' investigations of a topic. An example of how this topic might develop is outlined in Figure 1.9.

The series of questions that are elicited about democratic government provide a very thorough and well-developed sense of the topic "government." The challenge for teachers is to develop very powerful strategies for teaching each of these inquiry skills so that students have control over their learning (metalanguage) and strong strategies for increasing their independence as they learn.

In the sections of each chapter called Innovative Approaches in Your Social Studies Classroom we will demonstrate how to teach each of these inquiry skills and how to combine the use of some of these skills to get even more powerful inquiry happening in the classroom.

Figure 1.8 Inquiry Using Topic Elaboration

Inquiry Question	Inquiry Skill
What is it?	Concept clarification
How does it work?	Model building
What are its interesting characteristics?	Narration
	Description
	Map making
How do those characteristics change over time, place, etc.?	Comparison
What are those changes related to?	Correlation
What would happen if . . . ?	Causal reasoning
What could/should/can/will be done about it?	Decision making

Figure 1.9 Sample Inquiry Using Topic Elaboration

	Topic: Democratic Government	
Inquiry Question	**Inquiry Skill**	**Inquiry Question Applied to the Topic of Democratic Government**
What is it?	Concept clarification	What is a democratic government?
How does it work?	Model building	How is a democratic government organized?
What are its interesting characteristics?	Narration Description Map making	How does a democratic government get its power? How does a democratic government make laws? Who are the people who have power in a democratic government? What powers does each person have? What area does the democratic government govern?
How do these characteristics change over time, place, etc.?	Comparison	How would a democratic government operate with a party system and without a party system?
What are these changes related to?	Correlation	What pressures from society would cause changes in the structure of a democratic government? What pressures could cause changes in laws? Compensation structures? Senate appointments? Terms?
What would happen if . . . ?	Causal reasoning	What would happen to our democratic government if the party system was changed?
What could/should/ can/will be done about it?	Decision making	Should we change Canada's democratic government system to a non-party structure?

CASE STUDIES AND PROFESSIONAL ACTIVITIES FOR INNOVATION IN SOCIAL STUDIES

The following case studies are designed to help you consider how you will approach social studies planning for your own classroom. After reading the scenario, discuss it with your peers and examine how you would address each of the questions outlined below each scenario.

Ms. Côté's Dilemma

Ms. Côté is a first-year teacher and has just accepted a job teaching a Grade 4/5 combined class in a rural district. She hopes to start her curriculum development for her class by planning the social studies program because she knows she can tie in other subject areas to the story themes in the social studies course. Now that she has the curriculum guidelines for each of the two grades, she is ready to begin planning.

- What should she do first to start her planning?
- How will she ensure that her plans focus on learning, rather than on teaching?
- How will she determine what is expected for these grades in terms of values students should be developing?
- How can Ms. Côté ensure that she is being consistent between what she is planning for activities and what she is requiring that students do to demonstrate their learning?

Ensuring an Inclusive Learning Environment

Mr. Mattiazzi is starting to develop daily plans for his Grade 2 social studies course. His school is in a large multicultural city, and his students represent 19 different cultural backgrounds. He wants to make sure that his program for social studies stresses the concept of inclusiveness.

- How will he define inclusiveness for this group of students?
- What strategies could you suggest to help young children understand that inclusiveness means more than just letting everyone play together?
- How can Mr. Mattiazzi go about soliciting support from his diverse parent community to aid his efforts to teach this concept?
- How would you suggest that Mr. Mattiazzi respond to the parent who says that the school has no business trying to teach her child values . . . that's his job as a parent?

Planning Ahead

During the summer months, the school principal sent an email to all staff members asking each teacher to lay out their budget requests for social studies resources for the coming year to help them implement the new government guideline. The email directs teachers to identify what resources they already have and what resources they will need school funds to purchase. Mrs. Gervais wants to develop a clear outline that will meet the principal's requirements and her own planning needs.

- Develop a framework that Mrs. Gervais can use to plan her requests and her inventory to meet both her needs and the principal's request.
- List the electronic resources that you think should be available for you as a social studies teacher. Include specific software that you think is applicable to Grade 1–6 social studies classrooms.

CHAPTER REVIEW AND PROFESSIONAL DEVELOPMENT AS A TEACHER

Social studies is a multifaceted discipline. It is not stagnant or fixed; rather it is constantly changing and mirrors the fast-paced nature of the twenty-first century. Effective teachers know they must adapt their teaching to include relevant and up-to-date material that will meet the needs of all their learners so that their students may become well-adjusted and productive members of society. Through flexibility and adaptability teachers will be able to create dynamic social studies programs where various curriculum goals will be met and students will thrive.

- Social studies is relatively new as a subject in Canadian schools.
- Creating social studies curricula that is uniquely Canadian, and independent of American influence, is an ongoing task.
- Social studies is multidisciplinary in nature, drawing its knowledge and techniques of inquiry from many areas of expertise.
- There are major strands or key ideas that focus the specific objectives or expectations for any part of our social studies curriculum.
- Teaching social studies involves teaching appropriate values; character education initiatives are one way to do this.
- Critical thinking is a key skill in social studies and can be applied to the examination of moral dilemmas.
- Cognitive and social constructivism approaches help students make meaning of new experiences.
- Social values and norms evolve and our social studies curriculum needs to remain responsive to their evolution.
- Practising professional reflection is a desirable trait in a teacher and helps us focus our professional improvement efforts.
- The characteristics of transformative instructional strategies that are responsive to cognitive and social constructivism theories will create a dynamic social studies learning environment.
- Backwards design of the curriculum helps us to keep a focused match between what we are intending to teach and how we will ask students to demonstrate that they have learned what was intended.
- Both teacher modelling and directed activity have valuable roles in our classrooms.
- Social studies classrooms need to be resource rich.
- Reflective practice is a professional responsibility that focuses our instructional improvement efforts.

References for Further Reading

Parkay, F., Stanford, B., Vaillancourt, J. P., & Stephens, H. (2009). *Becoming a teacher*. (3rd ed.). Toronto, ON: Pearson Education Canada.

Gibson, S. E. (2009). *Teaching social studies in elementary schools: A constructivist approach*. Toronto, ON: Nelson Education Ltd.

Auger, W. & Rich, S. (2007). *Curriculum theory and methods*. Mississauga, ON: John Wiley and Sons.

Weblinks

Provincial and Territorial Curriculum Guidelines in Canada

Ministries of education across Canada set standards for their provinces and territories by developing and publishing curriculum documents. Curriculum documents characterize what students are taught in elementary schools. They detail the knowledge and skills that students are expected to develop throughout their educational experience.

www.library.mun.ca/cmc/wwwguide.php

Inquiry Models

This site focuses on providing teachers with various inquiry-based frameworks that will foster their students' ability to generate questions and use them to develop their investigations.

http://virtualinquiry.com/inquiry/models.htm

Values Clarification, Moral Dilemma Approaches, and Character Education

The following sites contain resources for teachers to encourage character education and human rights education for the classroom. With lesson plans, and hands-on activities geared for various age groups, teachers will have the materials required to implement a successful character education program.

www.goodcharacter.com

www.safehealthyschools.org/character_education.htm

Constructivism

Creating knowledge for students from their personal experiences takes sound planning from the teacher. The following sites provide support and guidance for teachers as they create classroom programs that foster internalization of new knowledge.

www.sedl.org

http://tip.psychology.org

Reflective Practice

Reflective practice is a process through which teachers can improve their teaching by thinking and re-examining their judgments and beliefs about what it means to "teach" through their own experiences in the classroom.

http://socyberty.com/education/reflective-practice-for-classroom-teachers/

www.nipissingu.ca/oar

www.infed.org/thinkers/et-schon.htm

www.ericdigests.org/2001-3/reflective.htm

Backwards Design

The Backward Design model is rooted in the planning of curriculum with the end in mind, instead of traditional planning, where teachers begin planning for interesting activities and then focus on meeting expectations.

http://digitalliteracy.mwg.org/curriculum/process.html

Modelling (also see references to "direct instruction")

Direct instruction provides carefully scripted and planned lessons that are taught explicitly by the teacher. Modeling is a process where the teacher introduces new concepts and performance skills before students have an opportunity to apply the new skills.

www.jefflindsay.com/EducData.shtml

www.teach-nology.com/teachers/methods/models/direct/

Space Geography

These sites explore many space-related topics, including civilian space travel.

www.kidsastronomy.com

www.nasa.gov

Social Studies for Kids

This site is especially geared for primary and junior learners to introduce them to fun activities based on budgets, trade, and the history of money.

www.socialstudiesforkids.com

Economic Lessons for Teachers

Full of lesson plan ideas, this site provides lessons from K-6 about needs and wants, goods and services, and teaches children about the importance of economics.

www.moneyinstructor.com

Environmental Education

This webpage provides numerous links to environmental education websites. Teachers please note that some of the advertisers at the bottom of the page are not suitable for students.

www.webdirectory.com/education/k-12

Chapter 2
Why Theory Matters: Moving From Theory into Praxis

Learning Topics

- Consistency of Approach in the Classroom
- Transmission, Transaction, and Transformation: Three Approaches to Curriculum
- Critical Thinking in Social Studies
- The Role of the Teacher
- Creative and Imaginative Instruction in Social Studies

Teachers play a vital role in ensuring that each lesson taught meets intellectual quality, is relevant to the students, is supported by the classroom environment, and recognizes the diversity of the learners.

Success, not failure

Fun, not fear

Excitement, not boredom

Activity, not passivity

Playfulness, not regimentation

Extensions, not limits

Pattern seeking, not just recognition

Cooperation, not just competition

Surprises, not just routines

Questioning, not just answering

Understanding, not just memorizing

Talking, not just listening

—**Author Unknown**

CONSISTENCY OF APPROACH IN THE CLASSROOM

Educational theory provides us with speculative or conjectural views of how the principles, ideas, and experiences we have as educators work together to help us make informed and reasoned decisions about the operation of our classrooms.

Educational theories come to us from developmental psychologists, behavioural psychologists, cognitive psychologists, constructivists, educational researchers, and brain researchers. Reflective analysis of these theories helps the classroom teacher form reasoned opinions and judgments about what is relevant in a theory to each classroom context. By applying strategies informed by a theory, we have immediate opportunities in our classrooms to determine the ways that theory will mold and shape our practice. This blend of practice informed by theory is called *praxis*.

I am convinced that children learn in more ways than I know how to teach.

—*Reinhart*

"Teachers are ultimately the people whose task it is to work creatively with their students and translate theoretical notions into practice" (Evans and Hundley, 2004). To be able to do this effectively, teachers must have both knowledge and skill. They must be able to absorb, refine, reshape, reject, and apply ideas in their personal context. Their experience allows teachers to make useful applications of ideas that are theoretical in nature. The professional habit of mind, which informs practice through the dual filters of experience and theory, is professional practice.

One framework that attempts to create this professional habit of mind is the Productive Pedagogies approach that originated in Australia (Lingard, Ladwig & Luke, 1998). Productive Pedagogies asks two reflective questions to guide teachers toward effective planning:

1. What classroom practices contribute to increased learning for *all* students?

2. What classroom practices contribute to more equitable learning for *all* students?

Maintaining a focus on the experiences that students have as a result of our actions is the strength of this approach.

Productive Pedagogies is not a strategy or a structure for learning. Rather, it is a systematic way of considering instructional planning choices in an effort to ensure that the final instruction produces active and transformative learning for every student.

Productive Pedagogies provides four dimensions (see Figure 2.1) that teachers can use to ensure that they plan curriculum that addresses the two guiding questions outlined above.

Figure 2.1 Productive Pedagogies: Instructional Planning Choices for Transformative Learning

Dimension	Explanation of the Dimension
1. Intellectual quality	■ Starts with the belief that all students can demonstrate their learning with high quality and attention to standards. ■ Promotes the use of problem solving, higher-order thinking, and constructing personal understanding. ■ Big ideas or enduring understandings are used to shape learning episodes. ■ There is minimal use of transmission to learn new information. ■ Development of metacognitive language (knowing what you know) is central to strong instruction. ■ Talk is a useful strategy to support developing understandings.
2. Relevance	■ The focus of the learning must be significant to the learner outside of the classroom context. ■ Deliberate efforts are made to connect new learning to past experiences. ■ Real issues and real problems are examined.
3. Supportive classroom environment	■ Diversity is respected. ■ A classroom climate of inclusion prevails. ■ Diverse learning needs are addressed. ■ Social and academic supports are used to help all learners succeed. ■ Students know and understand the expected performance criteria for success. ■ Clear direction is provided to support learning. ■ Supports to foster self-direction, metacognition, and metalanguage development are central to instruction.
4. Recognition of difference	■ Individuals are valued. ■ Cultural differences are valued. ■ Non-dominant cultural contributions are recognized and valued. ■ Strategies celebrate the learning traditions of other cultures to support the ethos of a group identity (e.g., narrative).

Productive Pedagogies

increased learning

equitable learning for all students

Universal Design for Instruction

In the Ontario context, planning for the needs of learners has, for many years, focused on how to provide effective instruction for special-needs learners. However, in 2005, the Ontario Ministry of Education released a seminal document called *Education for All*. The focus of this document was on providing a design for instruction that respected the inclusion of special-needs instruction within a broader framework of instruction that would benefit all learners (see Figure 2.2). The model for this instruction was called *Universal Design* and includes the concept of differentiation to meet the learning needs of any student. An updated version of this document, called *Learning for All*, is now in production.

The strength of this model is its clarity in identifying the three ways that teachers could make adjustments to their classroom practices to ensure successful learning for all students (see Figure 2.3). The model identifies possible changes to teaching methods.

The Universal Design model for inclusive instruction is based on three central principles to create differentiation. These principles are adapted from the work of C. A. Tomlinson as discussed in *The Differentiated Classroom: Responding to the Needs of All Learners*. These principles include

- the use of respectful tasks;
- flexible grouping to facilitate learning; and
- ongoing assessment and adjustment.

Figure 2.2 Planning for Inclusion

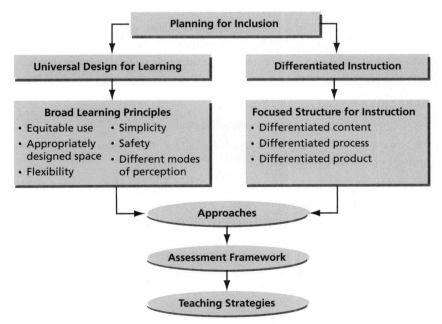

Source: Reprinted with permission of the Ontario Ministry of Education. Education for All (2005).

Figure 2.3 The Elements of Differentiation

Elements of Instruction that Could Be Changed to Meet Learners' Needs	Explanation
Differentiated content	The teacher could change what the student is learning to create a better match between interests, skills, and the curriculum.
Differentiated process	The teacher could change how the student is learning to build skills and approach new learning through preferred learning styles.
Differentiated product	The teacher could change how the student demonstrates their learning by providing options for assessment.

[handwritten margin notes: what, how, demonstrates, authentic instruction]

This model is reflective of the call for "thoughtful instructional choices" (Evans and Hundley, 2004) to promote thinking about curriculum design for social studies in holistic and integrated ways, rather than reflecting approaches that are a collection of all known strategies. Evans and Hundley encourage the use of a framework for effective curriculum design. They feel that the use of planning frameworks can support the teacher's understanding of theory and technical know-how in the design and development of effective instruction.

Other researchers who have worked with social studies curriculum design and delivery have provided guidance for teachers in three notable areas, including authentic instruction, the development of an inquiry-supportive classroom, and the development of culturally inclusive concepts in the classroom culture.

Newmann and Wehlage (2004) promote the use of *authentic instruction* that has three identifying characteristics. In their model, students

- construct meaning and produce knowledge;
- use disciplined inquiry to construct meaning, and
- work toward producing discourse, products, and performances that have value or meaning beyond success in school.

The parallels between the Newmann and Wehlage model and the Productive Pedagogies model are evident in their focus on relevance. Throughout this text, we will provide ideas for teaching disciplined inquiry in the Innovative Approaches in Your Social Studies Classroom section of each chapter.

Evans and Hundley (2004) incorporate ideas from several models to promote the use of inquiry in a supportive classroom environment. The inquiry-supportive classroom will be characterized by

- clarity in direction to students, including clear rules and procedures for how the classroom operates;

- social instruction embedded in lessons;
- social skill development feedback;
- a vision of inclusiveness that pervades the atmosphere of the classroom;
- challenging, respectful learning tasks that create student interest and engagement;
- systematic inclusion of alternative perspectives of the non-dominant cultures in the classroom or the community;
- blocked, flexible timetabling that allows for intense engagement;
- pre-identified and analyzed criteria for success;
- metalanguage instruction to create awareness and self-regulation of learning;
- structured reflection (in action and on action); and
- valuing and profiling of responsive and responsible action.

These characteristics create an environment for learning that is focused, embedded, and enriched.

Evans and Hundley also provide us with clarity about their view of cultural inclusion in the classroom. Again, through analysis of the work of other writers and researchers, they provide a vision of cultural inclusion that respects

- cultural knowledge—knowing what other cultures are about creates understanding of them;
- inclusivity—all perspectives are welcomed and encouraged, and perspectives of non-dominant cultures are sought;
- narrative—cultural traditions embedded in story are used in classroom investigations to create a climate of inclusiveness;
- group identity—teachers work toward creating connections that allow for productivity and inclusion of all perspectives within the classroom group; and
- active citizenship—students engage in learning tasks that extend their involvement beyond the classroom to investigate real issues and take action.

culturally
inclusive

embedded
in story

real
issues
take action

TRANSMISSION, TRANSACTION, AND TRANSFORMATION: THREE APPROACHES TO CURRICULUM

John P. Miller first introduced the notion of curriculum orientations to study the various assumptions and beliefs teachers hold, whether consciously or unconsciously, about how curriculum should be planned and taught. He called the three orientations transmission, transaction, and transformation.

The transformation approach to authentic instruction, inquiry, and cultural inclusion is reflective of beliefs about holism and holistic orientations to curriculum. Miller compared three orientations to curriculum and espoused a holistic approach in support of

Figure 2.4 Background to Curriculum Orientations: How Do We Know?

Atomism	Pragmatism	Holism
Reality is seen through materialism and the properties of bodies.	The universe is in process; all things are changing.	There is an interconnectedness of reality and a fundamental unity in the universe.
Reality can be reduced to logical components or atoms.	Experimental science is the best model for interpreting experience.	There is an ultimate connection between the individual's inner self and the unity of the universe.
We know through our senses.	Hypotheses tested by experience constitute the best form of knowledge.	To see the unity of the universe, we need to cultivate our intuition.
Empiricism can be used to develop a technology to control our behaviour and the environment.	The scientific method in the form of reflective intelligence should be applied to social experience.	Value is derived from seeing and realizing the interconnectedness of reality.
It is possible to control inquiry from a value-neutral perspective.	Values from a pragmatic perspective arise from particular contexts and consequences.	Realizing the interconnectedness of the universe and humans leads to social activity that is designed to counter human injustice and suffering.

Source: Adapted from J. P. Miller, *The Holistic Curriculum*, pp. 10–23.

its potential to make learning meaningful. Holistic approaches are a central tenant of constructivism, where students are engaged in learning actions that help them construct relevant knowledge (see Figure 2.4).

From the work of Miller, we derive alternative views of curriculum orientations that examine curriculum implementation by considering differences in the role of the teacher in relation to learning.

Teachers will find it useful to approach curriculum implementation from all three of these orientations, depending on what is being focused on as the desired learning at that point in the instruction.

Transmission—The teacher is the teller. Curriculum knowledge is delivered. This might be the approach used if a skill, such as how to read informational text, is being modelled or facts are being explained.

Transaction—The teacher guides practice of a skill after demonstrating it. Corrections are included to ensure students' success. Interaction between the teacher and student is ongoing and responsive to the students' developing understanding.

Transformation—The teacher is a guide. Students explore, inquire, investigate, and construct meaning. Transformational approaches are synonymous with constructivism. Meaning is made and reality and knowledge are subjective to the perspective of the learner. This transformational view of the curriculum is what Miller refers to as the holistic approach to curriculum.

Holism and Constructivism

It would be very easy for teachers to become confused about how holism and constructivism are similar and different. They appear to offer two terms for the same approach to curriculum.

Constructivist views of learning first surfaced in 1916 with the work of John Dewey, who explained that "education is a constant reorganization or reconstructing of experience." Similar approaches to thinking about the nature of learning were supported by the Swiss biologist Jean Piaget in the 1920s and 1930s and also by the Russian psychologist Lev Vygotsky in the same period. The works of both Piaget and Vygotsky remained relatively unknown until English translations of their works became available from the original French and Russian versions in the 1950s and 1960s (Slavin, 2000). Piaget first used the term "constructivism" to describe his theory of knowledge acquisition in young children. Since his theory focused on how children learned in interaction with their environment, Piaget also called his theory "interactionism." Piaget hypothesized that patterns of behaviour were evidence of thinking and the development of thinking schemes. From this conception, we derive our current concept of developing learning *schema*, or cognitive structures whereby learners build their understandings by either adding to or changing (assimilating or accommodating) existing schema.

At approximately the same time period, both Piaget and Vygotsky developed comparable views of how schema developed through the processes of assimilation or accommodation. Piaget approached the theory as a biologist, seeing the biological organism interacting with its environment. Vygotsky's approach was that of a psychologist, explaining mental structures in evolution. Both theorists felt that learning occurred when the learner faced situations that caused surprise or disequilibrium in their understanding. The resolution of this understanding is learning.

Piaget's theory provided the basis for our current view of constructivism, which is directly attributed to Jerome Bruner. Bruner used this concept to describe learning theories in the 1950s and 1960s. Bruner expanded this theory in two texts: *The Process of Education* (1960) and *Toward a Theory of Instruction* (1966).

An analysis of the contributions of these earlier works led to the development of a definition of constructivism that focuses on the process of the individual making meaning from experience as students learn.

Constructivism is the educational philosophy that learners must individually discover and transform complex information if they are to make it their own.

—Slavin, 2000

In 1992, D. H. Jonassen proposed a link between our approach to, or philosophy of, learning and the level of thinking needed to acquire new learning. Jonassen proposed that we consider levels of tasks for learning that could be viewed on a continuum.

Drill and Practice   Less Well Structured Tasks   Expertise Requiring Critical Thinking

Jonassen also proposed that these task levels could equate to Benjamin Bloom's levels of cognitive thinking in the following manner (see Figure 2.5):

Figure 2.5 Correspondence between Instruction and Levels of Thinking

Learning Continuum (Jonassen, 1992)	Corresponding Levels of Bloom's Cognitive Taxonomy
Drill and practice	Knowledge
	Comprehension
Less well structured learning acquired through apprenticeship and coaching (skill based)	Application Analysis
Expertise requiring critical thinking; learners rely on their own experience; become self-directed, critical thinkers	Synthesis/creativity Evaluation

We will focus on learning more about Bloom's ideas about cognition in later chapters.

The correspondence between Miller's Curriculum Orientations and Jonassen's Learning Continuum is striking. To apply Miller's terminology, Jonassen is suggesting that appropriate instruction for lower-level tasks could be achieved using transmission approaches. Mid-level tasks that require coaching or apprenticeship support to achieve skill acquisition can be achieved through transactional methods. Higher-level tasks, requiring synthesis and evaluation from the learner for them to make meaning of the experience, require transformational approaches where opportunities for structured experience, assimilation or accommodation, and reflection to create a meta-language connection, are provided. The question of instructional approach, in Jonassen's model, becomes a question of which approach to use at what time rather than a question of which approach to use in every situation.

To restructure the chart above to account for a blend of Miller's view of Curriculum Orientations, Bloom's model of a cognitive taxonomy of thinking levels, and Jonassen's model of approaches for a learning continuum, we present Figure 2.6, on the following page.

Some educators ascribe to relatively prescriptive methods of designing instruction that uses constructivist approaches. Gagnon and Colley (2001) present a six-step approach to constructivist teaching that directs facilitators to design learning that attends to these requirements:

■ Situation—The facilitator explains the goals of the activity and how students should develop their own opinions.

■ Groupings—The facilitator groups students for learning and sorts corresponding learning materials.

Figure 2.6 Matching Curriculum Orientations with Levels of Thinking

Curriculum Orientations (Miller, 1988)	Learning Continuum (Jonassen, 1992)	Corresponding Levels of Bloom's Cognitive Taxonomy
Transmission	Drill and practice	Knowledge
Transaction	Less well structured learning acquired through apprenticeship and coaching (skill based)	Comprehension Application Analysis
Transformation	Expertise requiring critical thinking; learners rely on their own experience; become self-directed, critical thinkers	Synthesis/creativity Evaluation

- Bridge—Students make use of their prior knowledge (activate prior knowledge) to inform new experience; students are presented with an introductory problem to solve or consider.

- Questions—The facilitator uses questions to guide and support critical thinking and metacognitive skill development, helps students ponder implications, and considers applications to a variety of contexts.

- Exhibit—Learners work actively and collaboratively to acquire deep understanding; they follow a process and may produce a product to demonstrate their learning.

- Reflection—Learners reflect on the learning process to learn from their experience and from the experience of other students; reflective language is developed to help learners access new learning in other contexts as appropriate.

The work of J. P. Miller, D. H. Jonassen, Benjamin Bloom, and Gagnon and Colley contribute to our understanding of how and when constructivist approaches are most effective to facilitate learning.

We offer the view that constructivism is a valuable approach to learning, but not the only approach we should consider for teaching. Instead, we propose the concept of *situational constructivism*. Situational constructivism is the philosophy of learning that promotes the appropriate and selective application of a teaching approach to reflect the intent of the learning goal or expectation. This approach will foster the most efficient and effective use of classroom time and effort on behalf of both teacher and learners.

Curriculum development is a complex professional skill, requiring teachers to consider the many interrelated aspects of curriculum, learning, and learner. One's belief and understandings about curriculum, the subject being taught, teaching and learning, characteristics of learners, the learning context(s), self, and how these factors interact are cited as important factors influencing one's instructional choices, and subsequently, one's impact.

Our best social studies teaching will be responsive to the complexities of curriculum design (see Figure 2.7).

Figure 2.7 The Complexities of Curriculum Development

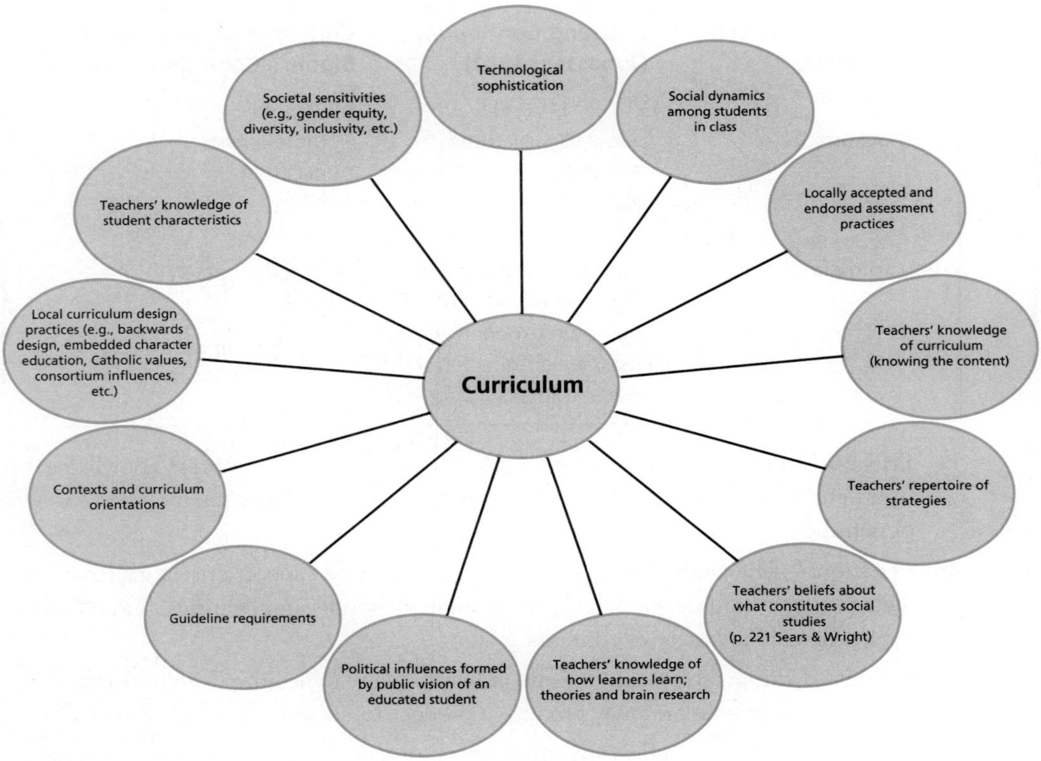

This selective approach to the way we deliver curriculum experiences for students is supported in the recent work of Evans and Hundey (2004) as well.

CRITICAL THINKING IN SOCIAL STUDIES

How we design and deliver curriculum in our classrooms is subject to many influences. A central consideration for curriculum development and delivery is to match *what* we teach with *how* we teach. These should be congruent. Bennett and Rolheiser (2001) refer to this as *instructional intelligence*.

Evans and Hundey (2004) observe that:

> A variety of educators and educational researchers offer a range of substantive evidence-informed instructional approaches that closely align instructional purposes and practices and attend to deep understanding. Underpinning these works is a sense that instruction has become increasingly complex and ought to be approached in a way that respects the relations between its elements: the teacher, the classroom or other contexts, content, the view of learning, and learning about learning.

Figure 2.8 Sample of Instructional Practices Referenced in Curriculum Guidelines

- Analytical shaping (making mental models)
- Binary opposites identification and exploration
- Case-based learning
- Community-based learning
- Constructing models
- Cooperative learning strategies and structures
- Critical challenges
- Ethical reasoning
- Experiential learning and service learning
- Informed decision making
- Internalizing through practice
- Internet-based inquiries
- Metaphors
- Mythical planning frameworks
- Public information exhibits
- Public issue research projects
- Role playing
- Simulations
- Story models
- Web searches
- Youth forums

Many provincial and territorial curriculum guidelines provide samples of instructional strategies as examples to point to the desired tone of instruction (see Figure 2.8).

While the list of strategies for instruction is virtually endless, those that are most valued in an effective social studies classroom will promote deepened conceptual understanding. New teachers enter the profession with a broader awareness of instructional possibilities than those taught to previous generations of their colleagues. It is an ever-present challenge for teachers to consider the sometimes conflicting messages of official curriculum goals and expectations that are provided in provincial or territorial guidelines, and the information about what constitutes the most powerful and effective forms of instruction that is evident from instructional research.

Deepened conceptual understanding will be the product of a range of enriched and sophisticated approaches that have, at their centre, a respect for and valuing of critical thinking. These strategies will encourage and facilitate " . . . deepened conceptual understanding; substantive public-issue investigation, from the local to the global; critical judgment and communication; building capacity for personal and interpersonal understanding; providing for community involvement and political participation" (Evans and Hundey, 2004, p. 219). The challenge for primary and junior division social studies teachers will be to provide this substantive approach to their curriculum in age-appropriate and meaningful contexts.

To retain the strength and integrity of an academically challenging and meaningful social studies program, teachers and curriculum developers must understand the concept of *critical thinking*. Critical thinking should be a central component of instructional goals and approaches for any age group of students. Critical thinking defines the quality of the thinking and is fundamental to the nature of social studies as a discipline. It is not, in itself, a single strategy, but rather a way of managing the acquisition and consideration of knowledge in the classroom.

Five elements of critical thinking are offered by Evans and Hundey (2004, p. 230). These elements define the habits of mind essential for an environment supportive of critical thinking in a social studies context.

1. Knowledge is not fixed, but always subject to re-examination and change.
2. There is no question that cannot, or should not, be asked.
3. Awareness of and empathy for alternative world views is essential.
4. There is a need for tolerance of ambiguity.
5. There is a need for a skeptical attitude toward text.

To this list of critical thinking elements, we would add the need to provide expert learner structures and strategies to the classroom environment so that students learn the skills that promote the development of their critical-thinking abilities. The teacher, as the expert learner in the classroom context, can model, scaffold, and promote practice of these skills with young learners.

> If you don't know where you're going, it is difficult to select a suitable means for getting there . . . Instructors simply function in a fog of their own making unless they know what they want their students to accomplish as a result of their instruction. (Mager, 1984).

Analyzing the characteristics of a learning environment that fosters critical thinking leads us to define critical thinking as habits of mind that cause a learner to systematically consider, analyze, question, investigate, and promote action in a productive, safe, and socially responsible manner.

To create a classroom where critical thinking is the norm and becomes part of the ethos of the learning environment, teachers need to attend to many elements of the physical environment of the classroom and the systematic planning of their social studies curriculum.

Instructional elements to develop a critical-thinking classroom include

■ promoting cooperative talk among students;

■ teaching social skills so that learning time is respected in a culture of inclusiveness and regard for differences of opinion;

■ teaching students to ask questions (see Figure 2.9);

■ teaching the difference between open-ended (deep) questions, and closed (factual) questions;

■ modelling critical thinking in your own approach to events;

■ structuring tasks that require cooperative problem solving and critical analysis with multi-variant dilemmas;

■ infusing daily learning with ambiguous thinking challenges that require "messy" analysis;

Figure 2.9 Question Stems that Students Can Learn

What is . . . ?	What can . . . ?	What will . . . ?
Where/when is . . . ?	Where/when can . . . ?	Where/when will . . . ?
Which is . . . ?	Which can . . . ?	Which will . . . ?
Who is . . . ?	Who can . . . ?	Who will . . . ?
Why is . . . ?	Why can . . . ?	Why will . . . ?
How is . . . ?	How can..?	How will . . . ?
What did . . . ?	What would . . . ?	What might . . . ?
Where/when did . . . ?	Where/when would . . . ?	Where/when might . . . ?
Which did . . . ?	Which would . . . ?	Which might . . . ?
Who did?	Who would . . . ?	Who might . . . ?
Why did . . . ?	Why would . . . ?	Why might . . . ?
How did . . . ?	How would . . . ?	How might . . . ?

- modelling your own approaches to "messy" challenges;
- using meta-language to create awareness of critical-thinking strategies;
- teaching students to identify and apply criteria to their analysis of tasks that require critical thinking;
- teaching students how to acquire background knowledge so they pursue informed investigations;
- teaching investigation skills and thinking strategies;
- teaching students to self-assess and to analyze their strategies for efficacy and effectiveness;
- teaching students how to identify implicit and explicit criteria;
- teaching students that to think critically is to consider both the quality and the processes they apply to situations; and
- teaching students to be critical listeners and to challenge non-critical thinking in respectful and productive ways.

Classrooms will vary in the intensity of their use of critical-thinking approaches. Initially, teachers may provide isolated critical-thinking experiences or events in their social studies programs. As success breeds success, more opportunities may be included, until the curriculum becomes infused with critical thinking. The process might look something like this:

1. Isolated use of critical thinking (a single, "trial" event)
2. Integrated use of critical thinking (an opportunity to try critical-thinking approaches in many contexts)
3. Embedded use of critical thinking (critical thinking becomes a common approach but isolated to a specific subject area)

4. Infused use of critical thinking (critical thinking becomes the accepted "way of being" in all contexts)

As critical thinking becomes more comfortable and familiar to both the teacher and students it will evolve as a way of life in the classroom and become infused into every aspect of how learners engage each other and engage new learning content.

To start the process of creating a classroom learning environment that supports critical thinking, the teacher will need to deconstruct learning opportunities to identify what skills or intellectual tools students will need to support their effective response to challenges that require the students' critical analysis.

THE ROLE OF THE TEACHER

In a critical-thinking classroom, the teacher must be flexible, responsive to the goals of the curriculum, and open to the changing circumstances of students' interests and developing skills.

The teacher will act as guide, model, and facilitator, all in short spans of time. Different students will require different types, levels, and timing of support. Teachers have to expect, plan for, and be responsive to these differing needs to create the classroom environment that will support inquiry and critical thinking.

The teacher's flexible roles can be seen as the following (see Figure 2.10):

Figure 2.10 The Changing Roles of the Teacher

Curriculum Goals	Teacher's Role
Require students to learn facts and memorize ideas	Provide sources; model new learning; organize the drill and practice
Require students to gain new skills as being demonstrated	Provide clear modelling of a new skill, analysis of its strengths and limitations, and consideration of its applicability to new contexts
Require students to engage in "messy" research and analyze issues then draw conclusions	Provide a critical-learning atmosphere and task directions and guidance to structure investigations

By being clear about what teachers are trying to achieve with each lesson, they can ensure the most effective use of different approaches that are part of their repertoire of instruction.

CREATIVE AND IMAGINATIVE INSTRUCTION IN SOCIAL STUDIES

In addition to creating a classroom culture where critical thinking becomes part of the way of life in the classroom, social studies classrooms must be permeated with creative and imaginative habits of thinking and ways of teaching. Since young students cannot experience many of the more abstract or geographically remote foci of interest, the teacher must develop ways to bring this learning into the classroom.

Consider this example:

Example

Two groups of students, one in Ontario, and one in northeast London, England, undertook a project together. They were asked by their respective teachers to investigate local bridges in their city and look for materials and construction techniques that were used. Through webcasting, students were able to share ideas, discuss their study, and examine each other's results.

With the technology available in many classrooms and most schools today, this type of engaging and imaginative approach is easily manageable. The uniqueness of the international link in itself becomes a powerful motivator for students' engagement and deeper research.

Another reason for ensuring that the classroom is imaginative and creative is that many students come to school with deficit background knowledge. If they lack life experience, they lack starting points for learning.

Consider this example:

Example

A teacher wants to teach her students about earthquakes but recognizes that this will be an abstract idea for most of her Grade 2 students. To start the study, she asks students to form two lines facing each other and holding hands. The teacher has asked that the group on the right jump up and down, make lots of noise, and jostle their neighbours to the right. The group on the left will simultaneously jump up and down, make lots of noise, and jostle their neighbours to the left. Since students are holding hands with people opposite them, partners will start to get pushed away from each other in the noise and confusion. After 30 to 40 seconds of this, students can return to a discussion area and list words that describe how they felt during this experience. Words such as "silly," "confused," "crowded," "hot," and "overwhelmed" might be listed. The teacher can then say, "These are some of the feelings that you might have if you were in an earthquake." This approach gets students started into investigations of the topic with a mindset about the abstract idea of "earthquake" that they can draw from to help them make meaning from subsequent learning about earthquakes.

A third reason to use imaginative and creative education approaches in the classroom is that social studies encompasses time spans that students cannot experience firsthand. So we need to create experiences in real time to build links to times past.

Consider this example:

Another example illustrates how creative and imaginative approaches help us to understand abstract or intangible ideas that relate to social studies with the resources and equipment available in an elementary classroom.

Consider this example:

Creative thinking in the classroom is about helping students make connections. These can be mind-body connections, connections over time, connections among students, or connections between abstractions and developing ways to represent them. Just as critical thinking is a way of "being" in relation to the way we think, so too, is creative and imaginative education a way of being in relation to how we teach. Creative and imaginative approaches in the classroom should be encouraged to help students

- create new perspectives;
- examine the outrageous as possible by asking "what if . . . ?" questions;
- extend their abilities to perceive and understand;
- maintain their focus and perseverance;
- maximize input from other learners;
- respect divergence; and
- value non-dominant perspectives.

One effective model of ensuring opportunities to examine issues through a creative or imaginative habit of mind is the Story Model, originally designed by Drake et al. (1992) as a model for developing integrated curriculum.

The Story Model is a curriculum model to promote the examination of implicit values. It uses a five-step approach to examine past practices critically, and contrast them with evolving practices that reflect different values. The five steps of the Story Model are:

1. Identify why the present story is changing or no longer valid.
2. Identify the values that are implicit, and sometimes explicit, in the old story.
3. Explore how the future might be if:
   a) the old story continued unchecked and values did not change; and
   b) the new story (ideal version with all barriers avoided) became true.
4. A new but practical and workable story is then designed to blend the necessary from the old and the desirable from the new.
5. Develop a personal story. This is the action step where the student creates a practical plan to put the new story into action in a manageable way.

An example of an old story is environmental harm caused by large, older, high-maintenance, gas-guzzling cars. The new story evolves into an examination of the environmental and health effects of the overuse of large, inefficient cars. The Story Model can help teachers sequence learning opportunities within a unit to investigate topics in critical and imaginative ways.

Story is at the heart of many topics of study in primary and junior social studies. Because of this, many curriculum developers suggest that curriculum integration start by planning around the main stories inherent in the particular time period or location being studied. This approach opens up many possibilities for the use of creative and imaginative language-based approaches in the study of social studies topics. Fictional text is available to match many social studies topics to support students' creative and imaginative engagement in social studies.

The research of Dr. Kieran Egan and colleagues in the Imaginative Education Research Group at Simon Fraser University in British Columbia is central to our understanding and valuing of creativity and imagination in our instruction. Creative and imaginative opportunities are, in Egan's words, "intellectual activity at its most engaged and energetic" (1989).

Earlier in this chapter we introduced the three elements of curriculum that can be manipulated to allow for differentiation. Each of these elements (the curriculum content, the process used for learning, and the products students create to demonstrate their learning) can be seen as opportunities to infuse the curriculum with creativity and imagination. Choice is key in promoting a classroom environment where creativity and imagination are valued and celebrated.

INNOVATIVE APPROACHES IN YOUR SOCIAL STUDIES CLASSROOM

In this part of Chapter 1 we provided an outline of a plan to use this section of each chapter to give direction for how teachers can use several complex inquiry skills, either alone or in combination, to teach social studies students to engage in inquiry at increasingly complex levels. In this chapter, we will provide direction about the skill of concept clarification.

Concept clarification provides an opportunity for students to examine any word they encounter to make its meaning clear. This approach can be used with either concrete words (those that allow us to form a mental image of an object), or abstract words (those that name qualities or intangibles, such as honesty).

Providing students with the skill of concept clarification will help them in several ways. Students will be able to

- identify what they do know about an idea;
- work with other students to compare their current knowledge to that of their peers and seek expansion or clarification from peers;
- write definitions that are meaningful to them and relevant to the context that is their focus; and
- use the components of a definition to generate criteria for other inquiry tasks.

All of these skills are valuable in an inquiry-oriented, critical-learning environment. The initial stages of learning concept clarification may feel very mechanical and procedure-based. However, as students gain experience with the skill, develop increased comfort with it, and begin to internalize it, they will be able manage and make meaning from the procedure. To start instruction in the skill of concept clarification (see Figure 2.11), teachers need to ensure that students have some experience with the idea in order to create a common understanding. To begin teaching this skill, work with concrete nouns and then move to more abstract concepts once students are familiar with the process. If experience is lacking, the first task is to create common experience.

Figure 2.11 Starting Concept Clarification with a Mind Map

The concept of community is a common concept in primary social studies programs. If the teacher wanted to teach concept clarification using this concept and the primary students did not have many experiences with community, the teacher could

■ take students for a walk in the community;

■ show pictures of buildings in the community;

■ invite guest speakers into the classroom to tell about their role in the community;

■ study community events and participate in some if possible; or

■ build community models.

After creating a common base of experience about community, the teacher is ready to use this example to teach the skill of concept clarification.

1. Start by writing the word "community" in the middle of the blackboard, chart paper, or SMARTboard.

2. Ask students, "What ideas come to mind when you hear the word 'community'?"

3. Print each word or idea that students respond with (brainstorm) around the word "community."

4. Connect all of the ideas that students generate to the word "community" as shown above.

5. Stop the brainstorming process when the generation of ideas slows. This is a good indicator that you are getting uncommon responses from those students who may have broader experience with the concept.

6. Ask students to put the word "community" into a class or group of things. Model how to determine the class of things by providing non-examples. Using your sense of humour with the types of non-examples you supply will help students to understand how to determine the class of things more readily.

Example

Ask "Is 'community' a type of animal?" . . . No
   "Is it a type of drink?" . . . .No
   "What group of things could we say 'community' belongs to?"

If students are initially unable to provide a response such as "a community is an area," provide this example. Students will be able to put other concepts into a class or group more readily once they get some practice.

7. Write "A community is an area" and stop.

8. Ask students to continue the definition by connecting any two ideas in a sentence.

Example

"A community is an area that houses family and friends."

9. Ask "What other ideas could you connect to make another sentence?"

Example

A community is an area that houses family and friends. A community has parks, schools, churches, services, and hospitals that are used by the people who live there. Community helpers serve the community. Communities provide activities, festivals, and special events for people who live in the community.

Most teachers would likely be quite happy to get this as a definition of community from Grade 2 students. Using this process for teaching the skill of concept clarification, this is very possible after just a few examples are used. Students will need opportunities to see this modelled several times and will need both teacher and peer support to develop concept definitions with increasing independence.

Anchoring skills will support skill development. To anchor the skill of concept clarification, the following chart would be helpful for students (see Figure 2.12).

In Chapter 3, we will examine how to teach the inquiry skill of *model building*.

Figure 2.12 Concept Clarification Procedure

1. Name the skill.
2. Write the word in the centre of a page.
3. Brainstorm all of the words and ideas you can think of, related to the main word.
4. Start writing a definition for the word by naming the class of things it is in.
5. Join any two or more ideas from the brainstorming chart and make a sentence.
6. Continue to join ideas and make sentences until all of the ideas on the brainstorming chart have been used.
7. Change the order of the sentences in your definition if necessary.

CASE STUDIES AND PROFESSIONAL ACTIVITIES FOR INNOVATION IN SOCIAL STUDIES

In the pre-service program, teacher candidates can be invited to use technology that enables them to outline abstract concepts. Concept-mapping software programs like SMART Ideas enable students to analyze and understand complex ideas by building multilevel interactive maps. The teacher can lead students through concepts one level at a time for greater clarity, and easily convert their concept maps into a multipage website for everyone to share (www2.smarttech.com/st/en-US/Products/SMART+Ideas/default.htm).

After downloading the SMART Ideas software, present information from a variety of perspectives using the diagram outline, global or presentation views. Encourage creative thinking by integrating interactive images such as clip art, connectors, patterns, and images. Enhance a social studies lesson by creating multilevel maps and multimedia that allow students to explore concepts through the use of engaging visual tools.

CHAPTER REVIEW AND PROFESSIONAL DEVELOPMENT AS A TEACHER

This chapter has examined the following ideas:

- Teachers need curriculum knowledge and skill, or instructional intelligence, to make effective decisions about planning and delivering a strong social studies program.
- Maintaining a focus on the benefits to students as we make program planning choices will strengthen their learning.

- We should focus on four elements of our program as we plan to ensure productive instruction or pedagogy:
  1. Intellectual quality
  2. Supportive classroom environment
  3. Relevance
  4. Recognition of individual student differences
- Universal design is a curriculum design concept that promotes focusing on planning program variations in content, process, and products to create learning success for every student.
- Authentic instruction has three characteristics:
  1. It allows for the construction of meaning.
  2. It uses disciplined inquiry.
  3. It works toward production of learning that has value outside of the school context.
- Curriculum orientations give us three perspectives on the relationship between the learner and the curriculum; these perspectives are called transmission, transaction, and transformation. Transformational approaches are synonymous with constructivist approaches.
- A strategic selection of the most valid approach to achieve each curriculum goal is the most effective way to apply different orientations to curriculum.
- Curriculum guidelines and support documents provide teachers with a range of effective strategies for social studies instruction. Teachers should use the strategy that is the best match for the lesson being taught.
- There are many factors that affect curriculum development.
- Critical thinking is a standard for the way we try to teach students to be analytical, reflective, and skeptical in their examination of resources and issues.
- There are many instructional elements that teachers can implement to support critical thinking instruction in their social studies programs. Research and experience inform these elements.
- The teacher's role changes with each approach or orientation to a learning episode. Teachers must remain flexible and responsive to the need to make these role shifts as learning needs change.
- Creative and imaginative instruction is an important approach for the development of strong social studies learning. Looking for ways to make mind-body connections in our teaching is one way to ensure creative and imaginative approaches are used.
- The story nature of social studies makes it a perfect vehicle for the integration of stories to support students' efforts to make personal meaning.

References for Further Reading

Amosa, W. & S. Cooper. (2006). *Schools matter, teachers matter: Exploring the links between teachers' work, school context, and quality teaching.* Paper presented at the annual meeting of the American Educational Research Association, San Francisco, April 7–11, 2006.

National Research Council Committee on Learning Research and Educational Practice. (2000). HYPERLINK *"http://www.amazon.com/gp/redirect.html?ie=UTF8&location=http%3A%2F%2F www.amazon.com%2FHow-People-Learn-Experience-Expanded%2Fdp%2F03 09070368%3Fie%3DUTF8%26s%3Dbooks%26qid%3D1180561918%26sr%3D1-1&tag=- httpwwwgame05-20&linkCode=ur2&camp=1789&creative=9325"How People Learn: Brain, Mind, Experience, and School: Expanded Edition.* Washington, DC: National Academy Press.

Sawyer, R. K. (Ed.). (2006). *The Cambridge Handbook of the Learning Sciences, Volume One.* Cambridge, NY: Cambridge University Press.

Schunk, D. H. (2007). *Learning Theories: An Educational Perspective* (5th Edition). New York, NY: Prentice Hall.

Weblinks

Many concept-mapping software programs provide live online demonstrations about how to use their software to engage students, encourage creative thinking, and enhance lessons. The demonstration software allows you to see all the major features of the software and have the opportunity to ask questions. Many also offer free trials.

Concept Mapping

SMART Ideas software brings the power of visual learning to your classroom. Students can better analyze and understand complex ideas by building multilevel interactive maps.

www2.smarttech.com

Thinkmap SDK

The Thinkmap SDK enables teachers to incorporate data-driven visualization technology into their lessons.

www.thinkmap.com

CMAP tools

This software empowers users to construct, navigate, share, and criticize knowledge models represented as concept maps.

http://cmap.ihmc.us/conceptmap.html

Inspiration 9 (Grades 6–12)

This software enables visual mapping, outlining, writing, and making presentations. It can help transform diagrams, mind maps, and outlines into polished presentations that communicate ideas clearly and demonstrate understanding and knowledge.

www.inspiration.com

The Concept Mapping Homepage

This concept-mapping site offers engaging information and resources.

http://users.edte.utwente.nl/lanzing/cm_home.htm

Chapter 3
Instructional Approaches for the Young Learner

Learning Topics

- Inquiry Learning in Social Studies
- Introducing Inquiry to Young Children
- Direct Instruction and Effective Modelling
- Activity Centres in a Social Studies Context
- Cooperative Learning in a Social Studies Context
- Independent Learning in a Child-Centred Classroom
- Computer-Facilitated Instruction
- Individual Instruction Options in Social Studies

A student uses a SMARTboard to examine historical photographs from the McCord Museum collection online.

INQUIRY LEARNING IN SOCIAL STUDIES

In the previous chapter we examined the concept of critical thinking as it applies to the social studies program. Critical-thinking considerations ensure that we maintain a focus on the standards of the discipline of social studies. Every discipline has its defining standards. It is helpful before planning a program in detail to be clear about what standards we are promoting within the discipline. In social studies, we might generate a list such as the following to identify the standards of the subject area:

- Consideration of the evidence
- Respect for the traditions of preservation within a culture (e.g., oral tradition, written tradition)
- Respect and consideration of perspectives
- Creation of a balanced perspective
- Respectful participation and productive functioning in a diverse society
- Responsible stewardship of resources
- Tolerance for ambiguity in the pursuit of knowledge
- Respect for the interdependence of people and places
- Appreciation for the nature of field research
- Creation of conceptual frameworks that aid understanding
- Encompassing expanding horizons in our considerations and deliberations
- Understanding fundamental concepts that inform thinking in history and geography (e.g., environment, culture, change, continuity)
- Clear communication
- Informed decision making
- Critical thinking
- Dynamic and informative inquiry

This list is not exhaustive. However, it does give an overview of some of the standards that permeate substantial programs designed within the discipline.

Dynamic and informative inquiry is both a standard and a strategy for social studies programs. Inquiry is a constructivist approach, defined as the belief that "understanding is constructed in the process of people working and conversing together as they pose and solve the problems, make discoveries, and rigorously test the discoveries that arise in the course of shared activity" (retrieved from www.galileo.org/inquiry-what.html; accessed January 19, 2009).

There are many reasons for ensuring that inquiry approaches are central to the strategies and culture in a social studies program:

- Facts change.
- Information is readily available.
- Our knowledge base is constantly increasing so knowing everything is not possible.

■ Since we cannot retain all knowledge, learning to be discerning consumers of knowledge is a desirable characteristic of an educated person.

Inquiry learning allows teachers to structure learning so that students can get and make sense out of large amounts of data. Students' involvement leads to deep understanding. Inquiry guides the development of skills and attitudes that permit students to resolve issues and questions that reflect their current level of understanding, in a reflective context. Students are shown how to convert information and raw data into useful knowledge and connections.

The content of inquiry needs to be engaging for students, involve serious investigation, and inform activity that promotes both the creation and testing of new knowledge against the standards of the discipline.

Models for this type of inquiry can be constructed to provide a visual representation of the process of inquiry for both the teacher and students to use as a reference and guide. In the classroom, this model could become an anchor chart that is posted for reminders and reference each time students engage in inquiry.

This model reflects a combination of what we know about how learners expand and retain their knowledge and create sustainable action (see Figure 3.1). The model

Figure 3.1 An Inquiry Model for Social Studies

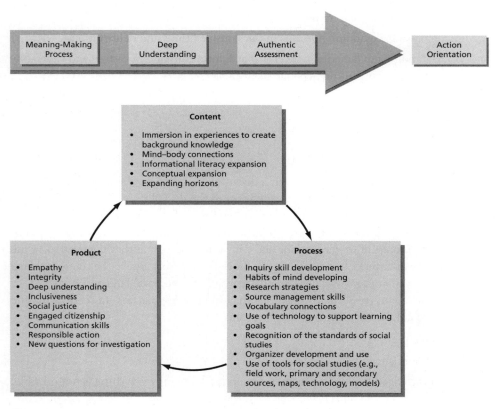

is based on developmental concepts, cognitive theory, constructivist theory, and brain research.

INTRODUCING INQUIRY TO YOUNG CHILDREN

Young children are naturally curious and explore with energy and interest. We can support the strengths of this tendency by inviting and supporting questioning in our social studies classrooms. However, students will also benefit from being taught how to question effectively. See the outline for question stems in Chapter 2.

Strong inquiry will include questions that

- have a context;
- help students to generate a framework for investigation;
- are focused;
- are higher level;
- have specific and contextually limited structure;
- build on the students' need to know;
- are open-ended and resolution oriented;
- foster inquiring attitudes so that they continue to cause students to generate and examine their evolving knowledge; and
- help students expand the boundaries between what is known and understood, to encompass new knowledge and greater inclusiveness.

Habits of mind are the unique perspectives brought to an inquiry from the discipline being studied. The perspectives of social studies focus mainly on history and geography, but may include aspects of art, science, religion, philosophy, etc.

Inquiry shifts the emphasis of instruction from what we know to how we come to know, by asking students to assume the role of reflective investigator. Content interacts with conceptual knowledge, inquiry skill development, and habits of mind. This develops in response to awareness of the standards of the discipline of social studies (see Figure 3.2 on page 52).

Very young students benefit from strong mental images for good questioning as a filter for judging the strength of their questions. Primary students can be taught to ask "fat" questions (see Figures 3.3 and 3.4 on pages 52 and 53). Fat questions would have the characteristics that would lend themselves to discussion, perspective taking, and age-appropriate inquiry.

Thin questions are not bad questions. They are just questions that serve a different purpose, which we should teach students to recognize. They have their place in helping learners to develop the background knowledge they require to undertake sustained inquiry. They provide a starting point for knowledge expansion and deep understanding.

Figure 3.2 The Role of Inquiry in Developing Social Studies Learners

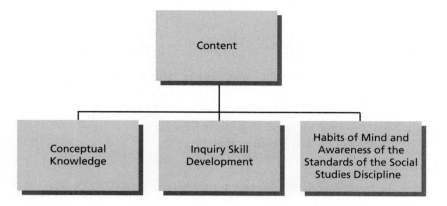

As students mature, they will resist the idea of using "fat" questions. Teachers' terminology for the same concept should "mature" with the students. Clifford and Friesen (2007) refer to these types of inquiry-sustaining questions as *essential questions*. They define essential questions as those that have the following characteristics:

- They arise from people's attempts, throughout human history, to learn more about the world(s) we live in. Essential questions probably intrigued the ancients as much as they puzzle people living today.

- Essential questions are so compelling that people have raised them in many different ways. Essential questions invite perspective to be brought to bear in order to develop deep understanding. For example, the question "What is light?" has scientific, mathematical, aesthetic, literary, and spiritual dimensions.

Figure 3.3 Recognizing Strong ("Fat") Questions

"Fat" Questions	"Thin" Questions
The questions are open-ended.	The questions are closed and have a specific answer.
The questions have ambiguous possibilities as answers.	The questions have clear, definitive answers.
Higher-order thinking is required (analysis, synthesis, creativity, evaluation).	Lower-order thinking will lead to an answer.
Many perspectives can be brought to bear on the question.	One perspective is dominant.
The questions are open to discussion and investigation.	Answers are straightforward and need no investigation.

Figure 3.4 Teaching Using "Fat" Questions

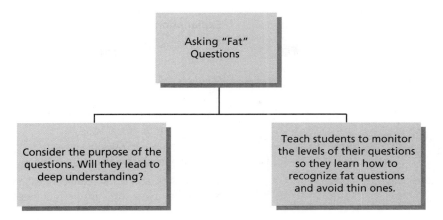

- Attempts to answer essential questions allow people to explore the connection between their personal, individual, unique experience of the world and its exterior, objective, held-in-common dimensions. In exploring essential questions together, people are able to find expression for their own strongest gifts and interests at the same time that they are able to establish a sense of community with others.

- Essential questions allow us to explore what knowledge is, how it came to be, and how it has changed through human history.

- An essential question is always poised at the boundary of the known and the unknown. While permitting fruitful exploration of what others before us have learned and discovered, attempts to answer an essential question open up mysteries that successively reveal themselves the more we come to "know."

- An essential question reaches beyond itself. It is embedded in ideals of freedom, strength, and possibility that permit people to "come to know" without becoming trapped in constructs that are oppressive or no longer useful. Essential questions arise from an implicit commitment to human efficacy—to a belief that individuals can make a difference, that knowledge can both be acquired and changed.

- An essential question engages the imagination in significant ways.

In Chapter 2 we examined several approaches to critical thinking. The Story Model approach uses the essence of essential questions to guide inquiry into deeper learning and understanding through the creation of a "new" story for personal action, based on improved understanding of the issues. This is the basis of good citizenship, a primary goal of studying social studies.

As students are being introduced to inquiry as an approach to learning, they may benefit from using a relatively prescriptive approach to inquiry. Barbara Woods (2001), from the Ministry of Education in New Zealand, promotes a "Knowledge Attack" approach to inquiry that models the use of inquiry steps (see Figure 3.5). In this model, Woods stresses

Figure 3.5 Woods' Model for Inquiry

Inquiry Step	Explanation
1. Knowledge Attack	Students are immersed in the topic to gain background information.
2. Essential Question	Students ask questions that: ■ are at a high level of Bloom's Taxonomy; ■ are relevant to students' lives; ■ can relate to global issues; ■ do not have an obvious answer; and ■ require research and critical thinking.
3. Subsidiary Questions	Students ask additional related questions to provide a base for answering essential questions.
4. Hypothesize	Students analyze their questions and subsidiary questions and group them to relate to each hypothesis.
5. Gather Information/Research	Students examine materials in search of answers. Materials include ■ rich resources; ■ all media Students are taught information literacy skills to support the use of rich resources.
6. Sift and Sort	Students sort answers to subsidiary questions and make collaborative decisions about the relevance of the information they have collected.
7. Synthesize	Students create and use an appropriate mind map or visual organizer for their information.
8. Report	Students assume responsibility for sharing information within a cooperative research group.
9. Answer the Essential Question	Students decide on an answer to their question(s), raise awareness of issues, and take action.

Source: Adapted from Barbara Woods, Ministry of Education, Wellington, New Zealand.

Asking QUESTIONS!

Sort ANSWERS

Visual ORGANIZERS

REPORT

the importance of ensuring that students have a strong knowledge background to help them benefit from the power of an inquiry approach. This model has nine recursive steps.

In the Knowledge Attack model, Woods makes it clear that good inquiry follows good information. Without first being immersed in knowledge about a topic, students cannot hope to engage in meaningful and substantive inquiry about issues related to the topic. In Chapter 2, we referred to this as the strategic and deliberate use of different orientations to teaching.

In the later years of the junior division, teachers may want to develop a more refined approach to inquiry by examining issues through specific filters within the broader realm of inquiry. This approach has been called *critical inquiry pedagogy*. Critical inquiry pedagogy is inquiry with specific foci and includes approaches of equity pedagogy, transformative pedagogy, engaged pedagogy, inquiry pedagogy, and critical theory (see Figure 3.6). Use of this framework would help more mature learners understand some of the social background and pressures related to how they consider issues.

When planning courses, the classroom teacher needs to be clear about the role of inquiry in their social studies program. The use of inquiry as a central program approach is affected by the teacher's beliefs about how students learn most effectively.

CRITICAL INQUIRY PEDAGOGY

Figure 3.6 Critical Inquiry Pedagogy

Pedagogical Approach	Explanation
Equity Pedagogy	Curriculum is adapted to facilitate the successful academic work of students from diverse racial, ethnic, cultural, socio-economic, and gender groups (adapted from Banks, 1995, p. 392).
Transformative Pedagogy	Curriculum examines power relationships implicit or explicit in the society.
Engaged Pedagogy	Curriculum promotes the reexamination of issues from inclusive perspectives (adapted from Hook, 1994).
Inquiry Pedagogy	Students (not teachers) formulate investigative questions, obtain factual information, then build knowledge and deep understanding to address questions; investigations may lead to further inquiry questions (adapted from Fecho, 2000, p. 194)
Critical Theory	Curriculum experiences provide a radical critique of knowledge by considering the situations, systems and structures, relationships, and interests that influence the construction of knowledge; support reflection both in action and on action.

Source: Adapted from www.scribd.com/doc/2897923/Incorporating-Critical-Inquiry-Pedagogy-in-Social-Studies-Curriculum; accessed January 19, 2009.

By examining how expert learners use inquiry, teachers can apply elements of an inquiry approach in the most effective way for the grade and age level of students. In an inquiry classroom environment, the teacher is the expert learner. As the expert learner, the teacher understands the messiness and ambiguity of inquiry as a learning process. Tolerance for the uncertainty of where inquiry in its most powerful forms will take the learner is an essential thing for teachers to understand prior to embarking on learning through inquiry. As the expert learner in the classroom, the teacher does not have to be the teller. Their role is to support the structure of the inquiry so that students come to know, through personal experience, the power of the approach. To do this effectively, teachers need a reflective view of their own contributions and skills.

Teachers should be aware of the following characteristics of themselves as effective adult learners:

■ They see patterns and meanings not apparent to novices.

■ They have in-depth knowledge of their fields.

■ Their knowledge is structured in ways that make it useful and accessible (e.g., they understand the big ideas of the discipline).

■ Their knowledge is structured to be transferable and applicable to a variety of situations.

■ They can retrieve their knowledge easily and learn information from their fields of expertise with little effort because they have structures in place to allow for ready accommodation of new ideas.

Source: Adapted from *How People Learn;* National Research Council, 1999.

By creating an active inquiry environment in their classrooms, teachers are shifting their role from teller of information to facilitator of learning. That does not mean that there is no room or place for modelling during these inquiry times. Teachers should remain responsive to students' needs, and many may need the teacher to guide and even direct their thinking in their early experiences with inquiry. Students' own experience with engaged inquiry will gradually replace the experience of the teacher and allow for more self-direction. When the teacher disengages from the expert learner role too early in the learning process, learning can become inefficient and unfocused.

In the primary and junior divisions, our efforts to provide inquiry-rich learning environments are validated by arrangements that the teacher makes. All arrangements should be made with the intention of supporting the learner. These include

■ performing a clear and purposeful pre-assessment of the learners (What do they know about the topic? What do they want to know? What misconceptions are evident?);

■ preparing an inclusive and respectful classroom culture that values inquiry and is risk tolerant;

■ offering students opportunities for ownership of the learning by asking "Who wants or needs to know or understand this?";

■ using interactive technology;

- providing a range of rich resources at appropriate reading levels;

- working with interrelated and integrated curriculum;

- having a clear view of the teacher's role in instruction (which is suited to the learning goals we have for each learning time block) including facilitation plans for times when students are engaged in inquiry; and

- providing authentic assessment and specific feedback.

Students will come to value those behaviours, habits of mind, and processes that we consistently assess in their learning. We need to ensure that what we assess is always aligned with what we intend for students to learn.

When we create a classroom culture that supports significant inquiry in social studies, we can expect that students will develop stronger information-processing skills, develop better understanding of the habits of mind or unique perspectives of social studies inquiry, expand their content knowledge, and develop stronger conceptual understanding, including an understanding of the interconnectedness of the natural and human world.

DIRECT INSTRUCTION AND EFFECTIVE MODELLING

Direct instruction is a term that has had different meanings in education during the last century. The earliest mention of direct instruction in educational literature referred to the use of scripted lessons. The thinking seemed to be that if every student heard the same lesson input, each student would learn the same things. We now know that better learning results from meeting the needs of the learner.

Recent literature uses the term "direct instruction" as synonymous with teacher modelling and the practice opportunities that follow it (Rosenshine, 1997). It remains the decision of each classroom teacher to decide when modelling should be used as an instructional strategy.

Modelling is beneficial any time students would learn from seeing an expert's thinking and behaviour in action. However, an essential component of modelling is how the teacher moves students from being dependent on his or her modelling for their learning, to being increasingly independent in the use of the knowledge or skills that were modelled. This process of developing increasing independence is often referred to as "gradual release of responsibility" (Pearson & Gallagher, 1983; Campione, 1981). The support that students receive while they are learning to be increasingly independent is called scaffolding (Bruner, 1996; Balaban, 1995), and is one of the central conceptions of constructivist approaches to teaching.

When students are learning through the teacher or other sources of modelling, there are instructional phases that ensure productive modelling and subsequent support are provided. These are often referred to as the "phases of instruction" (see Figure 3.7).

Figure 3.7 The Phases of Instruction

Phase of Instruction	Explanation
Motivation	The teacher gives the students a reason to attend to the modelling by peaking their interest. This may include reminders about previous information about the topic ("surfacing prior knowledge") or by creating a sense of wonder or dissonance ("this doesn't fit").
Modelling of the New Learning	The teacher shows, tells, and explains his or her thinking as he or she takes on the role of mentor to the apprentice students.
Consolidation	The teacher provides very closely monitored practice for students. Students' work is scaffolded and constructive feedback is provided to ensure success.
Application	The teacher provides additional practice in more complex contexts and with greater student independence. Constraints that add pressure to the learning are used to solidify the learning (e.g., time constraints).

Modelling is a valuable form of instruction, especially to demonstrate skills. In social studies, there are many skills taught (see Figure 3.8), and students will benefit from the use of this approach to learn these skills efficiently and effectively. Mastery of these skills provides freedom for the learner to focus on engagement in deeper learning through inquiry.

When using direct instruction for learning, teachers need to ensure that students attain the language that will enable them to recall, reuse, and adapt new skills to new applications. This provides students with meta-language (language to name their skills) and metacognitive awareness (awareness of what they know). That is, because they have mastered the skill and applied language to it, they can more readily retrieve the skill from memory and use it again. An effective lesson conclusion allows teachers to ensure that meta-language and metacognition are developing as expected.

By understanding the phases of instruction (see Figure 3.9 on page 60), teachers can ensure that students have the support needed to acquire new skills and understandings as they engage in new topics.

Figure 3.8 Skills Typically Taught through Primary and Junior Social Studies Programs

- Asking questions
- Comparing
- Creating models
- Determining relevance
- Developing personally relevant definitions for key concepts
- Drawing valid conclusions based on data and/or evidence
- Expressing personal viewpoints
- Identifying issues
- Making connections
- Preparing charts and graphs to present information
- Re-creating/re-enacting
- Relating studies to career opportunities
- Sorting information related to criteria
- Understanding and relating to global issues
- Understanding scale
- Understanding the difference between definitions and examples
- Understanding the role of time in causing change; creating timelines
- Understanding time zones

- Understanding relative positioning
- Understanding cause and effect relationships
- Using bibliographic conventions
- Using drawings to communicate
- Using factual (informational) texts
- Using flow diagrams to illustrate interactions and relationships (e.g., flow of goods and services)
- Using globe skills (including various projections of the world)
- Using graphic organizers
- Using media to communicate
- Using oral presentations to communicate
- Using standard and nonstandard units to measure distance
- Using written notes and descriptions to communicate
- Using illustrations to gather information (charts, pictures, graphs)
- Using primary sources
- Using secondary sources

ACTIVITY CENTRES IN A SOCIAL STUDIES CONTEXT

Teachers will use both direct instruction and inquiry approaches frequently in their social studies classrooms. In addition to these instructional choices, teachers might also elect to use activity centres, cooperative learning strategies and structures, independent learning approaches, computer-facilitated instruction, and individual instruction. These choices all use more indirect forms of teaching but may be equally viable and effective for achievement of the selected expectations. The role of a good teacher is to determine and use the most promising approach for the time and context of the learning.

Figure 3.9 A Graphic Representation of the Phases of Instruction

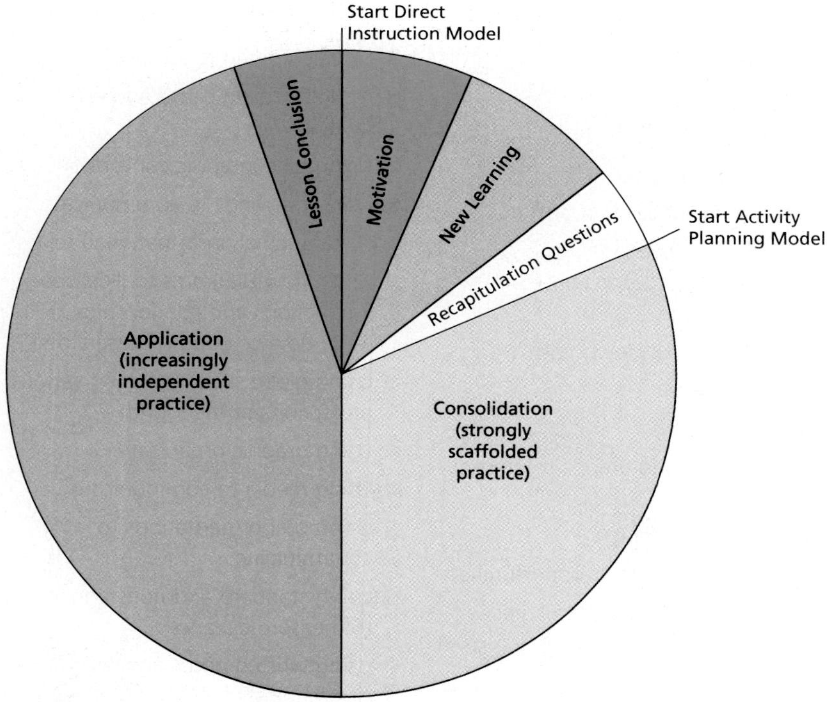

Source: Maynes & Scott, 2009.

Activity centres can serve many purposes in a primary or junior social studies classroom. Activity centres provide

■ a venue for developing background experiences to immerse a student in a concept as the first step toward deeper study through inquiry;

■ practice of a new skill through either consolidation (closely scaffolded) practice or application (increasingly independent) practice;

■ thought-provoking or dissonant experiences that lead to deeper understanding after investigation; and

■ exposure to examples that allow the student to touch, smell, and examine items to create stronger mind-body connections.

Regardless of which of these purposes is selected by the teacher for the use of activity centres in social studies, teachers will need to plan thoroughly for the set-up, maintenance, and safe use of each centre.

Activity centres provide a venue for developing background experiences to immerse a student in a concept as the first step toward deeper study through inquiry.

Students examine, touch, and smell fur samples as they listen to a tape about the role of the fur trade in Canada's early settlement.

Activity centres provide practice of a new skill through either consolidation (closely scaffolded practice) or application (increasingly independent practice).

Students practise the use of different types of maps to find information.

Activity centres provide thought-provoking or dissonant experiences that lead to deeper understanding after investigation.

Students examine a traditional Aboriginal dress through a web-based museum.

COOPERATIVE LEARNING IN A SOCIAL STUDIES CONTEXT

Cooperative learning is an ideal strategy for use in social studies instruction because it provides the social context for students to experience and practise concepts such as power and governance, diversity, and inclusiveness that may be rare opportunities in their school day.

Kagan (1994) developed the theory and characteristics of fully involved cooperative learning lessons and also developed many cooperative learning structures. Cooperative learning structures are strategies that can be used within a lesson to facilitate students' interaction and promote social learning contexts.

Many cooperative learning structures have become part of the repertoire of strategies used by teachers. Jigsaw strategies would be an example. With a jigsaw strategy, the teacher establishes a learning task and divides the content into pieces so that each member of a learning group learns one part and teaches other group members about their part. In return, the other group members teach that student about their parts so that everyone learns about the whole. In order to teach their peers effectively, students learn the information at a deeper level (analysis and synthesis) so they benefit from the time they spend teaching ideas to their peers. Jigsaw is only one of over 50 cooperative structures you could use to support students' learning in your classroom (see Figure 3.16 and Figure 9.7). Resources to help teachers learn more about cooperative structures are included at the end of this chapter and in the bibliography. We encourage you to examine them and learn more about the instructional power of cooperative learning strategies and structures.

INDEPENDENT LEARNING IN A CHILD-CENTRED CLASSROOM

One way to ensure that students receive instruction at the level of their ability and in response to their interests is to provide some opportunities for independent learning in social studies. Teachers can structure independent learning opportunities in small or relatively large blocks of time.

For example, students might become particularly interested in one aspect of pioneer life while studying that topic. A student who developed a particular interest in food preparation and preservation could study that topic independently at the same time that another student extended their learning about early settlers' farm implements. Both studies would lead to a better understanding of early settlement life, through divergent content.

If independent learning is going to be used in the primary or junior classroom context, teachers will need to ensure that

■   a rich variety of suitable reference materials at appropriate reading levels is available for research;

- large blocks of learning time are structured to allow for investigation;
- students are taught research and communication skills (written and oral) to support recording and reporting tasks about their research;
- students understand inquiry;
- students understand and have strategies for accessing common text structures; and
- progress is closely monitored.

Class monitoring posters can support the teacher's efforts to keep track of students while they pursue divergent, independent work (see Figure 3.10).

Figure 3.10 Monitoring Independent Inquiry Steps

Students	Independent Topic	Research Progress Check	Research Progress Check	Research Progress Check
Melissa				
Habib				
Madison				
Grant				

In a social studies classroom, teachers will want to monitor the independent study starting point to ensure that each student's focus encompasses big ideas and the search for deep understanding. Without this focus, there is a risk that time could be spent pursuing trivial and minute facts that fail to support deep understanding.

COMPUTER-FACILITATED INSTRUCTION

The computer is an essential tool for effective and efficient research and communication in a social studies classroom. The range of software programs, accessing capabilities, and virtual tours available through the computer will help teachers to provide information and mind-body experiences for young learners that may not otherwise be possible because of time, cost, or resource limitations.

Teachers can develop web quests and use snipping tools to provide clear direction that students can use to access sites with ease and recognize the correct site by matching paper and electronic photos. Students can create movies, slide presentations, and responses in many formats that include colour, action, and sound. We can anticipate that these capabilities will expand. Many school boards provide one or more in-class computers and, increasingly, mobile laptop labs are available to individualize access.

Teacher-developed web quests can lead students to the use of valuable research sites. There are also many sites that allow students to engage in simulated experiences online.

Web quests are an ideal way for students to navigate purposefully through the Internet, developing their geographic inquiry skills. Sites such as *Where in the World Are You?* (www.edina.k12.mn.us/cornelia/teach/sallyweb/intro.htm) offer clear direction for students to develop their own quest to share with their peers upon completion.

Many computer lab setups in schools include software that allows the teacher to monitor all computers from a single terminal in the lab to ensure safe and appropriate access to web-based resources as students work at separate computers. Web blocking management is also becoming common practice within school boards to block students' access to inappropriate or offensive material. In support of these security features, it is wise for the classroom teacher to address Internet security issues on a regular basis when students use computer sources for their research.

INDIVIDUAL INSTRUCTION OPTIONS IN SOCIAL STUDIES

Social studies programs can be managed at the individual student level as well. To do this, the teacher establishes a framework for study by defining the end product of the study—how students will demonstrate their learning.

Individual instruction has many benefits. Students are able to work at their own pace and pursue topics of personal interest. Their motivation is intrinsic; resulting from personal interest in aspects of a topic, so they tend to stay engaged and work diligently. Differentiation is facilitated by the use of individual instruction. Students are able to pursue their interest in respectful tasks that are inherently engaging to them. With individual instruction, teachers can provide options for what students learn (content) within a framework of the class work, for how students learn (process), and for how students demonstrate what they have learned (product). See Chapter 2 for a review of differentiation.

To promote individual instruction in social studies, the teacher would need to ensure many of the same conditions are characteristic of their planning for independent study. This should include opportunities to work with research and organize ideas using different types of graphic organizers (see Figure 3.11).

Figure 3.11 Graphic Organizers Support Text Structure Understanding

Text Structure	Explanation of Structure	Visual Representation of Structure
Enumeration	A listing of items or ideas specified one after the other	Lists or a sequence of numbers
Time Order	Lists a series of events in time	A timeline or bulleted series

Figure 3.11 *(Continued)*

Text Structure	Explanation of Structure	Visual Representation of Structure
Compare	Describes or explains similarities and differences between two or more things or events	A comparison chart or Venn diagram
Cause(s) and Effect(s)	Explains how events cause other events (effects)	One- or two-way arrows
Problem(s)/ Solution(s)	Explains the development of a problem and one or more solutions to it	Connected bubbles showing relationships or impacts
Description	A characterization of salient features or events intended to create a mental image of something experienced (e.g., a scene, a person, an object, an event)	Mind maps

As well, students should be taught skills for effective independent work and have many supervised opportunities to practise these skills. Inquiry skill mastery is a key skill for ensuring that students are able to benefit from the potential of individual study time. Research studies identify several conditions that should be ensured if students are to acquire a useful repertoire of skills that will support their learning, either individually or in concert with their peers (see Figure 3.12).

Individual study opportunities in social studies can add breadth to any topic because students will learn from the engagement of their classmates in diverse aspects of a common topic.

To ensure that students who undertake social studies in alternative ways to whole-class instruction retain intensity and integrity in their studies, students would benefit from having a set of criteria for judging the unique perspective of the sources they access. Kieran Egan provides a useful overview of four perspectives of history accounts that younger students could understand with examples (see Figure 3.13). These perspectives present four "layers" of historical understanding.

Figure 3.12 Strategies for Ensuring Skill Acquisition

- Name the skill.
- Show/model the skill step by step.
- Develop anchor charts.
- Provide guided practice.
- Practise, practise, practise.
- Use the skill in new contexts.
- Reflect on how the strategy worked (strategy efficacy).
- Build the learning wall by using strategy words and examples.
- Activate re-use of the strategy by renaming it.

- Enrich the strategy as students master each stage.
- Model systematic use first.
- Model concept-enriched use next (use the elements of the concept to create criteria for the skill).
- Model enriched use last (use the elements of the model to create criteria for the skill).

(Maynes, 2007)

Figure 3.13 Egan's Layers of Historical Understanding

Types of History Recounting	Explanation	Example
1. Mythic	Includes mythical accounts that help cement national or group identities; can be told with mythical elements (e.g., miracles) and in story form.	Aboriginal stories of creation
2. Romantic	Involves dramatic historical narratives that emphasize emotional content and affective involvement.	Dear Diary series of Canadian history
3. Philosophic	Characterized by history accounts that seek to provide patterns and generate theories about the possible underlying laws or processes of history.	Photo studies of an era that seek to examine underlying practices of early photography and how these practices can distort history
4. Iconic	The details and facts are examined for their own sake.	Typical textbook accounts of historical events

Source: Adapted from Egan, Kieran (1989). Layers of historical understanding. *Theory and research in social education*. 17.4: 280–294.

Providing this type of overview of possible approaches to examining social studies will support students' increasingly independent inquiry and research into topics of interest.

INNOVATIVE APPROACHES IN YOUR SOCIAL STUDIES CLASSROOM

This part of Chapter 3 will explain how to teach the skill of *model building* as a form of inquiry. In order to explain how things work, we often build models of the concepts we are trying to visualize. These models may include

- graphic organizers;
- physical models/constructions; and
- computer-generated/simulated models

Model building addresses the question "How does it work?" and is a critical aspect of understanding events and relationships in social studies.

There are many computer programs for generating graphic organizers to help students create relationship models. Teachers will need to expose students to the use and adaptation of these graphic organizers to help them make efficient and effective use of them. Students need to understand that graphic organizers are developed as a way to provide a visual representation of their thinking. Some sample graphic organizers for common types of text were presented earlier in the chapter.

By performing a web search for "graphic organizers," teachers will be able to access many samples of organizers that are applicable to many types of thinking. Sites that are particularly useful include

- www.teachervision.fen.com/graphic-organizers/printable/6293.html
- http://images.google.ca/images?hl=en&q=graphic+organizers&um=1&ie=UTF-8&sa=X&oi=image_result_group&resnum=5&ct=title

Students will need to be taught to be critical consumers of the organizers that are available to them online and to make use of samples in adaptive ways.

Physical models can also be helpful to support young students' understanding of how things work. Many types of models can be built in the classroom for low cost and reasonable effort. For example, young students could create model log cabins or sod houses to help them understand the lifestyle of early settlers. Simulations and reenactments also provide answers to the question "How does it work?" Some simulations can be created easily and allow students to gain understanding of abstract concepts such as fairness, honesty, sharing, resource management, and conflict.

An example of such a simulation is "Make Your Own," (see Figure 3.14) based on a geography simulation of greater complexity called "Unequal Resources." Young students can be involved in this simulation for about 15 minutes and learn several valuable abstract ideas.

Figure 3.14 Sample Simulation to Teach Complex Concepts

Make Your Own

Three countries have to complete the same tasks in a limited amount of time.

The countries are:

*Nicah

*Yenak

*Naadac

Nicah is a country of 20 people.

Yenak has a population of 15 people.

Naadac has a small population: the rest of the class.

Tasks include:

- Make up a four-line cheer to present to everyone.
- Using the resources given, make a country flag with three colours; your flag must be exactly 20 x 30 cm in size.
- Make one luxury item. Name it and be prepared to show how it is used.

Country	Resource Provided
Nicah	■ 1 sheet of white 8½ × 11 paper
Yenak	■ 1 ruler (cm)
Naadac	■ 6 sheets of coloured construction paper ■ Glue ■ Paper clips ■ Pencil ■ Elastics ■ Markers (3 colours)

Once groups have had about 15 minutes to complete their tasks, ask them to unscramble the letters in their country's name! Many students will experience an "ahhh" moment when they realize that the country names can be unscrambled as China, Kenya, and Canada. Unless they have chosen to raid the country of Naadac and steal their resources, or engage in diplomatic trading, the citizens of Nicah and Yenak will not be able complete all of their tasks because they lack the necessary resources. Even the resource-rich country of Naadac cannot complete the flag task correctly because they lack the ruler that would help them create a flag of the required size. Students come to realize that fair trade would have allowed all three groups to complete their tasks and that they collectively had all of the necessary resources to do this. Debriefing of the simulation can help students understand the abstract concepts of competition, fair trade, unequal resource distribution, social justice, competition, globalization, and social responsibility.

Computer-generated or simulated models are becoming increasingly possible and available as a classroom tool and computer software becomes more sophisticated and more widely licensed for educational applications. There are many software programs available that are accessible enough for primary classroom use. Students will need exposure and training to enable them to use such software in a manner that respects the need for efficiency in the use of learning time.

CASE STUDIES AND PROFESSIONAL ACTIVITIES FOR INNOVATION IN SOCIAL STUDIES

Try some of these cooperative learning approaches. More detail and resources to support each approach can be found at: www.teach-nology.com/‌ currenttrends/ ‌cooperative_learning/‌kagan.

Cooperative learning can be approached in two ways:

1. Through fully structured cooperative learning lesson *strategies*.

2. Through *structures* that include a small component of cooperation within the larger lesson.

Fully structured cooperative learning lessons use strategies that evolve through application of the following principles, referred to by Kagan as PIES (see Figure 3.15). The outline below will help you understand how to apply these principles to your own lesson plans.

Figure 3.15 PIES: Organizing Lessons Using Cooperative Learning Principles

Cooperative Learning	This Stands For	You Would Plan For This By . . .	Example	
P	Positive interdependence	■ Creating a climate of team spirit in the class; "I win if the team wins" attitude ■ Teaching social skills every day ■ Modelling what the desired interaction looks and sounds like ■ Developing and posting anchor charts for the social skills	■ Teach the skill of disagreeing in an agreeable way.	
			Looks Like	**Sounds Like**
			■ Look at the person who is speaking ■ Listen when others speak	■ "I understand what you are saying, but I think that. . . " ■ "Would your idea also include. . . ?"

(Continued)

Figure 3.15 (*continued*)

Cooperative Learning	This Stands For	You Would Plan For This By . . .	Example
		positive and less than positive interactions you witnessed during the lesson	
		■ Planning the group task so that no person in the group can do the task without relying on the other people in the group for their input	
I	Individual accountability	■ Holding students individually responsible for the new learning ■ Teaching in groups but test new learning for individuals ■ Treating group products as practice, not as evidence of learning; never assign individual marks for the group product	■ Give groups feedback about the quality of their group product. ■ Assess individual learning using strategies that focus on students' independent and individual understanding, following the group task.
E	Equal participation	■ Planning the lesson so that each group member must participate at all times to get the job done ■ Having the team share resources (e.g., one pair of scissors, one instruction sheet, etc.)	■ Add time limitations. ■ Add rewards (e.g., points for the team)if the task is completed properly. ■ Add rewards if the task is completed on time. ■ Teach students to develop and use a group "cheer" when group tasks are complete. ■ Have every group member sign the group product to attest to their agreement that they have contributed equally to the completion of the task.

Figure 3.15 (*Continued*)

Cooperative Learning	This Stands For	You Would Plan For This By . . .	Example
S	Simultaneous interaction	■ Assigning roles for each student to assume during the completionof the task (e.g., recorder, reporter,materials handler)	■ Rotate roles for each cooperative task. ■ Teach students how to manage each role successfully. ■ Keep records of roles each student has assumed in previous tasks. ■ Add outside stressors such as time limits, competition, and deadlines for completion.

However, structuring a lesson with a fully developed plan for cooperative learning requires a great deal of planning and is time consuming so may be possible less regularly than desirable.

To teach students how to be cooperative without the support of fully developed cooperative learning lessons each day, teachers can use *cooperative learning structures*. These structures involve using strategies that promote cooperation within an otherwise direct instruction lesson. In this case, the cooperative structures would be used to implement the *new learning, consolidation*, or *application* of the lesson.

Kagan, and other authors, present several cooperative learning structures that can be used within a direct instruction lesson (see Figure 3.16).

These are just a small sample of the many cooperative structures that can be used effectively in the classroom to promote interest, enthusiasm, and social skill development. Resources can be purchased directly from the Kagan website at www.kaganonline.com.

Figure 3.16 Sample Cooperative Learning Structures

Structure	Explanation	Examples/Cautions
Agreement Circles	■ Students form a large circle. ■ Teacher provides statements about which students will have an opinion (agree or disagree). ■ Students step into or out of the original circle to express	■ Teach multiplication practice using agreement circles. ■ Select activities for physical education through this type of voting procedure.

(Continued)

Figure 3.16 (*Continued*)

Structure	Explanation	Examples/Cautions
	their agreement or disagreement with the statement. ■ Teach students to match the size of their opinion (e.g., strongly disagree) with the size of their step into or out of the circle.	
Blind Sequencing	■ Provide students with some pieces of new learning that must be sequenced (e.g., numbers on a number line). ■ Have each team member sort the items on their own, then match their decisions with those of team members to reach consensus.	■ Create a number line. ■ Sort historical dates in relation to events. ■ Create a story line for a story they have just read.
Circle the Sage	■ One student in each group studies one aspect of the new learning and becomes the expert (sage). ■ Other students form a circle around the sage. ■ Students ask prepared questions of the sage and the sage tries to answer each in turn.	■ What are the ways that Kwanzaa is celebrated? ■ How are the three bears in the story made to seem appealing and cuddly in this story?
Corners	■ Students in each group of four select a number from one to four. ■ Corners of the room are assigned a number from one to four. ■ Each corner group is assigned to discuss one aspect of the topic then return to their original group to report what they learned.	■ Discuss a short story using the following questions, one assigned to each corner of the room: 1. What do you like about this story? 2. What do you dislike about this story? 3. What made the protagonist a hero in the story? 4. Was the ending of the story satisfying? Why? Why not?
Fan and Pick	Create question cards for the new learning.	■ What is the most appealing part of this story?

Figure 3.16 (*Continued*)

Structure	Explanation	Examples/Cautions
	■ Each team is given a set of questions with each question on a different card. ■ Students in each group of four take one role from among the following: 　■ Student 1 fans the cards. 　■ Student 2 picks the question from the fanned cards. 　■ Student 3 answers the question. 　■ Student 4 comments on the answer.	■ Apply to question cards that can be open to opinion or can have a specific answer that is provided on the card (e.g., The Prime Minister of Canada is?)
Find My Rule	■ The teacher proposes groupings of items in a graphic format (e.g., using boxes, paper mystery bags, number lines, Venn diagrams) ■ Teams of four are challenged to discuss the clues and decide on the category of items.	■ Teacher asks students to discover the rule of the organizer that has been used (e.g., "What is the Venn diagram showing us about these two historical figures?")
Find Someone Who . . .	■ Groups of students are given a worksheet requiring certain information that others in the class may have. ■ Students are given a limited amount of time to circulate and find the answers to their questions, filling them in on their worksheets as they circulate. ■ After the time is up, students can return to their original groups of four and share any answers that others have not yet acquired.	■ Find a person in the room who . . . (an introductory activity). ■ Fill out your bingo sheet by finding someone who can give you an answer to each question (e.g., timeline question on sheet). ■ Get a fact to answer each question on your sheet. Have the people who answered each question initial that part of your question sheet.

(Continued)

Figure 3.16 *(Continued)*

Structure	Explanation	Examples/Cautions
Find the Fib (also called Three Facts and a Lie)	■ Each team of four students is given a series of statements that relate to the topic, some true and some false. ■ Through discussion, students try to determine the truth of the statements by referencing resources about the topic.	■ Using the short story, quote parts of the story that provide evidence of why some statements are true and others are not. ■ Re-sort the items in the envelope to create a true number line. Discard the dates that are not applicable.
Flashcard Game	■ Pair students. ■ Provide each pair of students with a set of flashcards relating to the topic. ■ Have students take turns questioning each other using the flashcards. ■ This can also be done by using one questioner and three answerers in each group.	■ Apply to historical facts. ■ Apply to spelling or reading of word wall words. ■ Apply to facts of informational text reading small groups have discussed.
Formations	■ Apply this to students' understanding of shapes and spatial sense. ■ Using concepts of mathematical shapes, have students create the shapes by standing in various formations.	■ Stand in circles, squares, rectangles, triangles, etc., to represent military formations in different contexts.

CHAPTER REVIEW AND PROFESSIONAL DEVELOPMENT AS A TEACHER

This chapter has examined the following:

■ The standards of social studies are unique to the nature of the discipline.

■ The role and approaches to inquiry in social studies contexts are central to the subject area.

- Inquiry is used to engage students in making meaning of the ideas they encounter. Inquiry is a constructivist approach but requires immersion into the content of the topic in order to ensure that inquiry is focused and informed (situational constructivism).

- Inquiry can help students make meaningful connections between pieces of information.

- A model for inquiry can be taught to students and used by teachers to show flexible and recursive steps that inquiry might follow.

- Inquiry-rich classroom environments have characteristics that teachers can plan and provide.

- Direct instruction should be used in social studies when students would benefit from seeing how an expert learner would approach something they want to learn.

- The phases of direct instruction include the gradual release of responsibility for learning (scaffolded support) that is withdrawn over time as students become increasingly competent and capable.

- Indirect approaches to instruction, including activity centres, cooperative learning and cooperative structures, independent learning, computer-facilitated instruction, and individual instruction, can be used to engage students in social studies.

- Students benefit from being taught common structures for texts they may encounter during research and from being taught skills in ways that ensure solid learning of the skills.

- Teachers will need to exercise professional caution and diligence when they facilitate students' access to computers for research.

References for Further Reading

Bransford, J., Brown, A., & Cocking, R. (2000). *How people learn: Brain, mind, experience and school.* Washington, DC: National Academics Press.

Dewey, J. (1938). *Logic: The theory of inquiry.* New York, NY: Henry Holt and Co.

Kagan, S. (1994). *Cooperative learning.* San Clemente, CA: Resources for Teachers.

Kagan, S. & Kagan, M. (1998). *Multiple intelligences: The complete MI book.* San Clemente, CA: Resources for Teachers.

Rosenshine, B. (1997). *The case for explicit, teacher-led, cognitive strategy instruction.* Chicago, IL: American Educational Research Association.

Wells, G. (2001). *Action, talk and text: Learning and teaching through inquiry.* New York, NY: Teachers College Press.

Weblinks

Hands-On, Inquiry-Based Activities

This website from the McCord Museum offers students an excellent opportunity to engage with the material and build greater understanding of key concepts through online games, exhibitions, and resources. The McCord Museum also offers Keys to History, a web resource specifically geared for teachers. One of the most interesting activities at the site superimposes historical photos of specific historical sites with photos of their location today. Students can guide the icon and instantly see the changes that have taken place over time and can go back and forth between the scenes. A unique forward-looking and thought-provoking museum, the McCord explores contemporary issues through its collections and exhibitions, and offers stimulating public programming relevant to Canadians of all backgrounds and ages. The McCord is engaged with communities at the local, national, and global levels.

www.mccord-museum.qc.ca

The Learning Company offers software called Adventure Workshop with Where in the World is Carmen Sandiego? As agents for the world-famous ACME Detective Agency, student-sleuths must track down the ex-secret agent and her cohorts. As students pursue Carmen, they will explore dozens of the world's great cities and diverse cultures, guided by over 1000 clues about history, the arts, language, currency, and geography. Students can use the built-in database to research reports and focus on the country or region the class is studying.

www.riverofsoftware.com

Inquiry Learning

www.saskschools.ca/curr_content/bestpractice/inquiry/index.html
www.thirteen.org/edonline/concept2class/inquiry/index.html
http://education.alberta.ca/media/313361/focusoninquiry.pdf
www.scribd.com/doc/2897923/Incorporating-Critical-Inquiry-Pedagogy-in-Social-Studies-Curriculum
www.tki.org.nz/r/ict/ictpd/downloads/inquiry_learning.doc

Direct Instruction and Effective Modelling

www.nifdi.org/15/
www.centerii.org/techassist/solutionfinding/resources/FiveMeaningsOfDI.pdf

Cooperative Learning

http://help4teachers.com/MarthasResearch.htm
www.kaganonline.com

Independent Learning

www.cdli.ca/~acrawfor/lrc2b.html
http://webtest.sasked.gov.sk.ca/docs/policy/cels/el7.html
http://video.google.ca/videosearch?hl=en&q=independent+learning&um=1&ie=UTF-8&oi=video_result_group&resnum=10&ct=title#

Computer-Facilitated Instruction

http://portal.acm.org/citation.cfm?id=763180

Individual(ized) Instruction

www.eralearning.org/01/WhatIsII.phtml
www.dropoutprevention.org/effstrat/individualized_instruction/overview.htm

Independent Learning for the Junior Grades

The Canadian Geographic site contains animal facts, games, map puzzles, and stats on Canada.
www.canadiangeographic.ca/kids

Chapter 4
Deconstruction as a Critical Teaching Skill

Learning Topics

- Understanding Learning Goals and Expectations
- Goals as Observable Behaviours
- The Challenge for Social Studies Programs
- Deconstructing Goals for Learning
- Effective Lesson Planning in Social Studies
- Data-Based Decision Making for the Improvement of Instruction

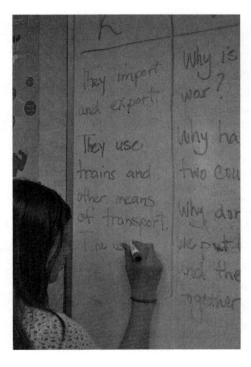

Teachers must select the appropriate tool to gather information about the student's prior knowledge. Using a KWL, the teacher can assess if the student's concepts are internalized incorrectly.

UNDERSTANDING LEARNING GOALS AND EXPECTATIONS

Planning a program for social studies must begin with identifying the goals of the program. However, unless the teacher has an academic frame of reference for the construction, origin, orientation, and connection among the goals that are stated or selected, the resulting program could become haphazard and create isolated and trivial learning situations. Clear, connected, and thoughtfully produced program goals are essential starting points for a well-developed program.

In most jurisdictions, program goals (see Figure 4.1) will be provided in curriculum guidelines. In this case, the teacher must take the time to examine the goals and determine the implicit or explicit structure of the goals. It is critical for the teacher to understand how these prescribed goals are oriented in relation to learning, the students, and the role of social studies in developing an educated person, prior to planning for units and lessons.

Knowing and understanding the goals for the program, while necessary, is not sufficient for the teacher as a basis for effective planning at the unit and lesson level. Well-stated social studies goals will "imply the kinds of learning activities that would be appropriate for achieving them" (Ornstein et al., 2003, p. 16). It remains the role of the effective social studies teacher to tie stated goals together into a comprehensive and effective classroom program.

Knowing how to examine, analyze, and use curriculum goals for social studies requires that the teacher have and use the following curriculum skills:

- Professional knowledge—to see the pattern and intent in each goal
- Pedagogical content knowledge—to know how to teach an idea, what students are likely to misunderstand, and how to use effective examples to support understanding
- Knowledge of the standards of the discipline—to ensure that learning time is connected and directed toward the attainment of high levels of learning related to significant knowledge

Figure 4.1 Learning Goals Have Many Synonymous Names

From time to time, our language in curriculum changes to reflect changing perspectives of curriculum writers and societal priorities. Teachers may find that goals are called different things in different guidelines and resources. Goals may also be referred to as

- aims
- competencies
- ends
- ends sought

- objectives
- outcomes
- purposes
- expectations

- A solid personal philosophy of learning—so that learning is going somewhere, rather than consisting of unconnected, low-level activities
- Experience—to know how to approach learning in the most beneficial and efficient manner
- Imagination—to manage learning experiences that help students transcend time and location to develop deep understanding
- Rich resources—so that teachers can select and provide for diversity and variety to promote breadth and detail in learning

Effective social studies teachers will not see goals as isolated from each other. Rather, they will understand and seek to manage goals as interconnected aspects of the program that connect *what* students learn with *how* they learn, and how they have *opportunities to demonstrate their learning*. The content, process, and products embedded within goal statements will be connected to inform strategy development. Individual goals cannot be seen as isolated, but must be in concert with the strategies that evolve from them (see Figure 4.2).

To create balance in the strategies that flow from well-defined curriculum goals, educational goals should reflect three factors: the nature of organized knowledge, the nature of society (its social values locally, provincially, and as a nation), and the nature of the learners (Tyler, 1949). These three factors are reflective of the categories of influence that we would consider when developing an image of the educated learner in Canadian society. Curriculum goals for social studies must reflect the concepts, principles, and processes of the discipline and be developed to reflect the ways of knowing that characterize social studies.

Figure 4.2 The Interplay of the Elements of Differentiation

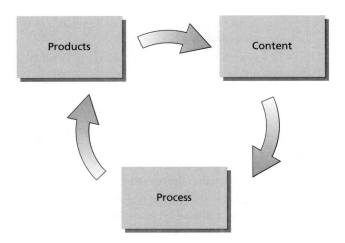

Most educational goals, and especially those that relate to attitudes, beliefs, and values that influence behaviours, are not exclusive to schools, but are a shared responsibility with the broader community. Similarly, many of the principles and processes of social studies share some characteristics with the principles and processes taught in other subject areas. It is for this reason that integrated units of study may be appropriate instructional approaches for some contexts. Integration will be dealt with in greater detail in Chapter 8.

Curriculum goals are most readily accessible to teachers when they share a common form. This common form will help curriculum developers make appropriate decisions when designing learning experiences for their students. Close inspection of the curriculum goals that are provided in provincial and territorial guidelines allows teachers to put each goal in perspective so that instructional time is allocated to those goals that reflect high-priority learning and promote deep understanding.

Goals may also be differentiated into levels to address the levels of planning that teachers engage in program development. Brandt and Tyler (2003) divided goals into four types (see Figure 4.3).

In some jurisdictions, goals for social studies fall into three main categories (see Figure 4.4).

Many factors influence the way curriculum goals are developed in social studies. Figure 4.5 identifies the interaction of these influences.

Figure 4.3 Types of Goals

System Goals	■ Reflect the goals of the entire program, including all subject areas at all grade levels
	Example: The student is able to apply inquiry to the investigation of events in the past and present.
Program Goals	■ Reflect the combined goals of all subjects within the program for a grade level
	Example: The student is able to use language conventions appropriately to describe events from the past.
Course Goals	■ Reflect the combined goals of all units within the subject of social studies for the grade level
	Example: The student is able to analyze the causes of an event and provide evidence to support his or her opinions.
Instructional Goals	■ Reflect the changes in knowledge, skills, and attitudes anticipated as the result of specific learning experiences
	Example: The student is able to identify four push and four pull factors that affected development of the Canadian prairies.

Figure 4. 4 Categories of Goals

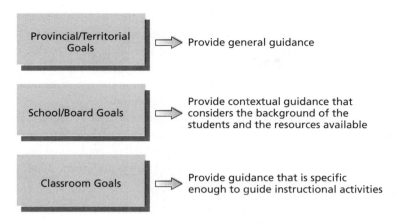

Provincial/Territorial Goals ⟹ Provide general guidance

School/Board Goals ⟹ Provide contextual guidance that considers the background of the students and the resources available

Classroom Goals ⟹ Provide guidance that is specific enough to guide instructional activities

Figure 4.5 Elements that Influence the Learning Goals of a Program

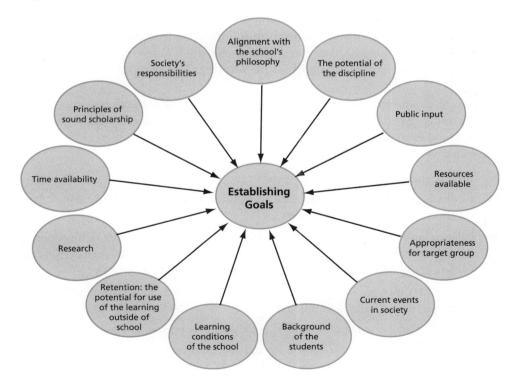

Society's responsibilities

Alignment with the school's philosophy

The potential of the discipline

Principles of sound scholarship

Public input

Time availability

Establishing Goals

Resources available

Research

Appropriateness for target group

Retention: the potential for use of the learning outside of school

Learning conditions of the school

Background of the students

Current events in society

GOALS AS OBSERVABLE BEHAVIOURS

Many of the goals of social studies will result in learning that is observable. However, this is not true for all goals. Goals that relate to developing students' capacity for thinking in certain ways, or being aware of certain things, are less likely to be readily observable. Mager (1962) suggests that goals should be written as observable behaviours while keeping a focus on big ideas. Hughes and Sears (2004) propose the use of *situated learning* to maintain a focus on big ideas in the social studies curriculum.

In situated learning approaches, social constructivism (see Chapter 1) is used to develop knowledge. Knowledge is considered to be a product of the culture where it develops and the emerging ideas that students come to understand are created and negotiated in the social context of the interactive classroom (Hughes and Sears, 2004, p. 260). In this model, situated learning requires two conditions:

1. The learner must be touched or engaged in profound ways that cause emotive responses to new learning; deep understanding comes about through embedded interactions that make the abstractions concrete and tangible in a social context.

2. The learner must interact with ideas that cause them to rethink/assimilate and reshape/accommodate their existing ideas.

If situated learning is to be a goal for social studies instruction, teachers must ensure that the learning is situated in two ways. First, learners must have experiences in learning as part of a group or community of learners. That is, the learning is socially situated. Second, the learning goals must centre on ensuring that students have discussion opportunities that will immerse them in key elements that characterize the important concepts and ideas that are the goals of the learning. The learning is situated in key content.

To create programs that have situated learning as a major goal, teachers must ensure that learning opportunities are filtered with "careful planning and skillful practice" (Hughes and Sears, 2004, p. 263). This will require that teachers focus on goals for their program that

■ involve students in collaborative consideration of problems;

■ facilitate connections between classroom activities and current thinking about questions that are being examined;

■ balance knowing the students' current level of knowledge with goals that encourage the refinement and extension of knowledge to help students gain perspective, find evidence, and accommodate new information;

■ use a variety of approaches to foster deeper understanding as anchors or springboards for deeper investigation and inquiry;

■ recognize that assessment is complex, collaborative, ongoing, and formative; and

■ make use of students' prior knowledge and address their preconceptions, misconceptions, and alternative frameworks (see Figure 4.6).

Figure 4.6 Three Types of Conceptions Students May Hold

Preconceptions—Students do not yet understand the concept fully.

Misconceptions—Concepts are internalized incorrectly when some aspect is misunderstood in the learning process.

Alternative frameworks—Concepts are internalized in unique, imaginative, and possibly misconceived forms because students relate embedded ideas in unanticipated ways.

Source: Adapted from Driver and Easley (1978), Pupils and paradigms: A review of literature related to concept development in adolescent science students, *Studies in Science Education* 5: 61–84).

When setting instructional goals for learning, teachers need to become aware of the conceptions students hold before instruction. This will allow them to use instructional time to build understanding that addresses preconceptions, misconceptions, and alternative frameworks.

In classrooms where teachers are unaware of students' interests and life experiences, they not only fail to build on local knowledge but essentially offer "disinvitations" to participate in classroom discourse.

—Windschitl, 2002, pp.151–152

Teachers can delineate students' prior knowledge of social studies concepts in a general sense and a more specific sense. By defining current knowledge in a general sense, teachers create a learning climate where they are ready to plan from students' current knowledge and to build in time to share what students know and value. Specific prior knowledge can be accessed through several powerful strategies that engage, honour, and invite learners to make sense of new ideas. Sample strategies for engaging or surfacing students' prior knowledge to support strong program goal setting include

■ prioritizing—identifying through students' consensus what they think is most important to learn;

■ using a KWL organizer to identify prior knowledge, conceptions, misconceptions, bias, etc. (K=What do you already know about this subject?; W=What do you want to know about this subject?; L=What new things have we now learned about this subject?);

■ using a RAN chart (Reading and Analyzing Non-fiction by Tony Stead) to offer students an opportunity to share what they think they know;

■ using mind maps and other graphic organizers to connect ideas and build frameworks that are commonly understood;

■ using brainstormed lists;

- connecting feelings (emotive) to ideas (cognitive) to surface bias and misunderstandings; and

- having students question their own ideas through commonly understood filters that serve as monitors of classroom discourse (e.g., Is this appropriate? Is this effective?).

Goals that promote the use of anchors or springboards in creating deep understanding of concepts allow teachers to plan learning situations that examine issues over time and across contexts to determine their current relevance and meaning.

Young learners benefit from the use of springboards (or touchstone stories) in social studies instruction because they have the features of story that create emotive connections for students. An additional advantage to using springboards is that they open up the possibility of integration with other subjects, which helps young learners make connections among ideas. Springboards and anchor examples can become the touchstone events or stories that help define the culture of the classroom by exemplifying desirable values and behaviours in story form.

If students are taught only to follow prescribed rules, they will be unable to deal with varied situations.

—*Brandt and Tyler, 2003*

Springboard stories in the social studies context
- address the "big ideas" or central concepts of a topic;
- provide strong and emotively engaging examples of ideas;
- are authentic in the sense that young learners find them understandable;
- are able to catch and hold interest through their vivid relating;
- promote dialogue that leads to deeper understanding;
- highlight inherent concepts and issues to start dialogue;
- promote examination of layers of meaning; are multidimensional and allow for many perspectives;
- are deliberately ambiguous to promote dialogue;
- are open to interpretation through personal values filters;
- invite comparisons that help to surface values and principles; and
- have breadth that can be extended across contexts.

Source: Adapted from Hughes and Sears, 2004, pp. 268–271.

Resources to support the social studies program need to be selected with specific goals in mind and provided to relate to the springboard experiences planned as central components of the social studies program. The big ideas or organizing concepts of social studies will be developed further in Chapter 5.

THE CHALLENGE FOR SOCIAL STUDIES PROGRAMS

The role of clear goals in social studies is to ensure that learning time is spent productively and efficiently. Without clear goals, classroom learning time can deteriorate to a string of unrelated experiences that are not structured to accumulate and promote deep understanding. Instead, experiences become a "parade of facts" (Parker, 1989) and disassociated events that provide knowledge at the exposure level only and fail to move understanding forward.

Students must acquire knowledge, yet the teaching must reach beyond transmitting factual information to developing thoughtful understanding. There is a need to involve students in mindful exploration of the world around them.

—*Smith, 1999, p. 7*

Our role in choosing educational goals at the provincial, school, or classroom levels is to ensure that they are educationally sound in reference to the overall standards of the discipline. Making meaning of experience must remain central when planning learning experiences. We cannot confuse level of activity with level of understanding by engaging students in "serial pop-up activities" (Smith, 1999).

Helping and guiding as students make important and sustained connections must be central to our program goals, as we help students draw conclusions from educational experiences and engage in reflective thought to make meaning from each experience. This layer of interpretation added to experience legitimizes active learning and separates it from activity. Reflection added to legitimate active learning helps students draw conclusions and make meaning through deep understanding. "Deliberate and comprehensive preparation" (Smith, 1999) is a necessity if we are to provide effective program goals and clear and effective instruction to achieve them.

Social studies seeks "to engage students in the study of society" (Horton, 1999, p. 123). To do this effectively, teachers will need to ensure that their programs have an underlying rationale that reflects what the teacher holds to be true about the discipline and its role in education, clear goals that social studies will pursue and promote, and strands (see Chapter 1) around which the discipline is organized to promote the desired goals.

DECONSTRUCTING GOALS FOR LEARNING

We must also recognize that guideline goals often are not classroom ready. They will usually need to be deconstructed or pulled apart to provide appropriate direction for designing learning activities and experiences. Often, teachers will find that guideline goal statements have many supporting skills embedded in them. These are the skills that are assumed to be present in students' repertoire, or that will need to be taught, prior to expecting successful learning of the stated goal.

Example

Grade 3 students will identify geographic and environmental factors that explain the location of various urban and rural communities.

In order to achieve this goal, students will also need to be able to

- identify what a geographical feature is;
- identify what an environmental factor is;
- identify an urban community;
- identify a rural community;
- generate criteria for a comparison;
- use actual, photographic, and electronic sources to identify and sort features;
- sort by criteria;
- recognize patterns and anomalies; and
- generalize.

If the teacher neglects to deconstruct the expectations that are provided in guidelines, and determine the underlying skills, knowledge, and attitudes that contribute to achieving the goal, they will be unable to provide the sequenced, accumulative, and substantial background to promote learning success.

In the words of Smith (1999, p. 7), "The concerns . . . are found in the manner in which students are cast into an extremely complex . . . context with insufficient background knowledge, concepts, and skills to analyze the issues competently." Failure to provide the background knowledge by deconstructing the goal for learning is to doom students to fail in their efforts to construct meaning from experiences. This will devolve the social studies program into a series of unrelated activities that fail to lead the learner to develop clarity about concepts and to draw supportable conclusions.

EFFECTIVE LESSON PLANNING IN SOCIAL STUDIES

In Chapter 3, we presented a diagram that promoted an overview of the instructional decisions that teachers need to make to provide effective learning experiences for students. This diagram presented the phases of instruction for lesson planning. Here we consider the term *lesson planning* to apply to the set of experiences designed to promote learning of a stated expectation or group of expectations. Lesson plans should not be bound by the time limitations of the instructional day set within an imposed timetable. Rather, we should think of lesson plans in a broader context, perhaps spanning many days.

A broader conception of lesson planning allows us to focus on inquiry and critical-thinking investigations as central components of a social studies program. Because these are demanding and involving program goals, large blocks and extensions of time are needed to achieve deep understanding using these approaches. Whether a lesson plan describes learning plans for one hour, or for several hours spanning many days, there are elements of an effective social studies lesson plan that are critical to successful and efficient learning (see Figure 4.7).

By ensuring that lesson-planning processes are strong, comprehensive, and reflect our professional beliefs about the discipline of social studies and its approaches to learning, we can evolve a program that promotes the overall goals of developing informed and responsible citizenship as our students engage in the study of society.

Figure 4.7 Lesson Planning in Social Studies

Components of an Effective Social Studies Lesson Plan	Explanation
Learning Goal	State the goals for the lesson as a function of what students will know, understand, believe, or do as a result of the new learning.
Social Skills Goals	Since lessons will benefit from students' interaction as they attempt to make meaning from their new experiences, they will need to be taught how to manage that interaction in positive, constructive ways. Social skills goals can complement the goals for learning the content and processes of the discipline.
Pre-assessment of the Learners	Determine what students already know about the subject under investigation and what pre-conceptions, misconceptions, and alternative frameworks may be structuring their current levels of understanding.
	Determine informational and technological literacy skills that may influence students' access to resources.
Motivation	Create a sense of curiosity, wonder, or cognitive dissonance that will cause students to attend and want to learn. This includes strategies to surface prior knowledge, hook students' interest, and create mind-body connections.
Orientation	Determine whether you will approach the new learning of the stated goal directly through modelling, or indirectly through strategies such as inquiry, activity centres, web quests, cooperative learning, etc. The chosen orientation should reflect the nature of the learning goal.

(Continued)

Figure 4.7 *(Continued)*

Components of an Effective Social Studies Lesson Plan	Explanation
Guided Practice	Provide for guided and supported practice that will ensure that students have time and structures to aid their understanding. Expose students to contexts that will test their new comprehension and help them solidify and internalize it. Challenge their understanding by posing ambiguous examples. Model the formation of generalizations. Build conceptual language.
Support Generalizations	Continue practice and exploration opportunities to allow students to gain enough exposure that generalization is possible. Attach language to concepts. Being able to name an idea supports further exploration and reflection. Anchor the learning with charts, symbols, exemplars, samples, etc. Promote social action.
Embed Assessment and Evaluation	Provide feedback that is detailed and specific as students are learning. Formative feedback will help them reflect as they investigate (reflection in action) and after they complete tasks (reflection on action).
Provide Exemplars	Provide a standard by which students can examine their own achievements, products, and conclusions. Clarity about expectations will help students achieve learning goals.
Promote Metacognition	Provide time and structure to ensure that students are aware of what they have learned. By creating metacognitive awareness, we ensure that students know what they know, and thereby ensure that they can retrieve what they know when they need to.

DATA-BASED DECISION MAKING FOR THE IMPROVEMENT OF INSTRUCTION

Our society values productivity. We expect our schools to meet identified standards of performance and support students' developing knowledge, skills, and attitudes. Competitive global markets and job situations require increasingly well-prepared employees. Beyond the scope of the marketplace, we value the attributes of an educated person.

In this social climate, schools are expected to show the quality of the work they are doing with students. Hard data is one way to do this. While many achievements in social studies programs do not easily lend themselves to data-based measurement, some of the outcomes may. Shifts in attitudes, increasing ability to sustain inquiry, or a personal ability to be inclusive may be difficult to measure. On the other hand, the ability to compare, discuss an issue, or select and use appropriate resources could be measured.

Today's schools are expected to allocate resources that ensure recognized improvements in the students' education. Basing decisions about resources, approaches, and timelines on the data that demonstrates a history of success is the essence of data-based decision making. While many models for data-based decision making are available in business cultures, the model proposed here reflects the culture of classrooms and schools (see Figure 4.8).

While applying such a business-oriented model for improvement to the complex task of teaching young children may be uncomfortable for some, the socio-scientific approach of such a model is flexible and can be adapted to maintain the data focus with all of the advantages of humanity considered in each context.

The public call for accountability in education has led to the use of this approach as a way to measure the successes of our schools. The potential of data to support the ability of the school to teach to its maximum capacity is one more support for teachers. It should always be used to complement the professional judgment of teachers.

Additionally, creating an ethos of social studies approaches within a school culture can have a powerful effect on colleagues and the ongoing culture of support for certain

Figure 4.8 Sequencing the Actions of Data-Based Decision Making

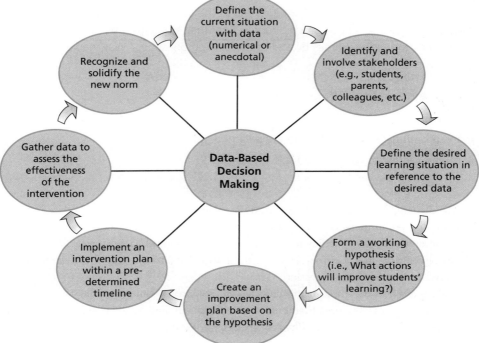

approaches. Data can also support the development and maintenance of the culture in the school. For example, if students have "always" experienced heritage fairs in their school, such an event becomes an established way in which that school approaches teaching a certain aspect of its social studies program. The community comes to recognize such an established event as part of the way that the school does business, and comes to expect, support, and value the event. By establishing prime roles for social studies in the school culture, teachers can influence the perceived role of the subject in the school's community and data such as that reflected by opinion polls can provide program direction.

INNOVATIVE APPROACHES IN YOUR SOCIAL STUDIES CLASSROOM

In the last chapter, we examined use of the skill of model making in many forms to help students investigate the general question, "How does it work?" Finding out about how something works can be followed by a closer investigation of its characteristics.

Inquiry investigations can start with the question "What are its interesting characteristics?" This question would guide students' inquiry supported by the skills of narration, description, and map making. To make use of each of these skills, students could be taught to tell stories, describe thoroughly, and use maps of many types to investigate a topic.

Example

Grade 3 social studies students are involved in the study of medieval times. They have identified the binary opposites (see Chapter 3) for their study. They will investigate wealth and poverty in medieval times by asking the guiding question, "Was medieval life good for everyone?"

Guiding questions should

- be short;
- focus on provoking analysis and evaluation; a judgment; and
- often include the word "good."

To investigate this topic using narrative, students will examine stories based on historical and geographic facts and interpretations to discover details about the lives of people in different strata of medieval society. They will read and write stories. Comparisons of daily lives will give them background information that will help them support their opinions about the guiding question.

To investigate the topic using description, students should consider the ways that authors and artifacts describe. Elements of time, location, and actions can be examined to promote thorough description. Physical, behavioural, and emotional descriptors can be examined. Students can be taught to use, and later to develop, graphic organizers that will aid their efforts to examine all of the elements of descriptive detail they are able to collect from a variety of sources. Using verbal descriptions, students can be challenged to construct examples of items that may have influenced life in medieval times, using similar patterns and construction materials. Items such as a catapult could be constructed and examined for applications authentic to the time period.

To investigate the topic using map making, students should have access to a variety of map projections and formats, both paper and electronic. Map skills should be taught in context as they are needed to support the examination of information.

Several of the map and orienteering skills and strategies outlined below (see Figure 4.9) include ideas that were summarized from the resource book *Orienteering and Map Games for Teachers*, by Mary E. Garrett (2004). This summary contains ideas for both early and later elementary students and some that may extend into the secondary program but could provide enrichment ideas for late junior level students. To supplement the ideas provided by Garrett, some additional ideas and details have been added.

Figure 4.9 Mapping Skills for Young Learners

Strategy	Skills Being Developed	Resources
The Picture Game		
Have children draw a picture of a space with several recognizable objects (e.g., front door, dog dish, big tree). Using one picture, mark brightly coloured circles or Xs on the map and hide "treasures" at each place, using the overhead machine or a large reproduction to show the map to the class. Challenge the children to find each item using the map.	■ Perspective taking ■ Relative space ■ One-to-one correspondence	■ Child's drawing ■ Brightly coloured markers ■ 3 or 4 "treasure" items per child
Tabletop Maps		
Cover a large tabletop with butcher paper or similar. Gather students around the table and distribute a pencil to each child. Lead students to gradually develop a picture of the classroom from a "face on" perspective. Start by drawing in three of the four walls of the classroom. Have the table placed with your back to the	■ Recognizing spatial relationships ■ Recognizing relative size ■ One-to-one correspondence	■ Pencils ■ Large drawing paper ■ Large tabletop that children can gather around

(Continued)

Figure 4.9 (*Continued*)

Strategy	Skills Being Developed	Resources
fourth wall. Model the placement of some items in the room. Gradually release responsibility to the children to have them add other objects. As you model, discuss why you are drawing some objects larger than others to show their actual different sizes. Post the finished classroom map in the room in preparation for the next mapping lesson.		

On the Ceiling

Strategy	Skills Being Developed	Resources
Use the classroom map from the previous activity. Ask students if there are things in the classroom they could not show on this map (e.g., the fourth wall, the things behind the desk). Ask where would the children have to be in order to see everything in the classroom (e.g., on the ceiling). Introduce students to names you will give to each of the four walls and show large cards displaying these as the four directions (e.g., North, South, East, West). Place these on the appropriate walls in the classroom so that they can be seen readily. Place another large sheet of drawing paper on the large tabletop and gather children around the table. Mark the four sides of the drawing paper to correspond to the direction signs placed around the classroom. Repeatedly point out these directions to students as you continue your demonstration. Ask students to focus on one object in the room (e.g., the teacher's chair) and think of what it might look like if you were	■ Aerial perspectives ■ One-to-one correspondence ■ Directions (cardinal) ■ Using symbols ■ Relative size	■ Tabletop ■ Large drawing paper ■ Several pencils ■ Chair or other object that is easily carried

Figure 4.9 (*Continued*)

Strategy	Skills Being Developed	Resources
looking at it from the ceiling. Ask students to lie down on the floor and carry a chair around to show them this perspective (e.g., holding the chair carefully above each child's head). Then, have the children discuss and decide upon a symbol they could use to represent the chair on a new map, as seen from the ceiling (e.g., a square with a small bracket behind it). Model the position of this symbol for the children on the large tabletop map. Gradually add other features of the room to this map, using symbols that children suggest. Post the finished map in the classroom.		
Taking a Trip On an overhead sheet, show the aerial map of the classroom that the children made last class. Have each child take a turn to show on this map where they are at the outset of the lesson (e.g., at their desk, on the carpet). Have a moveable, transparent, coloured item that is small enough to represent a child on the overhead machine. Place the item where one child is sitting. Then, as children watch, move the object to another spot and have the child move to the new spot as identified by the new location of the object on the overhead machine. Repeat this so that every child has a turn to move to a new spot. As this progresses, have children check and support each other with directions so that each child is successful getting to the new location.	■ Aerial perspective ■ One-to-one correspondence ■ Relative size ■ Relocation ■ Use of symbols ■ Relative location	■ Overhead machine ■ Overhead map of aerial view oF the classroom ■ Small, transparent, coloured object to represent a child(ren) on the overhead map

(Continued)

Figure 4.9 (*Continued*)

Strategy	Skills Being Developed	Resources
Visit a Friend Have each child sit at her desk. Using the overhead machine to show the aerial map of the classroom that was created earlier, place a dot where each child is sitting. Have each child take turns to move to another seat to visit with a friend. As each child moves, show their new location on the overhead map by moving their dot from one place to another. Gradually allow students to take responsibility for moving the dots as they start to understand the idea. (Variation: Have a small letter that represents the first letter of each child's first name instead of the dots.)	■ One-to-one correspondence ■ Relocation	■ Overhead machine ■ Aerial map of the classroom on an overhead sheet ■ Dots (or letter symbol) for each child
String Along Using the classroom tabletop map, displayed on the blackboard for easy viewing, show the starting location of one student by using a symbol or blackboard magnet to represent the student. Then, attach one end of a long, colourful piece of string to the map at the child's starting point. Now, attach the string to various other spots in the classroom to show where the student should move. As the student achieves success with the first relocation, ask students to help by giving directions for the student to find the third, fourth, fifth, etc., spots they are to move to in the classroom (e.g., turn left, go around this desk). Secure the string to the map at each new spot before the student begins to move so that all students can see it clearly. Encourage students to	■ One-to-one correspondence ■ Directionality	■ Aerial map of the classroom ■ String (coloured to be seen easily against the map)

Figure 4.9 (*Continued*)

Strategy	Skills Being Developed	Resources
use the terms north, south, east, and west as they give directions to classmates. As time allows, give each student an opportunity to be the student who moves.		
Crayon Game		
Have children gather around an aerial map. Place several crayons or other objects around the classroom. Have children take turns going to get each object and return to the map and add a symbol (e.g., X) on the aerial map where they found the object.	■ One-to-one correspondence ■ Directionality ■ Symbolism	■ Aerial tabletop map ■ Crayons of different colours (or other objects) ■ A coloured marker or plastic symbols (e.g., game pieces) to show locations on the aerial map
Make Your Own Map		
Have children draw their own aerial map of the classroom.	■ One-to-one correspondence ■ Relative size ■ Direction (N, S, E, W) ■ Symbolism	■ Paper ■ Pencils ■ Wall cards showing directions (N, S, E, W)
Learning Your Letters Game		
Place each of the letters of the alphabet around the classroom in various locations. Have children move around the room and use their own map (from previous lesson) to show where they have moved to find each of the letters, in order, to spell their own name. Mark each spot with the letter on their map. Emphasize that each child is to go to each letter of their name in order and ask other students questions to find out where their next letter is before moving toward it. As they find each letter, they should pause and mark their route from their last location to their current location on their map by printing the letter at the appropriate spot.	■ Symbolism ■ One-to-one correspondence ■ Reading a map ■ Recording location changes on a map ■ Relative location	■ Children's aerial maps of the classroom ■ Plastic alphabet letter set ■ Pencils

(Continued)

Figure 4.9 (*Continued*)

Strategy	Skills Being Developed	Resources
Storybook Maps		
Have children listen to stories with strong location elements in a read-aloud setting. Following the reading, have students assist with drawing an aerial map of the story location. As students develop confidence with this skill, have them work with increasing independence to complete their own maps. Gradually introduce standardized symbols for items represented in maps (e.g., for streams, churches, fields, buildings). Post standardized symbols around the classroom as per word-wall use.	■ Aerial perspective ■ Symbolism ■ One-to-one correspondence ■ Standardized symbols	■ Read-aloud books ■ Large paper for development of common map ■ Smaller paper for development of individual maps ■ Wall cards to display standardized map symbols
What's Wrong With This Map?		
Display a map of the schoolyard on an overhead machine, using moveable acetate or plastic coloured symbols for the features of the yard (e.g., soccer posts, basketball nets, grass, asphalt). Display these items in the wrong places on the map. Through questioning, starting with "What's wrong with this map?" ask students to help place the items in the proper spots on the map. This can later be set up as a temporary centre for students to review the concepts.	■ One-to-one correspondence ■ Symbolism ■ Relative size ■ Relative location	■ Blank overhead sheet ■ Coloured acetate or plastic pieces in shapes to represent an aerial view of the items in the schoolyard ■ Small box to store acetate/plastic pieces if a centre is being set up
Mapping Treasure Island		
Display and review standardized symbols for maps (e.g., fields, streams, trees). Post an anchor chart for these symbols. Provide each student with a blank island map showing a border area (surrounding water) and the symbols: N=North, S=South, E=East, W=West. Orally provide	■ Following directions ■ Using standard symbols ■ Using standard colours ■ Standardized spacing	■ Photocopied sheet of a blank "island" for each student ■ Pencils ■ Wall cards showing directions ■ Blackboard outline of the steps in developing the map

Figure 4.9 (*Continued*)

Strategy	Skills Being Developed	Resources
students with directions to gradually add features to the map. For example: ■ A long cliff runs along the south of the island ■ A trail starts in the northwest corner the island, goes south, and then runs east along the top of the cliffs; the trail then continues north again to the inlet where ships are moored ■ A cave sits in the middle of the island ■ A stream starts in the cave and flows to the inlet ■ There is a marsh at the west side of inlet where the stream joins it ■ There are many boulders near the cave in the centre of the island ■ Then give an instruction to get to the spot on the map where X marks the treasure. This activity can be done with the children using graph paper and examples for developing the map being given in spaces (e.g., Three spaces south of the cave is a tower). Also, students can be trained to colour the finished map using standard colours (e.g., blue for water).		(evolves as directions are given) ■ Crayons or pencil crayons
Orienting Your Map Teach students to orient their maps by modelling how you hold the classroom tabletop map so that your N point is facing the N point marked by posters on the classroom wall and/or the outdoor pylon or chair (see below). Use cues such as "Look at my map.	■ Orienting maps to directions	■ Classroom or schoolyard signs showing four directions (N, S, E, W) ■ Tape ■ Individual pages for students' maps ■ Pencils

(Continued)

Figure 4.9 (*Continued*)

Strategy	Skills Being Developed	Resources
I turned it so that the N on my map is facing the N on the wall marker (or chair or pylon). Please do the same with your map"). Teach children to turn their maps each time they change direction so that they are always in line with what they are facing.		

Outdoor Map Games

Strategy	Skills Being Developed	Resources
To teach children how to orient a map they are drawing, place four markers (use chairs or pylons) in appropriate spots on the schoolyard. Mark each one with the direction N, S, E, or W. Have students face each marker holding their paper in front of them to match its position relative to where they are standing. Have each student mark their paper with N, S, E, or W to correspond to the markers. Lead students, using a question/answer format, to mark the location of all of the schoolyard features on the map, using appropriate size and symbols.	■ Orientation ■ Symbols ■ One-to-one correspondence ■ Relative size	■ Orientation/direction markers to mark N, S, E, and W ■ Signs for directions (e.g., N North) ■ Tape (to attach direction signs to chairs or pylons) ■ Chairs or pylons ■ Separate sheet of paper for each student ■ Pencils or markers ■ Area of the schoolyard that contains several features to be mapped

String Orienteering

Strategy	Skills Being Developed	Resources
Lay out a course of hanging symbols in various places in the playground. Pictures can be drawn on paper or from more durable materials such as magic marker on brightly coloured plastic bottles. Lay out string or footprint shapes to lead to the hanging symbols in the order you want students to visit each station. Provide each student with a personal map showing the same number and location of the markers and string or footprint	■ Map reading ■ One-to-one correspondence ■ Symbol recognition ■ Organization **Note:** This activity could also be done in a small group so that students work as a relay team, with each member of the team responsible for one "leg" of the activity.	■ Station markers (e.g., flags, brightly coloured plastic bottles, pictures, etc.) ■ Individual maps for each student ■ Pencils ■ Crayons or markers ■ String to hang station markers

Figure 4.9 *(Continued)*

Strategy	Skills Being Developed	Resources
lines. As the students visit each location, have them draw the symbol or picture (e.g., flower, animal) that they find on the marker at each station. Variations on this activity could have students finding orienteering punches, pattern scissors, or colourful stickers at each station. They mark their paper in the prescribed way using whatever means the teacher has explained. Alternatively, students could collect a picture they are to colour from each station as they visit it. Courses can be made longer and more complex as students become more familiar with this skill.		
Graph Paper Game		
Provide students with a sheet of graph paper. Have each student mark N, S, E, W on their sheet and orient it to face the N. Have students locate a start point (e.g., draw a red dot at a spot five lines east and four lines south of the top left corner of your paper). Now, provide step-by-step directions so that students create a pattern developing from each direction you provide. Example: ■ Move one line northeast (introduce the word "diagonal") and draw on a dot; connect this dot with the last dot using a straight line. ■ Move one line east. Draw a dot and connect it to the last dot.	■ Directions ■ One-to-one correspondence ■ Graphing ■ Counting accurately ■ Auditory attention ■ Orientation	■ Graph paper for each student ■ Set of step-by-step directions to be spoken by the teacher ■ Pencils ■ Coloured markers or pencils for each student ■ Direction signs

(Continued)

Figure 4.9 (*Continued*)

Strategy	Skills Being Developed	Resources
Start to abbreviate your directions (e.g., one line south) as students become familiar with the pattern.		
You may want to sketch a picture related to a current theme you are studying. The picture that results from following these directions will gradually emerge as students place and connect each dot. Having students colour the picture at the end of the activity will allow you to check quickly for each student's ability to complete this skill.		
Battleship		
Provide each student with a file folder and a piece of graph paper. Have each student orient and mark directions on their paper (N, S, E, and W) and letter each line of their paper from the northwest corner (top left) (e.g., A, B, C, etc., across the top [N] of their paper and 1, 2, 3, etc., down the left [W] side of their paper).	■ One-to-one correspondence ■ Coordinates ■ Direction ■ Latitude/longitude (can be introduced using this activity)	■ File folder for each student ■ Graph paper for each student ■ Pencils ■ Coloured markers ■ Paper clip for each pair of students
Once the numbering is completed, assign each student a partner and give each pair a paper clip. Have students sit opposite each other and set their file folders up using the paper clip to connect them to create a barrier between partners. Each partner draws 10 (or more, depending on the amount of practice you want to provide) ships on their paper so that their partner cannot see what they have drawn. Students sit on opposite sides of the barrier and call out the coordinates of their missile strike and the partner answers "hit" or "miss." As each student's battleships are "hit" by the		

Figure 4.9 (*Continued*)

Strategy	Skills Being Developed	Resources
partners' coordinates, the other student uses a brightly coloured marker to draw an X through the downed ship. The game is won when one partner has had all of their ships hit.		
Variation: A more "world friendly" variation might be to have students "switch off" a light bulb on a partner's sheet.		
Line Orienteering		
Have each student set up a page of graph paper as per the directions for the graph paper game above. Give students coordinates and have them print a predetermined letter at each coordinate. The letters should be chosen to spell out a word that relates to a current unit. Now, give step-by-step directions for students to move around the page in a certain order so they "pick up" one letter at a time in that order to spell out a word or words. Once students can identify the word(s), the game is complete. Start with simple words of 6–8 letters and move to longer words or phrases as students gain experience with this approach.	■ Following coordinates ■ Latitude and longitude ■ Direction	■ Predetermined letters to form a word or phrase ■ Graph paper for each student ■ Pencils ■ Classroom direction signs (on wall ahead of time)
Variation: Students could record several letters, randomly picked by them, on the coordinates determined by the teacher and then, once some of these letters are "picked up" by following coordinate directions from the teacher, students could be challenged to make as many words as possible using these letters.		

(Continued)

Figure 4.9 (*Continued*)

Strategy	Skills Being Developed	Resources
Puzzle Map Create a map of the classroom, schoolyard, neighbourhood, or country. Photocopy the map then cut each one into puzzle pieces and place each set of pieces into a separate envelope. Have students reconstruct the map(s). This would work well as a centre activity after students are familiar with it.	■ Map making ■ Orientation	■ Drawn or photocopied maps ■ Scissors ■ Envelopes ■ Glue (optional) **Note:** Mount puzzle map pieces on cardboard and/or laminate them for reuse.
Contour Cut-Outs Teach students that contour lines show elevations on a map. Add the words "contour lines" and "elevation" to the classroom word wall. Provide each student with a large quantity of cardboard and have them create a layered contour map (i.e., one layer of cardboard for each level of elevation) to show sample elevations in a model approximating the size of the top of their desks. Have students colour the edge of each contour level so that it is easily visible on the model.	■ Contour lines ■ Elevation **Note:** Make a hallway or library display of the finished products.	■ Cardboard ■ Scissors ■ Glue ■ Coloured pencils or markers **Note:** Students can each be asked to bring a cardboard box from home for this activity if you plan ahead.
Trivia Orienteering Plan a tour to a local event or exhibit that relates to a current unit of study (e.g., a museum or science centre or school/local library or heritage site). Set up a map with questions at each site marked on the map and have students follow the map to collect information to report. Providing different maps for each student or group, while creating considerable planning for the teacher, presents more	■ Map reading ■ Orientation	■ Individual or group maps ■ Pencils

Figure 4.9 *(Continued)*

Strategy	Skills Being Developed	Resources
challenge for the students. If all students have the same map to follow, give each student a different starting point. **Note:** It may be necessary for the teacher to make an advance visit to the site to collect information to put on the map.		

CASE STUDIES AND PROFESSIONAL ACTIVITIES FOR INNOVATION IN SOCIAL STUDIES

1. The provincial/territorial government has announced that they are starting a review of the provincial/territorial guidelines for elementary social studies. With a group of colleagues, design a process to identify the training steps that the government should provide to the teachers who will write this new guideline to ensure that the writing team is viewing the process from a consistent set of beliefs about the teaching of social studies.

2. Preambles in provincial/territorial guidelines often contain a section that describes the purpose of the program for social studies. Examine this section of your local social studies guideline. Edit the section so that the revised preamble reflects what you believe should be the priorities for the program of social studies in your classroom. Using a highlighter, highlight those sections that reflect your beliefs. Compare your highlighting and editing to that of other colleagues and discuss those areas where common agreement is found and those areas where unique additions or editing have been suggested.

3. Examine a section of a local social studies textbook or related resource book designed for students. Find a section that provides a detailed description of a person, event, or location. Consider how you would model for your young students how to use a graphic organizer to sort out the details provided in the description.

4. Examine the mapping activities provided in the Innovative Approaches in Your Social Studies Classroom section of this chapter. Using the active strategies that are modelled for you in this section, develop one further activity you could do with young children to help them understand an aspect of making and using maps.

CHAPTER REVIEW AND PROFESSIONAL DEVELOPMENT AS A TEACHER

This chapter has examined the following:

- Clear and carefully considered goals for the social studies program guide orientation and strategies, and focus subsequent events.

- Teachers need sophisticated curriculum knowledge to analyze guideline goals and help them provide the intended program of social studies.

- Professional knowledge, knowledge of discipline standards, a personal philosophy of learning, experience, imagination, and access to rich resources help the classroom teacher analyze and implement the stated goals of the social studies program.

- Curriculum goals should be analyzed to uncover and clarify intended connections among the content, processes, and student products created in response to the curriculum.

- Education goals should reflect the nature of knowledge organized in the discipline of social studies, the nature of society, and the nature of the learner.

- Curriculum goals are often referred to by other names (e.g., aims, competencies, outcomes).

- Curriculum goals can be stated at different levels to provide direction for the province/territory, school system, and classroom.

- Many factors in the school, community, society, and learner influence the development of curriculum goals.

- Situated learning goals will provide transformative, constructivist learning direction for classrooms.

- Students may hold a variety of inaccurate conceptions about topics that will require the teacher's attention during instruction; goals for implementation should take these conceptions into account.

- Many strategies can be useful to surface students' prior knowledge about a topic before specific goals for new instruction are identified.

- Springboards are learning experiences that become memorable anchors for students' learning because they create strong emotive responses and address key concepts of the program.

- Resources need to be selected carefully to support program goals.

- Clear goals help to ensure that learning time can be used productively and efficiently.

- Goals must reflect the standards of the discipline of social studies.

- Goals stated in provincial/territorial guidelines need to be deconstructed by teachers to identify the embedded knowledge, skills, and attitudes that will need to be taught for the success of the student in achieving the overall goal.

- Background knowledge, concepts, and skills need to be acquired before students will benefit from engagement in complex learning tasks such as inquiry.
- A comprehensive conception of the interrelated elements of sound lesson planning will help teachers maximize instructional time.
- Data can support our decisions about how we approach social studies.
- The skills of narration, description, and map making will support students' ability to address inquiry that seeks to examine the characteristics of a situation or event.

Professional Development Opportunities

1. Use a local social studies guideline for this activity. Work with a small group of colleagues to examine the goals indicated in the guideline. Sort the goals into three groups: those that address a provincial/territorial vision, a school vision, and a classroom vision. Examine each group of goals by asking, "What vision do these goals support for the role of social studies?" Then ask, "Are these visions consistent across the three levels of jurisdiction?"

2. Using a local social studies guideline, photocopy all of the expectations for one unit of study. Then, cut them up so that each expectation is on a separate slip of paper. Now, write the words Content, Process, and Product on three separate pieces of paper and lay them out on a table next to each other. Sort the slips of paper with goal statements on them under each of these three headings. Now, match one slip of paper from each heading so that you group an expectation that identifies a content goal, an expectation that identifies a process goal, and an expectation that identifies a product goal. Using these matched goals, create an outline that you could use to direct students to undertake an inquiry to meet all three learning goals. Compare your ideas with those of other groups of colleagues and examine the strength and vibrancy of the proposed inquiry.

3. Use the inquiry idea that you developed in #2 to expand the possibilities that you could offer students for their investigation by giving them options that reflect differences in their learning interests, abilities, and readiness for deep learning. Explain your expansions to another group of colleagues and get their feedback about your ideas. Adapt your ideas based on their input.

Weblinks

The links below will take you to the provincial guidelines for each province.

British Columbia
www.bced.gov.bc.ca/irp/ssk7.pdf

Alberta
http://education.alberta.ca/teachers/program/socialstudies.aspx

Saskatchewan
http://www.sasklearning.gov.sk.ca/docs/elemsoc/elemsoc.html

Manitoba
www.edu.gov.mb.ca/k12/cur/socstud/index.html

Ontario
www.edu.gov.on.ca/eng/curriculum/elementary

Quebec
www.mels.gouv.qc.ca/DGFJ/dp/programme_de_formation/primaire/pdf/educprg2001/educprg2001-071.pdf

New Brunswick, Newfoundland and Labrador, Nova Scotia, and Prince Edward Island
www.gnb.ca/0000/publications/curric/social.pdf

Chapter 5
Central Concepts in Social Studies

Learning Topics

- Central Concepts in Social Studies
- Systems and Structures
- Interactions and Interdependence
- The Environment
- Globalization
- Change and Continuity
- Culture, Multiculturalism, and Multi-Racism
- Power, Governance, and Stability

Children need to have multiple and engaging multi-sensorial experiences to ensure sound understanding.

The best and most beautiful things in the world cannot be seen or even touched. They must be felt within the heart.

—Helen Keller

CENTRAL CONCEPTS IN SOCIAL STUDIES

The discipline of social studies offers a unique perspective organized around a set of fundamental concepts. These central concepts, although described by different terms, have common presence in the provincial and territorial guidelines across Canada. Using a spiral curriculum approach, guidelines revisit some concepts in different contexts and at different grades to allow students to make deeper connections to related ideas and understand each concept at increasingly sophisticated levels.

Fundamental concepts that are central to social studies include

- systems and structures;
- interactions and interdependence;
- the environment;
- globalization;
- change and continuity;
- culture, multiculturalism, and multi-racism; and
- power, governance, and stability

In the following pages we will examine one of these fundamental concepts—systems and structures—more closely by looking at four aspects of it:

1. The meaning/definition of the concept.

2. Expansions of the concept to identify related concepts.

3. Examination of provincial and territorial curriculum guidelines to identify sample units and topics where the concept is addressed.

4. Sample strategies for teaching each fundamental concept in primary and junior classrooms.

We will also provide definitions, expansions, and sample teaching strategies for the other fundamental concepts of social studies.

SYSTEMS AND STRUCTURES

"Systems and structures" refers to the cluster of concepts that relates to patterns in our environment and our society. These patterns may be natural, such as patterns of growth at different elevations in an environment. They may also consist of human-constructed patterns that are designed for convenience, socialization, protection, or economic trade and exchange. Patterns are closely tied to geography. For example, we may socialize, trade,

Figure 5.1 Systems and Structures

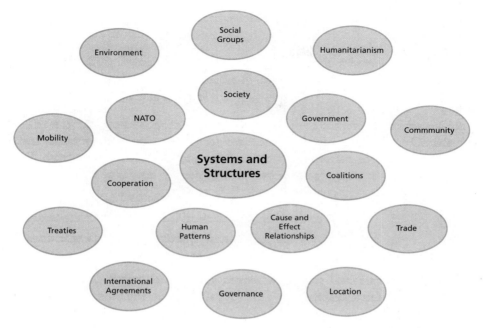

and protect ourselves within the boundaries of a country that is somewhat defined by geographic features such as lakes, rivers, oceans, and prairies.

We may develop the larger concepts of systems and structures with our students by having them experience them at a level that is more familiar to their daily experiences. Embedded in the concepts of systems and structures are many of the concepts shown in Figure 5.1.

By providing our students with exposure and study opportunities to examine these concepts, we can develop their capacity to understand the fundamental concepts that will contribute to their ability to generalize and draw conclusions.

Reflections of Fundamental Concepts in Provincial/Territorial Guidelines

While provincial/territorial guidelines are designed differently to reflect local preferences for the study of social studies as themes or as general topics, all provincial/territorial guidelines contain some units of study in the primary and junior divisions that reflect inclusion of the fundamental concepts of systems and structures. The chart below shows units in each provincial and territorial guideline that reflect these concepts.

The chart below does not incorporate all of the units that are identified for study in each grade across Canada. Rather, it seeks to identify a format that teachers can use to analyze and align their programs with the fundamental concepts of social studies.

Grade	British Columbia/ Yukon	Alberta	Saskatchewan	Manitoba	Ontario	Quebec	Atlantic Provinces	Northwest Territories and Nuavut
K	Characteristics of local, natural, and human-built environments	I belong	Identity	The People Around Me The World Around Me	Features of Communities Around the World	To orient self in space and time	Social Connections	Living in Our Community Working in Our Community
1	Similarities and differences among families Social Structures Symbols of Canada Purpose of Classroom and School Rules How the Environment Affects Daily Life Recognizing Maps of Canada	Introduction to the Concept of Community	Cooperation Family Meeting Needs and Wants Family, School Rules	Connecting and Belonging	The Local Community	To orient self in space and time To compare places and social phenomena here and elsewhere from the past and the present	Understanding the similarity and diversity of social and cultural groups, including Aboriginal People Identify the difference between needs and wants; factors that influence how these are met Understand how communities depend on each other for the exchange of goods and services	Family Relatives Community Cooperation

2	Group decision making Bodies of water and landforms; how the environment affects human activities	Canada's Dynamic Communities	Decision Making	Communities in Canada	Features of Communities Around the World	To construct his/her representation of space, time, and society To compare places . . . from the past and present	Economics	Living in Our Community
3	Characteristics of Canadian Society	Communities in the World	Identity	Exploring the World Communities of the World	Urban and Rural Communities	French Society in New France Around 1845 Canadian Society in New France Around 1745 Iroquoian and Algonquin Society Around 1500 Canadian Society in New France and Societies in the Thirteen Colonies Around 1745	People	Communities in Our Region Communities in the NWT

(Continued)

Table 5.1 (continued)

Grade	British Columbia/ Yukon	Alberta	Saskatchewan	Manitoba	Ontario	Quebec	Atlantic Provinces	Northwest Territories and Nuavut
4	Bartering; traditional technologies used in Aboriginal Cultures; technological exchange with European explores/settlers	The Land, Histories, and Stories	Identity	Canada and the North: Places and Stories Geography of Canada Canada's North	Canada's Provinces, Territories, and Regions		Explorations Exploring the World Today Exploring Canada Today	The Faces of the NWT
5	Immigration, Citizenship, and Rights Physical Regions of Canada	Histories and Stories of Ways of Life in Canada	Identity	First Peoples Early European Colonization (1600 to 1763) The British Colony to Confederation	Early Civilizations	Canadian Society Around 1800 Quebec Society Around 1980 Canadian Society in the Prairies and on the West Coast Around 1900	Societies Over Time Ancient Societies Social Structure: Medieval Societies Early Aboriginal Peoples: North America	The North's Resources

6	Federal Government, the Justice System, and the Charter of Rights and Responsibilities Role of Canada in the World	Citizens Participating in Decision Making	Canada's Relationship with its Atlantic Neighbours: Location and Physical Geography	Building a Nation (1867–1914)	Connections: Canada's Links to the World	World Cultures: Canada- A Multicultural and Multiracial Mosaic	Quebec Society and Canadian Society on the Prairies Around 1900 Micmac Society and Inuit Society Around 1980	Settlement and Immigration: Colonial French Societies The World in 1800	The Regions of Canada The Faces of Canadian Settlement

Teaching about Systems and Structures

Fundamental concepts of the discipline of social studies can be daunting for teachers to consider when planning a program because the concepts are expansive. We need to remember that many small experiences with ideas accumulate to create bigger and more comprehensive understanding. Some strategies that can help to accumulate experiences and help young students build an understanding of the concepts of structures and systems include

- using graphic organizers to show relationships in visual ways;
- using children's literature examples to develop generalizations;
- having students create models from concrete materials;
- using photo studies to help students imagine what they cannot experience firsthand;
- making comparisons;
- using the language of the discipline to identify examples of the concepts;
- teaching students the difference between examples and definitions (they will often give an example when you ask them to explain or define unless they are taught the difference between the two);
- teaching concept clarification as a study skill (see Chapter 2);
- creating opportunities to make mind–body connections as you teach abstract or not-yet-experienced concepts; and
- moving teaching from the known to the unknown, creating analogies as abstract ideas are introduced (e.g., "This is like . . . ").

The following pages identify the other fundamental concepts, provide working definitions that are accessible to later junior level students, and provide some strategies for teaching each concept.

INTERACTIONS AND INTERDEPENDENCE

When humans come into contact with other humans, with the environment, and with ways of doing things, they either adapt and accommodate the new contacts or they conflict with them. The forces that influence the developing relationships shape the impact that groups and systems have on each other when they come into contact. Successful contacts will result in productive interdependence. Unsuccessful ones will result in conflict. The impact of interactions can be identified and followed over time and space.

Interactions and interdependence are fundamental concepts in social studies. Concepts that relate to and support students' understanding of the concepts of interaction and interdependence include those listed in Figure 5.2.

Some strategies to help young students build an understanding of the concepts of interactions and interdependence include

- creating trade and movement maps that students can develop using strings or arrows to show how people and goods move around the globe;

Figure 5.2 Interactions and Interdependence

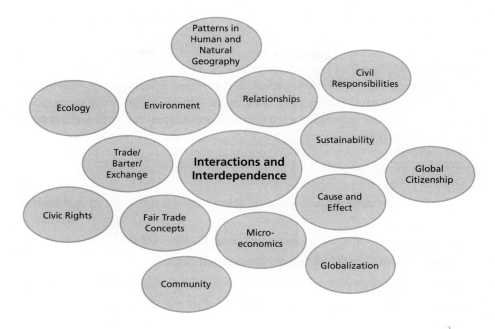

- having students develop a T-chart to identify their rights and responsibilities;
- teaching students how to generate criteria for a comparison;
- developing simulations to show students that some resources are being depleted;
- simulating fair trade exchanges and analyzing them to help students determine what fair trade means;
- studying near and far examples of communities to show how they are structured and interact to meet needs (ask probing questions such as "Whose needs are met?", "Whose needs are not met?", and "Why?");
- connecting social studies to science to examine examples of micro-communities and ecosystems;
- connecting social studies to language to tell stories about other communities the students have not experienced firsthand;
- exploring through field trips; and
- using media and technology to create opportunities to experience through the eyes of another.

These are just a few examples of effective strategies that will help social studies students to accumulate experiences to help them build their understanding of complex ideas. Professional brainstorming, supported by interaction with colleagues, can help teachers generate many of these effective strategy ideas.

THE ENVIRONMENT

The environment needs to be understood to include both the natural and the constructed elements of the earth and its atmosphere in dynamic interaction with each other. When we structure learning experiences for young students to engage their understanding of the environment, we must constantly return to the idea of interaction between human activity and its impact on the environment. Environmental issues cannot be adequately represented as linear relationships but must be shown as a complex web of cause-and-effect relationships. Students must be led to understand that human needs and wants have an environmental price.

The environment is a fundamental concept in social studies. Concepts that relate to and support students' understanding of the concept of the environment are depicted in Figure 5.3.

Some strategies that can accumulate to help young students build an understanding of the concepts of the environment include

- graphing activities that show per capita use of resources across cultures;

- performing web quests to examine and compare lifestyles;

- creating and analyzing graphics that demonstrate environmental trends and impacts;

- providing opportunities for cross-curricular experiences with the examination of ecosystems;

- building and studying terrariums;

- tracing transportation routes of common goods manufactured in other countries;

Figure 5.3 The Environment

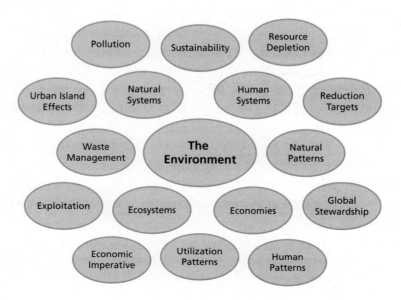

- differentiating between needs and wants; and
- developing perspective through stories exchanged with students in other countries (i.e., "A Day in the Life of . . . ") and analysis of the resources that are needed to sustain the lifestyle as described.

An integrated curriculum approach that examines environmental issues from many perspectives may benefit students' understanding.

GLOBALIZATION

Transportation and communication technology has made connections around the globe readily available and possible for many Canadians. While students may not have visited other countries they will all be aware of other countries through exposure to media and through secondary sources, such as parent trips. Students can be made aware of these connections by asking them to examine the labels on their clothing and the items in their desks. Connecting what they have and use every day to the origin of these items can help students understand the interrelationships that influence every aspect of our lives in Canada. We cannot, however, leave the concept of globalization at the level of trade relations. Students need to understand that globalization encompasses connections among the world's geography and its peoples in relation to economies, labour, conflict, peacekeeping, resource and waste management, common territories (e.g., oceans), political interfacing, technology, humanitarian interaction, immigration, and space exploration. Technology has increased our awareness of inequities across the globe in relation to lifestyles and resource use. In social studies, we study the environment from a global perspective for the purpose of becoming better stewards of it.

Globalization is a fundamental concept in social studies and touches on many related topics (see Figure 5.4).

Some strategies to help young students build an understanding of the concept of globalization include

- designing integrated studies that support social studies through stories about other peoples and places;
- using sustainable and resource-friendly classroom practices to heighten students' awareness of waste;
- providing opportunities for students to tell classmates about their travels to other countries;
- using documentaries and vignettes or video clips to expose students to living conditions in other countries;
- developing comparisons;
- creating management plans; and
- developing inquiry tasks that focus on "why" questions to examine implicit and explicit values in a situation.

Figure 5.4 Globalization

These strategies represent a few of the many ways that teachers can design engaging learning experiences to help students understand the complex nature of globalization and the impact of this reality of their lives.

CHANGE AND CONTINUITY

It is difficult for young students to conceptualize change over time and place outside of their immediate experience. Continuity may be even more difficult for students to understand because of their lack of a long engagement with events. Popular media will have created exposure to some historical and futuristic examples that students can draw upon to help them build generalizations. However, teachers will need to understand the impact of media on creating conceptions, misperceptions, and frameworks for guiding students' abilities to assimilate and accommodate new information about historical events or new conceptions about space. Whole generations of Canadian students grow up with certain conceptions because of their childhood exposure to popular media phenomena. For example, some students may have a romanticized view of wildlife predators in Africa because of their childhood experience watching movies such as *The Lion King*. Similar TV experiences watching a series such as *Anne of Green Gables* may create interesting but idealized views of both history and geography. The challenge for teachers of social studies will be to build on and adapt these romanticized versions of change and continuity to reflect reasonable and age-appropriate reality for young students.

Ultimately, social studies experiences should guide students in their understanding that *change* is manifested as differences over time. *Continuity* should be understood as consistency, stability, and connectedness over time and place.

To examine the concepts of change and continuity effectively in a social studies program, teachers will need to teach students about perspective, bias, and cultural filters that may distort and inflate factual information. We need to teach students about methods of critical literacy to help them examine events from many angles. Chapter 3 developed ideas about how to teach critical thinking in social studies. Students need to develop appropriate habits of mind to examine the concepts of change and continuity without bias and from the broadest possible perspective.

Change and continuity are fundamental concepts in social studies and touch on many related ideas (see Figure 5.5).

Some strategies that can help young students build an understanding of the concepts of change and continuity include

- re-enactments;
- pageants and simulations;
- imaginative recreations and plays;
- costume design and use;
- heritage fairs (see Chapter 17);
- magazine comparisons;
- critical analysis of artwork and photography;
- comparisons;

Figure 5.5 Change and Continuity

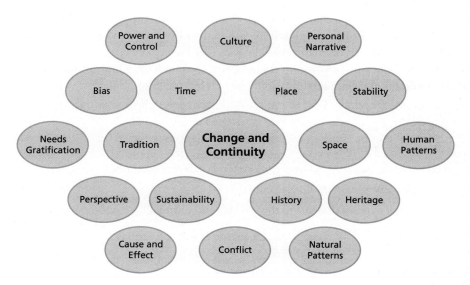

- debates related to historical or future studies issues; and
- readers' theatre.

These strategies will help young students examine change and continuity by supporting their thinking through the creation of mind–body connections. This will help them gain perspective on the ideas they encounter.

CULTURE, MULTICULTURALISM, AND MULTI-RACISM

Immigration has played a key role in defining Canadian society. It has influenced how the culture we call "Canadian" has evolved and how we describe that culture within Canada. The curriculum of Northwest Territories and Nunavut refers to the "faces" of settlement in those areas of Canada, personalizing the concept of culture. Canada's culture is changing as immigration, population, and urbanization influence settlement patterns. Economic fluctuations and job opportunities influence mobility. Population rates within cultural groups, and particularly within Native communities, influence the social priorities that define the culture of Canada. Terms to describe the nature of Canadian culture have evolved from concepts that emphasized a blending of cultures (i.e., melting pot), to those that recognized the differences within the society (i.e., cultural mosaic), to those that celebrate and encourage the preservation of various cultures within a harmonious whole (i.e., multiculturalism, multi-racism, pluralism). Our perspective on the nature of the evolving Canadian society, and our ability to view each culture with respect and inclusiveness, has put pressure on the evolution of the language we use to describe it.

Culture includes the ways that we choose to express our humanity within our Canadian population. Our culture is not static and is influenced by our interaction with the environment and with each other. Cultural values provide a filter for our perceptions of time, place, change, significance, and perspective. Culture defines our tolerance and refines our ability to appreciate that which is different from our personal experiences.

Culture, multiculturalism, pluralism, and multi-racism are fundamental concepts in social studies and touch on many related topics (see Figure 5.6):

Some strategies to help young students build an understanding of the concepts of culture, multiculturalism, pluralism, and multi-racism include

- investigations into the beliefs, values, customs, and lifestyles of all cultures that make up Canadian culture;
- cultural celebrations;
- banquet-style celebrations that explore foods of many cultures;
- guest speakers to explain diverse cultures;
- artwork that exposes students to the symbols and spirituality of non-dominant cultures;
- character education;
- teaching social skills to support group work;
- cooperative learning strategies and structures;

Figure 5.6 Culture, Multiculturalism, Pluralism, and Multi-Racism

- journaling before and after multicultural experiences to make personal awareness explicit; and

- comparisons.

These strategies will help young students examine culture, multiculturalism, pluralism, and multi-racism by supporting their thinking through experiences designed to generate respect and tolerance for diversity.

POWER, GOVERNANCE, AND STABILITY

World stability is a Canadian value. We support this value through global peacekeeping efforts and through membership in the United Nations. Some Canadians support world organizations such as Amnesty International and students may have opportunities to engage these organizations in classroom studies. The study of power, governance, and stability in social studies provides students with knowledge of the laws and rules that we value and support across Canada and as a member of the global community.

Power, governance, and stability are fundamental concepts in social studies and touch on many related topics (see Figure 5.7).

Some strategies that can help young students build an understanding of the concepts of power, governance, and stability include

- simulations that include conflict and opportunities for peaceful resolution to conflicts;

- mock parliamentary debates;

- mock elections;

Figure 5.7 Governance and Stability

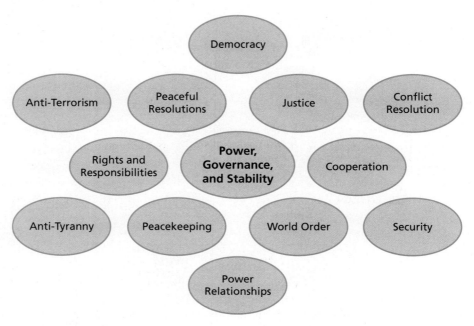

- democratic classroom meetings;
- graphic representations of government decision-making processes;
- community action;
- web searches about local, national, or international issues;
- projects; and
- justice circles.

These strategies will help young students examine power, governance, and stability by supporting their thinking through experiences designed to generate respect for the democratic process, the rule of law, and order in society.

By being aware of the fundamental concepts embedded in common or similar topics in Canadian curriculum in social studies, teachers can ensure their conscious and deliberate inclusion in a curriculum that respects the nature of the discipline and promotes deep and enduring understanding in learners.

INNOVATIVE APPROACHES IN YOUR SOCIAL STUDIES CLASSROOM

As you examined some of the strategies for identifying ways to help students accumulate experiences and understand the fundamental concepts of social studies, you may have noticed that the skill of comparison appeared many times. Comparison is one of the

Figure 5.8 A Sample Graphic Organizer (Venn Diagram)

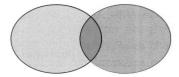

sequence of skills that can be used to help students undertake a thorough study of a topic using topic elaboration (see Chapter 1). Comparison addresses the inquiry question, "How does this change (over time, space, etc.)?"

Comparison in early primary grades is aided by the use of graphic organizers and visual representations (e.g., photographs, sketches) before students have developed a broader vocabulary. Venn diagrams (see Figure 5.8) are commonly used for comparisons where criteria are not identified for the comparison but students brainstorm similarities and differences between two ideas.

However, as students' language skills develop, they can begin to be introduced to the concept of criteria for a comparison. Comparison criteria such as location, purpose, actions, time period, nationality, achievements, and accomplishments can be introduced to students and used on a concept or word wall in the classroom to help students develop spelling expertise with these words. Process words such as *criteria* and *criterion* can be introduced in the mid-primary grades.

Once students understand the concept of criteria that can be used to balance a comparison (or make the comparison "fair"), teachers can begin to move away from the relatively unsophisticated comparisons allowed by Venn diagrams and start to teach students to organize comparisons on comparison charts that will allow them to see the items, events, or people being compared and the common criteria being used to structure that comparison. This also can be done effectively in the early primary grades but the content of the comparison will need to reflect the language development of the students and may require support from pictures and symbols.

As students develop increasing facility with completing comparison charts that the teacher has provided, they should be challenged to develop their own charts and to become increasingly independent with the skills that support effective comparison, including

- naming the class of items to which the things to be compared will belong (e.g., industries);
- generating appropriate criteria;
- physically structuring a comparison chart that will guide their research and that is large enough to serve as a recording page;
- developing comparison charts using a computer;
- managing files to import research information into a comparison chart;
- expanding comparison charts as data becomes more complex; and
- using words that highlight the three elements of comparison (i.e., similarities, differences, and cause/effect relationships).

Charts such as the one below provide a valuable reference (anchor) for students as they approach comparisons.

Sample Comparison Chart			
	Industries in Our Provinces		
Criteria	**Forestry**	**Mining**	**Fishing**
Product(s) of this industry			
Location of this industry			
Number of people employed in this industry			
Related employment			

Late primary and junior students can also be taught to use their comparison chart to structure writing to explain what they have compared. The comparison chart becomes their writing plan. Initially, such comparisons may be stilted and seem very mechanical. However, as with any skill, once students become more adept at the process, their writing will begin to flow more naturally and provide an opportunity for students to infuse their personal style into their writing. Providing students with connecting words such as those in Figure 5.9 will help them with this process.

For initial comparative writing efforts, students can be taught to use a writing procedure that will guide them to work through their comparison chart (see Figure 5.10).

Good teaching practice would require that teachers move students away from the lock-step approach to comparative writing as soon as possible and allow their own style to

Figure 5.9 Connecting Words to Identify Similarities, Differences, and Cause/Effect Relationships

Similarities	Differences	Cause/Effect
■ like	■ unlike	■ causing
■ as	■ different than	■ cause
■ similar to	■ dissimilarly	■ results in
■ just as	■ without	■ is affected by
■ also	■ but	■ because
■ as well	■ notwithstanding	■ is caused by
■ similarly		■ consequently
■ with		■ as a result
■ either/or		
■ neither/nor		

Figure 5.10 Comparative Writing Procedure

Opening Paragraph

1. Name the topic.

2. Name the things that will be compared (subtopics).

3. Name the criteria that will be used for this comparison.

Body Paragraphs

4. Rename the first criterion.

5. Write comparative sentences (using the connecting words provided in Figure 5.9) to talk about each thing that is being compared (subtopic).

6. Rename the second criterion.

7. Write comparative sentences (using the connecting words provided in Figure 5.9) to talk about each thing that is being compared (subtopic).

8. Continue as per steps 4–7 for each remaining criterion.

Closing Paragraph

9. Write a paragraph that explains what was compared and what criteria were used for the comparison.

10. Add one or more concluding sentences to the closing paragraph to explain overall conclusions that you have come to as a result of comparing.

---

develop through practice. This can happen once students develop a mental framework for comparisons that allows them to distribute information across all topics and criteria. Once that mental framework is in place, students' comparative writing will flow more naturally. It is, however, very important for early comparative efforts to be supported by visual frameworks, clear procedures, and teacher modelling (see Chapter 4). A framework also allows students to free up mental storage space to concentrate their attention on looking for similarities, differences, and cause/effect relationships in their information.

CASE STUDIES AND PROFESSIONAL ACTIVITIES FOR INNOVATION IN SOCIAL STUDIES

1. Ms. Griffin is a newly certified teacher and has just accepted a contract to teach Grade 4. She is eager to start planning her program. This week she will focus on plans for social studies. She knows that if she starts there, she may uncover some opportunities to integrate topics with what she is doing in language, art, and possibly music. She starts by examining the provincial/territorial guidelines for social studies. The preamble of the guideline directs her to focus on "habits of mind" and "fundamental concepts" of the

discipline as she designs her courses. She now turns to the first unit she will teach and examines the direction she is given there. Help her through this process. Using any unit in your provincial/territorial guidelines for Grade 4 social studies, match each guideline expectation to the fundamental concepts that are central to the discipline.

2. Ms. Griffin is aware that she now needs to develop comprehensive lessons that will attend to developing specific expectations as laid out in the guideline, as well as ensuring the development of fundamental concepts in her students. Throughout this chapter, strategies were suggested for approaching social studies in ways that include attention to ensuring the students understand the fundamental concepts of the discipline. Take any one of these ideas and develop it as an outline for a lesson (or a full lesson plan). Once you are done, form a cooperative group among your colleagues and share the approach you have developed.

3. Ms. Griffin would benefit from hearing your ideas. Form a group of four or five colleagues. Select one of the fundamental concepts of social studies that have been presented in this chapter. Write the name of the concept at the top of a piece of chart paper. In your group, brainstorm other strategies that you could use to develop this fundamental concept with your students. Once you have finished that list, add the ideas from this chapter that are different from those on your brainstormed list. Post the chart paper in the classroom for casual reference as you learn more about teaching social studies effectively.

4. Ms. Griffin wants to have her students participate in this eye-opening activity. First, she will have them add up the approximate value of everything they have on their body. If they are unsure what to include, she will ask them, "Did you come into the world with it?" Ms. Griffin explains to students that if they say they did not come into the world with the item, it has been purchased. Have students include items such as glasses, socks, bracelets, braces, earrings, etc. Assign an approximate dollar value to each item. Have them add up the total value. Now, have them calculate how many days, months, and years it would take them to earn enough money to buy all of these items at a developing country wage. For example, if the total on their body is worth $2000 then divide $2000 by $2.50. This will give you the number of days someone in Tanzania would have to work to pay for what they have on their body. Have students repeat these calculations for several other countries to appreciate the scope of global poverty.

CHAPTER REVIEW AND PROFESSIONAL DEVELOPMENT AS A TEACHER

This chapter has examined the following:

- The discipline of social studies focuses on fundamental concepts that are central to the nature of the discipline.

- The fundamental concepts of social studies include systems and structures; interactions and interdependence; the environment; globalization; change and continuity; culture, multiculturalism, pluralism, and multi-racism; and power, governance, and stability.

- Understanding these fundamental concepts can support teachers' development of a social studies curriculum that promotes deep understanding.

- Fundamental concepts are reflected in the topics identified for study in all Canadian provinces and territories.

- Systems and structures refer to the study of patterns in our environment and our society.

- Interactions and interdependence refer to the forces that influence developing relationships and the impact those relationships have on interacting groups and systems.

- Study of the environment must include both natural and constructed elements of the earth and its atmosphere and consider the dynamic interaction each element may have on the other.

- Globalization encompasses connections among the world's geography and peoples in relation to economies, labour, conflict, peacekeeping, resource and waste management, common interests, political interfacing, technology, humanitarian interaction, immigration, and space exploration.

- Change refers to differences over time.

- Continuity refers to consistency, stability, and connectedness over time and place.

- "Culture" refers to the ways in which we choose to express our humanity.

- The study of power, governance, and stability includes exposure to laws and rules valued in Canadian society, within Canada, and as a member of the global community.

Professional Development Activity

Observe as an experienced social studies teacher teaches a lesson. As you observe, monitor the lesson for reference to, or inclusion of, any of the fundamental concepts of social studies. As well, monitor strategies the teacher uses during this lesson to include expanding conceptions of these big ideas. An organizer such as the one below may help structure your observations.

Observation Organizer		
Fundamental Concept	**Supporting Concepts**	**How This Was Taught**

Take one of the ideas to develop fundamental concepts in social studies provided in this chapter and develop it into a strategy for a specific grade you may work with in the near future. Once you have tried the strategy, refine it to ensure that it is optimally effective. Write up your strategy on a single page and share it with your colleagues. Through this sharing process, you can start to build your professional references of social studies strategies for future use.

While the fundamental concepts that are presented in this chapter provide a comprehensive overview for you, you may find that additional concepts become central to the discipline as time and social sensitivities evolve. Discuss this with a group of colleagues. Are there other fundamental concepts that you think need to be addressed in social studies? Is there evidence in local guidelines that these ideas are intended for your local curriculum? What social forces are causing this (or these) new fundamental concepts to become priorities?

Weblinks

The Environment/Resources

This site allows children to explore and learn how to protect the environment. It contains games, pictures, and stories.

www.epa.gov/kids

This site is an online magazine that covers a wide range of current environmental issues and provides links to more detailed information on Environment Canada's website and to other valuable Internet sites.

www.ec.gc.ca/envirozine

The Teacher's Lounge at this site provides new lesson plans tailored to elementary curriculum. It also provides access to the national contest The Great EcoKids' Challenge.

www.ecokids.ca/pub/index.cfm

Multiculturalism and Diversity Resources

This site includes an extensive range of collections and learning modules to help teachers and students make use of the wealth of primary materials related to Canadian multiculturalism. It offers Canada-wide resources, regional history, and resources on specific cultural groups. It also links directly to over 30 different Canadian multicultural sites.

http://multiculturalcanada.ca

The Canadian Government

This Government of Canada website provides access to many online activities for elementary students, including quizzes, video gallery, and information regarding our nation.

http://canada.gc.ca/acanada/vwctgry.htm?lang=eng&f4nt=1&CId=105

Chapter 6
The Study of Controversial Issues in Social Studies

Learning Topics

- Global Thinking and Local Sensitivity
- The Ethics of Critical Thinking
- Understanding Community Norms and Values
- Gender, Sexuality, Age, Race, and Disability in Social Studies
- Teaching Social Justice and Social Action in the Primary and Junior Divisions
- Character Education, Restorative Justice, and Values for Young Learners

Teachers must always consider the ethics that underscore the critical-thinking skills they teach.

Social studies education was designed from the outset to get at these big issues of what it means to live together in a democracy, of working together to build a respectful and responsible community, of bringing together various cultures and peoples into a common whole, of giving the young the tools and insights to help create a better world.

—Wanda Cassidy, 2004

GLOBAL THINKING AND LOCAL SENSITIVITY

The complex interactions of technology, space, and ocean explorations, and the ease of global transportation have combined to make us more aware now than in any previous generation that our destinies as members of the human race are connected. The impact of actions in one part of the world may have profound and drastic implications for people thousands of kilometers away. At the best of times, these global impacts on each other may be felt as aid in times of crisis or empathy in times of disaster. At the worst of times, these global impacts may take the form of international conflicts, epidemics, and exploitation.

How we address the globalization of our world in our social studies programs with very young children has the potential to have dynamic and long-lasting impacts on how our students view their role as global citizens. It is for this reason that the development of the attitudes and behaviours of good citizens has become a central goal of social studies in many jurisdictions across Canada. Young children can have an impact on global events through the guidance of their teachers. It is, however, just as likely that young students will have many more opportunities to take action at the local level. Regardless of the focus of action, it is incumbent on teachers to develop global thinking capacity in students as they learn to ask challenging questions, explore issues, and propose solutions.

Through the sensitive and age-appropriate study of controversial issues, we can ensure that our students

- learn how to demonstrate care;
- understand their role as global citizens;
- understand legal issues in global contexts;
- develop appropriate personal and social values; and
- take appropriate and responsible action.

Teaching Students to Demonstrate Care

The backgrounds of our students are diverse. We cannot assume that they have common values or standards of consideration for others. By including goals and approaches related to developing our students' capacity for caring, we can help to nurture this aspect of their global citizenship education. Students can demonstrate care through attitudes and actions in relation to

- themselves;
- classmates;

- the school community;
- the local community;
- strangers from a distance;
- the natural world;
- other living things, including plants and animals;
- the human-made world; and
- diverse ideas and values.

To create a curriculum that will promote caring in our students, it is the obligation of social studies teachers to address controversial issues as they relate to the grade's curriculum. We can teach our students that caring is "a continuous search for competence. When we care, we want to do our very best for the objects of our care" (Noddings, 2003). A caring curriculum will promote respect and understanding of diversity in the human condition.

To create a curriculum of caring, social studies teachers will need to address controversial issues related to war, poverty, inequity, crimes, socio-economic disparity, racism, sexism, gender discrimination, marginalization, genocide, weapons proliferation, dissent, political participation, unfair trade, privacy, and national insensitivity. Many of these topics will create concern for parents in the school community. It is the role of the social studies teacher to ensure that the path toward the responsible treatment of controversial issues in the curriculum is paved through communication and sensitive handling.

Addressing controversial issues in the classroom is risky, requiring professional perspective and anticipation of the risks so that students, parents, and the broader community see the presentation of balanced perspectives. Classroom discussions have a role in the exploration of controversial issues. By anticipating the risks and responses to the discussion of issues, social studies teachers can ensure that they prepare themselves to manage these discussions with balance, integrity, professionalism, and sensitivity to local views. With young children, opportunities to address controversial issues such as fairness, rights, and responsibilities, may present spontaneously so teachers will have to consider ways to manage such points of discussion as part of the process of creating a tolerant and inclusive environment in their classrooms. Students need many opportunities to see their teachers in the role of people who care to develop a perspective on themselves as people who care.

[D]eveloping people with a strong capacity for care is a major objective for responsible education.

—*Noddings, 2003*

We need to recognize that, as teachers of social studies and teachers of young children, our role as caregivers can provide powerful models for children to become caring. We need to honour our roles and our ethical responsibilities to our students

Figure 6.1 Purposes of Citizenship Education in Social Studies

Purpose	Strategy	Explanation
Social Initiation	Strategy: Textbook-based approach	Teaching the understandings, abilities, and values needed to fit into a productive society
Social Reformation	Strategy: Values-based approach	Empowering students with the understandings, abilities, and values needed to improve their society
Personal Development	Strategy: Builds from the students' feelings, needs, values, issues, and problems	Fostering personal competencies and interests in students so that they develop fully as individuals and members of a society
Academic Understanding	Strategy: Promotes original historical or social science research; focuses on bodies of knowledge that define processes of the discipline through research and reasoning/critical thinking	Mastering the knowledge and processes (e.g., inquiry) of the social studies discipline as a form of organizer for making meaning of the world

Source: Adapted from Case and Clark, 2004.

in their growth toward their own capacity to become caring individuals. By addressing controversial issues as an adjunct of the social studies curriculum, we can maximize our opportunities to role model the caring adult.

Citizenship education is central to creating a curriculum of caring. Case and Clark (2004) identify four purposes of citizenship education in our social studies programs (see Figure 6.1).

Case and Clark (2004) suggest that "the most common and long-standing view of the purpose of social studies . . . has been to promote a core body of beliefs and instill a set of essential values and skills that are thought necessary to function in and contribute to society." This view is supported by other noted social studies academics. Alan Sears (2004) says that "Across Canada, preparation for democratic citizenship is widely acknowledged as a central goal for public schooling." Because of the nature of social studies as a discipline, it has been the subject area with the most obvious focus on promoting citizenship as a goal of its curriculum efforts.

Through the examination of controversial issues in social studies, supported by viable investigation techniques offered by the discipline, we can teach students that there is value in being able to support an opinion about something controversial to arrive at intellectual and defensible positions. This will teach students that we can disagree about an issue with respect and tolerance for differing opinions.

[C]itizenship is a complicated idea, affected by many factors, including where a person finds his or her sense of belonging and the degree to which he or she is engaged in the civic culture.

—Sears, 2004

As teachers of social studies, we need to clarify for ourselves the difference between being a citizen and demonstrating citizenship. Demonstrating citizenship includes active participation and exercising our rights as citizens to influence and provide direction within the democratic framework of our times. Through participation we mold and shape the democracy we want to share in our pluralist society to reflect the values, dispositions, and actions that define us as Canadians.

Sears notes the deficit in large-scale data about the extent to which our provincial and territorial curricula are meeting the stated goals of promoting citizenship in our students.

Since 1968, however, there has been no systematic, large-scale effort to evaluate civic education in Canada either by academic researchers or through provincial or national testing programs.

—Sears, 2004

It becomes the role of the individual teacher to ensure that they are selecting and designing curriculum strategies to address the attainment of noble goals. The context in which we address such goals—the democratic operation of our classrooms—can create the venue for modelling the citizenship ideals we are trying to inculcate.

Finally, it is the responsibility of the social studies teacher to give careful thought to the role of action in the pursuit of the discipline of social studies. In Chapter 1 we examined topic elaboration and found that the potential of a thorough investigation of a topic can lead the learner to ask, "What could/should/might/will be done about this?" Addressing this question will lead the learner to act. Action that is spurred by passionate beliefs and convictions is empowering and can engage and give meaning to academic studies. However, leading students to engage in action related to their studies requires thoughtful consideration by the teacher to examine the potential actions for pitfalls, and to consider the long-term consequences of action. Social action for the sake of being active may be misguided, despite the best intentions of the planners.

Case and Clark (2004) offer some useful guidelines for social studies teachers who want to consider the inclusion of a social action component in their curriculum planning. The following questions provide guidelines for teachers in selecting social action projects for their students:

- Will the project promote a sense of empowerment on the part of the students?
- Will the project develop a range of civic competencies?

- Will the project promote academic learning?
- Is there a high degree of student interest and personal commitment?
- Is the cost in teacher time worth the potential benefits?
- Is there a high probability of success in the eyes of the students?

Once teachers have considered these questions, they need to ensure that they become informed about the potential long-term impacts of the proposed action before engaging their students and the school community. Teachers will then need to teach students the skills that will ensure success when they invest in an action-based project.

Once a course of action is determined, teachers will need to

- acquire support from school administrators and affected colleagues;
- acquire support from the local community;
- gather related information about the proposed course of action, including possible long-term effects;
- provide students with a balanced perspective about the controversial issues or potentially controversial actions;
- anticipate resource needs, including research data, related to the proposed actions;
- anticipate consequences of the proposed actions, both short and long term;
- evaluate alternative courses of action;
- proceed responsibly; and
- engage students in post-action reflection to move their thinking from "Now what?" (the action) to "So what?" (the influence of their action); this step creates a sense of self-efficacy in students and the belief that their energies can make a difference.

By ensuring the consideration of these steps, teachers will help students to have early experiences in responsible social action that are ensured of success, while teaching them to remain sensitive to local issues.

THE ETHICS OF CRITICAL THINKING

In Chapter 2 we defined critical thinking as habits of mind that cause a learner to systematically consider, analyze, question, investigate, and promote action in a productive, safe, and socially responsible manner. The teacher who seeks to promote and support the use of critical thinking as a central approach in their social studies classroom will need to consider the ethics or morality issues of critical thinking. A classroom where critical thinking is the norm will respect both the engagement in critical thinking and the logical action-oriented results that will ensue because of that critical approach to examining issues.

We need to understand, and help our students to understand, that critical thought does not necessarily result in the same standards being applied to action. People can espouse one belief and act in conflict with that stated belief. Lawrence Kohlberg, noted for his theories of moral reasoning, suggests that a person's level of reasoning about an issue will always operate consistently with the highest possible level of their current moral reasoning development. However, moral actions and behaviours are highly situational and may not match the person's highest level of moral reasoning because of pressures brought to bear by the situation in which action is undertaken (Kohlberg, 1969).

Critical-thinking experiences in the classroom must take into account each student's development of moral thinking capabilities. "Since moral reasoning clearly is reasoning, advanced moral reasoning depends upon advanced logical reasoning" (Kohlberg, 1969). We can equate Kohlberg's conception of logical reasoning with the concept of critical thinking, a term used more widely in social studies.

Kohlberg promoted the use of moral discussions in the social studies classroom to advance moral thinking through the critical analysis of situations that pose moral dilemmas. Through both role-playing and modelling in the classroom, we can expose students to the structured consideration of moral dilemmas and guide their critical analysis of dilemmas to support their growth in moral reasoning capacity. The historical and environmental issues inherent in social studies will provide many opportunities for teachers to guide the moral development of their students to promote the growth of students' capacity to engage in citizenship. Through discussion of moral issues, students will reconstruct their understanding of situations and move to higher levels of moral reasoning.

These reconstructions occur in order to achieve a better match between the child's own moral structures and the structures of the social and moral situations he [or she] confronts. . . . In the cognitive-developmental view, morality is a natural product of a universal human tendency toward empathy or role taking, towards putting oneself in the shoes of other conscious beings. It is also a product of a universal concern for justice, for reciprocity or equality in the relation of one person to another.

—Kohlberg, 1969

Teachers will need to consider the advantages and disadvantages of various approaches to addressing morality or ethics in their treatment of critical thinking in social studies. Three approaches are in frequent use in classrooms. Each approach has its strengths and challenges. Social studies teachers should give careful consideration to each approach before deciding on strategies to be used to ensure that critical analysis in their classrooms is correspondingly infused with ethical characteristics. The approaches of character education, values clarification, and the cognitive-developmental approach espoused by Kohlberg are introduced below (see Figure 6.2).

Approaches to the moral aspects and ethics of critical thinking that the teacher uses in the classroom need to be considered carefully to assess the efficacy and purpose of the approach and its match to the stated curriculum goals.

Figure 6.2 Approaches to Addressing Morality and Ethics

Character Education	Values Clarification	Cognitive-Developmental Approach
■ Focuses on rules and values of the culture	■ Elicits the student's own values or judgments about issues through open discussion	■ Stresses open discussion of issues
■ Uses inculcation approach; telling, preaching, exemplifying, rewarding as the lowest level of application and academic understanding, through original inquiry as the highest level	■ Helps students become aware of their own values	■ Poses value-laden dilemmas to promote discussion
	■ Promotes the belief that there is no single right answer in issues	■ Models an open discussion, where the teacher's opinion is not that of an authority but another contributor
■ Considers some values to be universal (e.g., honesty, fairness)	■ Promotes the belief that values are relative to each person's perspective	■ Helps the moral reasoning development of each student to progress at a different pace; movement and growth, rather than convergence to a single opinion, is the goal of discussions
■ Promotes the teacher's values in the culture of the classroom		■ Values some judgments as being more adequate and defensible than others while respecting each student's current judgment
■ Relies on individual teachers for interpretation of the universal values		■ Restricts moral discussions to values that promote justice

UNDERSTANDING COMMUNITY NORMS AND VALUES

The school is a microcosm of the community in which it exists. It is important for teachers to operate with respect for the values and norms of the school community and to work with parents to develop curriculum experiences that will promote growth for students, and by extension, for the community.

Teachers can develop awareness of the norms and values of the school community by

- having early and frequent conversations with parents about the curriculum;
- holding curriculum nights so that parents can be exposed to the purposes of various parts of the curriculum;
- providing a curriculum column in classroom newsletters;
- posting sample strategies that relate to approaches for teaching critical thinking and ethical thinking on a classroom website;
- inviting parents to observe and participate in classes;

- promoting active involvement among parents as volunteers in the classroom;

- including parents as active participants on field trips; and

- providing parents with samples of work from a student's portfolio on a regular basis.

All of these strategies evolve to produce a climate of respect and trust between the teacher and the parent. As well, social studies teachers need to consider the role of studying the law in their courses to promote social literacy.

[S]ocial literacy to me involves some appreciation of the legal system.

—*Justice Bora Laskin, 1977*

Including law studies in the social studies curriculum can introduce new and interesting approaches to discussion in the classroom (see Figure 6.3). Such discussions will help students engage in the examination of controversial issues and plan social action with greater clarity about the values and norms that will support their decisions to act.

When choosing to address a controversial topic in the classroom, teachers should be fully aware of community demographics, including socio-economic status, education levels of parents, community hot topics, religious affiliations within the community, and other characteristics that may affect the sensitivity of a community to a particular issue. The age, maturity, and previous exposure of students to controversial issues should also be considered carefully. The norms and values of the community should be respected and honoured while still seeking to address those issues that have no easy or universally acceptable answers.

Figure 6.3 Approaches to Law Studies

Law Methodology	Explanation
Case Study	■ Apply an inquiry approach to examining the progress and outcomes of real or model/imaginary cases tried (or that could be tried) in courts
	■ Help students to see the many perspectives or sides to an issue
	■ Guide the sorting of relevant and irrelevant facts
	■ Role play or engage in written analysis to support examination of the case
Mock Trial	■ Assign roles for students to research and engage (e.g., prosecution, defence, key witnesses, court personnel, the media, jury)
	■ Encourage creative abilities (e.g., presenting findings in a role-play scenario)
	■ Use simulation experience to heighten students' emotional engagement
The Moot Appeal	■ Students form two teams (appellant and respondent)
	■ A judge is appointed to consider the arguments from each team
	■ The judge clarifies the inherent issues in each argument

(Continued)

Figure 6.3 *(Continued)*

Law Methodology	Explanation
	■ The judge questions each team
	■ A written decision is formed by the judge based on the uncovered issues
Mediation	■ Help students seek compromise
	■ Encourage listening, flexibility, other directedness, empathy, and solutions
	■ Use role-playing to immerse and engage students
	■ May employ Native concepts such as the "sentencing circle" to resolve conflicts
	■ Focus on fairness and justice

Source: Adapted from Wanda Cassidy, 2004.

Law-related education is all about issues, about competing values, about what is paramount in society, about how people should be treated, about what is meant by the common good, about the relationship between minority and majority rights, about the kind of society people want to have and the challenges they face in getting there. Law-related education in social studies (legal topics, the law-related perspective, legal methodologies) can provide a natural vehicle whereby important citizenship attributes may be addressed and cultivated in students.

—Cassidy, 2004

GENDER, SEXUALITY, AGE, RACE, AND DISABILITY IN SOCIAL STUDIES

Textbooks and support materials used for teaching social studies may be infused with stereotypical or biased information related to gender, sexuality, age, race, and disability. Such materials are designed within provincial or territorial guidelines but these guidelines may have unclear or even contradictory views of issues related to stereotyping. As well, many resources may be selective and non-representational both in what they include and what they omit as choices are made about what to highlight in text and graphics.

Teachers need to be critical consumers of text materials and teach their students similar standards, using texts with both sensitivity and critical analysis, to examine both explicit and implicit biases and perspectives that may cause inaccurate or romanticized views in relation to gender, sexuality, age, race, or disability.

Provincial/territorial policies may mandate some aspects of inclusion to reflect growing sensitivity to these issues. "The intention [of such policies] is to authorize only those materials that accurately depict the racial and ethnic pluralism of Canada and show people of various races and ethnic groups, both genders, the elderly and the disabled, making positive contributions to Canada, past and present" (Clark, 1999).

As Canada has evolved over the past four decades from a country of two predominant cultures to a pluralistic nation, our awareness of the need to represent the contributions of other groups in Canada, both racially and in terms of other demographics, has evolved. As well, our efforts to appreciate the complexities of an individual's identity, which can be defined in terms of race, sexuality, age, gender, location, economics, and religion, are evolving. Our ability to define a person through many filters simultaneously is becoming more suited to the pluralistic and complex nature of our social interactions.

Texts can present distorted images of people and their contributions in each of these contexts, can create gaps in accuracy of the representations of each group, and can overdevelop a single perspective on an event or people to the exclusion of more balanced perspectives.

To address these tendencies in textbooks, teachers in social studies will need to

- be critical and reflective about the text, graphics, data, and photographs they encounter in texts to uncover distortions and omissions;
- use a variety of other sources to support the text; and
- compare perspectives on the same issue or event from a variety of texts that offer differing perspectives.

Source: Adapted from Clark, 1999.

By teaching students how to examine many sources of information about events, teachers will expose students to the natural biases that place, distance, and perspective will lend to an account and teach students to look for hints of such bias as a habit of mind in their studies.

Instruction in the early primary grades is markedly different than the methodology for using sources that is possible during the junior grades. Students' ability to engage text is critical to their ability to analyze it. In the early primary grades, teachers can model their critical questioning techniques as they examine text and provide many and frequent opportunities to have students examine primary artifacts and photographs for evidence (see Figure 6.4). Attitudes and aptitudes for tolerance, sensitivity, and inclusiveness are approaches that can be successfully modelled by teachers.

Figure 6.4 Using Primary and Secondary Source Materials

- Present an account that contradicts another text for discussion of the inherent perspectives of each one.
- Use two or more sources.
- Supplement secondary sources with primary sources where possible.
- Teach students to ask "Why" questions.
- Expand the background information offered in the text to help develop and contextualize students' understanding.
- Have students use text sources then construct their own historical accounts. Attempts to personalize the story elements may help students uncover previously unseen issues.

(Continued)

Figure 6.4 (*Continued*)

> ■ Create related simulations that lead students to explore deeper meaning and emotions related to the issue.
>
> ■ Have students illustrate or otherwise render the meaning of a text into another communication format (e.g., radio broadcast, cartoon, slogan, legal bill) to help them search for what is missing from the text.
>
> ■ Relate the text and graphics of a source to prevailing social trends of the time it was created.

Teachers will also need to examine source materials for age appropriateness. It is unnecessary to promote full disclosure to the extent that young students are horrified and frightened by historical reality. By considering what is relevant to a student's current level of understanding, teachers can examine sources for their appropriateness.

TEACHING SOCIAL JUSTICE AND SOCIAL ACTION IN THE PRIMARY AND JUNIOR DIVISIONS

The concept of social justice springs from a global sense of fairness. The concept of social justice includes an understanding that

- the world's population is increasing;
- many resources we have come to rely upon are limited;
- some nations use more resources per capita to support their lifestyle than is typical of other countries; and
- poverty is a global issue.

Social justice is based on the concepts of human rights and equality. It is the belief that society should afford individuals and groups fair treatment and an impartial share of the benefits of society, including a distribution of the advantages and disadvantages within a society. Peace education mindsets provide some strategies for addressing social justice issues (see Figure 6.5). In its broadest context, society includes the population of the entire world.

Social action is the commitment to do something to create change toward the more equitable distribution of resources. In the primary and junior social studies classrooms, these can be difficult concepts to teach. In Chapter 2 we discussed strategies that promote the development of critical-thinking skills in students. Many of these strategies will also serve effectively to develop students' increasing awareness about the issues of social justice and promote their involvement in social action. Earlier in this chapter, we examined situations that the teacher needs to manage to engage young students in appropriate social action projects.

[B]ecoming educated is not simply, or even essentially, a matter of acquiring a body of knowledge. Equally important is the nurturing of personal and social values that will guide our decisions and actions in just and productive ways.

—*Case, 1999*

Figure 6.5 Peace Education Mindsets

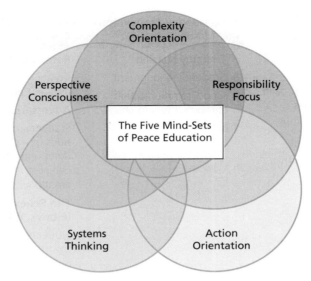

The Five Mind-Sets of Peace Education

- Complexity Orientation
- Perspective Consciousness
- Responsibility Focus
- Systems Thinking
- Action Orientation

Embedded in the concept of social justice is the concept of world peace. Peace education can foster a sense of social justice through awareness of the differing realities that young children face in unstable countries around the world. In studying the political conflicts in some countries, teachers will need to use sensitivity and professional discretion to select or develop informative activities that provide deep understanding, while balancing exposure so as not to create anxiety and emotional distress among students.

In the article "Peace Education: Politics in the Classroom," Susan Hargraves (1999) provides a five-part framework to identify the types of thinking, embedded skills, and sample strategies that can be effective in promoting broad understanding of peace and social justice in our classrooms. Hargraves stresses that these five mindsets are interrelated and draw upon each other in operation.

Teachers will find that while these mindsets can be developed across subject areas of the curriculum, social studies is uniquely suited to incorporate the systematic use of these strategies (see Figure 6.6 on page 142).

At various grade levels, teachers can also develop simple but powerful simulated experiences that will allow students to develop deeper understanding of the concepts related to social justice and social action.

CHARACTER EDUCATION, RESTORATIVE JUSTICE, AND VALUES FOR YOUNG LEARNERS

Increasingly, the traditions of restorative justice approaches are becoming used as a strategy for creating a more powerful sense of community in schools and society. When introducing character education, restorative justice, and controversial approaches to teaching values, teachers need to do so in ways that respect parental and community values (see Figure 6.7 on page 145).

Figure 6.6 Strategies to Develop Mindsets

Mindset Explanation	Skills Needed to Develop this Mindset	Sample Strategies to Develop this Mindset
Perspective Consciousness An awareness that each person sees issues somewhat differently because of our backgrounds and experiences; empathy	▪ Empathy building ▪ Suspending judgment ▪ Good communication through listening and questioning	**Retelling the Story** Creating a new story from a different perspective **Adversarial Roles** Students role-play both sides of a conflict to help them understand perspective taking in emotional situations. **The Believing Game (Elbow, 1973)** Students create reasons why the opposing point of view is valid, then explore the emotions and thinking behind each reason they were able to generate. Then students defend their own point of view and modify their reasoning to reflect their broadened perspective in consideration of the point of view they espoused earlier.
Systems Thinking Seeing patterns, structures, and interrelationships	▪ Recognizing that actions influence one another ▪ Finding patterns ▪ Developing graphic representations of relationships	**Breaking the Cycle** Students create a graphic, circular representation of the relationships in a situation under the three headings Feel, Think, and Do then they examine how a change in one aspect of the cycle will disrupt the rest of the cycle. More complex interrelationships can be created in graphic representations by older students. **Wooly Thinking** Students discuss an issue while each is unwinding a ball of colourful wool that passes to each speaker in

Figure 6.6 (*Continued*)

Mindset Explanation	Skills Needed to Develop this Mindset	Sample Strategies to Develop this Mindset
		turn. As the discussion progresses, students have a visual reminder that everyone's views are heard and add to our evolving understanding.
Complexity Orientation The expectation that issues are often more complex than they appear; the ability to move beyond stereotypes and overgeneralizations	▪ Good communication ▪ Listening ▪ Eye contact ▪ Maintaining open body language ▪ Asking open-ended questions	**Exploring Assumptions** Use a modified KWL chart to query "What do I know for sure about this?"; "What do I think I know?"; "How can I find out more?" The question sequence for older students can be more sophisticated (e.g., How do we know what we know? Whose facts are these? What biases are inherent here? What assumptions underlie this position? What is it about the individual who holds these views that has contributed to this position? What is it about me that makes me sympathetic/antagonistic to these views? What are the economic, social, cultural, historical, or environmental factors that are pertinent here? What are the interests behind the position?).
Responsibility Focus Developing a sense of appropriate ownership and a sense of commitment to address problems	▪ Seeing oneself as powerful to influence change ▪ The will to have an impact ▪ Experience with assuming responsibilities ▪ Experience with facing the consequences of personal actions	**Classroom and School Meetings** A problem-solving approach to school community events **Inner/Outer Scenarios** Examine a problematic situation from two perspectives, one where you believe you can do something about it and one

(Continued)

Figure 6.6 (*Continued*)

Mindset Explanation	Skills Needed to Develop this Mindset	Sample Strategies to Develop this Mindset
		where you believe you are powerless to control any aspect of what is happening.
		Charter of Rights and Responsibilities
		Create a classroom charter that will identify common expectations for how the group of students will interact with each other to create a productive learning situation.
Action Orientation The expectation of self to move beyond words to take socially responsible action; replacing apathy with action and a commitment to go beyond knowing about a problem to doing something about a problem	■ Learning to take a stand ■ The ability to change positions as new information arises ■ The ability to act in a climate of uncertainty	**Life Choices Map** Students role-play hypothetical actions to a situation(s) before committing to real action; the role-playing allows them to examine the consequences of actions in a risk-free scenario.
		Human Graph Students get opportunities to respond to prompts that require their opinion by sorting themselves into groups according to where they stand on a continuum of responses to an issue (e.g., strongly agree, agree, disagree, strongly disagree).
		Community Projects Students engage in productive action that demonstrates their commitment and the depth of the research into the issues surrounding a problem.

Source: Adapted from Susan Hargraves, 1999.

Figure 6.7 Connecting Community Values and Controversial Issues

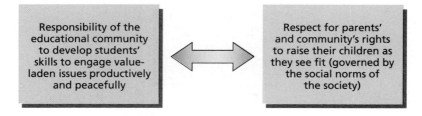

| Responsibility of the educational community to develop students' skills to engage value-laden issues productively and peacefully | ⟷ | Respect for parents' and community's rights to raise their children as they see fit (governed by the social norms of the society) |

Teaching values through the school curriculum is

- part of the school's mandate as outlined in provincial/territorial guidelines;

- a precondition for learning many other things (e.g., sustainability concepts);

- a unique opportunity in a school environment because it is a common experience shared by the children in a community; and

- an opportunity to create an environment that provides a microcosm of how the community operates as a whole to accommodate many differing opinions.

Source: Adapted from Case, 1999.

Values can be taught in the school through the explicit social studies curriculum or "caught" in the school through students' observations and experiences with how things operate in their daily environment. A democratically run classroom will help students see abstract concepts in action.

Three approaches to teaching values were outlined earlier in this chapter. Whether values are taught through character education, values clarification, or cognitive-developmental approaches, the teacher will need to engage students in discussions that are controversial to allow them to examine their views, consider the views of other students and adults, and experiment with broader conceptions that are informed by new knowledge (see Figure 6.8).

Figure 6.8 Reasons to Engage Students in Controversial Issues

- To instill sensitivity
- To lead students to make informed decisions and judgments after considering all options and many relevant criteria for considering each option
- To consider, and perhaps accommodate, alternative opinions
- To allow students to process information rather than imposing an external view
- To explore, clarify, and perhaps justify personal values
- To appreciate the freedom of opinion that typifies Canadian society where cultural and political pluralism are valued and protected

Figure 6.9 Nurturing Values

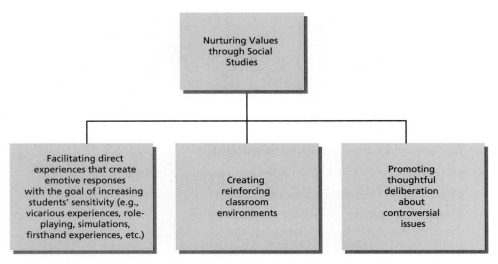

Source: Adapted from Case, 1999.

Teachers need to exercise professional caution when addressing values instruction in the classroom to avoid the possibility of indoctrinating students into our own value systems. This is a danger if teachers fail to reflect on what their personal values are and what approaches they intend to use to develop values among young students.

Nurturing the growth of appropriate values among students is a three-part process (see Figure 6.9).

A challenge for teachers of young children is to make the development of strategies to promote values accessible to the language skills and interpersonal skills that students have acquired. Through the use of pictures, discussions, and media, students can engage complex concepts without being hampered by complex language and literacy requirements.

It is critical to our classroom work with values that we teach students to consider both short- and long-term consequences of their actions that purport to help. Without foresight and thoughtful deliberation about consequences, students' attempts to act in socially responsible ways can exacerbate existing problems. When we teach social and ethical values to students, potential consequences can be considered using the framework laid out in Figure 6.10.

Figure 6.10 Considering the Consequences of Social Justice Actions

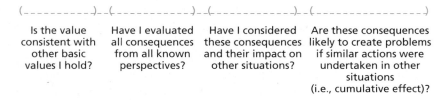

Figure 6.11 Social Action Continuum

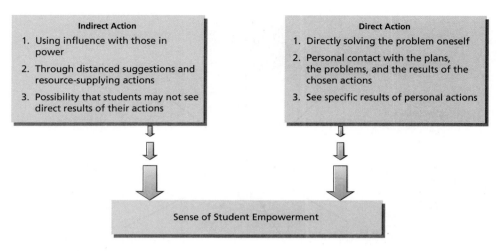

Indirect Action	**Direct Action**
1. Using influence with those in power	1. Directly solving the problem oneself
2. Through distanced suggestions and resource-supplying actions	2. Personal contact with the plans, the problems, and the results of the chosen actions
3. Possibility that students may not see direct results of their actions	3. See specific results of personal actions

Sense of Student Empowerment

Source: Adapted from Wade, 1995.

Teacher modelling of the thinking-through (think-aloud) process to consider each of these questions will support the development of these habits of mind in students as they have repeated exposure to action choices. The teacher's sensitivity and perseverance will be essential to the development of students' ability to gain deep understanding through the use of controversial, value-laden issues in the classroom.

In choosing to engage students in actions that are the extension of their values and beliefs, teachers will need to be cognizant of the feelings students bring to the experience. Engagement in a project that allows students to act on their values and pursue social justice perspectives will require that students experience firsthand a sense of efficacy. If they feel that they can make a difference through their actions because they have a viable combination of resources and abilities to make a difference, students will be more likely to engage in action (see Figure 6.11) and persevere in their efforts to complete related tasks (Kohn, 1990; Yaeger & Patterson, 1996).

In Chapter 8 we will address strategies that can be used with young students to help them consider action-oriented options in a systematic way with full consideration of the role of consequences in their decision-making processes (see Figure 6.12).

Restorative justice is a process that reflects consideration of the relationship between the offenders and offended. Increasingly, it is being used in schools as part of the regime of social problem-solving strategies that can help schools address personal relationships and help students take responsibility for their actions. Restorative justice promotes interpersonal respect and productivity by recognizing the nature and breadth of response to inappropriate actions that impact on an individual or a group. The processes of restorative justice can be used to help students interrogate their own action proposals to reflect

Figure 6.12 Informed Decisions

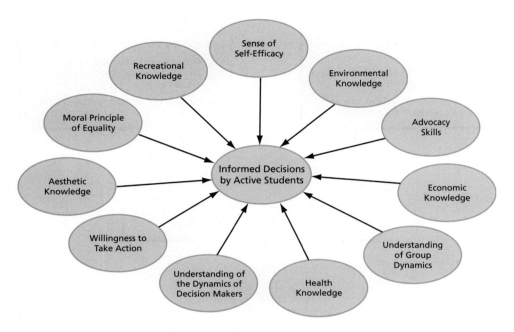

on their potential to create consequences for others. Restorative justice can be a vibrant component of a values education aspect of the social studies program because it stresses what it means to be social. However, social justice initiatives in schools will be most effective when

- an offender accepts responsibility for his or her actions and agrees to participate in seeking a resolution;
- the offended party freely agrees to participate in the program, without feeling pressured to do so; and
- teachers are trained in how to manage negotiation between parties.

Restorative justice processes can support students' understanding of ways to examine historical decision making and to clarify possibilities for creating more productive social options. Used as a way to influence the climate of the classroom and as a filter to examine what might have been done in some situations under scrutiny, students can apply restorative justice approaches as a way to expand their sense of global responsibility and local efficacy.

. . . the desired role of a citizen is to know what is going on, be a part of it, and do something about it.

—Chamberlin & Glassford, 1999

INNOVATIVE APPROACHES IN YOUR SOCIAL STUDIES CLASSROOM

In previous chapters, we examined some questions that will initiate various forms of inquiry. These have included

- What is it?
- How does it work?
- What are its interesting characteristics? or
- How do those characteristics change (over time, space, etc.)?

Another question in the topic elaboration inquiry scheme is "What are these changes related to?" This question would lead students to engage in inquiry through correlation. Data about two or more events could be examined to determine trends. This data could then be graphed to show the relationship between the events or phenomena.

Example

What are the changes in hurricane activity related to?

Using this question as a starting point, students could examine other weather phenomena to see if there is a tendency for hurricanes and other events to happen simultaneously.

Secondary questions to lead the investigation of these phenomena might include questions such as:

- Does the air temperature correlate with hurricane activity?
- Does surrounding ocean temperature correlate with hurricane activity?
- Does global volcanic activity correlate with hurricane activity?
- Does tectonic plate movement correlate with hurricane activity?

Students would then tabulate data for each event using a table such as the one below.

Correlation between Hurricane Activity and Other Geographic Phenomena				
Hurricane Activity	Air Temperature	Surrounding Ocean Temperature	Volcanic Activity	Tectonic Plate Movement

Once students have collected raw data, they can plot the data on a point graph, using time as the title for the x axis of the graph.

Example

Younger children can be taught correlation as well, using contexts that are based on experience and opinion rather than on researched data. Questions might include

- What are changes in our schoolyard play activities related to?
- What are changes in the size of our community related to?
- What are changes in my book choices related to? and
- How is a person's height related to their age?

By exposing students to the use of correlation early in their programs, we can help them to understand and distinguish between a correlation and a causal factor. (For an example of a correlation table, see Figure 6.13.) We can teach them that the tendency for two things to coexist does not mean that one thing caused another. Media studies related to the content of the social studies program would be a useful approach for teaching students the difference between correlation and causation since much of our advertising business relies on consumers failing to distinguish between the two.

Figure 6.13 Example of a Correlation Table

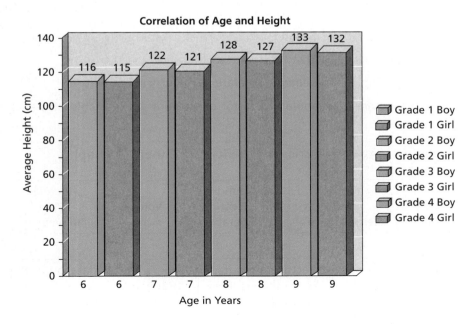

CASE STUDIES AND PROFESSIONAL ACTIVITIES FOR INNOVATION IN SOCIAL STUDIES

1. As a new teacher of social studies and a person new to the community, you have had only two months to settle in before starting your teaching duties in Grade 4. You feel that you are beginning to know the values and norms of the community but know that it would be wise to get input from other teachers who have taught in the community for many years before you engage in teaching about social action and controversial issues. You sit down with three colleagues and brainstorm what each of you believes about the community's norms and values.

    Do this on a single large sheet of paper with each person in the group of four taking a separate corner of the paper to brainstorm (this is called a "placemat" approach). Once each of you has had a few minutes to record ideas, discuss the similarities, differences, and examples each person has recorded. Determine how close you were as the newcomer to identifying the values and norms of your new school community.

2. Your class has been studying industry in the local community. As part of an inquiry, students have discovered that waste water is being released into a local stream after treatment to remove impurities. The company is in compliance with legal requirements but students who live in the area know that the part of the stream where the water is released is much warmer than surrounding water in the stream. They wondered how this temperature change affected wildlife in the stream and collected data to show that this area of the stream had many plants along the banks that can only be found within 200 metres of the waste water outlet. Students hypothesize that this is happening because of the higher water temperature. Students wonder if this is a good thing environmentally. They want to investigate further.

    As a community member, you are aware that many parents work in the company that is releasing the waste water. You want to encourage your students in their inquiry but you also want to be sensitive to potential controversy. Make a list of your next steps.

3. Citizenship development is a central purpose of the discipline of social studies. You are aware of all the concepts related to creating a strong sense of citizenship but you and your colleagues from other grades have not identified how what each of you is planning for your program might contribute to the end goal of creating a strong sense of citizenship in your students over the grades from JK to Grade 6.

    Work with a group of eight colleagues to develop a sample outline of each grade. For each grade, identify what you will study related to citizenship and provide three or four sample strategies you plan to use to develop this concept and related skills and attitudes in each grade. Sort this information into a chart.

4. Your students are quite upset about the condition of a large empty lot near the school, especially after studying the local community and many of the beautiful parks and

play areas. The lot that is near the school is full of trash, and is often used to dump unwanted items.

Your class wants to change this and make this lot as attractive as other park areas close by the school. Make a list of

- all of the possible benefits to your students of engaging in this social action project;
- all of the possible pitfalls of engaging in this social action project; and
- the next steps for you as the teacher if you decide to pursue this social action project with your students.

CHAPTER REVIEW AND PROFESSIONAL DEVELOPMENT AS A TEACHER

This chapter has examined the following:

- Social studies should teach our students that the destinies of all members of the human race are connected.
- Students need to be taught ways to demonstrate care and have opportunities to develop their capacity for caring.
- The study of controversial issues will create the venue to teach caring and expand students' capacity for caring.
- Our ethical responsibilities as teachers will guide our curriculum choices when we set about including deliberate attention to caring as part of our social studies curriculum.
- Developing citizenship skills is a necessary part of teaching students to be caring.
- Social initiation, social reformation, personal development, and academic understanding are purposes of citizenship education.
- Being a citizen is distinctly different from demonstrating the skills required for citizenship.
- The context of our classrooms can provide a model venue for citizenship education in a democracy.
- The ultimate goal of citizenship education is to encourage responsible social action.
- Teachers should consider some guidelines when examining their social studies programs for the possibility of including social action. These guidelines will help to ensure the success of classroom projects geared to social action.
- As teachers, we need to consider the ethics that underscore the critical-thinking skills we teach.
- Character education, values clarification, and cognitive-developmental approaches offer strategies for examining the ethics underlying critical-thinking skills.

- Social action projects in the classroom should reflect sound ethics and resonate with the values and norms of the school community.

- Discussions about controversial issues in the classroom can be informed by law study strategies, including case studies, mock trials, moot appeals, and mediation exercises.

- Text materials need to be used with professional discretion and awareness of the sensitivity each one offers to promote inclusion.

- Teachers can use a variety of principles and strategies to ensure that their social studies program offers inclusive perspectives.

- Valuing social justice concepts is critical to a social studies program that promotes productive citizenship as a primary program goal.

- Peace education needs to be addressed as a component of social justice.

- Many cross-curricular strategies can be used to promote mindsets that align with peace education.

- Character education, values education, and restorative justice practices help young students understand why actions that are ethically defensible are most desirable in a just social context.

- Values can be taught through thoughtful exposure to, and analysis of, controversial issues.

- Nurturing values through social studies includes the creation of a reinforcing classroom environment, facilitating emotive experiences, and promoting deliberation about controversial issues.

- Effective social action experiences in the classroom will teach students to consider the potential consequences of their actions from a moral and ethical perspective.

- Restorative justice practices have implications for social action projects; students can be taught to interrogate their own actions in consideration of the consequences they evoke.

References for Further Reading

Case, R., (1999). "Nurturing personal and social values," in *The Canadian anthology of social studies* (eds.) Roland Case and Penney Clark, Pacific Educational Press, Vancouver, Canada.

Clark, P. (1999). "All talk and no action? The place of social action in social studies," in *The Canadian anthology of social studies* (eds.) Roland Case and Penney Clark, Pacific Educational Press, Vancouver, Canada.

Weblinks

Law Instruction
This British Columbia–based website provides background information and teaching resources for teachers and students regarding Canadian legal issues such as Native land claims and treaties.
www.lawconnection.ca

Restorative Justice
This comprehensive resource is primarily for teachers to help them understand the role that restorative justice plays in our society. Although it is American based, it offers online videos and a multitude of links and resources.
www.restorativejustice.org

Character Education
This Ontario site is a community resource for advice, news, interactive tools, and the latest educational research for teachers, parents, and caregivers.
www.tvo.org/cfmx/tvoorg/tvoparents/index.cfm?page_id=145&action=article&article_id=321
Alfie Kohn's article, "How Not to Teach Values: A Critical Look at Character Education" is presented.
www.mega.nu:8080/ampp/kohn.html

Bullying Prevention
This site offers lesson plans and resources to help teach bullying prevention.
www.goodcharacter.com
This Government of Alberta website helps take control of the issue of bullying by giving teachers and parents the tools they need to prevent or intervene in a bullying situation.
www.bullyfreealberta.ca

Selecting Appropriate Resources
This site stems from the PBS.org/teachers' site. It offers a multitude of general resources for teachers that are separated by grade divisions. The link provides access to excellent guidelines to selecting on-line resources.
www.pbs.org/teachers/_files/pdf/Microsoft%20Word_FormattedInstTechDoc.pdf

Chapter 7
Aboriginal Education within a Canadian Context

Learning Topics

- Aboriginal Issues
- Treaty Rights and Provisions
- Culturally Responsive Teaching
- Resource Selection and Strategies for the Aboriginal Learner
- Community-Based Learning

At the Wikwemikon Pow-Wow, "the grand entry starts off the pow-wow with all dancers following the tradition of the Eagle Staff bearer and flag bearers as they enter the circle. Also during the day is the intertribal dance, where the audience is invited to try their hand at First Nations dancing" (Lori Henri, 2010).

. . . breaking down the barriers and increase understanding between individuals, communities, and cultures.

—*Windspeaker, 1997*

ABORIGINAL ISSUES

In recent years, students with Aboriginal ancestry have become the fastest growing segment of the student population in Canadian schools in many jurisdictions. Ministries and authorities are becoming more specific and active in the quest to meet the learning needs of these students in integrated settings and in reserve school settings. Typically, texts that have been used for social studies instruction in schools and experiences in teacher instruction in faculties of education have left the profession of teaching underprepared to deal with either teaching about, or teaching to, Aboriginal peoples.

In Canada, the term *Aboriginal* is inclusive of people of Native, Inuit, and Métis cultures and ancestry. The culture of each of these groups within Canadian society has been affected in both positive and negative ways through interaction with Euro-centred cultures that predominate throughout the provinces and some areas of the territories. Aboriginal leaders have focused recent attention on the socio-historical realities (Goulet, 2001) of Native and non-Native interactions, with a stress on actions to achieve social justice as defined through treaty rights.

Teachers must be cautious when teaching about Aboriginal issues. The range and diversity of issues is as diverse as for any other culture within the Canadian mosaic. However, the socio-historical background of these issues is poorly understood by non-Aboriginal cultures. We also need to guard against the tendency to overgeneralize and to treat all Aboriginal issues the same, regardless of the history or geographic origins of the group.

An Historical Perspective on the Issues

Historically, Native or First Nations peoples in Canada have been marginalized by a dominant Euro-centred settlement. Social, economic, and geographical development across Canada marginalized Native groups as expansion westward and economic development followed European models. Attempts at political and cultural control of Aboriginal groups in the late eighteenth century were compounded by disease, resource confiscation, illiteracy in the dominant language, and a systemic policy of assimilation of the Aboriginal culture. Residential schools were an institutionalized vehicle of assimilation. Until the 1940s the trend toward systemic assimilation continued. Aboriginal leaders began to voice concerns about historical injustices, Aboriginal rights, and the horrifying details of injustices became a focus for social change in Canada. During the 1980s and 1990s, Canadian awareness of Aboriginal issues became a catalyst in the national psyche.

Today, we recognize the need to prepare teachers in Canadian schools to deal honestly and effectively with appropriate instruction about Aboriginal history and current issues and to prepare teachers to provide effective instruction for Aboriginal students in various contexts across the country.

On June 11, 2008, Prime Minister Stephen Harper made a formal apology from the Canadian people to the Aboriginal people of Canada for the abuse and mistreatment many received in residential schools.

There is much to be done in revising our approach to curriculum and instruction to address teaching about, and teaching for, the Aboriginal population within Canada.

In order to teach about Aboriginal issues in the Canadian social studies context, teachers will need to address developing their own and their students'

- knowledge about traditional Native, Inuit, and Métis cultures;
- appreciation for traditional Native, Inuit, and Métis cultures;
- knowledge about contemporary Native, Inuit, and Métis cultures;
- appreciation for contemporary Native, Inuit, and Métis cultures;
- openness and respect for differing perspectives about Canadian historical events involving interactions between Native, Inuit, and Métis cultures and Euro-centred cultures.

A review of social justice concepts and strategies (see Chapter 6) may help teachers to design curriculum in the social studies programs that can impact these areas of their program.

Among the goals for understanding Aboriginal issues in the Canadian context is the need to understand the educational disparity between Aboriginal and non-Aboriginal populations. These goals include the need to examine and address the disparity in literacy between Aboriginal and non-Aboriginal students, the need to address disparity in school retention rates across Canadian cultural groups, and strategies for increasing graduation rates among Aboriginal students, including opportunities to progress to post-secondary education.

Analysis of Canada's 2001 Census data demonstrates some trends in education that show disparities by culture. Overall, the data demonstrates that the post-secondary achievement rates between Aboriginal and non-Aboriginal groups are affected most profoundly by the disparity in success with high school graduation. Also, the Census shows that Aboriginal students who have graduated from high school are more likely than non-Aboriginals to choose a college or trade post-secondary education than non-Aboriginal populations, with male Aboriginal students more likely than females to make this choice. It appears also that the schooling success of Aboriginal students living on reserves is less positive than for those Aboriginal students living in towns and cities (see Figure 7.1).

Figure 7.1 An Aboriginal Population Aged 15+ and 20–24 with Less than High School, by Area of Residence

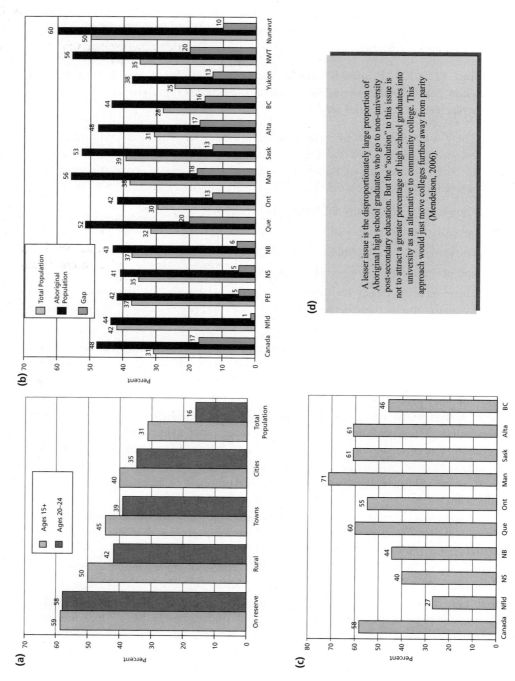

Source: Mendelson, Michael. (2006). *Aboriginal peoples and postsecondary education in Canada.* Copyright © 2006 by the Caledon Institute of Social Policy, Canada Census 2001.

Teachers will need to be taught, through pre-service and in-service sources, to develop instructional resources and instructional pedagogy that are responsive to the current realities of Aboriginal culture in its many Canadian forms. Treating all Native groups as one culture can be as destructive as past marginalization practices. Teachers will need a curriculum structure and an instructional repertoire that is inclusive, current, and representative of the social, educational, and economic realities of various Aboriginal groups across Canada.

This approach to Aboriginal issues in the Canadian context will represent understanding of the growing population of students of Aboriginal origins in Canadian schools and will respect the under-tapped resource of this hidden and marginalized culture in the Canadian landscape.

TREATY RIGHTS AND PROVISIONS

Treaty rights are respected by laws in Canada. Many of these laws are encompassed in the 1982 Constitution Act, Section 35. Both Aboriginal and non-Aboriginal people in Canada have rights under these treaties. The non-Aboriginal Canadian has access to land and its resources. Aboriginal treaty rights, dependent on the particular treaty, may include things such as reserve lands, farming equipment and animals, annual payments, ammunition, clothing, and hunting and fishing rights. By studying aspects of these treaties, teachers can develop empathy for the Aboriginal issues that are part of the Canadian social experience.

Teachers need to develop a personal understanding of how and why Aboriginal peoples have identified their issues with the development of Canada as significantly different from the issues of other groups within our pluralistic society. These differences are rooted in historical events. While the other minorities in the Canadian whole have chosen to be part of the Canadian pluralism, Aboriginal cultures were adhered through imposed and often poorly understood treaties.

Thus we do not have one archetypal Aboriginal identity nor do we have one vision or perspective that speaks for Aboriginal peoples, past or present.

—*Orr, 2004*

Teachers need to develop awareness about

- treaty processes; how and when they developed; how they are administered presently;
- Aboriginal dislocation from traditional lands;
- social policies related to economic development, education, and language;
- historical and contemporary accounts of racist policies and practices;
- diversity within Canada's Aboriginal communities and cultures; and
- Aboriginal contributions to Canadian and global societies.

Source: Seixas, 1999

By teaching students to relate the historical events of the past to the cultural conditions and issues of the present, we revitalize the study of the Canadian pluralistic culture in a climate of respect for those who have contributed to its development.

We cannot afford to leave events in the past, as this can serve to stereotype Aboriginal peoples as being peoples of the past.

—Seixas, 1999

WORLDVIEW

Canadian treaties with Aboriginal peoples have resulted in some common issues that are part of the heritage and the dilemmas of modern Aboriginal cultures. One of these issues is the difference in worldview between Native and non-Native cultures in relation to spiritual, educational, economic, social, political, and environmental directions. A second difference is that the predominance of Euro-centred language practices in Canada puts pressure on the use, viability, and preservation of Native languages and cultures. Finally, many of the social issues that characterize Aboriginal communities in Canada can be related to the cultural dislocation, identity transformation, and colonial policies and practices that are the product of treaties (Seixas, 1999).

It is important that teachers understand the relationship between treaties and the location of Aboriginal communities and between the location of Aboriginal communities and the community structures, including the governance processes in each community. In various treaties, allocations of land were exchanged for other concessions. Treaty lands, often referred to as reserves, were established in Canada by treaty with the British Crown. These lands were often in relatively remote and isolated areas, leading to the separation of Native and non-Native communities. This isolation, has, in turn, created the need for Native communities to evolve forms of self-governance that are workable for their remote and isolated conditions.

Self-governance serves many purposes in Native communities. Through self-governance, these communities can

- take control over decisions that impact the lives of people in each Native community;
- establish effective relationships with other governments;
- capitalize on economic development opportunities;
- improve programs and services available to the community; and
- enhance social and the economic wellbeing in each community.

The 2006 Canadian Census showed that over one million Canadians identified themselves as having Native ancestry.

The tendency to overgeneralize about the lifestyles of Native groups needs to be avoided as each community is evolving, maturing, and assuming self-governance roles at different rates. Self-governance is a critical process in the evolution of Native communities as entities with unique socio-economic characteristics. "Effective governance is the single greatest contributing factor to a community's socio-economic progress and its overall wellbeing" (www.ainc-inac.gc.ca/ap/gov/index-eng.asp; accessed November 6, 2009).

The first treaties in Canada were developed in 1701. Treaties were originally established to encourage peaceful relations between Native groups and early explorers and settlers. Some early treaties, in the Atlantic regions, were strategic alliances (Peace and Friendship Treaties) to support group interests against common foes. Between 1871 and 1921, the British Crown established many Numbered Treaties in Ontario, the Prairies, and the Northwest Territories. The numbers of the treaties evolved as settlement moved from east to west. In these treaties, land was exchanged for treaty rights.

Central to the expansion of knowledge about Aboriginal peoples in Canadian society is an understanding of the concepts of colonization and the reactionary concept of decolonization. Because the current structure and development of Aboriginal communities in Canada relates to their historical development in the treaties and early European contacts through colonization, many of the issues in contemporary Aboriginal communities are thought to originate from this practice. Colonization provides a framework for examining the historical origins of these Aboriginal communities within Canada and guides the examination of issues such as poverty and dislocation. Contemporary Aboriginal political initiatives attempt to eliminate socioeconomic gaps between the Aboriginal communities and other Canadian communities in relation to health, life expectancy, economic dependence, education, and per capita percentages of incarceration (Orr, 2004). By understanding the concepts of colonization and decolonization, teachers can help students to examine issues from the perspective of First Nations people.

CULTURALLY RESPONSIVE TEACHING

Effective teaching starts with consideration of the background of the child and how that background will impact the instruction being planned by the teacher. This is especially true when the culture of the teacher and student differ. It is even more true when the teacher is of a dominant culture and the student from a marginalized culture. When the marginalized culture of the student has also experienced systemic discrimination and acculturation efforts on a national scale, the teacher must be especially attuned to opportunities to be responsive to the student's cultural background and to the ways that background will influence the student's learning.

Culturally responsive teaching will start with a profile of every student to help the teacher understand the parameters that may influence the student's academic and social growth in the school context (see Figure 7.2).

Culturally responsive teaching should include the teacher's own knowledge of the child's culture. With Native students, this will include knowing about the origin and use of traditional teachings in the child's culture. Examples of some traditional Native teachings include

- the creation story;
- examples of how Native people lived together in the pre-contact era;

Figure 7.2 Culturally Responsive Teaching

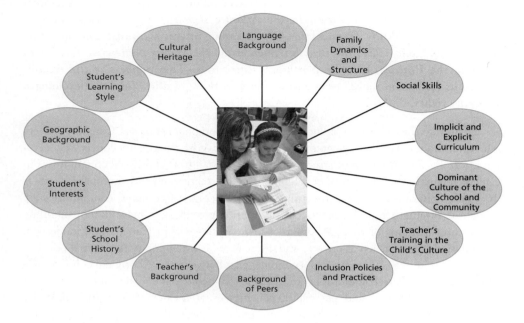

- traditional Aboriginal worldviews;
- the clan and tribal systems;
- Aboriginal languages;
- the interaction of Aboriginal language and culture;
- social norms within Aboriginal cultures;
- sewing and leatherwork;
- food planting, gathering, harvesting, and preparation;
- traditional survival skills;
- seasonal cycles and seasonal activities for survival;
- storytelling;
- humility, health, and healing; and
- holistic health and traditional medicines.

Teachers can learn more about their students by using systematically developed class profiles to study the nature of the class. Class profiles can be developed by

- considering the family, community, and personal background of each child (through school records, interest surveys, teacher-to-teacher conferences, parent surveys, class discussions, and observation);

- organizing the information from individual students into a profile of the class (e.g., cultural heritage, interests, English language skills, aspirations, social skills);

- selecting and designing instructional examples and instructional resources to reflect inclusion of all cultures represented by the children in the classroom;

- planning inclusively, including plans for differentiation of the content, learning processes, and learning products, to reflect the class makeup;

- continually reviewing efforts to provide inclusive, culturally responsive, and respectful curriculum experiences that reflect the makeup of the class; and

- Providing learning supports required for the success for every child.

Culturally responsive teaching must also be responsive to the many factors that influence the academic success of Native students in schools. These factors include

- teaching strategies that are appropriate to the cultural background of the Aboriginal learner;

- the use of resources that reflect aspects of Aboriginal culture;

- curriculum topics that reflect the perspectives and beliefs of the Native, Inuit, and Métis cultures;

- the availability and suitability of counselling and outreach services that respond to Native needs; and

- a school environment that encourages Aboriginal students and invites the engagement of their parents.

School curricula are constantly being revised and improved. As teachers examine their social studies curriculum, it is essential that efforts are made to

- learn about the various predominant learning styles that characterize students from Native, Inuit, or Métis cultures; we need to remember that, although there may be some trends across the culture, the specific variations are likely to be as broad and varied as for any other group of students;

- use a variety of instructional methods. This must include constant adaptations to methodologies so that student success is a constant focus. Method variations may include delivery accommodations such as altering the rate of learning, repetition, review, or exemplification, pre-teaching, verbal rehearsals prior to writing, oral and written instructions with models where possible, consistency in classroom routines and rules, moving from the known to the unknown, and providing peer support;

- incorporate the study of issues and events of significance to the Native, Inuit, and Métis students. This might include current events such as reserve issues or educational issues but should also include historical events examined from the perspective of the Aboriginal culture;

- support developing reading and writing skills to the level needed by each student. All of the elements of the student's profile will affect his or her skills in reading and writing. By using teaching strategies targeted to support the individual's development of these skills toward a preset standard, learning time can be used economically and students can begin to grasp the conceptual language of the discipline of social studies; and

■ develop the student's capacity for critical and creative thinking. These skills will allow the student to develop a breadth of perspectives.

The pluralistic nature of Canadian society demands that teachers acquire expertise in strategies that support many cultural backgrounds among our students. This support of recognition of the role of culture and learning and the inherent validation of the individual when the teacher recognizes and models respect for the culture of the student, creates a classroom climate that supports learning.

Canadian classrooms in urban centres can host students from a broad range of cultures. Culturally responsive teaching practices promote acceptance of, and support for, all cultures represented in Canadian society.

Culturally responsive teaching includes teaching that

■ uses the language and the culture of the students in the classroom;

■ is knowledgeable about the nature of the cultures in the school community;

■ recognizes cultural differences that may influence learning;

■ responds to cultural differences by teaching with culturally appropriate strategies;

■ recognizes that culture changes and responds to those changes through adaptations in the curriculum;

■ teaches both traditional and contemporary cultural examples when topics are addressed;

■ teaches cultural examples that represent the makeup of the class;

■ uses elders and leaders in the cultural community to provide examples of the lived experiences that exemplify curriculum concepts;

■ represents cultural differences as strengths and the students' experiences in different cultures as learning assets in the classroom;

■ prepares students for living in a pluralistic society while maintaining their own original culture;

■ provides opportunities to learn academic skills (process and product) through familiar cultural content;

■ uses authentic approaches; students have a real audience and a real purpose for their work;

■ uses teaching strategies that are holistic and synergistic (e.g., active learning, out-of-class learning, format variations, cooperative learning);

■ happens in a climate of inclusion and respect for all;

■ happens with a strong bond between the teacher and the student (e.g., warmth, caring, sensitivity, humour, classroom ethos, values, trust, high achievement expectations); the student trusts that the teacher has his or her best interests in mind at all times;

- makes use of effective, indirect, non-confrontational classroom management strategies;

- includes choice within the content, processes, and products of the learning themes;

- addresses difficult and emotional issues as part of the curriculum of inclusion; issues of culture, language, historical fairness, values, norms, power and governance, oppression, marginalization, poverty, and economic viability are included in class discussions and investigations; and

- includes self-monitoring for habits of mind that are self-aware, tolerant, inclusive, and respectful (e.g., reflexivity).

Teachers will recognize that all of these strategies represent good teaching in any context. For the child who comes from another culture and particularly for a child who comes from an historically marginalized culture within Canada, these strategies are essential to the academic success of the student. The inclusive and culturally responsive teacher will "harness diversity for enhanced teaching" (Seixas, 1999).

Through culturally responsive teaching, teachers can influence the evolution of students' tolerance and inclusivity and help them arrive at a deeper understanding of Aboriginal social issues. They can lead children to take a role in becoming an advocate for social justice within Canadian society.

Our responses as professionals to the need for culturally responsive teaching can be engaged at many levels. At an introductory level, students can experience *exposure* to the similarities and differences between their culture and that of another cultural group (see Figure 7.3).

Figure 7.3 Similarities and Differences to Address among Cultures

Similarities in . . .	Differences in . . .
Dress	Foods
Names	Clothing
Ways of doing things	Housing/shelters
Tolerance for safety and risk	Family structures
Occupations	Friendships
Foods	Community structures and relations
Physical appearance	Values (love, sharing, tolerance, cooperation, etc.)
Religious beliefs and observances	Laws and rules
Social norms	Government roles
Recreation	Health issues and needs
Conflict resolution strategies	Environmental issues and concerns
	Customs, observances, and traditions
	Arts and crafts
	Music and celebrations

A second level of engagement in the study of another culture is learning about the culture. At this level, students would have opportunities to delve into why cultures respond to environmental and social pressures as they do. After learning about a culture, students could engage studies to learn to respect the evolution and practice of the society's values and norms, including the laws of the society. At this level, students seek a deep understanding of the impact of pressures in many forms on the evolution of a modern society and its roots in historical and geographic contexts. Finally, students could engage the study of another culture through the lens of cultural appreciation. At this level, students have enough knowledge about the culture to engage in a study of its aspects with respect and integrity, bringing an attitude of inclusiveness and tolerance to their academic interests (see Figure 7.4).

As we engage studies at each level, the goal is to promote improved communications across cultures within the structure of Canadian pluralism. Studies encourage our students in communicating with others in ways that are positive, recognize others and self as worthwhile, create a respectful attitude toward human rights, focus on learning processes, and incorporate understanding and accommodation for various culturally characteristic ways of learning and communicating. We can teach students that cultures are always evolving and that assimilation and adaptation are cultural characteristics in all societies.

The culturally responsive social studies program will ensure that students learn about Aboriginal communities in Canada, along with other cultures that make up the pluralistic society in which we live. Strong social studies programs will also include opportunities for

Figure 7.4 The Seven Cs of Multiculturalism Policy in 1972

Celebrations—We learn about the norms and values of other cultures by watching and participating in the cultural celebrations of the group.

Curiosity—By studying the culture as both observer and participant and with emphasis on the commonalities across cultures, we can teach students to examine why cultural practices have evolved.

Contribution counting—We can examine ways that the practices and ideas from various cultures have contributed to the pluralistic nature of Canadian culture.

Case studies—We can examine specific instances through case studies allowing us to highlight similarities in values as demonstrated through people's responses.

Consciousness raising—We can examine issues through powerful group problem-solving techniques such as brainstorming, six-minute solutions, tutorials/jigsaws, group investigations and reporting, role-playing, inquiry, etc.

Communication—We can study our own communication practices to ensure that interpersonal and trans-cultural communications are always positive, worthwhile, sensitive, respectful, productive, and responsive.

Caring—Our studies of other cultures should always seek to promote the self-esteem of others through personal acceptance, awareness of the assets of each participant, respect for the cultural contributions of each participant, and acceptance of the challenges of each culture.

Source: Adapted from Friesen, J.W. (1999). Establishing objectives for a multiculturalism program. *The Canadian anthology of social studies*. Case and Clark (Eds.). Pacific Educational Press, Vancouver, B.C.

---

students to learn through various levels of engagement with information and through approaches endemic to Aboriginal culture.

RESOURCE SELECTION AND STRATEGIES FOR THE ABORIGINAL LEARNER

Earlier in this chapter we examined some strategies that are effective approaches for Aboriginal students because they reflect the traditions of Aboriginal cultural learning.

In selecting resources for social studies in the primary and junior division, teachers face the challenge of finding materials that are culturally respectful, promote deep understanding, and are still accessible to young students. Often, fictional text is most appropriate for young students to help them understand complex concepts. When choosing fiction for this purpose, teachers will need to ensure that

- historical fact is accurately portrayed;
- stereotypical text and pictures are avoided or analyzed to examine their biases and perspectives;
- text allows for examination from different perspectives; and
- opportunities to reflect on text sources from culturally responsive viewpoints are provided.

In selecting text and pictorial resources, teachers should consider the following questions:

- Is the source of information presented in this text and the pictures reliable?
- Are different perspectives on an event presented?
- Does the text/picture show respect for Aboriginal culture?
- Is there any use of inappropriate terms or pictures that show negative and stereotypical images in this source?
- Does the source recognize the differences between historical and contemporary Aboriginal culture?
- Is the source designed to foster deep understanding, inclusiveness, and respect for others?

Selecting photographs for use in social studies can be particularly challenging because they will require close examination to determine the explicit and implicit messages they convey. Clark (1999) encourages the use of photographs in social studies for their many advantages. Photograph study offers learners the opportunity to

- appreciate pictures as data sources;
- examine photographic images from a critical perspective by looking for the meaning underlying the images; and
- ask compelling questions about the photos and pictures.

Clark also offers criteria that social studies teachers can consider when using photographs as a source of information in courses (see Figure 7.5).

Figure 7.5 Details to Examine When Using Historical Photographs

Consideration	Explanation
Detail	Look closely; monitor the perspective.
Geographical data	Examine the photograph to determine the climate and landscape.
Historical data	Look at details in the clothing, hairstyles, furniture, and machinery to determine what these tell you about the times.
Sociological data	Students interpret specific contrasting historical events and analyze their unique characteristics. Have them question how race or ethnicity, class and gender, or various social problems are portrayed.
Emotional context	Determine the feelings that are depicted. Ask "Why?"
Aesthetic qualities	Identify the photographer's staging techniques. Look at how he or she has achieved appeal, the use of colour, light, texture. Ask "Why?"
Perspective and purpose	Determine who may have been the intended audience and what may have been the intended message. Ask "Why?"

Source: Adapted from Clark, P. (1999). Training the eye of the beholder: Using visual resources thoughtfully. *The Canadian Anthology of Social Studies*. Case and Clark (Eds.). Pacific Educational Press, Vancouver, B.C.

She cautions teachers to recognize that there are many types of historical photographs and recognizing the type we are using to gather information can support a solid interpretation of the images.

Photographs can be

- staged—these photographs may be intended to "sell" a particular message that may be inaccurate;

- selected focus—these photographs are a subset of staged photographs and present only part of the story by providing a limited perspective;

- unrepresentative images—these photographs may provide a misleading impression by overstating or understating, thereby leading to false generalizations; or

- altered photographs—these photographs may have been changed for a strategic purpose and create a false history.

With these cautions in mind, astute teachers can create appeal and interest in their social studies programs by including photographic study in a variety of ways.

Regardless of the strategies that are used to enliven and promote engagement in studies for and about Aboriginal culture, teachers need to ensure that their social studies program promotes and cultivates informed and critically analytical students who have "explored and clarified their place in honouring, respecting, and advancing the place of Aboriginal peoples within Canadian society" (Orr, 2004).

Instructional strategies for teaching the social studies curriculum should be carefully considered to reflect the age of the students, their instructional experiences in previous grades, the expectations focal to the lesson, and the learning traditions and approaches that characterize the cultural makeup of the class. Many of the strategies that, through research, have been identified as effective for Aboriginal students are also effective for students from other cultural backgrounds. That is, they work for Native students because they are characteristic of good teaching, as well as being reflective of historical approaches to teaching and nurturing in Aboriginal contexts.

The Adventures of Rabbit and Bear Paws *is a comic series that seeks to bridge the gap between students' Aboriginal culture and their urban reality. This series is written and illustrated by Chad Soloman, a First Nations graphic novelist, and Christopher Meyers.*

Some effective instructional strategies to teach to Native students and about Native culture include the following:

- Examine an issue by assuming the values of another person.
- Host someone from another culture for a classroom visit and investigate how to make the guest welcome by explicitly recognizing that person's cultural practices.
- Role-play being a guest from several different cultures and having to scrutinize the offerings of your host (foods, beverages, and activities) for their religious or cultural compliance. Follow up the decisions of the "guest" with discussion of the cultural background of these traditions and observances.
- Examine a current event and ask the question, "Who values what?" to determine the various perspectives represented in the report. Ask other "Who" and "Why" questions (see Chapter 2 for question stems).
- Use puppets to allow students to role-play in low-risk ways. Using the puppets, they can examine different perspectives without "owning" them.
- Cartoon a scenario after examining several political cartoons to see how exaggeration, satire, and humour are used to make them effective.
- Develop activity centres in the classroom to allow students to examine and familiarize themselves with items from other cultures and determine their use and significance.
- Undertake a comparative photo study; examine for similarities and differences across time, place, and context.
- Investigate multicultural literature (see Chapter 9) for books that support social studies in the primary and junior division.
- Use music from many cultures to manage transition times in the classroom. Over time, analyze the music for identification of the instruments.
- Use CDs and DVDs to expose students to stories told about other cultures in the voices of those cultures.
- Encourage volunteers from many cultures to work in the classroom.

- Hold food-related multicultural celebrations to recognize special days in various cultures represented by the classroom makeup.
- Host a multicultural fair.
- Teach decision-making structures so that students understand alternatives, options, and the complexities of multi-criterion decisions.
- Engage students in inquiry. Go beyond a descriptive history to ask "Why?" questions.
- Provide examples of concepts from many cultures (e.g., family, friendship, conflict).
- Teach students to understand ambiguity ("This is black, this is white, this is grey.").
- Teach students to understand and follow the progress of discussions about controversial issues:
  - This is what I think . . .
  - These are the differences between what each of us thinks . . .
  - These are the reasons for those differences . . .
  - Here is how we can show respect for those differences . . .
  - We want to . . . because peaceful coexistence is in everyone's best interest.
  - Ask yourself, "What did you learn from considering the other person's perspective?"
- Use conflicts and school cultural incidents to examine the values behind the incidents and teach alternatives to the conflict.
- Teach that culture is multifaceted and includes many commonalities across cultures (e.g., values, caring, families, protection, shelter, friendship, community, love, sharing, compromise, laws, survival, thriving, subsistence, progress, growth, sustainability, conservation, law, norms, values, cooperation, partnership, government, recreation, customs, traditions, art, celebrations, symbolism, language, habits, rituals, myths, stories, birth, death, grieving, offence, fairness, peace, justice, compromise).

Through the close and regular examination of many aspects of culture among both marginalized and more dominant groups within Canadian society, we can teach our students that culture is malleable and constantly evolving in a pluralistic society. As we participate in the study of other cultures, including Aboriginal cultures, we can validate practices that were unfamiliar to our students, negotiate transgressions among cultures and individuals, and become active participants beside our students in the evolution of Canadian culture. As we teach students to question their experiences and their underlying assumptions with a critical eye and an inclusive spirit, we teach them to participate in the evolution of Canadian society in a manner that can benefit all Canadians.

COMMUNITY-BASED LEARNING

The term *community-based learning* is often used interchangeably with the term *community-service learning*. Regardless of what it is called, the concepts are identical. Academic work in the classroom is strengthened with service work in the community, providing opportunities for the learner to apply their knowledge in community settings. Some teacher preparation programs offer opportunities for teacher candidates to complete part of their professional practica in remote parts of Canada, sometimes in reserve schools.

This type of community-based learning may not always be possible in elementary schools because of the transportation and safety issues related to the age of primary and junior children. However, all teachers can introduce concepts related to community-based learning right in their classrooms.

Community-based learning in the primary and junior social studies classroom can take the form of building connections with the local and more remote community so that students become aware of what characteristics define their local community or how their local community differs from other communities. Community-based communication efforts can help students experience cultural differences through virtual connections when they may not be able to experience them firsthand. Such connections will help young learners understand the differences between the reality of historical Aboriginal people and their contemporary counterparts.

Students can learn to build partnerships by participating in helping hands projects that partner their classroom and a local or remote Native school. Electronic communications have made this easy to accomplish.

Teachers can support community connectedness and the ethos of inclusiveness by

- involving students in age-appropriate community-based projects;
- using resources that represent accurate and unbiased views of Aboriginal and other cultures in their classrooms;
- building classroom displays that help familiarize children with many aspects of other cultures that are part of their community or more remote communities;
- teaching children greetings from other cultures and using these on a rotating basis in the classroom to model respect for other languages and cultures;
- including the study of efforts being made to preserve Native culture and language as part of the study of Aboriginal peoples; and
- including study and practice of Aboriginal crafts and arts through thematic units that support topics being considered in social studies.

If a Native Friendship Centre is located in the school community, teachers can partner with the staff of the centre to allow their students the opportunity to participate in special celebrations at the centre or in the classroom (e.g., sweetgrass ceremony, learning drumming rhythms). Native elders may be willing to speak to students or demonstrate traditional practices for young students who have been learning about Aboriginal culture. Opportunities to learn about crafts such as the setup of a full-sized teepee open up investigations into the ingenuity and resourcefulness of historical Aboriginal groups.

Community-based learning, in its many forms, provides an opportunity for exposure to people and their practices in an effort to increase understanding, and through understanding, respect.

INNOVATIVE APPROACHES IN YOUR SOCIAL STUDIES CLASSROOM

Causal reasoning seeks to consider what might cause another thing to happen. A generic causal question might be posed by asking, "What would/could/should/did happen (if/when) . . . ?"

By applying the generic question that focuses on causal reasoning, teachers can guide students to look at historical, current, or geographical data to determine evidence of cause and effect. Many data studies will lead students to see patterns. However, the tendency to confuse correlation and causation must be avoided.

Causation in social studies will present in two ways:

1. As hard numerical (quantitative) data. For example

   ■ Rainfall amounts causing flooding damage

   ■ Tectonic plate movement causing earthquakes

   ■ Mobility within a community affecting property costs.

   In these examples, causation can be determined by numbers.

2. As descriptive (qualitative) data. For example:

   ■ Opinions rated on a scale (e.g., Rate your opinion of the public services available in this community on a scale from 1 to 5).

   ■ Opinions related to feelings (e.g., Identify your feelings about this experience by circling one of the faces shown below).

   ■ Agreement circles (e.g., Step into the circle if you have . . . Step out of the circle if you have . . .).

It is helpful to students' investigations if they understand the difference between correlation and causation and if they can use both quantitative and qualitative forms of data to examine causal relationships.

A challenge for teachers is to have your students understand and appreciate the experience of marginalization. In age-appropriate ways, this can be done through experiences that are brief, evocative, and thoroughly debriefed so that the purpose of such experiences is fully realized by every student. For example, you might have students select team members for an event and ask students doing the selecting to leave one group until the end and then make vague comments and excuses about why their team has enough members and these marginalized students are not needed or wanted. While this is socially risky as a classroom strategy, it has the potential to have students really understand the emotional impact of such treatment. Immediate and effective debriefing is critical to getting the instructional value out of such an undertaking. After this experience, ask students questions such as the following:

- Who was included in the team choices?
- Who was not included?
- Why?
- What does marginalization mean?
- How were some students in our group marginalized by the team choices that were just made?
- What feelings did you experience if you were marginalized by this activity?
- What feelings did you experience if you were not marginalized by this activity?
- What marginalization experiences do Aboriginal people in our society face today?
- What feelings are they likely to have when this happens?

Following this discussion, have students determine ways they could identify team members in a fairer way to avoid marginalizing anyone.

CASE STUDIES AND PROFESSIONAL ACTIVITIES FOR INNOVATION IN SOCIAL STUDIES

1. Collect and display several comics from the *Rabbit and Bear Paw* series in a prominent place where students will see these frequently. Discuss the message of these comics as new ones are introduced to the display.

2. Invite guest speakers who teach Aboriginal students into the classroom to show you strategies they might use to motivate and engage students. Speakers such as Chad Solomon (author of *The Adventures of Rabbit and Bear Paws* comics) might be invited to speak to a group of teachers for a professional development/activity event to display the graphic artist's techniques used to motivate Aboriginal students.

3. Mr. Alexandre is a new teacher, trained in Ontario. He has just accepted a teaching contract to teach on a Native reserve in Northern Quebec. He has no background in Native education but is very open to learning about cultures and has travelled extensively. He is aware that he will need to prepare himself for this assignment. With a small group of teacher candidates, put together a preparation plan to help Mr. Alexandre prepare for teaching in this culture. Start by identifying many headings of preparation he will need to address. Then, flesh out each heading with some details for his plan.

4. You have an Aboriginal student in your class who is prone to outburts when upset and sometimes uses very improper language when doing so. The school population has about 15 percent Aboriginal students. Besides this student, there are four others with Aboriginal ancestry in your class. None of these other students act this way if they are

upset. You have worked hard to include culturally responsive strategies in your teaching and you always insist on a tone of respect and inclusion in your classroom. You have spoken to this student's parents previously about these outbursts and you have worked with the parents on creating a plan for action if this happened again. It has!

With a group of colleagues, outline specific actions that such a plan might include.

5. At the start of the summer, you receive your class list for the following school year. You know each of the students from their history in the school so you know quite a bit about the background of each student. Since your school is very close to a reserve area, you are looking forward to welcoming the Aboriginal students, who make up about 25 percent of your new class, into the Grade 5 classroom.

With a group of colleagues, design an action plan for preparing your classroom and your activities for the first day of school to make all of the diverse cultures represented by your class welcome into the classroom.

6. You have been able to find several colour and black-and-white photographs to help you teach about changes in Aboriginal culture in your area over the past 70 years. Plan a portion of the unit you will undertake, using the guide to historical photograph use from page 168. Use the list of approaches provided in Chapter 7 to plan lessons to teach your students each of the six criteria they should apply when examining historical photographs, including:

Photo Analysis Details	Lesson Ideas
Detail	
Geographical data	
Historical data	
Emotional context	
Aesthetic qualities	
Perspective and purpose	

CHAPTER REVIEW AND PROFESSIONAL DEVELOPMENT AS A TEACHER

This chapter has examined the following:

- "Aboriginal" includes people of Native, Inuit, and Métis culture.
- Teachers need to understand the socio-historical background of issues when they plan the study of historical and contemporary Native societies.
- Aboriginal culture was marginalized throughout the period of European settlement in Canada, starting in the early eighteenth century.

- Aboriginal leaders began to voice concerns about the marginalization of Aboriginal peoples in the 1940s.
- Teachers need to develop their background knowledge about Aboriginal peoples, both historically and contemporarily.
- There are disparities in educational achievement, retention, and access between Aboriginal and non-Aboriginal students in Canada.
- Teachers need knowledge and skills to develop curriculum about and for Aboriginal peoples to ensure that it is inclusive, current, and representative of the social, educational, and economic realities of various Aboriginal groups across Canada.
- Treaty rights in Canada are incorporated into the 1982 Constitution Act, Section 35.
- Treaty terms are different in each treaty.
- Treaty rights are being claimed by Aboriginal peoples to address socio-historical wrongs.
- Self-governance of Aboriginal communities serves many purposes, including providing opportunities for Aboriginal communities to determine their own socio-economic direction.
- Colonization in Canada led to the historic and contemporary marginalization of Aboriginal people.
- Culturally responsive teaching requires that teachers familiarize themselves with the cultural background of each of their students.
- Class profiles will help teachers become aware of the cultural makeup of their class of students.
- Teachers need to plan for, and manage, the factors known to influence student success in schools.
- Culturally responsive teaching is good teaching in any context.
- Culturally responsive teaching includes social justice advocacy.
- Students can study other cultures, including Aboriginal cultures, at many levels of engagement.
- J. W. Friesen (1999) promotes strategies for learning about other cultures.
- Teachers need to analyze historical fiction resources for suitability of content and perspective when considering their inclusion in a social studies program.
- Photographs, used carefully, can provide a valuable resource for learning about the historical background of Aboriginal peoples.
- Historical photographs can be staged, include underrepresented images, be altered, or provide distorted perspectives.
- Many traditional teaching approaches in Aboriginal culture are effective with students from other cultures.
- Teachers can introduce community-based learning, in age-appropriate ways, in their primary/junior social studies classrooms.
- The spirit of community-based learning can be brought into the classroom through what the teacher models and intercultural experiences made available through the curriculum.

Professional Development Activities

1. Before planning a program to be culturally responsive, it would be valuable to be aware of your own knowledge and attitudes about different cultures. With a focus on Aboriginal culture, make a two-column list. On the left side of the list, in point form, write everything you think you know about how to teach effectively to Aboriginal students. On the right side of the list, again in point form, write at least one idea for each of the points in the left column to explain why that approach will be effective with Aboriginal students. Once you have brainstormed your list for about 10 minutes, join a small group and discuss the ideas you have listed and the ideas they have listed. Now, return to your work spot and revise your list to add any ideas you have learned from colleagues.

2. Attend a pow-wow celebration. This provides a rich opportunity to collect resources, ideas, and an understanding of the Aboriginal culture.

3. Make a chart to identify the actions that characterize culturally responsive teaching. On the left side of the chart, list the 19 characteristics of culturally responsive teaching. On the right side, provide spots for notes beside each characteristic. Now, examine and recall the last lesson you taught to a group of students. On the right side of your chart, identify what specific things you did during your lesson that were culturally responsive. Discuss what you found out with a colleague who has also completed this exercise. Now, re-plan the same lesson with this framework for culturally responsive teaching in mind. Again, discuss the new plan with your colleague. Focus on identifying what you would do differently in this lesson when you keep the ideas related to planning for culturally responsive teaching in mind.

4. Visit a Native Friendship Centre in your area. Identify the resources that you can use to enrich your program with characteristics that welcome and recognize the unique culture of the Aboriginal students you teach.

5. Have an open-ended discussion about this topic with your colleagues. If you are going to teach on a Native reserve, how would you prepare differently than if you were teaching in a diverse multicultural area where you have two or three students in your classroom with Aboriginal ancestry and many other cultures represented among the students?

6. Plan a social studies unit for your class that incorporates strategies from the 7Cs of multiculturalism.

Weblinks

Native Languages of the Americas

Students can navigate the site and learn about the various Aboriginal languages of Canada. It offers translation tools, links to Ojibwe language resources, culture, and historical directories and fact sheets for students.
www.native-languages.org/ojibwe.htm

Health Canada First Nations and Inuit Health Branch

Students can navigate this site and learn about Health Canada's role in working with the First Nations people and Inuit to improve their health.

www.hc-sc.gc.ca

Canadian Geneaology

This site facilitates the research and history of tribes of Canada.

www.canadiangenealogy.net/indians

Indians.org

The American Indian Heritage Foundation helps to "build bridges of understanding and friendship between Indian and non-Indian people." It offers articles about today's Native North Americans.

www.indians.org

Assembly of First Nations

The Assembly of First Nations is the national organization representing First Nations citizens. This comprehensive site offers detailed information about their policies and history. They provide links to all provincial and territorial First Nations' organizations.

www.afn.ca

McGill First Peoples Library

McGill University's site offers books, videos, periodicals, and journal articles related to Aboriginal issues. This site is recommended for teachers.

www.mcgill.ca/fph/library

Native Self-Governance, Aboriginal Peoples and Communities, Urban Aboriginal People

This government website contains links to the topics as well as links to the Royal Commission Reports on Aboriginal Peoples.

www.ainc-inac.gc.ca

Chapter 8
The Methodology of Social Studies: Unit Design

Learning Topics

- Independent Inquiry Units of Study

- Combined (Split) Grade Planning for Social Studies

- Integrated Units: Combining Units around Process Skills

- Integrating Social Studies and Historical Novel Studies

- The Power of Story in Social Studies: Using Literature to Complement the Theme of a Social Studies Inquiry

Independent work offers flexibility and creativity to the learning process.

INDEPENDENT INQUIRY UNITS OF STUDY

Inquiry can take many forms in primary and junior social studies contexts. In Chapter 3, the theories and approaches used for inquiry were outlined and explained in detail. Additionally, Chapter 1 outlined many of the issues that are relevant to social studies. These should be reviewed before teachers plan units of study within the discipline.

A unit is any related group of learning episodes that are arranged around a theme. Units can be aligned with a single discipline and relate to one theme. They could also be integrated across subject areas. This is a common practice in the primary and junior grades and has the added advantage of conserving instructional time and helping students make links among ideas in their program. Units can be developed for single grades or used to span two or more combined (split) grades. Single-theme units can also draw resources from other disciplines. This is often done in the primary grades with language resources being used to support students' understanding of concepts in social studies. The story elements from language resources help young students to make personal meaning from the social studies concepts they are studying.

Regardless of the type of unit being developed, there are some common elements regarding planning units that should be understood. These include

- understanding the provincial/territorial requirements for the grade(s);
- having a clear overview of the standards of the discipline;
- understanding models for inquiry; and
- being familiar with procedures for unit development that incorporate the previous three elements.

Students' learning is facilitated when teachers view them as learners who have experiences, ideas, and home and community resources that can be built upon to help them master new knowledge and skills.

—James Banks, et al., 2005

Getting Learning Expectations Right

In social studies, there are a number of basic skills and approaches to presenting ideas for learning. Once the teacher has identified *what* to teach the students, the question of *how* to teach them must be considered.

In many jurisdictions, the question of what and how to teach for each grade is outlined in local curriculum guidelines. This guidance may be provided to the teacher in the form of topics to be addressed or in the form of specific and detailed expectations for students' learning that explain and describe the learning outcomes for students at each grade. Even if specific learning expectations are provided in a social studies guideline or curriculum document, they may need to be refined by the teacher to represent what the teacher is able to have students learn during that day's lesson.

Example: Refining Expectations

The guideline expectation states:

"Students will be able to use primary and secondary sources to locate and assess information about pioneer life."

A refinement to identify what students will be able to learn in the upcoming lesson may be restated as "Students will examine samples of implements from a pioneer kitchen and explain the use of each implement in labelled diagrams."

If specific expectations are not provided for the teacher, the teacher's planning task is a bit more challenging. In this case, the teacher will need to "tease" the appropriate expectations or learning objectives out of the topic. This can be done by creating a brainstormed "web" around the topic to surface the ideas the teacher has about where exploration of the topic could lead. The example provided below (see Figure 8.1) might represent such an effort to brainstorm the possibilities for the topic "Me and My Family in Our Community." This topic was chosen because it reflects the intent and focus of many primary social studies units (Kindergarten or Grade 1) in several provinces and territories.

Figure 8.1 Creating Concept Webs

Figure 8.2 SMART Goals

Acronym	Characteristic of the Expectation
S	Specific
M	Measurable
A	Attainable
R	Realistic
T	Timely

Once the possibilities for the unit are identified by brainstorming, the teacher would translate each of these possibilities into learning expectations or objectives.

Learning expectations or objectives should have certain characteristics that make them powerful guides for the teacher to use as directions for instruction. All learning expectations/objectives should be written to include the characteristics of SMART goals by Gene Donohue (see Figure 8.2). SMART goals are

■ specific—every expectation should say exactly what is to be learned; be written in terms of what students will know, believe, or be able to do;

■ measurable—every expectation should be able to be assessed using one or more approaches to determine if, and how well, students have achieved the intended learning;

■ attainable—every expectation should be able to be learned by all students in the class, given appropriate time and support;

■ realistic—every expectation should describe precisely what is reasonable to expect of students, given the reality of the time, resources, and other material to be learned.

■ timely—every expectation for learning should "fit" neatly into the whole curriculum package being prepared for that class for that year; this allows the skilled teacher to make connections across subject areas and those connections support students' understanding.

A careful examination of these characteristics of expectations for learning will allow teachers to realize that the focus of the expectations is *on the students' learning, not on the teacher's teaching*. All learning expectations should describe what the student will come to know, be able to do, or believe following instruction.

The acronym SMART has been used to describe the characteristics of well-written learning goals (see Chapter 1). Business organizations use variations on the SMART goals to keep their enterprise moving forward in a productive way. The SMART acronym may help teachers to remember the five characteristics of strong learning expectations.

An example of a SMART goal for learning is given below:

Students will be able to formulate questions to guide research and clarify information on study topics (e.g., What are the effects of physical features on land use? How are goods transported from one province or territory to another?)

Figure 8.3 Categories of Expectations

Knowledge	Skills	Affective
facts	cognitive	beliefs
concepts	social	attitudes
propositions	physical	values
theories		

This learning goal is *specific*. It says that the student will "formulate questions."

It is *measurable*. The teacher will be able to determine if the question(s) asked by the student is one that will lead to effective, inquiry-based research.

It is *attainable*. With the appropriate instruction, support, and resources, the student should be able to formulate questions.

It is *realistic*. Again with appropriate instruction, support, and resources, the student should be able to develop and refine questions to guide research.

It is *timely*. The teacher who identifies this as a learning expectation for a student would be designing research assignments that the students can engage in to find answers for their questions. The questions are being asked for a purpose and are connected to other learning.

Some curriculum guidelines support teacher's development of units by separating the list of expectations into categories by type of expectation (see Figure 8.3).

Another categorization approach for expectations recognizes the three variables in planning lessons and units for instruction. The teacher can vary the *content* within a unit or lesson; what the students will know and understand. The *process*, or thinking approaches, by which the students learn the content can be varied. Also, the teacher could vary the *product* that is required of students to demonstrate evidence of their learning; products give evidence of the student's ability to communicate ideas and apply them in various contexts (see Chapters 3 and 10).

Application of these three instructional variables to the categorization of learning expectations may yield a system of categorization such as the one outlined in Figure 8.4.

Although these categories for learning expectations and instructional variables are not linked this way in any curriculum guideline, an analysis of guidelines and support documents can reasonably yield such a connection.

Learning expectations sorted under this categorizing system might look something like Figure 8.5.

Teachers also recognize the need to teach students social skills so that productive, promotive interaction is facilitated while students learn together (see Chapter 3). Unit expectations that specifically identify social skills that will be addressed should be developed if they are not provided in mandated guidelines.

Figure 8.4 Analysis of Guidelines and Support Documents

Instructional Variable	Category for Learning Expectations
Content	Knowledge and understanding (will include mapping and graphic skills in social studies)
Process	Thinking and inquiry
Product	Communication and application

Figure 8.5 Sorted Samples of Learning Expectations

Knowledge and Understanding:

Students will be able to identify the physical and social needs of residents in an area.

Thinking and Inquiry:

Students will be able to brainstorm and ask simple questions (e.g., Who? What? Where? When? Why?) to gain information about their local community.

Communication:

Students will be able to use appropriate words to describe relative locations of various objects or sites within their community.

Application:

Students will be able to construct a model of their local community to show how a person's physical and social needs are served within the area.

Earlier chapters outlined strategies to be considered to ensure that the standards of the discipline of social studies and methods of ensuring an inquiry approach within units of study were provided. Once these are reviewed, a procedure for unit development can be applied. The advantage of following a procedure for this purpose is that a procedure has embedded assumptions and theories implicit in its steps (e.g., backward design, active learning, formative assessment).

Unit Development Procedure

1. Consider the title of the unit as provided in the provincial/territorial guideline.
2. Create a guiding question to focus the overall intent or "big ideas" in the unit.
3. Create a culminating task that addresses students' current understanding of answers or ideas related to the guiding question.

4. Deconstruct the culminating task to identify all of the sub-skills and knowledge students will need to learn in order to be successful with the culminating task.

5. Identify how you will assess the culminating task.

6. Identify how you will evaluate the culminating task.

7. Brainstorm to identify substantive inquiry-based activities you can have students complete to learn about the topic.

8. After brainstorming, check each activity against the initial list of learning expectations that you identified or that were given in a guideline. Code the activities to match the corresponding learning expectations (e.g., 1, 2, 3).

9. Generate additional activities to address any learning expectations that were not addressed through brainstorming.

10. Deconstruct each activity to identify sub-skills and knowledge that will be taught to ensure students' success with each activity.

11. Identify the assessment strategy you will use to assess students' learning for each learning expectation within each activity.

12. Identify the recording device you will use to record students' achievement in relation to each learning expectation.

13. Order the activities in the sequence they will be completed.

Having a procedure such as this as a starting point for planning will help teachers manage the task and retain focus on all of the interrelated components of unit planning. School boards often provide templates for unit planning that reflect current initiatives or priorities within the Board.

COMBINED (SPLIT) GRADE PLANNING FOR SOCIAL STUDIES

In many jurisdictions, a reality for the school is that there are many classrooms with combined (split) grades. Most frequently, these will be combinations of proximal grades such as Grade 2/3 class or Grade 5/6 class. Less frequently, a teacher may be challenged to provide instruction for a class with more than two grades (e.g., a Grade 1, 2, 3 combination) or a combined (split) class with grades that are not proximal (e.g., 3/5 combination). In most cases, such choices reflect the numbers of students and the assigned staff allocation and space in a school. However, in some jurisdictions, such arrangements may also reflect deliberate choices of instructional structures, such as a "house" system, where students are combined in less traditional ways for the purpose of social interaction within the school or creating student-to-student mentorships. In some jurisdictions, students are cross-assigned for academic instructional structures that allow the school to reallocate the students for part of the day for instructional purposes (i.e., putting students into single grade allocations for certain subject areas like reading or math or science/social studies).

Whatever the reason for the creation of a combined (split) grade class, the social studies teacher is faced with choices about how to present appropriate curriculum for the different grades in the classroom. This chapter is designed to help you do that in a productive, efficient, and deliberate way.

Once learning expectations are identified, the teacher can turn attention toward the planning of units of instruction for the social studies classroom. However, the planning process is more complicated when the teacher is providing instruction in a combined (split) grade.

There are four ways to address unit design for combined (split) classes:

1. Teach both grades the same content, using the same process, and requiring the same products.

2. Design process-based units.

3. Use a contract learning approach to instruction.

4. Plan for "out-of-phase" delivery of instruction to manage two distinct topics at one time. (See Chapter 3 for a review of the phases of instruction.)

In the pages following, each of these approaches to combined (split) grade instruction will be explained.

Teaching Both Grades the Same Content, Using the Same Process, and Requiring the Same Products

Quite often, when faced with a combined (split) grade with one year separating the grades (e.g., a Grade 3/4 or a Grade 5/6), the teacher will choose to manage instruction as though the class was a single grade. This is best done through long-term planning (and in collaboration with other members of the school team) for the group of students so that projections are made about what units of study will be addressed in social studies over several years. This approach can help to avoid having students repeating the same units.

The most obvious disadvantage of this approach lies in the mobility of families. A student who starts the school year in one school in Grade 3, studying the Grade 4 unit for social studies, could move partway through the unit and start at a new school where a Grade 3 unit of study is already underway. If the student is moving into a school where the grades are not combined, he or she might also begin study of an already familiar unit at the start of their Grade 4 course in the upcoming year.

Process-Based Instruction: The Mega-Unit Approach

Process-based units are designed around the conception that the skills students use for thinking and inquiring in social studies are common across grades (see Chapters 3, 5, and 11). These skills develop and become more sophisticated as students mature and receive additional instruction and experience with the skills. The skills become refined and personalized as students adapt them to new situations.

However, the common theme of selected skills across grades makes it possible for teachers to design *process-based* units of study, which build on the learning skills of thinking and inquiry. Analysis of a social studies guideline with expectations for Grades 5 and 6 shows these common processes as examples (see Figure 8.6).

When process skills are so similar across grades, units can be planned so that direct instruction focuses on teaching the process skills followed by independent opportunities to apply these skills to different content.

Figure 8.6 Common Processes

Grade 5 Process (Thinking and Inquiry Skills)	Grade 6 Process (Thinking and Inquiry Skills)
Formulate questions to develop a research focus	Formulate questions with a statement of purpose to develop research plans
Use primary and secondary sources to locate information about early civilizations	Select relevant sources and identify their point of view
Use graphic organizers and graphs to sort information and make connections	Use and construct a variety of graphic organizers to clarify and interpret information
Compare maps of early civilizations with modern maps of the same area	Read, interpret, and compare modern and historical maps of an area to determine accuracy
Use knowledge of map-making techniques and conventions to analyze map sites of early civilizations	Use models and draw and label various forms of maps, using cartographic symbols and a legend
Use media works, oral presentations, written notes and descriptions, drawings, tables, charts, maps, and graphs to communicate information about early communities	Observe bibliographic conventions, use media works, oral presentations, written notes and reports, drawings, tables, charts, and graphs to communicate the results of inquiries about the effects of early contact between First Nations peoples and early European explorers
Use appropriate vocabulary	Use appropriate vocabulary
Make connections between some elements of modern life and similar elements from early civilizations	Identify some present-day issues concerning First Nations peoples that relate to results of early contact
Report on the relevance to modern society of selected scientific and technological discoveries made by early civilizations	Explain how cooperation between First Nations peoples and early explorers benefited both groups

There may be some process learning expectations that are not common across grades and the teacher would then plan for separate activities and learning episodes to address them.

Once the expectations for a unit are identified and the process expectations are matched, the teacher can follow a procedure for generating the unit. A procedure for developing a process-based unit for social studies is outlined in Figure 8.7.

Activities should

■ include choice;

■ focus on inquiry;

■ provide individual, small-group, and large-group variety;

■ get students focused because they are inherently interesting;

Figure 8.7 Process-Based Combined (Split) Grade Unit Development Procedures

1. Consider the titles of the two separate units and create another title to blend the focus of the two separate units (e.g., Grade 5: Early Civilizations. Grade 6: First Nations People. New title: Characteristics of Early Settlements).
2. Create a guiding question.
3. Identify the overall expectations, or big ideas, for both units.
4. Create a culminating task for each grade.
5. Deconstruct the culminating task to identify all of the sub-skills students will need to learn in order to be successful with the culminating task.
6. Identify how you will assess the culminating task.
7. Identify how you will evaluate the culminating task.
8. Brainstorm to identify substantive inquiry-based activities you can have students complete to learn about the topic; keep the process and product the same for the activities; vary the content.
9. After brainstorming, check each activity against the initial list of learning expectations that you identified or that were given in a guideline. Code the activities to match the corresponding learning expectations (e.g., 1, 2, 3).
10. Generate additional activities to address any learning expectations that were not addressed through brainstorming.
11. Deconstruct each activity to identify sub-skills that will be taught to ensure students' success with each activity.
12. Identify the assessment strategy you will use to assess students' learning for each learning expectation within each activity.
13. Identify the recording device you will use to record students' achievement in relation to each learning expectation.
14. Order the activities in the sequence they will be completed.

- use a wide range of resources;
- allow for centres or activity areas (e.g., model making);
- include career investigations;
- go beyond the textbook;
- help students learn to manage time effectively;
- be built around strong and well-understood routines;
- include talk among students; focused, on-task discussion;
- help students make connections; include mind-body connection opportunities; and
- be fun!

Teachers could use the unit planning template provided below to plan a unit for social studies (see Figure 8.8).

Figure 8.8 Sample Unit-Planning Template

Grade: _____   Guideline Topic: _____

Integration Opportunities: _____

Overall Unit Learning Expectations/Big Ideas/Enduring Understandings:

- _____

  _____

- _____

  _____

Inquiry/Guiding Question for the Whole Unit:

_____

_____

_____

_____?

Social Justice Values/Actions Central to This Unit:

_____

Figure 8.8 (*Continued*)

Specific Expectations	Inquiry Question	Inquiry Activity (individual, small group or whole class)	Skill Deconstruction (identify all skills that will need to be taught, practised, and scaffolded to support learning success)	Assessment *For* and *As* Learning and Evaluation *of* Learning
Knowledge	What is it? Specific to the topic: _____ _____			
	How does it work? Specific to the topic: _____ _____			
	What are its interesting characteristics? _____ _____			
Understanding	How do these characteristics change over time/place/ circumstances, etc? Specific to the topic: _____ _____			
	What are these changes related to? Specific to the topic: _____ _____			
Valuing	What would/will/ could happen if . . . ? Specific to the topic: _____ _____			
Social Action	What could/should/ might be done about it? Specific to the topic: _____ _____			

Contract Learning: Teaching by Guiding Independent Work

If the units you need to teach in a combined (split) grade are very different in process skills, as well as content, contract learning may be an approach that would work best to achieve the learning goals for both grades.

Contract learning is an approach to unit delivery that emphasizes the products that students are to produce and individualizes the instruction needed to achieve success with each product (see Figure 8.9).

Contract learning can be a very effective form of instruction in some circumstances. However, there are some components that must be in place first to allow contract learning to work. These include

Strong classroom management skills—Students must come to each task with the attitude that it must be handled seriously, given their best effort, and with the knowledge that they will be held accountable for demonstrating their learning. Promotive interaction is essential among students for contract learning approaches to function well.

Effective procedures—Many activities in a classroom at one time can be chaotic unless the students know and use the procedures the teacher has taught so that learning time is handled efficiently and with consideration for others.

Instructional literacy skill levels—Students need to have a level of content literacy and information text skills (see Chapter 13) that allows for independent reading and comprehension. Differentiation approaches are a critical part of ensuring that all students benefit from this approach (see Chapter 10).

Task monitoring strategies—The teacher needs to have an overview of all of the tasks that are required by students for the whole unit (or for some part of the

Figure 8.9 Managing Contract Learning

To manage contract learning, the student needs . . .	To manage contract learning, the teacher needs . . .
A clear idea of the tasks they are to complete	Strong classroom management
Self-monitoring skills	Strong classroom procedures and routines
Time-management skills	"Withitness"—an awareness of what is happening elsewhere in the classroom
Informational text skills (see Chapter 13)	Task-monitoring strategies and multitasking skills
An understanding of expected standards	Clear standards that they communicate to students frequently.
A functional level of literacy to address tasks	The confidence to try contract learning!

Figure 8.10 Monitoring Contract Learning Tasks

Contract Learning for Grade 1/2 Class: Me and My Family in Our Community				
Students' Names	Task 1: Title Complete this by:	Task 2: Title Complete this by:	Task 3: Title Complete this by:	Task 4: Title Complete this by:
Brandon				
Haley				
Anna				
Allie				

unit that will be addressed through contract learning). It is most effective if this overview is also displayed for students to see, and if they are taught to monitor their progress with completion of all tasks.

Multitasking skills—The teacher needs to be able to scan the classroom regularly to see what students are doing and to identify where closer monitoring and support may be needed.

Clear standards—Students need to have examples of high-quality work, in many formats, shown and explained to them so that they understand what is expected when they engage in a task.

Contract learning is based on a clear picture of what students can do that will aptly demonstrate their learning (see Figure 8.10). At the outset of each unit, the teacher will focus on clearly identifying what tasks will form the substance of the unit. These will form a list that the teacher will provide in a displayable format in the classroom. The display should be designed to give the teacher an "at a glance" view of students' progress through the tasks.

The teacher's next instructional task will be to determine what skills individual students may lack but are necessary to help them complete the tasks successfully. However, unlike direct instruction, the teacher's role in a unit managed through contract learning is that of a guide and mentor. The teacher will teach to individuals and small groups when students are required to know more in order to complete high-quality tasks to demonstrate their learning. Using this approach, learning becomes personalized and precise. Large-group instruction time is minimal. This is differentiation (see Chapter 10) at its instructional best because the teacher will teach what is needed for immediate tasks as students address each task and the students will have a need to know.

One considerable advantage of the use of contract learning is its motivational value. Because students have some choice about when, how, and with whom they work on specific tasks, they tend to be strongly motivated and on-task behaviour increases. Along with this, misbehaviour and off-task time decreases. The tone of the classroom often changes and students will be noticeably more relaxed and less anxious.

The key to successful use of contract learning with every age group is the teacher's ability to organize the learning space, the tasks, and the resources, in an environment where strong routines and promotive interaction skills are already in place.

Out-of-Phase Delivery of Instruction: Managing Two Distinct Topics at Once

In Chapter 3, the phases of instruction model was introduced. Teachers can use either direct or indirect methods of instruction. Indirect methods include approaches such as activity centres, contract learning, independent study/inquiry, cooperative learning, and web quest learning. Details about how to select and structure lessons for each of these processes was provided in the Chapter 3.

The phases of instruction diagram reminds us about the role of the teacher as either model or guide in the learning process. These roles fluctuate throughout learning and are responsive to individual students' needs as they engage in learning.

Figure 8.11 illustrates where the teacher would start the phases of instruction, including motivation, modelling new learning, recapitulation, consolidation, and application, if the lesson was being delivered in a teacher-directed/modelled approach and if it was being presented indirectly, through some form of an activity-based approach.

When working with a combined (split) grade, the skilled teacher will implement both of these approaches simultaneously. While the teacher works with one grade to

Figure 8.11 Phases of Instruction in a Direct-Instruction Model and with Use of an Activity-Planning Model

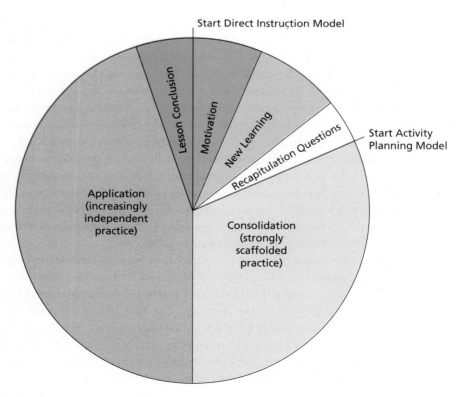

model a new concept or skill in social studies, the students in the alternate grade will be working independently to consolidate and apply a concept or skill that was modelled previously. This is "out-of-phase" instruction.

The success of out-of-phase instruction depends largely on the teacher's ability to multitask and to display "withitness," which is often defined as the ability to be aware of all things happening in the classroom while focusing attention on a specific thing.

Success with managing two distinct units in a combined (split) grade class is also heavily dependent on the teacher's establishment of productive, time-saving routines that keep the classroom focused, and preserve valuable learning time.

Example of Out-of-Phase Instruction in a Combined (Split) Class

Mrs. Groenweld has a Grade 4/5 classroom. She has taught social studies all year using different approaches. However, she has selected an out-of-phase approach for the latest unit of study. Her Grade 4 students are learning about Canada's provinces, territories, and regions, while the Grade 5 students are learning about government and citizenship in Canada.

Yesterday, Mrs. Groenweld had her Grade 4 students work with her to name the provinces, regions, and territories of Canada. She showed them many examples of political maps of Canada and ended her lesson confident that the students understood that different areas of Canada have different names, locations, and resources.

Today, the Grade 4 students will work in two small groups. In one group, they will work with velcro map pieces to create a map of Canada by fitting puzzle pieces together, then adding samples of resources for each province, territory, or region on their map. They have several reference books to check to ensure that their choices are correct before they complete their map.

At the second centre, students will select paper cut-outs of the provinces, territories, and regions of Canada from various envelopes on the table and glue them together to form a map of Canada on a large sheet of paper. Then, students will label the political areas of each map, using a list of labels they must include. Atlases are available at the table for them to check their work before they use glue.

Directions for both of these tasks are given in print form on the tables where the supplies for each activity are provided. When students have completed each task they have been directed to take their work to a third table, where samples of high-quality products for each task are located in an envelope. They are to check their work against these models and make any adjustments they think are necessary to improve their work before they put it in the "Work Completed" bin.

Meanwhile, Mrs. Groenweld is working with the Grade 5 students. She has shown them the levels of government in Canada, using a PowerPoint presentation. As she has explained the different levels and responsibilities of government to the Grade 5 group, students have been invited to come to the board and sort the list of words randomly displayed there. The final product they see at the end of their teacher's discussion represents a list that matches each level of government in

Canada with the responsibilities of that level of government. This process takes Mrs. Groenweld about 20 minutes to complete. At the end of that time, Mrs. Groenweld directs the Grade 5 students to create a chart in their social studies notebooks and to copy and give examples of each level of government responsibility.

As they get underway with this task, Mrs. Groenweld goes to the activity tables to check the two tasks that are being completed by the Grade 4 students. She has the group come together to quiz them about the names of the political divisions in Canada, using an unnamed map tacked to the chart stand.

This example of out-of-phase instruction for combined (split) grade social studies teaching can be examined by looking at each phase of instruction as represented in Figure 8.11. A sample schedule is provided below (see Figure 8.12).

Figure 8.12 Out-of-Phase Instruction for a Combined (Split) Grade Class

Grade	Phase of Instruction	Time	Activities Being Performed
4	Consolidation	1:00–1:40	Grade 4 students are: ■ fitting political map pieces together and matching pieces to resources after checking texts ■ making paper cut-out copies of a political map of Canada
5	New Learning	1:00–1:40	Mrs. Groenweld is: ■ using a PowerPoint presentation to explain the levels of government in Canada ■ having students demonstrate their understanding of her explanation by creating a chart on the blackboard, constructed from paper words that are randomly placed and matching levels of government with the responsibilities of each level
4	Application	1:40–2:00	Mrs. Groenweld: ■ brings Grade 4 students together to check the map they have created and labelled ■ questions various students about their knowledge of the names of the various political divisions shown on the unlabelled map
5	Consolidation	1:40–2:00	Grade 5 students are: ■ working at their desks to copy the chart they have created on the blackboard into their notebooks. At the end of this task, they will each have a record of the responsibilities of each level of government in Canada

The successful use of an out-of-phase approach requires a great deal of organization and preparation by the teacher. However, this approach has many advantages. Using out-of-phase instruction, students learn

- time management;
- task focus;
- independence;
- responsibility
- cooperation and promotive interaction
- innovation

All of these skills and attributes will only be learned by the students if they are taught each skill, and held accountable for showing them in context when needed.

The Necessity of Routines and Rules for Social Skill Development in the Social Studies Classroom

Effective routines are essential to the smooth operation of any classroom. Teachers will need to be clear in their understanding that rules and routines are not the same thing. Rules should be few and should represent the teacher's "bottom line" for what is expected in the classroom. Rules should be easy to remember and should operate like a classroom mantra that students will understand as being the incontrovertible "do not cross" line. Rules create a tone of respect in the classroom. A sample of suitable rules might be:

Respect Yourself

Respect Others

Respect the Environment

Routines or procedures have a different purpose in your social studies classroom. They are established to maximize learning time and ensure that your classroom runs smoothly, with the highest possible degree of time-on-task. They help students to be clear about what is expected of them and this helps everyone to be more relaxed. Examples of routines that you might use include

- how to enter the classroom;
- what to do when you've entered the classroom;
- how to pass in papers;
- sharpening pencils;
- asking permission to speak;
- getting into groups;

- what to do when you get into groups;
- how to get out of groups;
- how to break for lunch;
- how to exit the classroom;
- how to throw paper away;
- how to use in-class study time;
- how to take a test;
- how to work on computers;
- how to make notes about homework; and
- what to do/where to go when you need help and the teacher is unavailable

Strong teachers include instruction of social skills in their everyday direction (Johnson & Johnson, 2009). Being attentive to how students work together is the key to identifying next steps for ensuring that students are taught the skills they need to improve in group efforts and to maximize their learning in cooperative situations.

Through observation, teachers can identify the skills that are lacking, deconstruct the situation to identify skills that could be taught, and plan for systematic instruction in these skills. Students will need time to consider what newly introduced social skills will look like and sound like when they operate in small-group situations. The teacher can support this developing awareness by

- naming the social skill;
- discussing what the social skill will look like when it is observed in the classroom;
- discussing what the social skill will sound like when it is observed in the classroom;
- creating anchor charts for display in the classroom to demonstrate examples of what the skill looks and sounds like in context;
- recognizing students' efforts to use the skill;
- allowing group processing time at the end of group tasks so that students can discuss how well they worked together and can focus on how well they managed interaction using the new skill; and
- revisiting target skills each time group work or cooperative/collaborative work structures are used to complete classroom tasks.

When instructing students about the use of a new social skill, a T-chart is very useful. It allows the teacher to identify, in an economical format, what the skill looks and sounds like and can provide an easy reference to be posted in the classroom.

A sample T-chart for the social skill of "disagreeing in an agreeable way" might look like Figure 8.13.

Teachers should expect that progress with the development of social skills will be nonlinear. Students will seem to understand what is expected one day, but not demonstrate the social skills on another. Keep at it! This is a technique that needs a long-term commitment

Figure 8.13 Sample T-Chart

Disagreeing in an Agreeable Way	
Looks Like	**Sounds Like**
■ calm	■ quiet, respectful voices
■ looking at the speaker	■ asking for examples and clarification
■ waiting until the speaker is finished	■ ensuring that the speaker's ideas are understood by rephrasing (e.g., "Do you mean . . . ?")
■ determining ways to reach consensus	■ building on each other's ideas
■ taking turns to speak	

from both teachers and students, with the teacher's leadership. Over time, students will come to value the skills the teacher values and respond to the positive encouragement to use the skills in group work contexts.

The teacher will need to determine what social skills need to be taught to create a classroom that functions productively and that mirrors social justice values in this microcosm. Social skills, like any cognitive or physical skills, have a context. They should be taught when they are needed to improve students' chances for success with an academic task. Grouping students to get a job done is just the beginning. Teachers need to structure the groups for success by grouping students strategically and supporting their success by teaching them the skills that are required for that task. Through careful analysis of interactions, teachers can systematically teach students the skills that are lacking.

See Figure 8.14 for an extensive but not exhaustive list of the social skills that may be needed by primary and junior students.

When teaching social skills for group tasks, teachers should ensure that they focus on the skills needed by their students. This will help students to recognize respectful use of

Figure 8.14 Social Skills to Teach in Social Studies

- ■ staying on task
- ■ contributing to the group task
- ■ developing, expanding, or building on each person's ideas
- ■ accommodating or assimilating ideas
- ■ speaking to others with respect
- ■ expressing opinions in a way that will be attended to by others
- ■ using appropriate body language
- ■ taking turns speaking
- ■ explaining ideas with examples
- ■ suggesting more effective wording
- ■ motivating others
- ■ providing genuine praise
- ■ planning against group timelines
- ■ developing organizers that will help group members visualize the task
- ■ using eye-to-eye contact during discussions
- ■ obtaining and sharing task materials

(Continued)

Figure 8.14 (*Continued*)

- ensuring that group members can hear what is said
- requesting clarification
- rephrasing
- rephrasing
- ensuring group understanding of the task
- ensuring group consensus on the approach to the task
- coaching other group members to ensure common understanding
- checking task progress, including using task check points, against a schedule
- providing evidence to support an idea or opinion
- setting performance standards for the group
- praising

- keeping materials and workspace organized for efficient work
- sharing input time
- requesting clarification or rephrasing
- understanding and using the strengths of different group members to complete tasks effectively
- evaluating the process of working together in a group
- evaluating the group's products
- goal setting
- checking for understanding and agreement
- group editing
- summarizing ideas
- initiating reflection on group work and products
- responding positively to negative behaviour

their time and they are more likely to be receptive to learning the skills if they see them as something they need.

INTEGRATED UNITS: DESIGNING UNITS AROUND PROCESS SKILLS

Integrated units are units that draw expectations, standards of the discipline, and strategies from the subject areas that are integrated. When units are integrated around process skills, teachers need to examine the thinking, inquiry, and communication skills that are to be taught for each subject area. Common skills across the subject areas are highlighted in the development of the unit. The procedure used for the development of a unit for a single grade can also be used for developing integrated units built around process skills.

INTEGRATING SOCIAL STUDIES AND HISTORICAL NOVEL STUDIES

In Chapter 9, ideas for the use of novels and short stories to complement instruction about social studies concepts is developed. There are many excellent novels that can be used to help immerse students in ideas they are studying. Through the concurrent use of novels and historical or geographical references, students develop a clearer picture of situations

Students can develop a deeper understanding of social studies concepts and historical and geographical facts through historical novels and stories.

and learn to consider motivations, varied circumstances, values, and priorities that were influenced by different times in Canada's history, and the way that history and geography have impacted individual lives.

By integrating social studies and historical novel studies, teachers gain classroom time and support students in their quest to make connections. Novels and short stories should be selected carefully for accuracy and detection of bias.

THE POWER OF STORY IN SOCIAL STUDIES: USING LITERATURE TO COMPLEMENT THE THEME OF A SOCIAL STUDIES INQUIRY

Students can develop a deeper understanding of social studies concepts and historical and geographical facts through story. They can learn through the study of stories and through writing their own stories in response to new learning.

It is critical that teachers clarify for themselves what they want to achieve by using stories as a vehicle for learning. Teachers will need to examine stories as supplementary resources to ensure that they portray issues with accuracy and cultural sensitivity. The misuse of stories may create bias and misrepresent information rather than support deep understanding.

Writing about new learning through story can help students personalize their understanding of places and situations and examine their understanding of motivations and values. When using story writing to help students construct meaning, teachers will need to guide students' ability to represent the story elements to extend their language skills and guide their ability to represent valid understanding of social studies concepts.

Local libraries and commercial bookstores often have extensive holdings of books that relate to social studies concepts in the primary/junior curriculum. Bookstore staff are often very familiar with the books and can be helpful in selecting those that relate to themes in courses. Using these resources will help teachers to conserve learning time and integrate learning across subject areas so that students can make connections within their learning. Teachers should be sure to evaluate the reading level of any books that are being used to supplement the curriculum to ensure ease of access for learners.

Multiple literacy approaches should also be considered and optimized. Literacy through media, text, photographs, artifacts, activity, and interaction, alone or in any combination, should all be considered when the teacher engages in unit planning.

INNOVATIVE APPROACHES IN YOUR SOCIAL STUDIES CLASSROOM

Earlier chapters have introduced and developed the instructional concept of topic elaboration. This approach to a topic develops a sequence of related inquiries that support skill-based investigation.

The final skill in the sequence of topic elaboration is *decision making*. Decision making is focused on addressing questions such as "What could/should/might/will be done about it?" This is a very useful skill for students as it draws abstract ideas towards ownership and emphasizes each student's role in contributing to our society in responsible and socially just ways. Cultural responsiveness is dependent on students' age-appropriate internalization of skills that lead to responsive and sensitive multicriterion decision making.

Initially, decision-making skills should be taught in low-content contexts where students are already familiar with the content and can focus their attention on learning the skill. Cognitive theory leads us to connect the skill of decision making to a visual framework to support memory of the interrelated skills. Using known content and a visual framework, supported by a clear and sequential procedure for the skill of decision making, makes this skill easily adaptable for young students. Grade 3 learners have both the language skills and the conceptual development to use a decision-making framework with ease.

Figure 8.15 is an example of a social studies procedure for decision making. A decision-making procedure is provided before the example to show the order of the steps to be followed in teaching this skill.

When using this very mathematical approach to decision making, students will need to have several exposures to the process to develop comfort with identifying decisional questions, identifying options, and stating relevant criteria for the question. They will also need to understand that there are many types of decisions, and a process such as this is only suitable for more complex decisions when many criteria and many options or perspectives are relevant to making a good decision. Also, students will need to be taught that they may use such a process and arrive at a decision mathematically but the decision may not "feel" right to them. In this instance, they will need to understand that there are other criteria that are important to their decision that were not identified

Figure 8.15 Decision-Making Procedures

1. State the decisional question. (Note: Students will need to be taught the difference between a decisional question and an informational question.)
2. State the options. (If only two choices are possible, these are called alternatives rather than options.)
3. State the criteria.
4. Identify the relative importance of each criterion by assigning a number value (weight) to it (e.g., from 1 to 3, with 3 being the most important criteria).
5. Evaluate each option against each weighted criterion and assign each a number.
6. Total the columns.
7. State the decision. When two totals are close and a split decision is possible, consider that possibility.

before they applied the procedure. Role-playing and cooperative learning structures such as Corners and Agreement Circles (see Chapter 3) can be used as strategies for having students identify criteria so that the results of the mathematical process are also satisfying emotionally.

Figure 8.16 provides an example of the results of applying this procedure to a typical social studies context. The question, "What should B.C. do about their political affiliations?" is used for this example. The smaller numbers in each cell show the order of the options in relation to each other while the larger numbers show the weighted value of each option in relation to the specific criterion being considered in each row.

Using a Decision-Making Chart to Write an Argumentative Essay

Using the chart to support complex decision making can be very successful for very young students. Research with Grade 3 students has shown excellent writing results in argumentative formats when students are taught the procedure for decision making, shown how to apply it to the development of the chart, then shown through modelling how to use the chart to guide the development of their writing to explain a decision.

- The opening paragraph of the essay is written by following the steps that lead to consideration of the decisional question, the options, the criteria, and their weighting.

- Decisional question—students ask a decisional question that will lead them to the consideration of several options.

- Options row—the options are stated and placed across the top of a piece of paper, side by side. Any number of options can be stated. Each option will be the topic of a separate paragraph in the writing.

Figure 8.16 Decision-Making Chart

Decisional Question: What should B.C. do about their political affiliations?				
Criteria	Weighting	Stay Independent	Join Confederation	Join U.S.
What would provide the best economic advantages? **3**		1 **3**	2 **9**	3 **6**
What would give them the most power? **2**		1 **2**	3 **6**	2 **4**
What would give them the most political stability? **1**		1 **1**	3 **3**	2 **2**
What would give them the best trading options? **3**		1 **3**	2 **6**	3 **9**
Totals	Totals are determined by multiplying the preference order of each option by the weighting given to that option.	**9**	**24**	**21**

- Criteria column—this column provides an outline for a sentence or two that explains the criteria that the students feel are important in arriving at a decision.

- Weighting column—students examine the criteria. They decide which criterion is the most important. They assign criteria a weight to show the relative importance of each criterion in their judgment.

The body paragraphs of the essay are written by considering each option in descending order. The chosen option forms the topic of the second paragraph; the next most popular option forms the third paragraph, and so on until all options have been explained in writing.

The closing paragraph is written to review all of the options that were considered and summarize the reasons why the selected option was preferred. Using the key phrase "Review and react" helps students remember to consider both of these elements in their closing paragraph.

Using this process for argumentative writing applied to the decision-making chart example provided above, the students will have a six-paragraph essay (see Figure 8.17).

It is helpful to students to post an anchor chart in the classroom to identify the steps they can follow to develop their argumentative writing. As students develop fluency with this style of writing through experience and formative feedback, they will move away from the set procedure and begin to develop a more personalized style that builds on the systematic strength of the initial procedure. When students are ready to expand their style they can be taught to enrich each point within their paragraphs by providing examples for each point. The following exemplar can be provided for reference as students write.

Procedures for Writing an Argumentative Essay

Opening Paragraphs

1. State the topic.
2. State subtopics/options.
3. State criteria.
4. Explain each weighted criteria in relation to each option.

Figure 8.17 From Planning to Writing: An Introduction to the Argumentative Essay

Part of Essay	Description
P1: Introductory/Opening Paragraph	The opening paragraph will state the question and the options (neutral, Confederation, and join the U.S. in our example) and explain the criteria that will be considered and their respective weights.
P2, P3, P4, and P5: Body Paragraphs	Each option is explained against each criterion in a separate paragraph.
P6: Closing Paragraph	Students state their decision and explain the other options that were considered but discarded. They react to their feelings about the decision and explain other interesting reactions to the decision (e.g., next steps for action).
Subordinate Clauses	Strong writing should include sentences written in many styles. Students can be taught to write compound and complex sentences and subordinate clauses without getting bogged down by grammar terminology. By using the chart and simply asking students to provide a sentence that combines ideas from two or more cells of the chart, they will provide compound and complex sentences in their writing. Analysis of the grammar can follow competency with its practical use.

Body Paragraphs

4. Write an opening sentence for each paragraph (1 per option).

5. Write sentences to explain that option against each criterion.

Closing Paragraph

6. R and R (review and react). Students might also be taught the popular responding phrase for examining stories (retell, reflect, react) and use that sequence to guide writing for the closing paragraph.

By starting with the decisional question "What could/should/might/will be done about this?" students can be taught powerful decision making and argumentative essay writing skills that allow them to consider and express thoughts about difficult and controversial issues. It is critical that students are taught these skills in the context of studying a topic in depth so that they are not addressing complex decisions frivolously and from an uninformed stance.

CASE STUDIES AND PROFESSIONAL ACTIVITIES FOR INNOVATION IN SOCIAL STUDIES

1. Identify the social studies unit titles specified for a selected grade in your jurisdiction. Post each unit title on a piece of chart paper and tape these around a room. With professional colleagues, brainstorm approaches and strategies that could be used within each unit and have each person write their ideas on the chart paper in random order as they circulate the room. Have people rotate every three or four minutes during brainstorming. This will give you a good range of strategies to consider for your units as you plan connected ideas related to solid inquiry. It also opens the door to professional discussions with other social studies teachers about approaches and ideas for a strong program.

2. Identify a unit for social studies. Put the title of that unit in the centre of a sheet of chart paper. Around the title, write all of the "big ideas" or central concepts that students should understand by the end of the unit of study. Jot ideas that relate to the central concept around that concept name. Now, write a report card comment of four to five sentences that you would use to report the strongest learning results for this theme/unit. Check your final comment against the brainstormed cluster of "big ideas" or central concepts. Discuss the congruency between the reporting comment and the "big ideas" that you brainstormed with colleagues engaged in the same exercise.

3. Develop a poster that you could use in a primary or junior classroom to remind students of the steps of good inquiry approaches so that they have a reference for use when they engage in a contract unit. Use symbols and pictures to support reading of your poster. Compare your poster to those developed by other colleagues. Discuss the strengths and areas for growth in each model poster you examine.

CHAPTER REVIEW AND PROFESSIONAL DEVELOPMENT AS A TEACHER

This chapter has examined the following:

- Strong social studies units are designed around inquiry approaches.

- There are many approaches to unit design; approaches reflect the grade demographics, available time, and guideline mandates for the province/territory.

- Curriculum guidelines may provide expectations for units.

- Mandated expectations may require refinement to make them applicable to the lesson.

- When specific learning (not teaching!) expectations are not provided by guidelines, teachers need to expand topics to determine the scope of the topic as they develop it into a unit; then they need to develop learning expectations from each sub-topic they have identified.

- Learning expectations or objectives should always be written to ensure that they are specific, measureable, attainable, realistic, and timely.

- Guidelines from different jurisdictions present expectations in different groupings (e.g., knowledge, skills, and attitudes or content, process, and products); teachers need to analyze their local guidelines so that they understand the groupings that govern expectations for their curriculum; understanding these groupings can help teachers to combine learning expectations into vibrant learning experiences.

- Units can be developed by applying a procedure that keeps the focus on big ideas, inquiry processes, and connected inquiry activities.

- Unit planning for combined (split) grades can be approached in four ways, each using variations of a basic unit-development procedure.

- Activities within a unit should have many characteristics that ensure attainability of the overall learning goals.

- Contract learning is a valuable approach to inquiry once students have attained a functional literacy level to allow them to engage resources independently.

- Effective contract learning requires strong classroom management, effective classroom procedures, functional literacy among students, systematic task monitoring and multitasking by the teacher, and clear standards for students' performance.

- Contract learning can be monitored effectively by charting and assessing products through a chart system specifically designed for the unit.

- Effective contract learning will include provision for differentiated skill instruction in context.

- The choices available to students when a contract learning approach is used are inherently motivating for students.

- Promotive interaction is an essential social skill for effective contract learning involving group work.

- "Out-of-phase" approaches allow teachers to manage direct instruction effectively in combined (split) grades.

- Social-skill development is essential for students to engage any unit of study to its optimal potential; strategies to teach social skills must be considered when teachers plan units.

- A systematically organized decision chart can be used to guide young students' initial efforts to write in argumentative formats.

- There are many social skills that should be taught within the context of social studies and other subjects in the primary/junior grades.

- Units of study in social studies can be planned around process skills, historical stories and novels, and many forms of literacy (multiple literacies).

- Decision making is an essential skill for students to learn as they develop the capacity for social responsibility and awareness of the elements of a socially just and culturally responsive society.

- Systematic decision making can be taught to young students using a procedure and an organizational framework that support memory and consideration of many interacting elements of a situation.

Professional Development Activities

1. What guidance is provided in your jurisdiction for the learning expectations of students?

2. Refine the social studies expectations (as they may be stated in a guideline or curriculum document) in Figure 8.18 to reflect SMART goals for learning that could be accomplished in a specific lesson.

3. Explain the process of developing a unit for social studies in a combined (split) grade class.

4. Develop a unit for social studies for a combined (split) grade using the procedure defined in this chapter.

Figure 8.18 Practice with Refining Learning Expectations

Expectation	Refinement
Students will be able to identify traditions and celebrations and their roots, as they are celebrated in their local community.	
Students will be able to identify the provinces, territories, and regions of Canada.	
Students will be able to identify the responsibilities of each level of government in Canada.	
Students will be able to explain reasons why people immigrate to Canada.	

5. Develop an outline for students' use for a unit organized using a contract learning approach and reflecting all of the learning expectations for a unit in social studies.

6. Explain out-of-phase instruction in terms that will make the approach clear to a parent.

7. Discuss the rules and routines you would institute in your classroom to support management of a combined (split) grade unit of social studies. Explain the benefits of each rule and routine you identify in terms of support for improved learning.

8. Create a scope and sequence of social studies topics and skills for each grade in your school. If such a scope and sequence is provided in a guideline for your local use, map the scope and sequence so that relationships among topics and skills can be examined.

9. Talk about how each teacher or division in your school is handling instruction in combined (split) grades. Consider if the most appropriate strategies are being used. Are all teachers aware of all of the options for managing instruction in combined (split) grades? What supports are needed to make everyone aware of the options?

10. What social skills are being taught in each grade/division? How can the school staff collaborate to maximize their efforts to improve students' social skills?

Weblinks

Writing Learning Goals
This site helps teachers and students improve their goal-development skills.
www.eduhound.com

Story Writing Tips
This site offers access to thousands of webpages. They are child and family friendly.
www.blackdog4kids.com
Author Corey Green provides a detailed website that promotes writing primarily for junior grades.
www.coreygreen.com

Children's Creative Story Writing
This site provides support for parents and their children; includes story writing tips, interactive writing, text analysis, and publication.
www.Midlandit.co.uk/education/index.htm

Unit Development
These sites will provide support for unit development in many formats and with various levels of support.
By typing "Unit Planning Template" into a search engine, like Google, users have access to a wide range of templates from many jurisdictions.

Story Writing for Young Learners
This site provides several resources for teaching various forms of writing to young children, especially those with an ESL background.
www.englishraven.com/ttoolswritingworkshop.html

Chapter 9
Motivational Methodology in Social Studies

Learning Topics

- The Construction of Knowledge in Social Studies
- Integration in the Social Studies Classroom
- Narrative in the Social Studies Classroom
- Cooperative Structures in Social Studies
- Simulations, Drama, and Dance in the Primary and Junior Classrooms

Engaging resources and strategies are essential to create deep understanding of social studies themes, issues, and contexts.

THE CONSTRUCTION OF KNOWLEDGE
IN SOCIAL STUDIES

In earlier chapters, you have read about the standards of the discipline of social studies. These standards help teachers to guide the selection and creation of strategies for their social studies programs. Use of the strategies that support the standards of the discipline helps to ensure that the program is viable, dynamic, and interesting for students, while providing the basis for both deep understanding of complex concepts and a platform for questioning and inquiry.

To consider the ways that teachers can most effectively approach the construction of knowledge in social studies, we can use the elements of differentiation (as discussed in Chapters 2 and 10). To provide appropriate differentiation in a classroom, teachers must consider instructional variations in the content, the processes, and the required products students are to provide as evidence of their learning (see Figure 9.1).

These three elements of differentiation provide us with a useful framework for identifying the possibilities for effective instruction in social studies.

Figure 9.1 Instructional Variations to Support Success

Differentiation		
Content	**Processes**	**Products**
Identified through provincial and territorial guidelines	Inquiry that is teacher directed, or could be partially or fully student directed	Teacher identified Student identified
Usually expressed as a measurable or observable action that would identify students' learning	Formulation of questions Use of sources, both primary and secondary, to locate and examine information	Negotiated between teacher and student Demonstrate deep understanding of concepts and relationships, cause and effect, change over time
Often described as a theme (e.g., local community, medieval life) in primary and junior contexts	Analytical and critical viewing Classification and comparison Analysis and interpretation of information	Provide opportunities for ongoing growth
Can be connected to learning in other subject areas through integration of the curriculum	Using and creating graphic organizers to sort, classify, connect, examine, interpret, discard, highlight, and construct new understanding	Are non-intrusive; the products students provide as evidence of their learning evolve as part of the learning and develop over the course of the learning; learning and the assessment of the learning are seamless
	Exploring and using a variety of communication techniques (e.g., bibliographic conventions, media, graphics, tables and charts, oral, visual,	Reflect the questions that directed the student's work

(Continued)

Figure 9.1 (*Continued*)

Content	Processes	Products
	and written combinations, displays/posters, drama and simulations)	Authentic; the products have personal meaning for each student and reflect that student's current level of understanding
	Connecting the language of the discipline to concepts; developing appropriate vocabulary	Acknowledge the limitations and purposes of formal testing
		Focus on assessment for learning rather than assessment of learning
		Make use of assessment to provide new learning opportunities

Authentic Assessment

Authentic assessment is crucial to effective learning. The students must be provided with opportunities to demonstrate what they know and understand about the topics being studied, in ways that match their dominant learning styles.

Authentic assessment includes assessment for three purposes:

1. Assessment to find out what the student already knows and understands about a topic (diagnostic assessment)

2. Assessment to find out how the learner is progressing in understanding as learning opportunities evolve (formative assessment) so that strategies for learning can be adapted as needed

3. Assessment to determine the student's cumulative learning related to the topic (summative assessment)

Authentic assessment is substantively different from assessment that stems from the belief that social studies is a set body of information that students must learn (often called a knowledge acquisition approach to assessment).

Summative assessment is often problematic for teachers. We all have a tendency to teach as we were taught and earlier practices with summative assessment led to assessments that were paper-and-pencil driven, designed for one approach to be used for all students, and applied at the end of a unit of study. Only through engaged reflective practice can we ensure that more effective approaches to assessment are used in our programs. More effective summative assessments will provide ongoing opportunities for students to develop understanding, provide specific ongoing feedback as students work toward demonstrating their understanding, and give support to achieve the targeted learning, to the level that each student requires (see Figure 9.2). This type of very effective assessment celebrates what students have learned rather than measuring what they have failed to learn.

Figure 9.2 Assessment Approaches

	Knowledge Acquisition Approach to Assessment	Authentic Assessment Approach
Beliefs about Learning Social Studies	Knowledge is assessed at one point in the learning Data is collected from a single source There is an important body of social studies information that all students should acquire	Knowledge, understanding, and skills are assessed throughout the learning and detailed feedback from peers and teachers provides the student with information to improve their understanding and the demonstration of their understanding Data collection is ongoing; the highest and most consistent level of achievement is sought Social studies is viewed as a transformative discipline and understanding is individually constructed through guided experience
Tools of Assessment	Tend to be paper-and-pencil tests Require lower-level learning (e.g., memorization of facts, selected responses), "glorified recall" Terminal; tend to happen at the end of a unit of study	Many approaches to collection of a variety of assessment data Student has input into what is assessed and when that happens Examines deep understanding and evidence of higher-order thinking (analysis, synthesis, evaluation, and creative efforts) Assessments respect and reflect the student's learning style preferences; choice is evident Ongoing; the student has many opportunities to adjust evidence of their learning and pursue individual preferences about what to learn within a topic

(Continued)

Figure 9.2 *(Continued)*

	Knowledge Acquisition Approach to Assessment	Authentic Assessment Approach
Use of the Assessment Data	Provides a single mark to measure level of success	Evidence of learning is collected from many sources
	Summative; tells the students how well they did with attaining the preferred body of information	Assessment is formative and ongoing; learning does not stop so that assessment data can be collected; the assessment and learning remain seamless

Handwritten margin notes: "formative vs summative"; "Can inquiry build from Grade to Grade?"

Questioning and Product Options to Support the Construction of Knowledge in Social Studies

Teaching young students to ask questions at increasingly complex levels of understanding is a pivotal skill in social studies learning. In Chapter 2 we examined the variety of question stems that can be taught to young students to help them develop a questioning habit of mind.

Bloom's Taxonomy of questions can also be aligned to appropriate products that will allow students to develop diversity in how they demonstrate learning and also, eventually, allow them to select a product that will focus their thinking at higher levels.

The framework provided in Figure 9.3 was developed to use with young students to allow them to match the required level of thinking with a product option that holds appeal for them. The framework contains three concentric arcs that can be matched to align content, process, and products.

To use the Bloom's Taxonomy Wheel to identify a *product* for assessment, the teacher or student can choose a product from the outside arc, a *process* from the middle arc, and match it to the *content* for a particular topic at the Bloom's thinking level identified by the inside arc.

Examples:

Develop a model (product) to record (process) the lifestyle of an early prairie farm family in Canada (content).

Create a questionnaire (product) to survey (process) the class to determine the heritages represented in the class (content).

Draw a cartoon (product) to create (process) a pictorial representation of one or more of the hardships faced by fur traders in Canada's north (content).

Write a news item (product) to recommend (process) action that could be taken to save a local greenbelt area from development for commercial uses (content).

Figure 9.3 Using Bloom's Taxonomy to Select the Process and Product

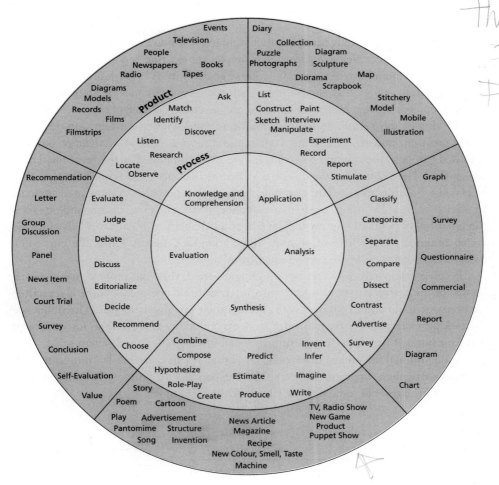

With modelling and practice, students can learn to use this graphic to generate many options for ways they can display their learning. Allowing this choice within the social studies program is very motivating for students, giving them a sense of control and purpose with their studies. Opportunities to demonstrate learning at the synthesis and evaluation levels will also promote creativity and respect diversity within the classroom.

INTEGRATION IN THE SOCIAL STUDIES CLASSROOM

Chapter 8 focused on approaches to unit design in social studies. A sample unit template and a procedure for developing both segregated (single grade) units and combined (split) grade units were provided. One of the strengths of social studies as an area of study is its focus on telling the stories of our developing nation. Because story is central to the discipline, social studies also provides a unique vehicle for the development of integrated units of study.

Integrated units of study are those that combine learning expectations or goals from more than one subject area. Consider the example strategy that is outlined in Figure 9.4.

This is a rich and interesting activity. Its strength is in its breadth and the inclusion of learning from many other subject areas. Science (physics) concepts are integrated in the development of toys. Historical concepts are developed as students do research about the clothing of the period. Mathematics concepts and science concepts are developed in the creation, making, preserving, packing, and serving of foods. Language skills are practised through research and the comparative tasks completed at the museum. This is integration. The book *If the World Were a Village: A Book about the World's People* (2002) by David J. Smith is an excellent example of a book that provides an integrated approach to social studies by using mathematics concepts to enhance understanding about the potential of population growth. The computer simulation "Real Lives" also provides a rich resource for teachers to promote integration of concepts across the curriculum (www.educationalsimulations.com/products.html).

Because integrated tasks can be so rich and varied, they can provide many starting points for the engagement of students with interests in diverse areas. There is something for everyone to do and to connect with through their learning strengths. The richness of the task provides many entry points for students and many opportunities for students to make meaning of new experiences through social interaction with classmates.

An additional advantage of integration is that it can conserve learning time. In a crowded curriculum, opportunities to use one experience to promote learning in many areas afford the teacher some flexible and creative use of time.

Figure 9.4 Pondering Early Settlers

Students are asked to engage in a Thanksgiving exploration at the local museum. The teacher has spent the last two weeks helping students to make early settler outfits to represent the style of dress of the early 1700s. They have created and tested many recipes from the time period and packed their foods for a picnic lunch.

Students will engage in traditional games on the lawn area beside the museum and have made some of the toys they will use for this purpose from authentically available tools and materials.

While at the museum, students will engage in a quest to find examples of clothing, foods, utensil, tools, and toys that they can identify. They will be asked to examine each authentic artifact for its similarities and differences from those they have researched and created.

NARRATIVE IN THE SOCIAL STUDIES CLASSROOM

Students of all ages love a good story. In social studies, teachers have many opportunities to use story to demonstrate an idea, to exemplify a concept, to provoke controversy, and to challenge complacent thinking.

Literature designed for any of these purposes can provide a rich source of support materials for social studies. Teachers will need to assess each story resource for the following:

- Age appropriateness (If the resource is to be used independently, is the reading level appropriate?)

- Presentation style (Will students know all of the fiction or non-fiction conventions that are used in the resource? If not, how will you address learning about newly introduced conventions?)

- Themes (Is this an efficient resource to support the intended learning?)

- Level of engagement (Will this story interest these students?)

- Range of perspectives (Is this story effective for representing desirable goals of inclusiveness? Tolerance? Stewardship? Conservation? Other concepts central to the values of the discipline? Are many perspectives on the problem and possible solutions tolerated? Invited? Denigrated?)

- Are the facts represented in the story true? If not, is the fiction intentional and not a misrepresentation of fact?

- Is the story conceptually accurate and does it use appropriate social studies terminology?

When using printed narrative to support the social studies program, teachers will also need to be mindful of the reading requirements of special-needs students. Often, the careful selection of stories and the carefully thought out use of printed resources can make wonderfully powerful stories accessible to all students.

Thoughtful and engaging discussion can enrich the classroom when students have an opportunity to examine many stories that present different perspectives and they can discuss the differences to help them arrive at their own views. Discussion is often remembered by students as among the peak experiences they encountered in their learning. Good literature sources that support social studies concepts can ensure that powerful discussion is part of the primary and junior social studies experience.

It will be important to teach the conventions of both fiction and non-fiction materials (see Figure 9.5) as students begin to use each type of resource to examine social studies concepts and issues. These reading skills will support the students' ability to access this rich literature in productive and accurate ways.

Teachers need to be aware of the desirability of providing balanced perspectives in resources when they are selecting story text to support learning about a social studies concept. Students should use these resources to enrich their understanding of such key concepts as

- the history of some of Canada's social problems;

- context influenced historical decisions;

FICTION ←→ NonFiction (handwritten)

Figure 9.5 Characteristics of Fiction and Non-Fiction

Characteristics of Fiction Text for Children	Characteristics of Non-Fiction Text for Children
■ Exaggeration	■ Represented as factual
■ Animals may have some human characteristics	■ May contain bias or distorted perspective
■ Timelines may be distorted	■ May include some fictional narrative to illustrate a point
■ Characters may be fictional to represent rather than report	■ Characters are historically real
■ Solutions to problems may seem to come easily	■ Solutions to problems may not be presented
■ Illustrations are closely tied to text	■ Illustrations are likely to be loosely connected to text
	■ May contain valuable information in formats other than text (graphs, charts, tables, timelines, maps, etc.)
	■ May include conventions from other sources (e.g., political cartoons)
	■ Key concepts may be bold or italicized
	■ Definitions may be provided
	■ Cross-references may be embedded in the text
	■ Will include text characteristics such as glossaries, appendices, indexes, etc.

■ individuals can cause social change;

■ historical events can influence current events;

■ authors always bring a perspective to their narrative and part of understanding the narrative is understanding that perspective;

■ empathetic responses to situations that have some similarity to the reader's experiences;

■ avoiding stereotypes by digging deeper into the lives of individuals within a society;

■ power, race, social class distinctions, culture, challenge, survival, heroism, and gender;

■ using productive approaches to problem solving and decision making; and

■ cultural awareness.

Some powerful fiction and non-fiction texts that can support primary/junior social studies instruction are listed in Figure 9.6.

When preparing to use literature and nonfiction texts to support social studies concept development, each selection will need to be examined for negative stereotypes and for the potential of the selection to develop deeper understanding of issues, perspectives, and values.

Figure 9.6 Fiction and Non-Fiction in the Primary/Junior Grades

Book	Author	Focus
Stand Up, Speak Out (2001)	Peace Child International	Rights of the child are explained through poetry, reports, and pictures
For Every Child (2000)	Caroline Castle	Rights of children
O Canada (1992)	Ted Harrison	Ethnic diversity across Canada
My Arctic, 1, 2, 3 (2001)	Michael Kusugak	People of Canada's north
Fort Chipewyan Homecoming: A Journey to Native Canada (1997)	Morningstar Mercredi	A photo story told about a 12-year-old boy discovering his Native ancestry
Free the Children (1998)	Craig Kielburger	The story of how a 12-year-old fought international injustice against child labourers and started a world-renowned non-governmental organization as a result
Marvelous Mattie (2006)	Emily Arnold McCully	The story of a young inventor who developed the modern paper bag
Supermarket (2001)	Kathleen Krull	The supermarket is presented by including concepts related to gender, socioeconomics, culture, and occupations
Against the Odds (1998)	Joe Layden	The story tells about several basketball players who face challenges on their path toward becoming professional sports players
The Flying Canoe (2004)	Roch Carrier	The story of the time that a young boy spends with lumberjacks and the adventures he experiences
Can You Catch Josephine? (1987)	Stephane Poulin	A young girl chases a cat through a school; can be used to motivate students' learning about aerial views and mapping perspectives
Town Mouse, Country Mouse (1994)	Jan Brett	Two mice learn about each other's lifestyles when they change locations and experience rural and urban challenges
Niki's Walk (1987)	Jane Tanner	The book provides a pictorial community walk through Niki's neighbourhood; mapping skills can be introduced
Island of the Blue Dolphins (1960)	Scott O'Dell	This story, in novel format, explores adventures and survival on an island that is described in vivid detail

(Continued)

Figure 9.6 (*Continued*)

Book	Author	Focus
Underground to Canada (1978)	Barbara Smucker	This novel describes the escape of two young girls from slavery and their rescue through the underground railroad
Stealing Freedom (1998)	Elisa Lynn Carbone	A young girl escapes slavery in the United States using the underground railway to Canada
The Last Safe House: A Story of the Underground Railroad (1998)	Barbara Greenwood	The role of Canadians in assisting escaped slaves through the underground railroad is told
The Kid's Book of Black Canadian History (2003)	Rosemary Sadler	The story of many roles played by black Canadians in Canada's history
Last Days in Africville (2003)	Dorothy Perkins	The story of a young girl who grew up in a black community in Halifax
A Proper Canadian (1980)	Alice Downie	A story about a young Bostonian who moves to Acadia in 1754 and his involvement in events that led to the War of 1812
Goodbye Sarah (1981)	Geoffrey Bilson	The story of two young girls whose lives are affected by the Winnipeg General Strike of 1919
Just a Dream (1990)	Chris VanAllsburg	The story of the dreams of a young boy who discovers the value of recycling by imagining the impact of failing to recycle in his dreams
A Child in Prison Camp (1971)	Shizuye Takashima	The true story of an 11-year-old boy's experiences living in an internment camp on Canada's west coast during WWII
Naomi's Road (2005)	Joy Kogawa	A fictitious story of a child living in a Japanese internment camp in Canada
An Ocean Apart: The Gold Mountain Diary of Chin Mei-Ling (2004)	Gillian Chan	A family is separated and the father and 12-year-old daughter work to pay the government's head tax on immigration to reunite the family in Canada
Sparks Fly Upward (2002)	Carol Matas	The story of a young Jewish girl in the early 1900s and her life in Winnipeg

Figure 9.6 (*Continued*)

Book	Author	Focus
Hana's Suitcase (2002)	Karen Levine	The real story of the life of a child who lived during the Holocaust
Anna Is Still Here (1995)	Ida Vos	The fictional story of a young girl who searches for and finally finds the family she was separated from during the Holocaust
A Picture Book of Anne Frank (1993)	David Adler	A picture story of the diary of Anne Frank tells how a young girl hid in Amsterdam from the Nazis during the Second World War
Shabash! (1994)	Ann Walsh	The story of a young Sikh boy who deals with prejudice when he joins a small-town hockey team
Tess (1995)	Hazel Hutchins	The story of a young girl living in poverty on the Canadian prairies and how she deals with her feelings about the family's poverty
Prairie Willow (1998)	Maxine Trottier	The story of the struggles faced by a family who come to homestead on Canada's prairies
Knots on a Counting Rope (1987)	Bill Martin	The story of the aspirations and dreams of a young Aboriginal Canadian boy and his struggle to deal with his self-consciousness
Catching Spring (2004)	Sylvia Olsen	A young Aboriginal boy looks for ways to circumvent discriminatory practices that exclude him from a fishing derby because he is Native
Thomas and the Métis Sash (2004)	Bonnie Murray	A young boy uses an artifact to learn about Métis culture when he has a presentation for school
The Polar Bear Son: An Inuit Tale (1997)	Lydia Dabcovich	An Inuit woman struggles to decide how to manage the conflicting needs of her community and herself and meets many local people who model good citizenship in the process
From Far Away (1995)	Robert Munsch	The true story of a young Lebanese girl when her family immigrates to Canada

(Continued)

Figure 9.6 (*Continued*)

Book	Author	Focus
Petranella (1980)	Betty Waterton	The experience of Canadian immigration is described
A Prairie Boy's Story (1994)	Jim McGugan	The experiences of a young boy living on the Canadian prairies are described
The Sandwich (1975)	Ian Wallace	The story of discrimination against an immigrant boy at school is told
The Sugaring Off Party (1995)	Jonathan London	The story of the traditions and the maple syrup industry experienced by a young French Canadian boy are told
Mary of Mile 18 (2001)	Ann Blades	Life for a young Mennonite girl growing up in remote northern British Columbia is connected to the natural environment in profound ways
The Sky is Falling (2000)	Kit Pearson	British children experience life in Canada during the air raids on London in WWII
Kiss the Dust (1991)	Elizabeth Laird	The story of a young girl who lived in Iraq during the Iran/Iraq conflicts in the 1980s
Ghost Train (1996)	Paul Yee	Chinese immigrants tell the story of the hardships they endured during the building of the Trans-Canada Railway
Hatchet (1987)	Gary Paulsen	A novel about a young boy who survives a plane crash and a winter alone in the Canadian wilderness
The Killick: A Newfoundland Story (1995)	Geoff Butler	The story told by a young boy of how he and his grandfather survived an Atlantic storm in their boat
Raven: A Trickster's Tale of the Pacific Northwest (1993)	Gerald McDermott	The customs and beliefs of the Native people of the northwest coast of Canada
The Song within My Heart (2002)	Dave Bouchard	The story of a young Cree boy preparing to attend his first Native powwow

COOPERATIVE STRUCTURES IN SOCIAL STUDIES

In Chapter 3 we introduced cooperative learning as a powerful instructional strategy to use in social studies. We also introduced cooperative structures, developed by Kagan (1994). While cooperative learning is a way to use social interaction to develop all of the new learning within a lesson, cooperative structures can be used at any point in a lesson to introduce social dialogue and support in order to learn more within a single aspect of a lesson. Cooperative learning structures are strategies that can be used within a lesson, at any point in instruction, to facilitate students' interaction and to promote social learning contexts.

While structures such as jigsaw are commonly used in schools, many other structures can also benefit students and help them develop deeper understanding, gain perspective, and establish empathy. While it is beyond the scope of this text to provide instruction in all cooperative structures that are useful in the discipline, some of the most dynamic are introduced in Figure 9.7. Teachers are directed to the many resources about cooperative learning structures available from the Internet as outlined in Chapter 3.

The cooperative learning structures outlined below (in addition to those described in Figure 3.16 on page 72) are effective for motivating, introducing new learning, consolidating

Figure 9.7 Sample Cooperative Learning Structures

Structure	Explanation
Four-S Brainstorming	■ Assign a topic to students (e.g., Create an exciting opening sentence for this story).
	■ Provide each group of four with several slips of paper on which each person can identify ideas by rapid response.
	■ Give groups a limited response time (e.g., three minutes).
	■ Have students individually record their ideas on separate sheets of scrap paper, one idea per sheet, and contribute each idea to the growing pile in the centre of the group table.
	■ Have the group consider and discuss each idea and select, through consensus or voting, which idea will represent the group's response.
	Note: You could also make this more interesting for students by giving students in each group different silly "S" names that would encourage each student to take on a different role within each group (examples include "Silly Sam," "Synergy Sue," "Sergeant Support," and "Speed Supervisor").
Idea Spinner	■ Provide each group with a spinner with numbers from one to four on the face of the spinners. These can be purchased in teacher stores and written in with markers.
	■ Assign a "selector" and a "spinner" for each group.
	■ Have students in each group number off from one to four.
	(Continued)

Figure 9.7 *(Continued)*

Parent Night (handwritten)

Structure	Explanation
	■ Provide a question box related to the topic for each group (based on levels of Bloom's Taxonomy).
questions based on Bloom's (handwritten)	■ Have the spinner spin the card. Students with the selected number will choose a question from the question box to answer.
	■ Individual scores can be kept within the group. (This task may be assigned to a group recorder.)
	■ Develop a strategy (e.g., pass option) for situations where students may need help or where the same number is spun frequently (e.g., pass to the right).
Inside/Outside Circle	■ Divide students into teams of four. Match up two teams.
	■ Give one team a set of question cards with answers recorded on the same side of the card (e.g., provinces/ territories and their capitals).
	■ Have students stand in circles around students from the other team so that the inside circle is facing out and the outside circle is facing in.
	■ Have the students stand facing a partner in the opposite circle and ask the first question, then have either circle rotate (e.g., the outside circle moves one spot to the right).
Jigsaw Problem Solving	■ The task is divided into four parts, with each group member being given one part of the information to study and become "expert" about.
	■ Once individual study is done, the experts join their group and become the teachers to the rest of the group about their part of the topic.
	■ Alternatively, students can meet with students from other groups who are responsible for the same content. They can study together to learn the new ideas before returning to their groups to share their new learning (jigsawing).
Value Lines	■ Students are assigned to line up on different sides of the room in response to a statement by the teacher to show their agreement or disagreement with the statement.
Folded Lines	This approach will help students to develop their understanding of different perspectives.
	■ Have students stand in a straight line.
	■ Divide the line in half (fold it) and have one side of the folded line take the positive view of a given statement and the other side take the negative view of the same statement.

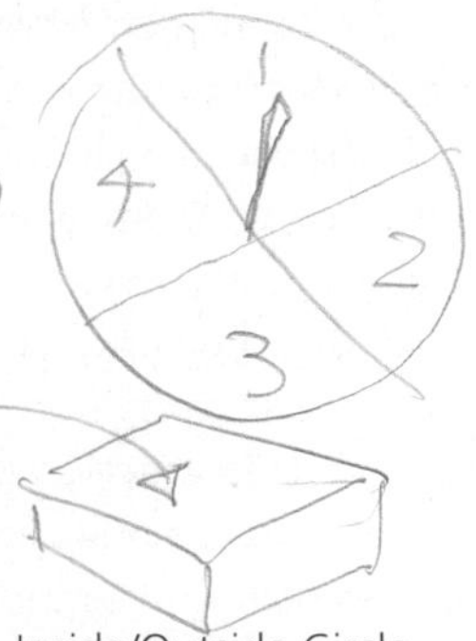

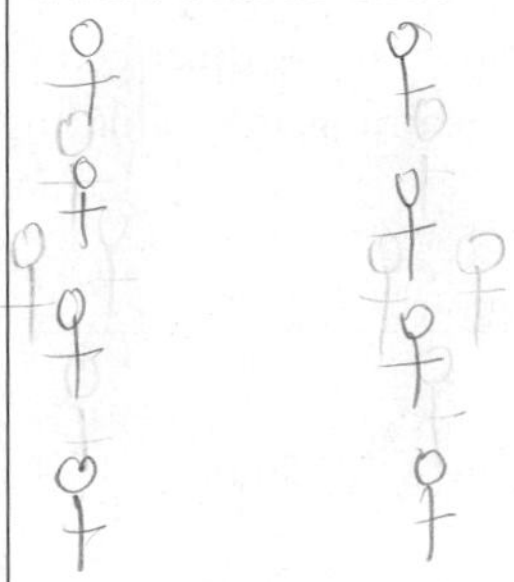

Figure 9.7 (*Continued*)

Structure	Explanation
	■ Once the line is folded, give students a limited amount of time to "argue" the issue from the perspective they are given.
Lyrical Lessons	■ Have students work in teams to create a lyric to a familiar tune to help them memorize the content of a new lesson.
Match Mine: Draw What I Say	■ Provide each pair of students with a barrier they can place between then (e.g., two file folders with the sides held up with paper clips to create a barrier).
	■ Have one student give directions to the other to draw what is being described.
Match Mine: Build What I Write	■ Have students work in partners as above with dividers between their worksheets.
	■ Have one partner describe in words what the other partner will build on the other side of the barrier.
Mix-Freeze-Group	This is a strategy to have students form random groups quickly.
	■ At a pre-determined sound (e.g., bell), have students rush to form a group of a pre-identified size.
	■ Predetermine a spot in the room that will serve as the" lost and found" spot where all students who did not get into a group quickly enough can report for group assignment.
Mix-Pair-Discuss (also called "Elbow Partners")	This is a quick grouping strategy to have students surface knowledge as a method of getting deeper discussion for the topic. Students turn to the person beside them for a brief directed discussion of a topic.
Mix and Match (also called "Snowball").	This can be used as a grouping strategy or as a way of having students assume responsibility for randomly assigned parts of a larger body of information.
	■ To group students, create two copies of each question. Crumple them up and give one to each student so that they do not know the content of what they have been given.
	■ Have students imagine a divider in the classroom (e.g., a volleyball net) and toss their "snowball" across the room.
	■ Another student will pick up a snowball, unfold it, then search the room to find a partner with the same question.
	■ Partners will then work to research or answer the question.
	Alternatively, have students catch snowballs of questions created by the teacher. This will become their question for the research task.

(Continued)

Figure 9.7 (*Continued*)

Structure	Explanation
Numbered Heads Together	■ Students work in groups of four to coach each member of the group in specified content. ■ Once students have had group coaching time, they assign a number (one to four) to each member of the group. ■ The teacher rolls a four-sided die or spins a four-point spinner and the students with that number are responsible for answering the question for the team. ■ The teacher may elect to assign a group point for each correct answer to reinforce the value of peer coaching and the nature of positive interdependence.
One Stray (can also be Two Stray or Three Stray)	■ Students work on a task as a group of four. ■ At different times throughout the task, the teacher calls out "one stray" (or "two stray" or "three stray"). ■ When this is called out, one or more students stray to other groups to borrow their ideas and bring them back to their group.
Pairs Check	■ Students are paired by the teacher or by random grouping (e.g., elbow partners, or mix-freeze-group). ■ Students have a task(s) to complete and partners are asked to coach each other to complete it successfully. ■ Partners create a quick way to celebrate each others' success and do that regularly throughout the work period (e.g., high five).
Pairs Compare	■ Students work with assigned or random partners to generate ideas and solve problems where many possibilities can be correct. ■ Once ideas are collected by partners, each pair recombines with a second pair and works in a group of four to share ideas and generate the maximum number of ideas.
Paraphrase Passport	This strategy is designed to encourage active listening. ■ Students work in groups of four. ■ Have students take turns discussing an idea assigned by the teacher. ■ Before each student can add their ideas, they must summarize (paraphrase) the comment that was made by the previous student.

Figure 9.7 (*Continued*)

Structure	Explanation
Partners	▪ Have students work in groups of four. ▪ Assign a task and have students work with one other member of their group to complete the task. ▪ After a predetermined time, have students combine with the other pair of partners in their group and share their ideas and strategies.
Poems or Songs for Two Voices	▪ Students work with a partner and alternate reading lines on assignments.
Q-Spinner	▪ Write questions on a spinner, using the starters from the question stem choices (see Chapter 2); this matrix is also referred to as a Bloom's Taxonomy Q-Matrix; Q for question). ▪ Spin the spinner for the whole class or for the students working in small groups. ▪ If students are working in groups, they can support development of each other's answers.
Rally Robin	▪ Students working in partners pass a "speaking token" to signify that they are taking a turn to speak.
Rally Table	▪ Students share one answer sheet for partners or small groups and pass the sheet to add parts of the answer(s). ▪ Limit the number of pencils or pens so that students have to take turns.
Pass and Praise	▪ This is done the same way as Rally Table but the receiving student must receive and read the last students' entry, praise their work in a genuine way, and then add their ideas.
Reading Boards	▪ Assign students to mixed ability groups. ▪ Provide each group with a page for reading (or singing). Have students use a game piece or pointer to track the reading or singing as it is done in a choral manner.
Rotating Review (also called "Parking Lots")	▪ The teacher posts aspects of the topic to be reviewed on separate sheets of chart paper. ▪ Students rotate individually or in partners to each piece of chart paper and record their ideas on each aspect of the topic.
Rotating Peer Review	▪ During times when students are presenting information to the class, feedback can be achieved in written form by having students record information on various posted charts for their groups around the room.

(*Continued*)

Figure 9.7 (*Continued*)

Structure	Explanation
Round Robin	■ Students take turns by passing items, tossing a paper wad, or using numbers to "schedule" their input within the group.
Round Table	■ Students work in small groups and the teacher limits the resources (e.g., number of papers, books, pencils) so that students must rely on each other to get the task(s) completed.
Sages Share	■ The teacher provides a topic for students to brainstorm about.
	■ Students record all ideas on the same sheet (recorder) and then students initial the ideas they could explain to the whole class.
	■ The class can then select "sages" from the group who have initialed the idea to explain their contributions.
Same-Different	■ Students work as partners.
	■ Students each have a picture, photo, map, or word list with some similarities and differences on each.
	■ Students ask each other questions in alternate turns and get ideas about what is similar and what is different on each list.
	■ Students can record similarities and differences in Venn diagram format.
Send a Problem/ Trade a Problem	■ Students create a problem that they send around the class for solving.
Part of the Problem	■ Create heterogeneous, mixed ability groups of four students.
	■ Have each take one piece of the problem from a random pile of paper strips (all strips taken together describe the problem in all its aspects).
	■ Have each group member read the problem strip they have and then have group members work on a common page (one paper, one pencil) to solve the problem.
Showdown	■ Students are divided into groups of four.
	■ The teacher gives the class an oral question or problem. Each member of the group writes their answer on an individual sheet.
	■ When the teacher says, "Showdown" each member of the group displays their answer to the rest of the group.
	■ Students compare and verify their answers.

Figure 9.7 (*Continued*)

Structure	Explanation
Similarity Groups	■ This is a group formation strategy. Students form groups based on similarities. For example, students whose favourite sport is soccer might form a group.
Spend a Buck	This strategy is used to have students make a quick "vote" about some issue or choice.
	■ Options are laid out so that all members of the group can see a written copy clearly.
	■ Each group member has the same number of tokens or coins (e.g., 4) to spend in making a choice.
	■ When the teacher poses the question, students each lay down a coin to vote on their choice.
Spin and Think Along the Thinking Trail	■ Teach students that a "thinking trail" includes the steps of reading the question, answering the question, paraphrasing the answer, and discussing the answer taking other perspectives into account.
	■ Provide thinking trail anchor charts to create thinking trail stations in the classroom (one for each step).
	■ The teacher randomly selects a student at each station to answer prompts and probes about the original question.
Stir the Class	■ Students are placed in heterogeneous, mixed ability groups of four, numbered from one to four.
	■ All groups then join a large circle.
	■ The teacher poses a question.
	■ The group members huddle in groups of four to discuss the question and pose an answer.
	■ The group then prepares for the next question by having one numbered person from their group join the next group that is placed clockwise in the larger circle, to participate in answering the next question.
Talking Chips	■ Students are placed in heterogeneous, mixed ability groups of four.
	■ Students are assigned to discuss some issue and given a predetermined number of talking chips to "buy" their way into the discussions of the group.
	■ Once students spend one chip to speak to the group, they must wait until every other member of the group has spoken before they can spend a second chip.

(*Continued*)

Figure 9.7 (*Continued*)

Structure	Explanation
Team Chants	This strategy aims to support cognitive growth through the use of kinesthetic and auditory means. ■ Small groups of students create chants and physical actions to help them with a memory task.
Team Interview	This is a peer coaching strategy. ■ Students are divided into heterogeneous, mixed ability groups of four. ■ Students are given material to learn and they coach each group member to learn it. ■ Before some form of individual accountability is applied (e.g., test), students interview and question each group member to ensure their readiness for assessment.
Teammates Consult	■ Students are divided into heterogeneous, mixed ability groups of four. ■ Each group receives four sheets of paper and four pencils. ■ The teacher poses a question and provides a predetermined amount of time for students to discuss the question. ■ Once the teacher gives a predetermined signal, students each take a pencil and write their individual answers.
Team-Pair-Solo	This strategy promotes progressive independence in students. ■ The teacher organizes a set of practice opportunities of similar types for students. Practice opportunities are separated into three categories, including team tasks, partner tasks, and solo tasks. ■ Each group member has several opportunities to practise the new learning in small groups, then with a partner, then individually.
Team Stand and Share	■ The teacher assigns a complex task to a heterogeneous, mixed ability team of four. ■ All students stand up. ■ The teacher leads sharing of ideas. As ideas are shared, students record information from all teams on their team's record sheet. ■ All team members sit down when they have shared all of their ideas. ■ Once all students are sitting, students work on the development of a final answer for submission.

Figure 9.7 *(Continued)*

Structure	Explanation
Team Statements	This is a multi-level strategy for synthesizing information. ■ Students are divided into heterogeneous, mixed ability groups of four. ■ Have students state an opinion, discuss it in pairs, then present an individual written statement (in turns) in their groups. ■ Once all individual written statements are presented, students work in a whole group to write a group statement that incorporates all of the most important elements of the individual statements.
Team Word Web (Mind Map)	■ Students work in heterogeneous, mixed ability groups to brainstorm ideas on a single sheet of paper. ■ Each student uses a different colour of marker to add their comments to the sheet to allow them to monitor their input into the group product. ■ The central concept of the brainstorming is written in the centre of the sheet and students build ideas and connections around the main idea.
Telephone	■ The class is required to learn a concept or skill so that they can teach it to another student who is not present for the original instruction. ■ The teacher can structure this so that one student agrees to be the person taught by the rest of the class.
Think-Pair-Share (or Think-Pair-Square)	■ Students discuss an answer with a partner then present their ideas, or their partner's ideas, to the class. ■ Ideas could also be discussed in groups of four then shared with the class.
Three Pair Share	■ Students are required to explain their ideas to three other students in their group. Questions and responses of the group members should enrich each telling.
Three-Step Interview	Students discuss a topic using the following three steps: ■ The first group member explains their answer to a partner. ■ The partner explains their answer to the first group member. ■ The partners team up to explain their collective answer to the other members of the group.

(Continued)

Figure 9.7 *(Continued)*

Structure	Explanation
Timed Pair Share	■ A student works alone to create an answer and then partners with another student to share their answer.
	■ In turn, the partner shares with the first student. Time is limited by the teacher for each sharing session.
Who Am I?	This strategy allows students to ask questions to use characteristics to determine the nature of an item.
	■ Students have a word taped on their backs and must circulate around the classroom to question others about what their word is by asking variations of the question "Am I . . . ?"
	■ Students are finished questioning each other student when they get a "no" answer or get three "yes" answers in a row but still haven't guessed who they are/what their word is.
	■ Circulation and questioning continues for a preset time.

Sources: Kagan, S. Cooperative Learning: 1-800-WEE CO-OP: Growing Collaboratively, Niagara District School Board, Prentice Hall.

and practising new skills, or applying new ideas. Creative approaches developed by the teacher can also allow these structures to be useful for assessment and evaluation.

SIMULATIONS, DRAMA, AND DANCE IN THE PRIMARY AND JUNIOR CLASSROOMS

Gibson (2009) synthesizes the key ideas about how to use social constructivism to guide effective teaching. Gibson summarizes these ideas into five main principles, including

■ incorporating students' prior learning into new learning opportunities through the use of brainstorming, class discussions, and graphic organizers that relate ideas;

■ supporting knowledge construction by helping students make connections, see patterns, and discern inconsistencies;

■ engaging learners actively to allow them to restructure current schema to assimilate or accommodate the new learning by teaching them to examine their views critically and to undertake inquiry;

■ recognizing the important role social interaction has in learning by allowing opportunities for discussion, comparison of ideas, and perspective building; and

■ reflecting on learning to help students internalize ideas through both formal and informal processes.

In this summary the role of activity—in the cognitive, social, and physical sense—is evident. In social studies, simulations, drama, and dance can provide venues for these modes of understanding new learning.

There are many simulations available to teachers on the Internet. For the primary and junior student, the reading level of web materials, and the content of each site, needs to be managed carefully by the teacher to ensure suitability and safety. Increasingly, museum websites are being made available to allow for virtual interaction with exhibits. Teachers can use such sites to create simulations that enable interaction with artifacts that would otherwise be inaccessible.

Discussions that follow simulated experiences are as important to the learning process as the simulation itself. These discussions are often referred to as debriefing and they allow students to move from experience to understanding. These debriefing discussions are also opportunities for students to learn conceptual language to describe and make meaning from simulated experiences. Debriefing is often essential to ensure that simulations benefit students by providing understanding of the fundamental concepts of the social studies program. The simulated experience helps the student to understand answers to the question "What?" (e.g., What is conflict? What does an earthquake feel like?). The discussion or debriefing after the simulation allows the student to consider the question "So what?" (determining the meaning of the experience) and "Now what?" (the opportunity to engage in active citizenship).

Drama and dance are both methods of active learning and characteristics of the cultures being studied. As a method of active learning, teachers can provide opportunities for students to demonstrate their new understandings by performing in either drama or dance modes. The reflective and social interaction elements are part of creating a drama or a dance. If drama or dance is being learned as elements that reflect a particular cultural tradition, opportunities to examine the methods of each medium within the cultural context are critical to representing the culture accurately and examining it thoroughly. Teachers need to have clear goals for the inclusion of drama and dance in their social studies program so that the role of these elements in various parts of the program is achieved.

Simulations, drama, and dance have a strong role in the delivery of effective social studies programs. These strategies can provide the link that allows students to make mind-body connections to support their growing understanding, particularly where abstract concepts are being examined.

INNOVATIVE APPROACHES IN YOUR SOCIAL STUDIES CLASSROOM

In Chapters 1 through 8 we focused on introducing and exemplifying the skills of topic elaboration. Topic elaboration allows teachers and students to develop many aspects of a topic thoroughly and systematically, using a sequence of inquiry questions that direct investigations.

Each of the following chapters will develop additional skills to support inquiry and build your repertoire of strategies to support innovative approaches in your classroom. In these chapters, the following topics will be addressed:

- Providing choice
- Connecting inquiry to correlation
- Analyzing perspectives and using newspapers in the classroom
- Interactive processing on informational texts
- Pre-teaching analysis: Map and globe skills
- Community connections
- Celebrating project work through communication
- Test and quiz preparation
- Student-led parent-teacher conferences

Each of these chapter segments is designed to strengthen your growing awareness of strategies to develop students' skills and knowledge.

CASE STUDIES AND PROFESSIONAL ACTIVITIES IN SOCIAL STUDIES

1. Mr. Thorough planned to include authentic assessment in his social studies program for his Grade 5/6 class this year. He had learned that there were many types of assessment strategies he could use. He made a list of the possibilities for his own reference (see below).

Assessment Strategies

Classroom presentations	Performance Tasks
Conferences	Portfolios
Essays	Question and answer (oral)
Exhibitions/demonstrations	Response journals
Interviews	Select response
Learning logs	Self-assessment
Observations	

Mr. Thorough wanted to be sure that he understood each of these strategies for assessment so he developed a way to research and review each strategy. He started to record his notes on the framework provided below.

Assessment Strategies Summary			
Name _____			
Assessment Strategy	**Brief Summary of Strategy**	**When This Strategy Would be Useful**	**Example**
Example: tests/ quizzes/exams	Questions are asked by the teacher in a variety of formats; students demonstrate learning through a response to each question, usually without the support of any resources	Mainly useful for testing students' memorized knowledge or comprehension	Name the provinces and territories of Canada from west to east.

Work in a small group to complete this chart to review all of the strategies that could be used for assessment in Mr. Thorough's classroom.

2. Mr. Thorough also realized that he could use several recording devices with each assessment strategy so he could keep detailed records of each of his social studies students' progress. He found that there were four recording devices commonly used:

- Anecdotal records
- Checklists
- Rating scales
- Rubrics

   In a small group, work together to create a chart to record a description, and sample applied to social studies, for the use of each of these recording devices.

3. Review the model for instruction in Chapter 3 (see Figure 3.9). Examine the use of the three types of assessment that teachers use: diagnostic, formative, and summative. Create a chart for your notes about when in the phases of instruction each type of assessment is used most productively.

4. Now, form a group with two other colleagues. In your group of three, create examples of diagnostic, formative, and summative assessments that you might use in your classroom to develop learning for any one expectation you have selected from a guideline.

5. Collect several examples of social studies work that students have produced for summative purposes/marking. In a small group, examine each piece of work separately and create specific formative comments about the work that you could provide to the student to help him/her improve the product. Be prepared to explain to other teacher candidates what you would expect students to improve in their product as a response to the formative feedback you have provided.

6. Develop three examples of integrated strategies that address social studies expectations, and some expectations from other subject guidelines from your jurisdiction. Write each strategy in the centre of a sheet of chart paper. Create a web around the strategy that shows the other subject areas that are being integrated with social studies, and the expectations from each other subject area that are being addressed by this strategy.

7. Select one fictional story or novel that relates to a social studies theme that is part of the local mandate for social studies in your jurisdiction. After reading this narrative, jot down a list of at least 10 ideas that you can use from the story to relate to themes, ideas, and values that are central to the social studies mandate.

8. Select one cooperative structure that is useful for addressing a single expectation from a social studies guideline. Develop and demonstrate the use of that cooperative structure to your fellow teacher candidates.

9. Select, plan, practise, and demonstrate at least one example of a simulation, drama approach, or dance application that relates to the social studies curriculum in your jurisdiction. Be prepared to explain to colleagues how you would use this strategy with a chosen age group of primary or junior students.

CHAPTER REVIEW AND PROFESSIONAL DEVELOPMENT

The chapter has examined the following:

■ Instructional variations in the program's content, processes, or products can provide many possibilities for designing effective instruction in social studies.

■ Authentic assessment provides students with opportunities to demonstrate their learning in ways that match their learning styles.

■ Authentic assessment can be used for diagnostic, formative, and summative purposes.

■ Authentic assessment includes the provision of ongoing, specific feedback as students investigate and seek to demonstrate their learning.

■ Authentic assessment approaches are substantively different from knowledge acquisition approaches to assessment in their beliefs about learning, the tools used for assessment, and the ways the assessment data is used.

■ Bloom's Taxonomy can be applied to teach students how to identify appropriate products and processes to demonstrate their learning.

■ Integration of social studies and other subject areas in the primary and junior curriculum can help to engage students in rich and diversified experiences.

■ Integration can conserve learning time.

- Narrative literature can be used in social studies to deepen students' understanding by providing opportunities to connect personal experience with a story.

- Fiction and non-fiction text each have specific characteristics that will need to be taught to students to allow them to engage each type of text with success.

- Many children's stories and novels can be identified to align with fundamental concepts and topics in social studies.

- If literature is selected to be used in social studies, it needs to be examined carefully for negative portrayals and stereotypes.

- Cooperative structures can be components of social studies lessons to incorporate the social interaction and reflection opportunities that are critical to help students make meaning of their learning.

- Kagan (1994) provides many examples of cooperative structures that can be used or adapted to the social studies classroom.

- Social constructivism promotes activity in the cognitive, social, and physical sense to help students process new ideas.

- Simulations, drama, and dance can support learning by providing cognitive, social, and physical stimuli to help students process new ideas and make mind-body connections.

References for Further Reading

Beane, J. (1996). On the shoulders of giants! The case for curriculum integration. *Middle School Journal*, 28.1.

Berson, M. J. (1996). Effectiveness of computer technology in the social studies: A review of the literature. *Journal of Research in Computing in Education*, 28.4.

Camp, D. (2000). It takes two: Teaching the twin texts of fact and fiction. *The Reading Teacher*, 53.5.

Darling-Hammond, L. (1995). *Authentic assessment in action: Studies of schools and students at work.* Columbia University, NY: Teachers' College Press.

Deasy, R. J. (Ed.). (2002). *Critical links: Learning in the arts and student academic and social development.* Washington, DC: Arts Education Partnership.

Drake, S. (1993). *Planning integrated curriculum: The call to adventure.* Alexandria, VA: Association for Supervision and Curriculum Development (ASCD).

Kagan, L., Kagan, M., and Kagan, S. (2007). *Cooperative learning structures for class building.* Heatherton, Australia: Hawker Brownlow Education.

Krathwohl, D. (2002). *A revision of Bloom's taxonomy: An overview.* Accessed online April 27, 2009 at www.jstor.org/pss/1477405.

Marzamo, R. J. (2001). *Designing a new taxonomy of educational objectives.* Thousand Oaks, CA: Corwin Press Inc.

Schechner, R. (1988). Performance studies: The broad spectrum approach. Accessed online April 27, 2009 at *www.jstot.org/pss/1145899. 32.3.*

Tomlinson, C. A. (1999). *The differentiated classroom: Responding to the needs of all learners.* Alexandria, VA: The Association for Supervision and Curriculum Development (ASCD).

Wiggins, G. (1990). *The case for authentic assessment.* Prepared for the California Assessment Program.

Weblinks

Centres are an excellent way to foster inquiry in your classroom. Dynamic centres allow students to apply their knowledge and skills to new and interesting situations using technology. For example, when teaching a unit on early settlers, have students develop a script describing how they travelled through time to a settlement where they are invited to take three modern innovations along with them to share with the settlers. Have them incorporate into their script the reactions of the settlers. Then have them record their skit and download into movie-making software, such as iMovie. This way, they are able to apply what they know to a completely new context and showcase their understanding in a short movie presentation!

Here are a few other examples:

■ After creating a castle as part of a medieval times unit, have your students create a real estate webpage to help sell their castle.

■ Encourage your junior students to participate in a "digital debate" with another class using an online conferencing system and have them take a position on a particular controversial topic.

■ Invite your primary students to select images from their community photo library using Photostory Le3. They can select which buildings or landmarks they see on their way to school. Have them select the music that best represents their feelings as they travel (e.g., Wheels on the Bus).

Chapter 10
Differentiation in the Social Studies Classroom

Learning Topics

- Defining Differentiation
- Respectful Learning Tasks
- Learning Styles and Social Studies Strategies
- Choice within and Inquiry Approach

The focus on differentiation for all students must be seen to include differentiation for the students who are gifted and talented as well as for those who may struggle to attain learning success.

DEFINING DIFFERENTIATION

In the context of an average classroom, there are many more differences than similarities among the learners. A typical public school classroom will have an average of 27 students, with smaller numbers usually typical of the early primary grades. Within this combination of learners, the academic performance span of students will stretch across five grade levels (Latz, Neumeister, Adams & Pierce, 2009). These characteristics bring into question what we mean when we talk about a typical student in a typical grade.

Earlier chapters introduced the concept of differentiation as an essential element of good teaching. The terminology "to teach" seems to present a focus of the actions of the teacher as the central feature of a strong professional practice. Through experience and reflection, teachers come to realize that a focus on the actions of students as they learn is the most critical feature of creating a strong professional practice. During a teaching career, teachers learn to shift their focus from their teaching to their students' learning. Recent support documents in education are highlighting the nuances of this shift in focus. For example, in Ontario, the 2005 support document for differentiation was titled *Education for All*. The updated 2009 version is titled *Learning for All*. Focusing on what students learn when we determine what we will teach is a critical element of effective differentiation.

If the culture of the teacher is to become part of the consciousness of the child, then the culture of the child must first be in the consciousness of the teacher.

—*Bernstein, 1972*

Clarity in the professional definition of differentiation is essential to social studies teachers. This will help to identify actions that are appropriate to ensure effective differentiation. A study for the Scottish Research and Intelligence Unit examined respondents' input to a variety of questionnaires and interviews attempting to identify a common conception of "good differentiation." At the conclusion of their study, the researchers accepted the definition proposed by Smith (1981) as providing the best sense of the variety of differentiation practices that the researchers encountered. Smith defined *differentiation* as "any process which divides pupils into subgroups which are then exposed to different educational experiences. Differentiation then covers a great range of phenomena from the allocation of pupils to different classes, subjects, sets, streams, bands, or tracks within the same school, to the different treatment of pupils within the same classroom."

Learning for All (Ontario Ministry of Education, 2009, draft copy, p. 49) promotes differentiation as the process whereby students are given "the best possible opportunities to learn and to maximize their potential. This is a matter of equity and social justice." Fullan, Hill, and Crevola (2006) promote a breakthrough system whereby teaching that is *personalized* and *precise* is used to address the particular needs of each student to maximize their learning potential.

In the social studies context, teachers must clarify their own conception of differentiation that is responsive to the school cultural priorities of their respective jurisdictions. Regardless of jurisdiction, the focus of differentiation efforts must always remain on professional efforts to create optimal learning for every student. Darling-Hammond (2005) identifies differentiation in social terms to reflect the reality of the United States context with diverse cultures in strong evidence in many classrooms. She argues that we should be focusing on changing our professional meta-narrative so that we see the diversity among our students as the norm of a classroom makeup rather than the exception. She also sites many studies that have identified disparities in the allocation of resources across economic and racial divides and argues for equity of access as a critical feature of socially just efforts to ensure optimal learning for all students. The trend toward mainstreaming of students with special needs also increases the need to develop professional expertise with differentiation.

The focus on differentiation for all students must be seen to include differentiation for the students who are gifted and talented as well as for those who may struggle to attain learning success. For the strongest students, differentiation must allow for different work to meet learning needs, rather than just more work to ensure that students are occupied while others catch up.

When teachers start the process of planning for social studies, the challenge of teaching effectively for diverse learners must be foremost in the process. Only by addressing the diversity in learners that comes from their different readiness, interests, social and economic backgrounds, ethnic histories, educational histories, learning styles, and interest in the current topic can teachers maximize the experience of each social studies class. By changing our personal meta-narrative to reflect the belief that all learners bring differences to the classroom and by seeing differentiation as extending beyond a special education scope, we can ensure that we plan optimal experiences for learning.

The challenge of teaching diverse learners starts the moment teachers begin planning ways to connect their students with the subject matter they intend to teach.

—*Darling-Hammond, 2005*

Differentiation is key to students' learning success. *Education for All* (Ontario Ministry of Education, 2005, pp. 4–5) provides some focal principles that are essential components of all teachers' instructional efforts to maximize the use of differentiation as a seminal strategy for instruction. Teachers must not only believe in each of these principles but must be prepared to make these operational as central tenants of their social studies instruction. These principles include the following:

- All students can succeed.
- Universal design (for effective teaching) and differentiated instruction are effective and interconnected means of meeting the learning or productivity needs of any group of students.
- Successful instructional practices are founded on evidence-based research, tempered by experience.
- Classroom teachers are the key educators for a student's literacy and numeracy development.

- Each child has his or her own unique patterns of learning.

- Classroom teachers need the support of the larger community to create a learning environment that supports students with special education needs.

- Fairness is not sameness.

Teachers can use these principles to guide the development of an inclusive social studies program that reflects commitment to the learning success of all students (see Figure 10.1). The broadest sense of differentiation will include an expansive array of approaches that will support special needs learners, respect cultural diversity, and recognize the uniqueness of each learner. This approach to differentiation will allow teachers to provide effective instruction in the complex environments of today's schools.

Teachers' commitment to differentiation in the classroom may be difficult to implement for many reasons (Latz, Speirs-Neumeister, Adams & Pierce, 2009):

- Teachers may not receive administrative support for differentiation efforts.

- Teachers fear that straying from the mandated curriculum may result in lower test scores on provincial or territorial testing.

- Teachers experience classroom management or behavioural problems.

- Teachers resist long-term changes in their teaching style.

- Teachers lack a plan for differentiation.

- Teachers fear negative parental reaction to differentiation.

It will be helpful to teachers to coordinate the development of their classroom differentiation plan in concert with other staff in the same school, and particularly in the same division. Collegial efforts can provide support to surmount many of the typical reasons for ineffective differentiation.

RESPECTFUL LEARNING TASKS

Students understand when teachers are filling time and when they are optimizing learning with tasks that promote deep understanding and personal development. When students feel that their time is being wasted with insignificant tasks, engagement and behaviour become classroom issues. It is, therefore, the first task of any teacher to commit to an unrelenting respect for every second of learning time available in the classroom. The teacher must strive to protect all learning time from intrusion and interruption and must project his or her belief in the sanctity of learning time with energy and consistency.

"Research confirms that gaps in student achievement can be closed and overall improvement in achievement attained if the responsibility for making these changes is shared by all partners in the education system—students, parents, educators, and community partners (Campbell, Comper, & Winton, 2007; Kober, 2001; Mortimore & Witty, 1997; Willms, 2006). Progress is seen where there has been a sustained and deliberate focus on individual students' strengths and needs, assessment for learning, and precision

Figure 10.1 Universal Design for Learning

Learning Principles	Explanation of Core Principles
Equitable use	Instruction in planned with a clear view of the learning needs of all students rather than starting with a "teach to the middle" and adapt for the rest approach.
Appropriately designed space	Physical space, resources, adaptive devices, technology, and learning tools are available as they are needed by each learner. Classroom space is organized to promote and celebrate a focus on learning.
Flexibility	Instructional approaches are varied so that students have optimal access to learning. Recognition that some students may learn at a different pace is built into instructional approaches. Re-teaching is achieved through many modalities to support all learners.
Simplicity	Instruction is clear and focused, precise and personalized, to allow all students the "breakthrough" experience of learning success. Learning goals are deconstructed effectively to ensure that sub-skills are learned to support success with overall goals. Students know what they are learning and why.
Safety	Classroom environments minimize safety risks and maximize learning potential.
Different modes of perception	The organization and presentation of all elements of instruction are established with optimal learning as a goal. Approaches to many aspects of learning are considered with respect to each student's preferred way of learning. Teachers vary ■ the expectations and the learning objectives of each learning encounter; ■ their teaching strategies; ■ learning materials and resources; ■ technology supports; ■ the products required of students to demonstrate their learning; and ■ assessment approaches and timelines.

Source: Adapted from Ontario. Ministry of Education. (2005). *Education for all: The report of the expert panel on literacy and numeracy instruction for students with special education needs, kindergarten to grade 6*. Toronto: Author. Ontario. Ministry of Education. (2009). Learning for all K-12 Draft. Toronto: Author.

in instruction through evidence-informed interventions" (Ontario Ministry of Education, 2009, draft copy, p. 12).

In order to create a positive classroom environment and positive interpersonal inter-actions among students and between students and teachers, teacher skill and a clear sense of direction are needed. The instructional methods that are used in the classroom will influence the values that students develop (Johnson & Johnson, 2009).

To establish the positive classroom climate that is essential to support learning, teachers need to consider the research about ways to promote positive interactions among the com-munity of learners. Johnson and Johnson (2009) call this type of classroom environment *promotive interaction*. In contexts where promotive interaction is prevalent, the individuals

- act in trusting and trustworthy ways;
- exchange needed resources, information, and materials, allowing them to process information efficiently and effectively;
- provide efficient and effective help and assistance to group mates;
- are motivated to strive for goals that are of mutual benefit;
- engage their efforts to achieve mutual goals and advocate for such efforts;
- have a moderate level of arousal, low anxiety, and low stress;
- try to influence each other's efforts to achieve the group's goals;
- provide group mates with feedback to help improve performance;
- challenge each other's thinking to improve subsequent performance on tasks; and
- take the perspective of others, thus being better able to explore different points of view.

Each element of promotive interaction relies on the systematic development of students' social skills.

Strong classroom management skills are critical to every teacher's success in provid-ing a classroom environment that will support the pursuit of respectful learning tasks and the maintenance of promotive interaction among learners. Many resources for establish-ing positive classroom management skills are available to new teachers. Annette Breaux and Todd Whitaker (2006) provide specific guidance about classroom management in the book *Seven Simple Secrets: What the Best Teachers Know and Do*. This is a companion text that new teachers should consider for their professional library. A brief summary of their "secrets" for managing a promotive classroom environment follows.

1. If you want to have a great lesson, you need to plan a great lesson.

    - Over-plan subsequent activities and make them increasingly challenging (not the same level as the initial practice activity)
    - Plan in short segments that reflect the phases of instruction
    - Be responsive to students' ability to stay focused
    - Be flexible and responsive to the day's events
    - Have clear goals for every lesson

- Promote activity (60/40 rule; students talk 60 percent of the time and the teacher talks 40 percent of the time)
- Be proactive about discipline; anticipate typical problems and plan to avoid them

2. See yourself as an effective teacher.

- Maintain an organized room
- Present lessons with enthusiasm
- Promote discussion
- Set and maintain routines and procedures
- Use consistent consequences
- Avoid interrupting the learning to maintain control
- Be proactive
- Plan thoroughly and clearly
- Tell students what they will learn and why
- Monitor actively; move around the room
- Use worksheets and textbooks sparingly
- Be consistent in how you address behaviour infractions
- Handle situations calmly; don't show frustration
- Differentiate as needed
- Use lots of positive reinforcement
- Smile
- Establish routines that save learning time
- Reduce the number of rules (3–5 maximum)
- Teach and expect learning every minute of the day (bell to bell; holiday to holiday)
- Be clear about your bottom line(s) (e.g., "It's never okay to interrupt our learning" or "It's never going to be acceptable to make fun of someone")
- It is never acceptable for you to yell and scream; be firm and clear but always calm—the more out of control the student is, the more in control you must become

3. Teach for real life.

- Relate the skills you are teaching to students' current lives
- Plan for intentional, active student involvement
- Believe that every student can succeed
- Project your belief that every student can succeed
- Teach enthusiastically

- Project a love for everything you teach
- Assess what you've taught
- Plan tasks and assessments with a level of support that will guarantee every student's success
- Move lessons along briskly
- Model and provide practice; scaffold and gradually release responsibility for learning

4. Control your attitude.

- Be positive
- Avoid gossip, especially in the staff room
- Expect positive attitudes from your students; support them in getting it right
- Treat every piece of students' work as a very important piece of evidence of their learning; mark all students' work (no "trading papers")
- Act responsibly; respond to things that are not right
- Don't buy into negativity from a coworker; walk away
- Maintain positive contact with parents
- Act in recognition that parents are doing their best, care deeply about their children, and want to trust their care to you; show that you deserve that trust!
- Be a faculty model for a positive attitude

5. Project your professionalism.

- Dress professionally
- Be cordial to everyone
- Differentiate between chitchat and gossip
- Maintain the dignity and privacy of your students
- Look for solutions
- Never see yourself as a victim
- Maintain self-control
- Think . . . then act
- Be cool and calm
- Continue to grow professionally
- Maintain your professional dignity
- Believe that you must do your best, not be the best
- Make sure your decisions benefit your students
- Focus on your students' needs
- Keep assessment authentic
- Know your students

- See yourself as one of many in the school providing service to your students
- Take an "across the curriculum" approach to all skills; all teachers are responsible for all subjects

6. Discipline effectively.

- Be aware of (if/when) your students may be "pushing your buttons"
- Appear calm
- Be consistent
- Have a discipline plan; use it!
- Manage your stress
- Use your psychology knowledge to manage your classroom; know what your students will respond to and use it
- Choose the better (not the bitter) path
- Treat students with dignity
- Hold students accountable
- Act, don't react
- Look for what is causing misbehaviour
- Talk to students about their wants and needs
- Control yourself!
- Find the good in every child; if they feel good, they are less likely to misbehave

7. Motivate and inspire your students.

- Create contagious excitement
- Keep your personal problems and concerns out of the school; maintain professional boundaries
- Make every student feel special
- Show personal interest in every student
- Know students' backgrounds, both personal and academic; maintain your focus on having and using such knowledge solely for the purpose of the improvement of instruction
- Give lots of specific and genuine praise
- Teach students that "fair" is not necessarily "equal"; believe it yourself!
- Work on motivating unmotivated students
- Don't give up on any student, any time, anywhere, ever!
- Monitor your own moods and motivations; stay positive

It takes time and practice for new teachers to develop these skills and to implement them consistently. Effective classroom management sets the climate of respect needed to maximize the effect of differentiation efforts in the classroom.

The development of respectful learning tasks in social studies will work in concert with other elements of effective instruction to promote learning. A high-quality curriculum, flexible groupings, continual assessment, and a sense of community among learners will support the students' engagement in and commitment to the pursuit of respectful tasks.

Respectful tasks in social studies should have the following characteristics:

- They build on previous learning. This will foster students' growing sense of independence if they can meet success because they have the basic skills and knowledge required for success with new tasks.

- They engage through a sense that the outcomes matter. Students are challenged through applications that require thought, perspective taking, and a sense that their efforts are going toward something worthwhile.

- Inquiry skills are engaged. Students have opportunities to explore ideas, and apply analysis, synthesis, and evaluation skills to information in order to relate to it in meaningful ways.

- Students are aware of what and how they are learning. Extra care is taken to ensure metacognitive development as students apply new learning to increasingly complex contexts.

- Tasks are supported by meaningful and ongoing formative feedback that is both detailed and specific. This will help students to understand what they need to improve and how they should go about it.

Tasks can be tailored to students' interests, readiness for the topic or skill, and their approach to learning as identified in their evolving learning profile. The principles of differentiation indicate that students will require different levels and types of support to meet success with their learning efforts. Differences in supports required can be achieved by

- preplanning support requirements based on knowledge of the student (interests, readiness, and learning styles);

- establishing shared and clearly understood learning goals for each specific learning episode;

- identifying students' needs and closely monitoring progress as they attempt greater levels of independence with tasks;

- providing measured and sensitive amounts of support to ensure success while promoting independence tailored to individual growth;

- supporting the students' focus on their learning goals through the creation of a focused classroom environment and emotional support for achievements as required;

- providing formative feedback so that each student is receiving ongoing information about personal progress in relation to the expected learning;

- providing and building strong promotive interactions among students and between student and teacher to help minimize risks and promote comfort as students engage in tasks;

- providing timely opportunities to practise new learning and apply it to meaningful contexts with growing independence;

- providing opportunities to apply appropriate language to the knowledge, processes, and products as students engage in tasks, thereby promoting the development of metacognitive awareness;

- providing opportunities for students to generalize new skills by considering other contexts for application; and

- providing time and structure for discussion of issues that promote controversy and generate alternative points of view so that students are frequently exposed to multi-faceted issues.

The overall benefit of ensuring the use of respectful learning tasks in social studies (see Figure 10.2) lies in the student's ability to acquire, over time, a repertoire of effective learning approaches (strategy efficacy). Teaching learning strategies takes time and is an essential part of the curriculum. Teachers must be committed to ensuring that time is spent to the level required by each student. While this may seem self-evident, statistically over 27 percent of teachers never spare curriculum time for teaching learning strategies. Only 44.6 percent of teachers spend time teaching learning strategies in every lesson (Ozel, 2009). To make the most effective use of instructional time, teachers need to teach learning strategies consistently and frequently and revisit these strategies often to ensure their development in students.

Each of these respectful task examples asks students to make personal meaning through engaging experiences.

Figure 10.2 Respectful Learning Tasks

Respectful Social Studies Learning Tasks	Less Viable Tasks
Students are asked to learn about the characteristics of a pioneer cabin by creating a photo story with captions during and after a visit to a pioneer village. Interviews with reenactment personnel are analyzed to formulate generalizations about resource use for each student's photo story.	Students look at textbook photographs of a pioneer cabin and tell what they can see in the cabin.
Students create a cardboard topography model to illustrate their understanding of foothills and mountains in a specified location.	Students look up elevations of various locations and record what they find on worksheets.
Students create a play to illustrate how families of many cultures would address a sample family crisis and add dialogue that illustrates the values of the culture that are brought to bear on each issue that is examined in the play.	Students are required to memorize a list of the main cultural and religious beliefs of several cultural groups who live in their area.

The overall goal of curriculum differentiation is to provide for learning success for every student. We can ensure that this happens in our classrooms by maintaining a focus on learning rather than a focus on teaching. This shift in focus will ensure a student-centred curriculum. A student-centred curriculum, a high degree of differentiation, coaching and feedback provided by the teacher, and the ways the teacher shows clarity on desired student behaviour, are key factors in successful lessons (Smetts & Moojt, 2001). These approaches create respectful learning environments.

LEARNING STYLES AND SOCIAL STUDIES STRATEGIES

Gardiner's learning styles theory initially identified eight learning styles and later included spiritualism as a style of learning as well. It is important to develop awareness of these learning styles and of learning styles theory as this is one element to consider when planning for differentiation in social studies.

In addition to Gardiner's theory of learning styles, teachers should consider other models to provide differentiation. The Big 6 process (Jansen, 2009; Eisenberg & Berkowitz, 1997) provides a learning styles approach that builds on inquiry processes and can support students' developing awareness of their strategy repertoire as well. The title of this process is easy to recall for young students, again supporting strategy efficacy. The Big 6 approach also incorporates elements of Bloom's Taxonomy of cognitive thinking so the connections across strategies that students are learning will support the extension to this model.

The advantages of the Big 6 model for differentiating is that it follows the general outline of differentiation through changes in content, process, or product; it is easy to remember and to establish as a classroom poster; and it focuses each question as a "we" question, thereby affirming a commitment to promotive interaction among students as they work together.

The Big 6 process allows for seamless differentiation by interest, readiness, and learning profile.

—*Jansen, 2009*

Additionally, students' social connections within the classroom group will often influence learning preferences. The teacher may also choose to frame or limit the choice options that are made available to students. This may be done to promote effective management in a busy inquiry environment. The choices the teacher offers may also be based on assessment of the learner's profile. A learning profile for any task can be developed by

- identifying the learning goals;
- breaking elements of the learning goals into components (e.g., content, process, and products);
- imagining the levels that students may exhibit in their learning behaviours for each component of the learning goals;

Table 10.1 The Big 6 Model of Differentiation

Big 6 Skills	Focal Question	Differentiating Instruction
Task Definition	What do we need to do?	Students identify areas of personal interest within the scope of the topic and contribute inquiry questions to pursue individually or as part of a class inquiry.
Information Seeking Strategies	What can we use to find what we need?	Students identify best sources, with teacher support to focus on reading level accessibility. Sources to support individual learning styles are sought.
Location and Access	Where can we find what we need?	The teacher and support personnel (e.g., librarian) work with individuals and small groups to teach, review, and extend library and media accessing skills.
Use of Information	What information can we use?	Students determine what note-making strategy and organizer(s) they would like to use to fit their learning goals.
Synthesis	How can we show what we learned?	Students select an option for a product to demonstrate what they have learned and to share learning with others.
Evaluation	How will we know if we did well?	Students can self-evaluate or conference with adults to determine their achievement of the goals in relation to previously communicated standards.

- developing a growth scheme for the learning goal in relation to each component;

- plotting the existing level of achievement for a student onto the growth scheme;

- planning for the student's learning by creating personalized and precise (breakthrough) strategies to extend the student's current learning; and

- using the growth descriptors on the student's learning profile to monitor their progress toward the goals and support extensions of the pre-instruction level of learning.

Teachers need to know when and how to use specific approaches and choice options to support the achievement of learning goals in a range of circumstances. This can be done through a careful assessment of each student's abilities and through professional knowledge of which instructional strategy can most effectively lead the student to the level of understanding as identified by the learning goal (Darling-Hammond, 2005).

Figure 10.3 provides an example of a learner's profile for social studies.

Figure 10.3 The Learner Profile

Learning Goal: Students will be able to explain how and why relationships, rules, and responsibilities may change over time and in different places.

Student's Name

Area of Differentiation	Goal Description Deconstructed	Level 1	Level 2	Level 3	Level 4
Content: What is being learned?	Student understands that relationships, rules, and responsibilities are contextual.	All rules seem to be understood as applying to everyone equally.	Understands that age can influence rules that apply but shows no comprehension of the societal context for rules, relationships, and responsibilities.	Shows a beginning understanding that rules, relationships, and responsibilities are contextual and influenced by many factors.	Shows a thorough understanding that rules, relationships, and responsibilities are contextual and influenced by many factors.
Process: How is it being learned?	Student compares relationships, rules, and responsibilities from different time periods and in different societies to determine patterns.	Student is unable to take a perspective that allows for comparison of rules, responsibilities, and relationships over time periods and in different societies.	With organizational support, the student is able to undertake a simple comparison of rules, responsibilities, and relationships over time and in different societies; needs strong support to draw conclusions.	The student is able to undertake a simple comparison of rules, responsibilities, and relationships over time and in different societies; needs minimal support to draw conclusions.	The student is able to undertake a multifaceted comparison of rules, responsibilities, and relationships over time and in different societies; needs minimal/no support to draw conclusions.

Product: How will student demonstrate what has been learned?				
Student creates a diorama to demonstrate understanding of roles in their family and in the families of other cultures represented by the makeup of the class.	Student is unable to demonstrate clear understanding of the roles in their family and others' through diorama.	Student is able to demonstrate clear understanding of the roles in their family through diorama but is not able to role-play roles of other families.	Student is able to use a diorama to demonstrate understanding of roles in their family and the families of other cultures represented by the makeup of the class, with minimal support.	Student is independently able to use a diorama to demonstrate understanding of roles in their family and the families of other cultures represented by the makeup of the class.

Source: Adapted from Ontario. Ministry of Education. (2005). *Education for all: The report of the expert panel on literacy and numeracy instruction for students with special education needs, kindergarten to grade 6.* p. 118. Toronto: Author.

By comparing students' learning performance to these learning profile descriptors, teachers can support growth.

A repertoire of rich and varied teaching strategies that are effective with individual students, small groups, or whole class groups will help teachers to support effective differentiation in various circumstances. When the teacher chooses strategies they should be

- effective—including explicit or direct strategy instruction and opportunities to name strategies and reflect on their effectiveness (metacognition);

- relevant—connecting to students' interests, previous learning, and personal learning goals within the framework of the overall topic;

- responsive—based on the students' current knowledge, the knowledge of individuals within the group, and the learning gaps that may exist in students' knowledge (content), understanding of learning strategies (process), or facility with demonstrating their learning (product); and

- engaging—involve a variety of strategies over time to maintain students' interest, develop their repertoire of learning to learn strategies, and maintain sophistication in each strategy so that the strategy is viable enough to support deep understanding of complex concepts.

Strategies for differentiation that can apply to all students can be changes to the learning context through either 1) instructional approaches, 2) environmental changes and adaptations, or 3) changes in the processes used for assessment and evaluation. These strategies are often referred to as accommodations (see Figure 10.4).

Some of the accommodation strategies should be available as options for all learners. They will support maximum access to the curriculum. By varying the size of tasks, input amount, time, level of support available, difficulty of the task, expected student output to demonstrate learning, degree of traditional participation, and learning goals, all learners can be supported to achieve to their potential.

Since the diverse makeup of the classroom is constantly changing, teachers need to be open to the expansion and refinement of their strategies for addressing diversity through differentiation. Instructional decisions need to be based on information collected through careful and sensitive observation as students engage classroom tasks.

CHOICE WITHIN AN INQUIRY APPROACH

Choice is a powerful motivator for students. Success with past choices leaves the student with a feeling of accomplishment and a growing sense of independence. For the student, choices can be based on the student's readiness, interests, and learning style.

In Chapter 3, we examined inquiry as an approach in social studies. In this chapter, the use of choice as a strategy to support differentiation has been examined. We have also considered how the tone of the classroom is established through specific strategies for management. Once the management of the classroom is working productively and the teacher is able to spend very little time on management tasks, students will be ready to

Figure 10.4 Accommodations to Maximize Learning

Instructional Approaches

- Assistive technology
- Augmented or alternative communication systems
- Buddy system
- Colour cues
- Computer use
- Concrete learning aids
- Cooperative learning
- Dramatization
- Duplicated notes
- Extra time
- Figure/ground changes to unclutter text
- Font size changes
- Graphic organizers
- Learning contracts
- Manipulatives
- Mind maps
- More frequent breaks
- Non-verbal signals/gesture cues
- Organizational instruction
- Peer tutoring
- Reinforcement incentives
- Repetition/rewording/ rephrasing
- Spatially cued formats
- Structured activities
- Taped texts/text-to-speech software
- Time management support
- Tracking sheets
- Visual aids
- Word retrieval prompts

Environmental Changes and Adaptations

- Alternative work space
- Assistive devices or adaptive equipment
- Minimizing background noise/quiet setting
- Proximity to teacher
- Reduction of stimuli (audio or visual)
- Special lighting
- Strategic seating
- Study carrel
- Use of headphones
- Voice projection equipment

Processes Used for Assessment and Evaluation

- Assistive devices or adaptive equipment
- Assistive technology
- Attention prompts
- Audio taping
- Augmentative or alternative communication systems
- Choice of ways to demonstrate learning
- Colour cues
- Computers
- Extended time limits
- Extra time
- Font size changes
- Frequent formative feedback
- More frequent breaks
- Ongoing, non-disruptive assessment
- Oral responses
- Product models
- Scripting/scribing
- Spatially cued formats
- Task modification or reduction

engage complex inquiry. Through modelling and repetition of use, students will develop automatic responses to inquiry opportunities. Teachers can then build choice into inquiry opportunities because students will be managing much of the process for learning and have access to skills that will enable them to engage content from different sources and produce a variety of products to demonstrate their learning.

It is wise, however, to introduce choices gradually so that you can develop effective strategies for monitoring progress. Tables, wall charts, computer charts, and visuals can be adapted to assist with tracking the myriad choices that students may make. By introducing students to the Bloom's Taxonomy Wheel (see Chapter 9), teachers can open up the options for demonstrating learning through a wide range of available products.

Most jurisdictions will mandate a core component of the program that all students are expected to master. Beyond this core, teachers can provide options. Within a unit of study, this could allow teachers to provide introductory lessons about a theme then use a project approach or cooperative learning (see Chapter 8) to have students branch out from the main topic to investigate questions of personal interest related to the main theme. The development of communication skills will allow the smaller groups or individuals to bring their discoveries back to the classroom as a whole through reports in various formats.

The average person cooperating (i.e., working in a cooperative learning group) was found to achieve at about two thirds of a standard deviation above the average person performing within a competitive or individualistic situation . . . Cooperative experiences promote more frequent insight into and use of higher order cognitive and moral reasoning strategies than do competitive or individualistic efforts . . . Cooperators tend to spend more time on task than do competitors or participants working individualistically.

—Johnson & Johnson, 2009

Allowing students to choose social and working groups within the classroom will help to avoid the risk of exclusion from peer groups (Darling-Hammond, 2005). The teacher will need to model and expect inclusive practices among students. By using an observant diagnostic approach to each learning episode, teachers can troubleshoot and provide differentiation and scaffolding that will ameliorate potential problems both socially and academically. Promotive interaction skills will need to be taught to students as they progress in their ability to manage new contexts, new groupings, and increasingly complex and ambiguous learning tasks. Socially skilled teamwork is the goal of cooperative interaction combined with promotive interaction.

[G]roup membership in and of itself is not sufficient to produce higher achievement and productivity . . . [K]nowing that one's performance affects the success of group mates seems to create responsibility forces that increase one's efforts to achieve.

—Johnson & Johnson, 2009

Individual feedback about the development of the student's social skills in promotive interaction contexts is important to the development of their relationships in the working group. When students are taught social skills, observed, then given individual feedback about the frequency of their engagement in the skills, their relationships within the working group became more positive (Putman, Rynders, Johnson & Johnson, 1989).

Awareness of the many ways that teachers can differentiate and build age-appropriate choice into opportunities for learning stretches teachers to develop deeper diagnostic skills and more breadth in their instructional repertoire. Managing choice productively provides access to learning for a wide range of interests and abilities among students. This breadth in the teacher's instructional skills expands opportunities for *all* students and allows teachers to assess both what students learn and how they go about learning it through as many avenues as possible.

INNOVATIVE APPROACHES IN YOUR SOCIAL STUDIES CLASSROOM

When teachers use choice as a method of differentiation for instruction, tracking the choices students make and the progress they make towards achieving learning goals is essential. Charts and tables will help organize such information. As students mature in their ability to participate in monitoring their own progress, they will be able to help keep track of communication about their progress if monitoring charts are created as wall charts that each student can access. The teacher must guard against creating monitoring systems that are easy to use and publically available and balance this with each person's right to privacy. Records of individual achievement should never be openly available. However, records of an individual's progress can be posted for student access.

When providing choice to address individual learning needs consider the categories of options for areas of choice first:

- Choice of what to learn—This is often quite limited because of provincial and territorial mandates for curriculum that define what should be learned by all students. However, it is often possible to give students the option to choose branches of study within a topic. For example, if the topic is Canadian resources, students may choose to work individually or in groups to explore information about a particular resource, such as diamonds or forestry products.

- Choice of how to learn—This is an easily managed way to differentiate within the classroom. Students can be provided with options about

  - Who they work with, whether alone or in a small group with common interests; if students choose to work in small groups, productive social interaction skills will need to be taught so that promotive interaction is achieved by the group

  - The resources they choose to learn from and examine for information

- Choices in how they present or demonstrate their learning—Again, this is an easily managed way to differentiate within the classroom. Students can be provided with options of format for displaying learning for the teacher's examination and should be taught presentation skills to allow productive sharing of their learning with students

Figure 10. 5 Monitoring Choices Chart

	Resource Focus	Exploration Background	Rights Acquisition Background	Harvesting and/or Development	Manufac-turing Back-ground	National Trade Partner-ships Back-ground	Inter-national Trade Partner-ships Back-ground
Groups							
	diamonds						
	aerospace technology						
	forestry products						
	food						

Topic: Canada's Trading Partners
Learning Goal: Students are to identify the processes involved in resource exploration, rights acquisition, harvesting, manufacturing, and national and international trade practices related to the resource.

in the class who have pursued the study of different subtopics within a theme. Exposing students to a wide range of possible products suitable to the learning goals is necessary to expand students' growing awareness of their learning options.

Sample Tracking Chart for Monitoring Choices

By examining the structure of this tracking chart (see Figure 10.5), teachers will see that the columns are headed by the products that students will need to produce to see the range of learning, and a reasonable sequence that students might follow to build toward the overall learning goal achievement. Building a tracking chart requires that the teacher break down, or deconstruct, the overall learning goal into sub-products that will accumulate to allow for the production of the final product.

CASE STUDIES AND PROFESSIONAL ACTIVITIES FOR INNOVATION IN SOCIAL STUDIES

1. You have just accepted a position teaching a Grade 5/6 split class in a rural community. There are 36 students in the class. Overall class achievement is weaker than average in literacy but approaching average on some measures of numeracy skills. Make a list of the steps you will take before meeting your new students to ensure that you are prepared to meet students' learning needs and that you have a differentiation plan to address these needs.

2. Create an opportunity to observe a social studies lesson in a primary/junior classroom. Record what you observe teachers doing to provide support for

differentiation during the observed lesson(s). Write each strategy you observe on a separate sticky note. Later, work with a peer group to sort your observations and theirs into four piles:

- Strategies that address differences in students' background knowledge (including related to cultural background)
- Strategies related to students' differences in process skills or preferences
- Strategies related to students' differences in product production skills or preferences
- Strategies related to students' social networking and social skills as part of the class group

Once you have sorted the observations into these four piles, determine the incidence of differentiation you observed using mathematical calculations (e.g., 18 percent of the time differentiation was addressed by students having a choice of groups to work with). Finally, draw some conclusions from your observations.

3. Interview an experienced teacher and ask about how he or she goes about providing for differentiation in his or her classroom. By analyzing the teacher's responses, determine if the teacher was talking about differentiating from a special education perspective or differentiation for all students to maximize their learning potential. Discuss your observations with colleagues.

Consider:

- Why might a teacher consider differentiation as an exclusively special education issue? *Meeting outcomes uniformly goal*
- Why might some teachers have a view of differentiation that allows them to consider optimizing learning through differentiation for all students? *Students might require diff. strategies to engage*
- What are the challenges teachers face in trying to implement a consistent and effective program of differentiation for all students? *I am not striving to be a teacher but striving to create learning for learners*

CHAPTER REVIEW AND PROFESSIONAL DEVELOPMENT AS A TEACHER

This chapter has examined the following:

- Academic performance in an average classroom spans across five grade levels.
- In education, our focus is shifting from teaching to learning.
- Differentiation is any process that divides students into subgroups, which are then exposed to different educational experiences.

- Differentiation is necessary to provide the best possible opportunities for students to learn and to maximize their potential and ensure equity and social justice.

- Teaching must be personalized and precise to maximize students' learning potential.

- Differentiation must include efforts to recognize diverse cultures and their impact on classroom learning.

- Mainstreaming of students with special needs means that all teachers must develop expertise with differentiation to optimize learning for all students.

- Teachers' meta-narratives need to include the belief that all students bring differences to their learning that must be addressed.

- Several focal principles must be adopted to ensure that teachers implement differentiation practices that place differentiation at the centre of learning rather than considering it an adjustment to plans for the "average" learner.

- Respectful learning tasks will optimize students' engagement and efforts to learn.

- Promotive interaction in the classroom can be achieved when students are taught, and regularly practise, social skills.

- Classroom management skills can be learned by teachers.

- Successful classroom management includes attention to what is taught, how it is taught, and how students interact with each other and the teacher when it is taught.

- Many factors can influence teachers' efforts to provide differentiation in the classroom.

- Good planning and effective communication with students, parents, colleagues, and supervisors can surmount obstacles to effective differentiation.

- Respectful tasks have six characteristics that teachers can ensure.

- Differentiation requires differences in the supports required for achievement; these supports can be used in combination to optimize learning.

- Teachers need to teach and reinforce learning strategies for all students.

- Learning styles can be used as one method of providing differentiation.

- Strategy frameworks such as "Big 6" and Bloom's Taxonomy can be used to support differentiation. Choice is an option to support differentiation.

- A learning profile can help teachers determine the most effective ways to differentiate.

- A learning profile can also operate as a growth scheme to provide guidance for future instruction for a student.

- Teaching strategies should be effective, relevant, responsive, and engaging.

- Methods of differentiation can include combinations of instructional approaches, environmental changes and adaptations, and processes used for assessment and evaluation.

- Information to guide differentiation needs to come from teachers' careful and sensitive observation as students engage classroom tasks.

Weblinks

Software programs can be applied to many uses in the social studies classroom. Many well-designed programs promote literacy development and are very motivating for students. Interest in the capabilities of the software may motivate students to focus on tasks they might otherwise find very difficult. Investigate some of the software programs identified below. Using a flow chart, brainstorm some applications of a selected program to a particular lesson in a social studies class at a selected grade level.

Software Selections

Program Title	Most Appropriate Divisions	Application
Say It Save It and Write Out Loud	Primary, junior and intermediate	Say It Save It allows the student to use text to speech to read aloud and save it as an as an MP3 audio file.
		Write Out Loud allows text to speech and can support basic word processing.
EasyBook Deluxe	Primary, junior	EasyBook Deluxe creates storybooks with words and pictures
The Print Shop	Junior, intermediate	The Print Shop provides desktop publishing capabilities
Geometer's Sketchpad 4	Junior, intermediate	Geometry support
Math Trek 1, 2, 3 and Math Trek 4, 5, 6	Primary, junior	Multi-strand math activities
Music Ace and Music Ace 2	Primary, junior, intermediate	Teaches basic music skills
Comic Life	Primary, junior, intermediate	Allows creation of comic books, storyboards, and other visual literacy devices
Kid Pix 4	Primary, junior	Allows the development of creative presentations

Chapter 11

Developing the Learner's Skills for Effective Inquiry: Examining Structured Thinking in Social Studies

Learning Topics

- The Role of Inquiry in Social Studies
- Knowledge-Based Skills
- Critical Thinking and Inquiry Skills
- Communication Skills
- Application Skills
- Metacognition

Opportunities for interaction support structured thinking.

THE ROLE OF INQUIRY IN SOCIAL STUDIES

The way that we view the learner will influence the approaches we take to planning and delivering instruction in our classrooms. Students report that they find it valuable when their teachers create classrooms that encourage active involvement, when they understand the usefulness of what is being learned, and when their teachers demonstrate enthusiasm as they teach. Using inquiry in the classroom can support students' engagement because students have opportunities to pursue the study of issues and topics that interest them, within the framework of the topic being considered.

When inquiry is used in the classroom, neither the teacher nor the student will know how the investigation of a topic will end, nor what answers they are likely to find during investigation (Obenchain & Morris, 2007). Topics may lead to controversial discoveries by the student. Students are engaged because inquiry approaches allow them to draft a plan for their own learning based on their interests. Rich resources allow the students to consider issues with depth and substance, ensuring academic rigour in students' investigations. Inquiry skills ensure that students are able to take responsibility for the intense nature of rigorous inquiry.

Sustained inquiry will require that students achieve a high level of knowledge about the topic, think critically about issues, communicate their findings, and apply their ideas and findings to produce a product that demonstrates their learning. Skills related to attaining knowledge, thinking critically, communicating ideas, and applying new learning to create an inquiry-based product will be the focus of instruction in an inquiry-based learning environment. The level to which teachers engage their students in inquiry will reflect their view of the learner and their beliefs about the learning process.

While the terms we use to describe learners may evolve during different educational eras and vary by jurisdiction, the academic debate over how to teach students seems to have clarified the value of articulating how we see the learner operating in relation to what is being taught. During the 1980s, J. P. Miller (1983) identified three approaches to teaching learners of any age. He called these orientations or approaches *transmission*, *transaction*, and *transformation* (see Chapter 2). Miller's work started an era of debate about the most effective approaches to instruction that have lasted well into the new millennium. The most conservative of the approaches (transmission) is most valued when society determines that students are lacking in their knowledge of basic facts. Calls toward improved skill levels for graduates to help ready them for the workforce often renew interest in teaching by transactional methods. More stable political and economic times foster greater interest in transformational approaches. Recent views about learning and the learner relate the transformational approach to the concept of constructivism.

TRANSMISSION, TRANSACTION, AND TRANSFORMATION

Transmission—The teacher is the teller; knowledge is imparted; emphasis is on the acquisition of facts and knowledge.

Transaction—The teacher is the coach, guiding the student to develop reproducible and transferrable skills.

Transformation—The teacher is a guide, supporting students' structured efforts to make meaning and understand new learning; the support that the teacher provides is often referred to as scaffolding.

It is important to recognize that Miller's orientations talk about how to teach; they are not suggesting different theories about how the student learns. Constructivism focuses on how students make meaning of their experiences, regardless of how those experiences come about.

Miller's work on these curriculum orientations sparked a debate about which is the best approach to teaching. We would argue that all three approaches are valid and should be selected to reflect the goals for the immediate instruction.

While educators would probably agree about many of the goals for a strong social studies program with differing emphasis, students may express more immediate and personal ideas about what makes social studies effective and enjoyable as part of their school program. Students report that active involvement, the usefulness of what is being learned, and the teacher's enthusiasm affected their views of the value of the subject area (Chiodo & Byford, 2004).

A study of practices of the most effective elementary social studies teachers (McCall, 2006) found that they

- articulated clear goals for their program;
- had a strong sense of purpose;
- actively involved students;
- challenged students' thinking;
- supported meaning making by ensuring that they made local connections and made ideas relevant;
- focused on current events;
- integrated social studies with other subjects, especially through the use of literature; and
- engaged in professional development to improve their practice.

The students' views about effective social studies programs are consistent with the challenging nature of a classroom rich in inquiry.

Various resources provide steps that students should engage to be successful with the use of an inquiry approach (see Figure 11.1).

This approach to inquiry parallels a scientific method. Students might also engage in inquiry processes that seem less structured but with each stage of the process guided by the teacher to maintain the academic rigor of inquiry.

To ensure that inquiry is academically rigorous in the primary and junior classroom, teachers will need to teach knowledge-based skills, critical thinking and inquiry skills, communications skills, and applications skills so that students can engage information from many sources analytically.

Figure 11.1 Steps to Inquiry

Inquiry Steps	Explanation
Identifying an inquiry focus	When studying a topic the student may encounter something that challenges their thinking, raises interest, or creates doubt. This may be the product of using texts that provide limited treatment of a topic, generating students' interest in delving deeper.
Identifying a problem	Students create a clear statement or question that evolves from their interests or doubts about a topic. The teacher helps students refine and clarify their question or focus so that ensuing investigations have a focus.
Formulating hypotheses	Based on their interests, students generate questions that will guide their inquiry. A central, guiding question will guide the selection of resources and define the limits of the inquiry so that it is manageable.
Collecting data and evidence	With guidance from the teacher, students collect, evaluate, and select resources in many formats to help them answer their initial question(s). Non-textbook resources and primary sources are valuable for answering inquiry questions.
Evaluating and analyzing data	With teacher guidance, students assess and evaluate the evidence they have collected and attempt to use it to answer their initial question(s).
Testing the hypothesis	Students develop a product that presents their inquiry question(s) and their research to their teacher and peers. Opportunities to present information in critical forums challenge students' understanding of their topic and extend their analysis and synthesis of their research.

Note: Chapter 10 presented the Big 6 skills that provide questions to guide younger students through these inquiry steps.

KNOWLEDGE-BASED SKILLS

Determining the knowledge that will garner our attention and classroom time is much more sophisticated a consideration than merely identifying what we are told to teach in provincial and territorial guidelines. Guideline expectations are typically stated in broad, general terms. It is the role of the teacher to determine what specific examples and investigations are used to teach the specified knowledge and what knowledge gets emphasis of time and place in the curriculum. As well, teachers will determine which knowledge-based skills are taught to students to enrich their engagement with the curriculum.

Figure 11.2 Relating Program Rationale, Goals, and Strands

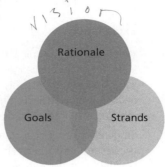

To determine what knowledge gets emphasis within a program of social studies, teachers must have a well-considered sense of the rationale, goals, and strands required in their program. Some provincial and territorial guidelines may provide the rationale and goals but strands are typically only implied, if addressed at all, in such documents. Without a strong sense of the rationale, goals, and strands desired in a program of study, teachers would find it difficult to develop a program that is coherent and directed by a consistent vision of the subject area. The rationale, goals, and strands of the program should reflect each other and intersect to promote clear direction (see Figure 11.2).

Rationale refers to the clear and well-articulated vision of what the course in social studies adds to the growth of the student. The vision may include a focus on any combination of reasons why social studies are taught. These visions may include emphasis on the role of social studies to initiate citizens, reform society, develop personal potential, or ensure academic understanding. *Goals* give the course a sense of purpose by defining what is to be achieved through the study of social studies. *Strands* provide a vision for determining how the rationale and goals will inform the emphasis of content and approaches.

In provincial and territorial guidelines, when examples are provided to give guidance about instructional strategies, they often promote mixed visions of the strands that might inform a program. Strands in a program of social studies could be

- discipline based—knowledge and knowledge-based skills for the program are drawn from any of the complementary disciplines that form aspects of social studies (e.g., history, geography, economics, politics, anthropology);

- dimensional based—knowledge and knowledge-based skills for the program are focused from the perspective of social roles, personal horizons or spheres of influence, social phenomena, institutions within society, or geographical areas (see Chapter 1); or

- concern based—knowledge and knowledge-based skills for the program are drawn from commonly viewed issues of the society (e.g., environmental concerns, social justice concerns, human rights concerns, peace initiatives, equity concerns).

Source: Adapted from Case & Clark, 1999.

The nature of the student experience within the social studies program could vary greatly depending on the rationale, goals, and strands that the teacher identifies for the program. Differences in these three dimensions of planning will determine where time is spent, which resources are available, and what instructional approaches are used.

See Figure 11.3 for a list of knowledge-based skills common in primary and junior social studies programs.

While this list of knowledge-based skills may not be exhaustive, it does emphasize the concept-based nature of knowledge-based skills. Teachers should examine local guidelines to ensure they understand the knowledge-based skills that may be embedded in expectations.

CRITICAL THINKING AND INQUIRY SKILLS

The call for strengthened focus on citizenship education in schools has renewed interest in the nature of critical thinking. Critical thinking has been defined by many researchers and organizations. It is a concept that changes with social situations and developing issues.

"Critical thinking is the intellectually disciplined process of actively and skillfully conceptualizing, applying, analyzing, synthesizing, and/or evaluating information gathered from, or generated by, observation, experience, reflection, reasoning, or communication, as a guide to belief and action" (Scriven, 1996).

"Most formal definitions characterize critical thinking as the intentional application of rational, higher-order thinking skills, such as analysis, synthesis, problem recognition and problem solving, inference, and evaluation" (Angelo, 1995, p. 6).

"Critical thinking is thinking that assesses itself" (Center for Critical Thinking, 1996).

Figure 11.3 Knowledge-Based Skills Common in the Primary and Junior Programs

- Descriptions of social structures
- Legal descriptions of rights and responsibilities
- Social processes (e.g., elections, ceremonies)
- Services and securities
- Roles and historical figures
- Knowledge of symbols, practices, and places
- Knowledge of concepts
- Knowledge of imposed structures used to classify and sort (e.g., physical regions)
- Knowledge of relationships between the natural and constructed elements of the world
- Knowledge of environments
- Knowledge of exchanges, relationships, traditions, and influences
- Knowledge of theories
- Knowledge of ascribed attitudes and their origins
- Knowledge of trends, advances, and patterns
- Knowledge of the relationships between change and time

"Critical thinking is the ability to think about one's thinking in such a way as to 1) recognize its strengths and weaknesses and, as a result, 2) recast the thinking in improved form" (Center for Critical Thinking, 1996).

Guideline foci during the 1970s and 1980s used various terms to describe the need for critical thinking as an approach to values education in social studies. Moral dilemmas, values clarification, moral reasoning approaches, and critical thinking can all be applied to develop strategies to improve our instruction in social studies.

Figure 11.4 outlines essential aspects of critical thinking as discussed in B. K. Beyer's book, *Critical Thinking* (1995).

Later chapters of this text will focus on connecting the inquiry approach to learning, critical-thinking strategies, and societal values and their evolution. As noted in an earlier work by Joseph Kirman (2008, p. 30), "As teachers, we have a duty to train our students to be thoughtful people able to correctly interpret reality and to make valid decisions . . . a major objective of teaching thinking and thinking skills."

In a world where daily events lead us to question the gap between socially acceptable values and the actions of some people and factions in our society and in the international community, being clear about the visions held by productive and valued members of a democratic society is a role uniquely suited to social studies. The resources and strategies we select will have an impact on the quality of our students' critical thinking in societal

Figure 11.4 The Essential Aspects of Critical Thinking

Dispositions: Critical thinkers are skeptical, open-minded, value fair-mindedness, respect evidence and reasoning, respect clarity and precision, look at different points of view, and will change positions when reason dictates.

Criteria: To think critically, a person must apply criteria. They need to have conditions that must be met for something to be judged as believable. Although each subject area has different criteria for inquiry, some standards apply to all subjects. ". . . an assertion must . . . be based on relevant, accurate facts; based on credible sources; precise; unbiased; free from logical fallacies; logically consistent; and strongly reasoned" (p. 12).

Argument: A statement or proposition with supporting evidence is required. Critical thinking involves identifying, evaluating, and constructing arguments that will stand up to close evaluation of the evidence.

Reasoning: Reasoning includes the ability to infer a conclusion from one or more premises. To do so requires examining logical relationships among statements or data.

Point of View: The way a person views the world, which shapes their construction of meaning, constitutes their point of view. Critical thinkers view phenomena from many different points of view to shape personal understanding.

Procedures for Applying Criteria: Critical thinking makes use of many procedures and processes to apply thinking criteria effectively. These procedures include asking questions, making judgments, and identifying assumptions.

Source: Beyer, B. K. (1995). *Critical Thinking* identifies essential aspects of critical thinking. Adapted from www.uts.edu/Administration/WalkerTeachingResource Center/FacultyDevelopment/CriticalThinking/index.html; accessed July 7, 2010.

contexts. Part of our role as social studies teachers is to create a classroom atmosphere where deep inquiry is the norm, where values can be questioned, where an inquiry environment is common practice, and where students can develop "shared conceptions of citizenship that will best advance democracy" (Levesque, 2004).

Critical thinking is often equated to inquiry skills in provincial and territorial guidelines and includes the ability to

- formulate research questions;
- use primary and secondary sources;
- analyze, classify, and interpret information;
- represent ideas in other formats (e.g., graphically);
- research;
- make connections; and
- use specific vocabulary.

Each of these skills applies to more sustained skills that engage learners through different ways of knowing. These skills were identified in Chapter 1 and are elaborated in several chapters of this book. These critical-thinking abilities can be applied to students' efforts to engage in concept clarification, model building, narration, description, map making, comparison, correlation, causal reasoning, and decision making.

COMMUNICATION SKILLS

Students need to be able to communicate to learn and demonstrate their learning. An examination of the social studies curriculum guidelines across Canada yields several common treads that inform how the subject is to be addressed because of its unique multi-disciplinary nature, and the nature of communication skills within the discipline. These commonalities include

- recognition that social studies draws from the approaches of many disciplines;
- an emphasis on historical and geographical content;
- the interconnectedness of people with their environment, including evolving concepts of global stewardship;
- a focus on using ideas related to self, family, community, country, and world to understand the present and develop a perspective on the future;
- guidance for students as they develop a broadening understanding of their role in local and global contexts through extended experiences that help them construct their reality; and
- a vision of the role of social studies as one vehicle to manage the development of students' citizenship skills for productive participation in a democratic society.

What all of these foci have in common is their direction to plan programs that help students construct or develop their own meaning. This is *constructivism*. Constructivism is an approach to teaching that focuses on the learner having experiences and opportunities to process and having time and structure to reflect on experiences to draw meaning from them.

There are two elements to constructivism: cognitive constructivism and social constructivism.

Cognitive constructivism focuses on how the individual makes meaning. Through interaction with the environment, the individual constructs meaning. Predictable developmental stages evolve with maturation; natural maturation opens gateways to learning and new insights that create further learning opportunities. The psychologist Jean Piaget described cognitive development as a biological process with key stages of development that align roughly to ages of the learner. As students experience new things, they either change existing understanding (accommodate) or they expand and enrich current understandings (assimilation).

Social constructivism focuses on how the individual, within a community of learners, negotiates understanding to arrive at a new reality. Reality is subjective and negotiated through social consensus. Social interactions allow the learner to arrive at a negotiated understanding that has contextual integrity (it's true for the current circumstances), and is useful and relevant to the learner. Russian psychologist Lev Vygotsky (1929) developed a theory of social development that is often considered to be the forebear of the current theory of social constructivism. In social constructivism, students advance their own learning as they explain and interpret ideas for others, assimilating or accommodating their ideas through social interaction. This requires well-developed communication skills. Conceptual development is related to language acquisition as the learner becomes more capable of attaching language to new realities and understandings. The teacher becomes a support to the student as the student experiments and molds the new experiences to extend their own understanding. This support is called *scaffolding*.

Developing new values in students is influenced by the type of exposure students get to value laden concepts and experiences, the amount of time and structure they get to process their exposure and experiences, and the accumulation of experiences that cause either the affirmation of what they know (assimilation) or the adjustment of what they know (accommodation). When students are first introduced to new learning, they may develop new attitudes. Further exposure that confirms these new attitudes will lead to the development of new beliefs. Then, further experience after a belief is in place will allow students to develop value structures that can be articulated and that will stand the test of new circumstances being introduced. In our social studies classrooms, it is the opportunity to have multiple exposures to new and more sophisticated concepts that is central to the approaches we choose for instruction.

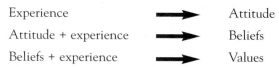

Experience ➡ Attitude

Attitude + experience ➡ Beliefs

Beliefs + experience ➡ Values

Social constructivist approaches, where students have opportunities and scaffolded guidance to produce complex products that communicate their learning, allow teachers to create the rich and respectful learning environment that will support the development

Figure 11.5 Applications for Learning

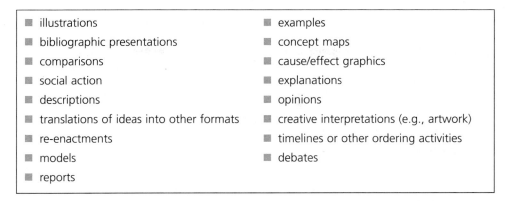

- illustrations
- bibliographic presentations
- comparisons
- social action
- descriptions
- translations of ideas into other formats
- re-enactments
- models
- reports

- examples
- concept maps
- cause/effect graphics
- explanations
- opinions
- creative interpretations (e.g., artwork)
- timelines or other ordering activities
- debates

of desired values appropriate to a strong democratic society. Students' opportunities to communicate with teachers and other learners as experiences influence attitudes and beliefs will support their development.

APPLICATION SKILLS

By understanding the developmental characteristics of students, teachers can work toward planning applications that suit developmental levels and appeal to the learners. Cognitive and social development changes during maturation and is influenced by many factors in the environment. Recent brain research also points to many physiological factors that impact on human development.

See Figure 11.5 for typical applications that support opportunities for learners to demonstrate their learning.

Many resources about teaching can be accessed to help teachers understand developmental theory. Auger and Rich (2007) have effectively summarized much of the recent research about cognitive development (see Figure 11.6) and present an effective and easy-to-reference outline.

METACOGNITION

Transformation means change. When we talk about transformative strategies for the social studies classroom, we need to consider strategies that have the potential to change students. But how do we want to change them?

To start the planning of your social studies program, you need to be clear about what this portion of all that the student will study is contributing to developing the educated student. Earlier, we considered the characteristics of an educated student from a constructivist perspective. When teachers start program planning, they also need to study the vision of the learner as it is described in appropriate provincial guidelines. As guidelines in any jurisdiction are revised and updated, the vision may be adjusted to include more current features

Figure 11.6 Cognitive Development in Young Children

Early Primary	Late Primary/Early Junior	Late Junior
■ movement and multisensory involvement are essential	■ begins to reflect consistently on past events	■ sorts and classifies ideas and information as well as objects
■ learns by manipulating and changing things	■ continues to use real objects to assist reasoning	■ focuses and sustains thoughts
■ uses trial-and-error approach	■ has enhanced and more objective use of language	■ extends interest to many different areas
■ impulsive; "labels" after action	■ repeats experiences to verify ideas from previous situations	■ continues to need concrete referents to support ideas
■ perceives from own point of view	■ begins to coordinate and interrelate ideas	■ refines notions about time and space
■ thoughts are governed by physical appearance of objects or situations	■ becomes increasingly aware of patterns	■ uses models, graphs, and symbolic forms to solve problems
■ has extremely concrete orientation to learning	■ begins to focus on more than one perspective or viewpoint	■ begins to think in increasingly logical ways
■ begins to make comparisons	■ increases ability to express and receive ideas in symbolic form	■ reasons and explains ideas associated with change
■ memory is personal, linked to particular actions or experiences	■ able to reverse thought	■ thinks about different dimensions of a situation
■ listens for general rather than specific detail	■ better able to predict change and anticipate outcomes before action	■ makes and carries out plans
■ language is not always clear to the listener but may seem clear to the child		■ becomes increasingly concerned with accuracy and realistic representations
■ begins to develop awareness of space and time		■ becomes consistently aware of how and why they learn (metacognitive)
■ begins to develop "reversibility of thought"		

and initiatives that reflect changes in our society. Current guidelines give attention to visions that reflect the concept of good citizenship and global interaction in a sustainable environment. It is likely that future guidelines will continue to stress the need for global citizenship and will include visions that refer to universal exploration initiatives as well.

In the context of social studies, transformation means that we are moving students toward the values and behaviours of a responsible citizen in a democratic society. Transformative instructional strategies are those that engage students and promote in them a desire to invest energy and their abilities in the topics of current focus. Transformative strategies combine all of the techniques that apply to address both constructivism and social constructivism. To create this type of learning environment for social studies, the teacher needs to consider the qualities of an active, transformative learning environment.

What would a student's favourite learning situation look like? When this question is posed to teacher candidates, they consistently develop a list of characteristics that they feel students would include if they had the advantage of the curriculum language that the candidates themselves are developing (see Figure 11.7).

A product of the transformative learning environment is happy, fulfilled, and self-directed students. The students know that they are learning and have opportunities to reflect on their learning because of the classroom atmosphere of inclusion and acceptance. Time is built into lessons to create awareness of what has been learned throughout the day. Students are aware of their academic growth. The knowledge that they are learning and the opportunities to reflect on their learning create opportunities for *metacognition*. When students are deliberately metacognitive, motivation and integrity characterize their learning.

Figure 11.7 Transformative Strategies

- Students are active.
- Choice is provided in how to learn and how to demonstrate learning.
- The classroom is resource rich.
- Students often work in groups.
- Groups are flexible, and respond to current learning needs.
- Talk is valued.
- Technology is readily available to support students' investigations.
- Questions are asked and investigated.
- Controversial issues are examined.
- Action in relation to findings is an option.
- The teacher is modelling, guiding, and supporting.
- Social interaction skills are taught, recognized, and reinforced.
- Divergence is valued.
- Depth and breadth in relation to examining a topic are encouraged.
- Furniture is portable and there to serve the tasks as needed.
- Students regularly get detailed, positive feedback from peers and teachers to guide personal improvement.
- Differentiation is always promoted.
- A positive, respectful tone is maintained at all times.
- Learning time is preserved from interruption.
- Large blocks of time are available to promote inquiry.
- Achievement is shared and celebrated.
- Parents are welcomed to share in their child's learning.

The teacher's role in a transformative learning environment demands sensitivity and flexibility. The teacher will sometimes provide direct instruction to model for students. At other times, the teacher provides direction and guidance during structured inquiry. Always, the teacher is responsive to current learning needs.

In a transformative learning environment, teachers need to provide access to the world for every student. This is available through electronic sources and media in many forms. Students must feel connected to the global reality as they expand their horizons in the ever-widening scope of their curriculum. Metacognition should be a component of every learning opportunity.

Once students have had many experiences with inquiry, they can begin to be more aware of the skills they are developing to increase their awareness of their strengths as learners. Teachers need to help students make connections between the inquiry steps and the types of expectations that typify directions in social studies guidelines (see Figure 11.8).

The more students are aware of the skills they are using in their daily learning, the more able they are to control their own learning and advance those skills, and the more they become intentionally metacognitive.

A Sample Inquiry Approach for the Primary Classroom

Grade 3 students have been studying pioneer life in Canada. They have looked at examples of pioneer lifestyles in Upper and Lower Canada, the Maritime provinces, and the prairies. They have found that governments at the time provided different types of support for settlers in different regions. A small group is interested in determining if the government supports provided for settlers in different regions seemed to influence the success of settlements. They determine to try to find out.

Figure 11.8 Seeing Inquiry Steps in Guideline Expectations

Inquiry Steps	Categories of Expectations
Identifying an inquiry focus	Knowledge-based skills
Identifying a problem	Critical-thinking and inquiry-based skills
Formulating hypotheses	Critical-thinking and inquiry-based skills
Collecting data and evidence	Critical-thinking and inquiry-based skills Communication-based skills
Evaluating and analyzing data	Critical-thinking and inquiry-based skills Application-based skills Metacognitive skills
Testing the hypothesis	Critical-thinking and inquiry-based skills Communication-based skills Application-based skills

Their teacher asks them to start their inquiry into this topic of interest by laying out a plan and maintaining notes about their plan as their inquiry progresses over the next two weeks. This is the plan they develop to keep track of what they are doing and what their next steps are. See the example below.

Inquiry Plan Group members: _____, _____, _____,

Inquiry focus: The success of early settlements in Canada

Problem we want to investigate: Settlers were given different things by the government to help them settle in new areas. Did these differences in supplies allow some groups to be more successful than others?

Hypothesis: Practical farming supplies would be most supportive of new settlements.

Data/Evidence:

Evaluation of the Data/Evidence:

Return to our hypothesis/Were we right?

INNOVATIVE APPROACHES IN YOUR SOCIAL STUDIES CLASSROOM

Chapter 6 introduced the skill of correlation. The inquiry question, "What are these changes related to?"was provided as a generic question that can be adapted to specific content in social studies. The topic of correlation is developed further here with examples of questions that would lead to correlational investigations.

Correlation is a skill that is central to thinking in social studies. Correlations examine the tendency of two or more things to happen at the same time. This is different from causality where one thing can be said to cause another to happen. Correlation opens the door for deeper questions because the tendency of two or more things to happen at the same time may suggest causality but requires further investigation through other means. Causality is a more scientific investigation than is typically undertaken when determining correlations.

Data to determine correlations can be collected through many means. Young students can ask questions such as, "What are these changes related to?" For example, in the primary/junior social studies curriculum across Canada, students could consider such inquiry investigations, using correlation, as:

What are mobility patterns across Canada related to?

What do educational opportunities across Canada relate to?

What are changes in trade related to?

What are economic indicators related to?

These examples demonstrate the far-reaching nature of investigations using correlation. They require students to collect, examine, and compare data from many sources and to consider ways of looking for patterns in the data.

The results of investigations using correlation are often shown in graph format so that relationships can be identified pictorially and points of intersection are readily seen. Even very young students can be guided to use correlation to investigate data that relates to their experiences.

Example

Grade 2 students have noticed that there are many more problems on the schoolyard at the end of the day's recess than are typical earlier in the day. They wonder if this has anything to do with classmates being more tired by that time of day. They ask classmates to record a "tiredness index" on a scale (see below) each day for two weeks. They also record all of the incidents they notice on the schoolyard involving classmates. As a group, students create a line graph of their data. They conclude that incidents increase as students report being more tired. They cannot, however, say that the tiredness causes the incidents.

Exposing students to the use of tally charts and tables, bar graphs, line graphs, and pie graphs will help them collect and sort data to engage in the use of correlations. Electronic software to generate such graphs makes their completion both interesting and easy for students. Junior students can be taught to use more sophisticated accounting software and spreadsheets to create tables and graphs.

CASE STUDIES AND PROFESSIONAL ACTIVITIES FOR INNOVATION IN SOCIAL STUDIES

1. **Grade 3** students are asked to open a resource booklet about castles in the middle ages, read several pages, examine the pictures, then answer a number of questions about castle life. This approach is transmissional. Using the same content as a starting point, develop a one-paragraph description of how this could be taught from a transactional orientation and how it could be taught from a transformational orientation.

2. Examine a unit of study from a local guideline. Identify all of the expectations for learners from a single unit in the guideline. Photocopy all of the expectation statements and

cut them into strips so that each expectation statement is on a single sheet of paper. Now, sort these expectation statements into five piles under these headings:

- Knowledge-Based Expectations
- Critical-Thinking and Inquiry-Based Expectations
- Communication-Based Expectations
- Application-Based Expectations
- Metacognition Expectations

3. This chapter discussed the importance of scaffolding while students practise new learning. In a small group, discuss the role of homework as it relates to the need for scaffolding during practice. When should homework be given? When should it not be given? What role does homework serve in the development of primary/junior students?

4. Metacognitive development is a critical part of the student's ability to become increasingly independent in their learning. The phases of instruction require that lessons conclude formally with a metacognitive component. Choose one lesson that you have taught or expect to teach and explain how you will ensure that a metacognitive component is included in the lesson. What did (will) you do during the lesson conclusion to ensure that students know what they have learned during the lesson?

CHAPTER REVIEW AND PROFESSIONAL DEVELOPMENT AS A TEACHER

This chapter has examined the following:

- Inquiry engages students' interest.
- Inquiry can be open-ended, with uncertain discoveries during the course of the inquiry.
- Inquiry allows students to pursue their own interests within a topic.
- Inquiry skills give students the academic tools they need to engage rigorous investigations.
- Transmission, transaction, and transformation identify three different orientations to curriculum.
- Transformational orientations to curriculum support sustained, student-centred curriculum.
- Constructivism is a transformational orientation that focuses on teaching in ways that encourage students to make meaning from their learning.
- All three orientations to the curriculum have a place in the classroom.

- Approaches should be chosen to create the strongest match with the learning expectation(s) for each lesson.

- Effective elementary social studies teachers use techniques that reflect clear learning goals and challenge students' thinking.

- Sustained inquiry experiences challenge students' thinking.

- Inquiry can progress through defined steps that mirror the traditional scientific approach.

- Strong inquiry skills have a foundation in the development of students' knowledge-based skills, critical-thinking and inquiry skills, communications skills, application skills, and metacognitive awareness.

- Classroom teachers make choices about the knowledge that gets emphasis within the classroom.

- The knowledge that gets emphasized in the classroom depends on the teacher's rationale, goals, and strand choices for their social studies program.

- Program strands are the teacher's view of how the program should unfold and include a discipline-based strand, a dimensional-based strand, and a concern-based strand.

- Analysis of provincial/territorial guidelines leads to the identification of relatively common lists of knowledge-based skills, critical-thinking and inquiry skills, communications skills, application skills, and metacognitive skills.

- Critical-thinking skills are skills linked to values.

- Critical thinking is an inherent aspect of inquiry.

- Critical thinking skills are part of the skills of concept clarification, model building, narration, description, map making, comparison, correlation, causal reasoning, and decision making.

- To communicate their learning, students must first make meaning of their learning experiences. This meaning making is called constructivism.

- Both cognitive and social constructivism have value in the creation of meaning and the values are linked to incorporating new meaning into reality.

- The accumulation of experiences expands the learners' attitudes into beliefs and solidifies their beliefs into values.

- Applications should be designed to suit the developmental characteristics of students.

- A wide variety of learning products can be used by students to demonstrate their learning.

- Transformative learning environments engage students and motivate them to learn.

- Metacognition is the students' awareness of their own learning through reflection.

- All categories of expectations provided in provincial/territorial guidelines align with the scientific model of inquiry often used in social studies.

- Correlation is the tendency of two or more things to happen at the same time.

- Correlations often develop by graphing data to show patterns.

Professional Development as a Teacher

1. Examine the local social studies guideline for a unit of your grade of choice. Determine if the guideline implies or overtly demonstrates adherence to one approach in the way it is presented. In a small group, discuss approaches that may be evident in other units and the influences that may have caused these approaches to be chosen for this guideline.

2. Explain which approach to social studies instruction makes the most sense to you and why that is so.

3. Analyze one guideline unit from a local document. Determine the values that are implied or stated in guideline goals for that unit. Determine how you would teach one of those values at the grade level you chose.

4. Create a series of experiences in outline format that you would arrange for your students to have them learn one of the knowledge-based skills. Do the same for any one of the critical-thinking and inquiry skills, communication skills, application skills, or metacognitive skills.

Weblinks

Inquiry is supported by ready access to a variety of resources that delve into topics more deeply than is possible through conventional textbooks. Many of these resources will be available to students through the Internet. Classroom libraries should also be rich in informational text to support inquiry. Whether students have access to inquiry resources through print or electronic sources, they should be taught accessing skills so that text structures are readily accessible as they engage in research. (See Chapter 13 for more information about the skills that students need to be taught to access each of these types of resources.) In addition, students will need to be taught skills related to accessing primary sources of information through interviews, documents, and photographs.

Internet sources that will support inquiry will be enriched on a regular basis as websites expand and ways of navigating websites become even easier. Teachers should always be aware of safety and security issues, reading levels, and exposure to offensive information that is biased or not credible when facilitating the use of internet sites for student research.

Interactive Online Historical Case Study
Students piece together the lives of ordinary people in the past. It is an experimental, interactive historical case study.
www.dohistory.org

Human Rights: Amnesty International
This site gives teaching guides and lesson ideas in the area of human rights.
www.amnestyusa.org/educate/page.do?id=1102117

Arab and Islamic Culture
This site provides inks to resources in the area of Arab and Islamic studies and culture.
www.awaironline.org

Primary Source Documents

This site gives a list of books and primary source historical resources.

www.historywiz.com

This site provides a vast amount of primary source historical resources.

www.jackdaw.com

Primary Source Documents—Canadian

The National Archives of Canada website provides a multitude of primary and secondary source historical material.

www.collectionscanada.gc.ca/index-e.html

Chapter 12

Classroom Discussion to Promote Effective Inquiry

Learning Topics

- Controversial Issues and Classroom Discussions: The Teacher's Role
- Pre-Discussion Strategies to Clarify Thinking
- Facilitating Classroom Discourse
- Questioning to Promote Student Inquiry through Discussions
- Summarizing Classroom Discussions: From Discussion to Action

Electric security fencing with glass infused concrete barriers surround a home in Iquique, Chile. Students are invited to discuss some of the differences found in various cultures regarding lifestyles and freedoms. How might these differ from Canada?

CONTROVERSIAL ISSUES AND CLASSROOM DISCUSSIONS: THE TEACHER'S ROLE

Social studies is a subject area that has developed from our practice of examining ourselves in many social contexts. Self-examination leads to differences of opinion. When opinions differ significantly, controversial issues arise. Self-examination of our society takes place through constructive dialogue. Freire (1970) defines dialogue as "the encounter between men [people] mediated by the world . . . to name the world." This definition highlights the role that dialogue about controversial issues can have in the elementary classroom since naming concepts is critical to developing ideas with children. By leading and promoting discussions in the classroom, teachers can support students' evolving sense of their role as mediators of truth and interpreters of events. Students can develop a deeper understanding of the complexities and subtleties of issues by having opportunities to explore their perceptions and those of their classmates and the adults involved in their learning.

Perhaps through these approaches, subsequent studies, and further refinements, we can realize Dewey's (1940) vision and avoid the dangers of forbidden thought."
—*Misco & Patterson, 2007*

Classroom dialogue about controversial issues provides support for students' developing sense of competency to address cultures and contexts they encounter on their own path toward participation in shaping their society as citizens. When students have early exposures to discussions about issues and come to realize that there are many sides and perspectives about controversial issues, their role as sense makers and personal mediators of the ideas they consider helps them to understand the nature of controversy and the role of open and honest discussion in a democratic context.

In Chapter 6, ideas for addressing controversial issues in the classroom were presented. This chapter will focus on using discussion as the vehicle of instruction to address controversy with young children and adolescents. Teaching about controversial issues is both a predictor of civic participation and a strategy for the development of democratic values and critical thinking skills (Torney-Purta, 2002). Students generally respond positively to opportunities to address controversial issues through discussion, recognizing their importance as peak experiences in their education about dealing with controversy (Hess & Posslet, 2002).

The benefits of discussions about controversial issues in the classroom are many:

- The experience positions students to become agents of change.
- Students feel that they are actively engaging in decisions in the social context.
- Students are able, through discussion experiences, to recognize, celebrate, and accept diversity in their experiences with society.
- Students can appreciate diversity among groups and within their own social contacts.

Source: Crossa, 2005

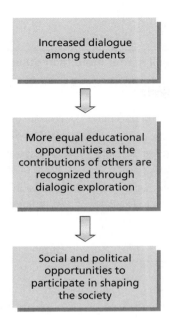

Increased dialogue
among students

⬇

More equal educational
opportunities as the
contributions of others are
recognized through
dialogic exploration

⬇

Social and political
opportunities to
participate in shaping
the society

Classroom discussions among young children also support the development of their multiple literacy capacities, strengthening their abilities to speak, listen, envision, and exemplify.

However, managing the discussion of controversial issues in the classroom requires skills and professional strategies on the part of the teacher. While there are many controversial issues that can be discussed in a social studies context, teachers must take into account the dynamics of their classroom when structuring and planning for this approach. When members of a classroom group do not share common interests among the social structures in the group, sharing views about difficult issues is a complex undertaking. The inability of everyone in the group to experience, know, or share the perspectives of others in the group may cause divisions within the class group and may lead to withdrawal of those who feel underrepresented or misunderstood within the group.

In choosing to use discussion of controversial issues in the classroom, teachers must first understand the age appropriateness of the topic. Successful engagement of students' interest in the topic also means that students need immersion in the content of the topic so that discussion is informed by knowledge. Finally, teachers need to recognize that some controversial issues matter more than others (see Figure 12.1). The relevance of a particular issue will relate to its timeliness within the society, and other factors that reflect time, place, and social dynamics.

Classroom discussions among young children also support the development of their multiple literacy capacities, strengthening their abilities to speak, listen, envision, and exemplify.

Figure 12.1 Controversial Issues

Some controversial issues will matter more than others because . . .

- they are timely issues in the society.

- students have studied the topic and have a critical mass of background knowledge on which to base opinions.

- many students in the group feel passionately about a particular issue.

- the need to engage in a discussion has arisen from the students' need to examine aspects of an issue, rather than from the teacher's choice of discussion as an imposed methodology.

- action is possible.

- the issue has longevity; it will make a difference if students understand different perspectives that may impinge on the issue.

- the issue is comprehensible by the age group of students.

- discussion of the issue has the potential to influence students' cohesion as a group, sense of efficacy as a social group, and/or sense of empowerment as young citizens.

However, managing the discussion of controversial issues requires skills and professional strategies on the part of the teacher. While there are many controversial issues that can be discussed in a social studies context, teachers must take into account the dynamics of their classroom when structuring and planning for this approach. Jackson (2008) cautions teachers to be aware of the social inequities and hierarchies that exist in any social group and to recognize that a group may not accept each participant's input with the same value. When members of a classroom group do not share common interests sharing views about difficult issues is a complex undertaking. The inability of everyone in the group to experience, know, or share the perspectives of others in the group may cause divisions and lead to withdrawal of those who feel underrepresented or misunderstood within the group.

When choosing to use discussion of controversial issues in the classroom, teachers must first understand the age appropriateness of the topic for the students involved. Successful engagement of students' interest in the topic also means that students need immersion in the content of the topic so that discussion is informed by knowledge. Finally, teachers need to recognize that some controversial issues matter more than others. The relevance of a particular issue will relate to its timeliness within the society.

Information to further students' knowledge about the issue must be available to them and accessible at their literacy level.

Teachers may avoid the opportunities that are available for introducing classroom discussions of controversial issues for many reasons. The teacher's sense of academic freedom is a major factor in the determination to provide opportunities to openly address controversy in the classroom. If the teacher feels confined by the social context of the school community, the choice to engage in discussions of controversial issues can risk conflict within the school and between the teacher and the school community.

A teacher's academic freedom is his/her right and responsibility to study, investigate, present, interpret, and discuss all the relevant facts and ideas in the field of his/her professional competence. This freedom implies no limitations other than those imposed by generally accepted standards of scholarship. As a professional, a teacher strives to maintain a spirit of free inquiry, open-mindedness, and impartiality in the classroom. As a member of an academic community, however, the teacher is free to present in the field of his or her professional competence his or her own opinions or convictions and with them the premises from which they are derived.

—Statement of Academic Freedom from the U.S. National Council for Social Studies, 2007

In pursuing academic freedom by presenting controversial issues for discussion in the classroom, teachers must first consider the following questions:

- Do I know enough about this topic?
- Do my students have sufficient academic background about the nuances of this topic to benefit from an exploration of each other's perspectives about an issue?
- Is the school community open to the exploration of this issue?
- Is there any imminent reason why it would be unwise to explore this issue at this time?
- Do I have administrative support and understanding of my use of discussions of controversial issues?
- Is prior communication with parents about the intention to discuss certain issues necessary?
- What are my beliefs and values about this issue?

Each of these questions will guide teachers toward purposeful and sensitive use of discussions as a strategy in the classroom.

Classroom discussion opportunities may be structured with some ground rules that will help to support the flow and equality of a discussion (see Figure 12.2). Teachers cannot assume that because they set ground rules in the classroom all students will feel equally valued in expressing their opinion. Classrooms are unequally structured, with those students who feel educationally confident and socially secure being the most outgoing and engaged in opportunities that require risk (Jackson, 2008).

Different voices pay different prices for the words they choose to utter.

—Boler, 1994

However, by establishing some ground rules for discussions and using strategies that encourage inclusion and heterogeneous exposure to classmates, teachers can optimize the opportunities for discussion for all students.

Ground rules for discussions in the classroom will vary with the students' age and their experience with controversy, group work, and social action projects. Students' age will be a critical aspect to consider when introducing discussions. Students' imperfect knowledge of

Figure 12.2 Sample Ground Rules for the Teacher to Consider When Presenting a Discussion

- Students have opportunities to define what they consider to be controversial and worthy of discussion.
- Time is provided for students to prepare for discussions; they are not discussing topics "cold."
- Pre-discussion strategies are taught and practised to surface students' knowledge about a topic (e.g., four corners). See Chapter 3 for cooperative learning strategies that support preparation to engage in discussions.
- Students understand the language of decisions (e.g., options, criteria, etc.).
- Classroom rules and procedures are used effectively to ensure an atmosphere of respect and to ensure that learning time is respected and used effectively.
- The teacher is prepared to model the roles of thoughtful speaker and sensitive listener/respondent as required.

themselves, other students, and social norms, especially in emotionally charged situations, will require that teachers monitor and engage the progress of discussions carefully. Some ground rules for classroom discussions will help (see Figure 12.3).

While it is important that teachers operate with full professional awareness of the school culture and that of the surrounding community, it is also important to engage

Figure 12.3 Students' Ground Rules for Discussion

- Understand the two roles you have in a discussion: the role of thoughtful speaker and the role of sensitive listener/respondent.
- You may be passionate and emotional about the issue; you may not be abrasive in the way you express your passion and emotion.
- Equality is not sameness; while everyone may wish to speak about this issue, your decision not to speak will be respected.
- Be prepared to support your opinion with ideas that can be discussed.
- Be prepared to accommodate the opinions of others.
- Stay focused on solutions and social justice actions.
- Recognize that what causes an issue for you may not cause an issue for fellow students.
- While you may question another student's opinion, you may not question a student's option not to express one.
- Ridicule is never acceptable.
- Discussions may have time limits.

effective discussions in the classrooms by reflecting your personal opinion and commitment to the social change in question.

We enter educational settings with pedagogical frameworks reflecting our commitments to various sorts of social change. One should not hide or repress such interests by attempting to enter classrooms as apparently neutral facilitators."
—*Jackson, 2008*

The line that will need cautious attention is between making your views known when that becomes appropriate as part of a classroom discussion and making your views known for the sake of trying to convince others to align with your opinion on an issue. Teachers must always be cautious about using their influence appropriately with young children. However, if teachers avoid including their views in a classroom discussion, they risk children not taking the value of the discussion seriously, which in turn will result in disengagement and static beliefs and values, and finally the perpetuation of the existing uninformed prejudices. The inclusion of controversy through discussion as a component of the curriculum must be for the purpose of furthering education within a pluralistic democracy to perpetuate attitudes and develop skills for a free, participatory, and harmonious social coexistence.

[F]reedom of mind, freedom of thought, freedom of inquiry, freedom of discussion is education, and there is no education, no real education, without these elements of freedom.
—*Dewey, 1928*

Many external forces on education can attempt to sterilize the curriculum and work against children's natural curiosity about their teacher's position about issues under discussion. These external factors may include

- ideology;
- politicized cultures; teacher's fear of a negative response from the school staff, administration, and/or parents;
- government influence on the school curriculum;
- limits on academic freedom;
- the teacher's lack of knowledge about the issue; and
- the teacher's lack of professional confidence in using discussion as an educational strategy.

When teachers do not use discussion techniques to make students aware of the existence of controversy, they risk students' acceptance of the presented narrative as the single possible interpretation of events and fail to expose students to the nuances of multiple perspectives. Students are "instead exposed to materials that are purported narratives of their nation and locality, which limits beliefs and entrenches singular narratives" (Hein & Selden, 2000). When teachers take an artificially neutral stance on a controversial issue, students may interpret the issue as being value free or unimportant. By using social studies content to examine the influences on modern life and the values that are espoused by certain practices, teachers provide a meaningful curriculum that has current relevance as it allows students to examine how we came to function as we currently do. Social education becomes integrated with the social studies content and values that have supported the development of our society are explored for their legitimacy, breadth, and sustainability.

Topics closed to reflective thought can certainly result in sustained unexamined beliefs and the formation of decisions that are based on blind impulse, emotion, or prejudice.
—*Misco & Patterson, 2007*

When teachers choose to use discussions as a strategy to explore controversy in social studies, they must do so with full awareness that societies generally have silenced histories and taboo topics (Misco & Patterson, 2007) and that many topics of discussion may introduce emotional responses that reach beyond the classroom. Some issues may be avoided both in the school curriculum and in the broader community. The use of discussions that are preceded by academic preparation to engage in them effectively, and communication within and beyond the school to ensure support for the approach, can ensure a curriculum that goes beyond the "general tendency toward neutral and value-free learning experiences" (Misco & Patterson, 2007). By exposing students to discussions that allow them to experience making reasoned judgments, teachers help students increase their civic efficacy, improve their critical-thinking skills, develop stronger interpersonal skills, explore their role in political activity, develop tolerance, and create greater interest in current events, social studies, and social issues (Remy, 1972; Goldenson, 1978; Curtis & Shaver, 1980; Harwood & Hahn, 1990).

PRE-DISCUSSION STRATEGIES TO CLARIFY THINKING

Students of all ages will benefit from having opportunities to clarify their own thinking before they engage in classroom discussions. The strategies used to support pre-discussion preparations will depend on the age and literacy level of the students. In the early primary grades, open whole-class discussions may be preceded by partner or small-group discussions. These approaches allow students to practise stating an opinion and facing requirements from their peers to explain their thoughts without the complication of trying to write about what they think. Their oral language skills are usually more developed than their written language skills, so a greater breadth of ideas may emerge when small-group and partner pre-discussion approaches are used.

Primary students will benefit from the consistent use of phrases that require them to engage in pre-discussion reflection orally. For example, many teachers direct students to turn to their "elbow partner" and explain what they think about ideas that are about to be discussed. Consider the interaction outlined below.

Teacher: Boys and girls, we have a small problem with our bird feeding project. We have been filling the three bird feeders in our schoolyard regularly throughout the winter to help small birds get enough food while there is snow and ice around. However, our feeders are also attracting mice and raccoons that are causing other damage around the property. Mice are getting into the school and raccoons are getting into the outdoor garbage bins and scattering garbage all over the schoolyard. The school caretakers are upset about the mess and extra work this is causing. What do you think we should do about this? Please turn to your elbow partner and explain what the problem is.

Teacher (two minutes later): What is the problem?

Tessa: The birds aren't getting the food we have put out for them because the mice and raccoons are taking it.

Michael: The mice are getting into the school.

Sacha: The raccoons are making a mess with garbage on the schoolyard.

Eriksen: The caretakers are upset about the garbage and mice and all the extra work this creates for them.

Teacher: So, you have told me that you see four problems here that have been caused by our bird feeder project. Let's write those four problems on our chart paper so we can look at each one together.

Teacher speaks aloud as she writes:

> The birds aren't getting enough food.
>
> The mice are getting into the school.
>
> The raccoons are making messes in the schoolyard.
>
> The caretakers are upset about the mess and work created by the mice and raccoons.

Teacher: Is there anything that we can do to solve any or all of these problems? Please take this sheet of paper and gather in groups of four. Use "four corners" to write or draw what you think we should do. Remember, in four corners you must explain the ideas written or drawn in each corner before you pass the page to the next person in your group. We will have 10 minutes to share ideas through four corners before we consider everyone's ideas.

Using this pre-discussion strategy, the teacher allows young students to

- understand that some problems have many aspects to them;
- realize that not everyone sees the same aspect of a problem as being the most important aspect;
- see that a solution for one group (the birdfeeders) may be a problem for another group (the caretakers);
- use a comfortable literacy approach to engage the task (i.e., students are given a choice among speaking, writing, or drawing); and
- develop their sense of efficacy by engaging them in finding a solution(s).

Review the cooperative learning structures presented in Chapter 3. Many of these cooperative learning structures can be used prior to discussions to help students understand the situation, identify problematic areas, brainstorm possible solutions, and systematically evaluate solutions against criteria. Review the decision-making strategy in Chapter 8. This approach will help students to review ways of addressing big decisions by allowing them to consider each option in the light of each criterion they identify. Even very young students could use a modified version of this approach by replacing numbers with happy, neutral, or sad face sketches in the cells of the decision-making framework.

Graphic organizers will also help students see the value of connecting their thoughts visually before they engage in an open discussion requiring them to explain their thinking. Teachers will need to use and model graphic organizers frequently and in different formats to help students develop their fluency with using these visual supports. Students should be allowed access to their graphic organizers during discussions to help them remember ideas. If graphic organizers are also available to students during discussions, students can be taught to use their graphic displays to follow the ideas presented by their peers and to record and connect those ideas to their own initial thoughts.

Computer software and websites have many examples of pre-structured graphic organizers available to teachers. When using pre-structured graphic organizers, teachers will need to ensure that they have considered the ways students are likely to record on the organizer and teach students to expand and adapt organizers as their thinking requires.

Teachers see several barriers to presenting controversial issues for classroom discussion. Primary concerns that prevent discussions of issues in the classroom include the teacher's lack of knowledge about the issue, and its relevance or timeliness. However, many teachers feel comfortable dealing with issues that are considered public issues (see Figure 12.4).

Figure 12.4 Issues Teachers Feel Comfortable Discussing in Their Classrooms

Issues	Percentage of pre-service teachers who said they would be comfortable having classroom discussions about these controversial issues
Political conflict	39 percent
Racial conflict	26 percent
Sexual orientation	24 percent
Sexual harassment	16 percent
Religious conflict	16 percent
Source: Adapted from Misco & Patterson, 2007, p. 539	

Figure 12.5 Controversial Issues in the Classroom: The Teacher's Perspective

Teachers' Stance on Controversial Issues in the Classroom	Explanation
Exclusive neutrality	The teacher tries not to introduce topics that the broader community may find controversial.
Exclusive partiality	The teacher seems to suggest that a correct position on the controversial issue exists and the role of the discussion is to uncover the correct view.
Neutral impartiality	The teacher structures classroom discussions about issues but does not present their own views in the discussion.
Committed impartiality	The teacher explains his or her own beliefs about the issue and their thinking to support their beliefs to avoid disingenuous discussions.

Because of the practical considerations of comfort, and knowledge of the nuances of current issues, many social studies teachers are, at least initially, more comfortable dealing with discussions about historical issues, which may lack relevance for students. More controversy will often arise when teachers introduce critical examination of social aims in the society (Thornton, 2005).

Without doubt and controversy, there is no judgment—only perception and recognition.
—Misco and Patterson, 2007

Awareness of your personal approach to controversial issues and discussions in the classroom will help you to examine ways to expand your use of this strategy. Kelly (1986) examined teachers' approaches to introducing controversy to the classroom and found that teachers' stances could be sorted into four categories (see Figure 12.5).

Prior to introducing classroom discussions as a strategy in social studies, engagement in a school staff discussion about such controversy may help each teacher to clarify the stance they support, the stance that will be supported within the school culture and the broader community, and the range of controversial topics that may provide a starting point for classroom discussions as the school and community experience first exposures to the approach. Awareness of persistent issues of our society that engender controversy (see Figure 12.6) may help teachers grapple with which of these they should address at various grade levels and within various course topics.

By engaging informed controversy through substantive classroom discussions, teachers promote classroom curriculum experiences for social studies that "reach beyond the lowest levels of content coverage and factual learning and aim for deeper, more meaningful conceptual growth and understanding" (Evans, 2007).

Figure 12.6 Samples of Controversial Issues

- Racial conflict
- Conflict over education
- Activism
- Religious conflict
- Gender identity/sexual orientation conflict
- Political conflict
- Restriction of freedom for national security
- Conflict among economic groups

- Conflict over health
- Welfare
- Domestic abuse
- Sexual harassment
- Homelessness
- Citizen apathy
- Ethnic conflict
- Public protests
- Poverty

Source: Oliver and Shaver, 1974; Parker, 2003

Most (65 percent) of pre-service teachers believe that they should have the academic freedom to design their courses to include discussions of controversial issues. They believe that the academic freedom to address controversy is important in social studies because

- teachers should have trust to use their professional judgment about issues;
- academic freedom to discuss controversy is part of strong citizenship education;
- students need opportunities to practise higher-order thinking skills;
- students need opportunities to shape their own opinions; and
- students will be more strongly motivated to learn if ideas are presented in meaningful ways.

Source: Misco & Patterson, 2007

To maximize the use of discussions of controversial issues in the classroom, teachers should ensure that they are aware of their academic freedoms within the context of their school community and culture. Once choices are made to engage in discussions that include the potential for controversy, teachers need to

- provide a wide variety of resources available through multiple literacies (text, visual, auditory) so that students have access to information on which to base informed opinions;
- provide frameworks that will support students' consideration of multiple perspectives about an issue;
- help students select or design graphic organizers in order to organize their arguments prior to discussions and to uncover and record alternative perspectives and supporting ideas;
- expose students to strategies that support productive, homogenous group work;
- help students access underlying opinions and criteria related to controversial issues in stories both told and read;

- teach students age-appropriate debate structures to help them explore and reach consensus when faced with controversy; and

- ensure pre-discussion immersion in the topic so that discussions are informed and respect the use of valued learning time.

If it is engaged at its most profound level, social studies, by its nature, inserts controversy into the classroom. Teachers should help students engage in the search for answers to the most challenging and persistent controversies of our society. Learning to manage the controversy to benefit students' learning is a critical skill for social studies teachers to master.

FACILITATING CLASSROOM DISCOURSE

Students who regularly take part in classroom discussions show a greater tendency to

- vote in later life;
- support basic democratic values;
- take part in political discussions;
- follow political news in the media;
- be interested in the political process; and
- have confidence in their ability to influence public policy.

Source: Barton & McCully, 2007

Rationalist approaches to controversy in the classroom support opportunities for students to examine issues by carefully weighing evidence and controlling emotive interactions during discussions. The ground rules provided earlier in this chapter will help teachers create the instructional environment needed in the classroom to use this approach to discussions. Once ground rules are in place to set the tone for interactions in the classroom (during all interactions, including discussions), teachers should face discussions that have the potential to elicit strong emotions by

- providing structure for personal reflection on a controversial issue before discussions;
- reviewing ground rules before substantive discussions and posting anchor charts so that ground rules are visible to students throughout discussions;
- remaining calm when students respond and interact emotionally;
- challenging personal disrespect;
- allowing the expression of all opinions, even extreme ones;
- being forthcoming with your opinion without imposing it on students;
- establishing the time available for the discussion that day; revisiting the topic another day if student interest warrants it; and
- providing decompression time to have students calm themselves and reestablish social equilibrium in the classroom before students leave the room each day.

Reflective writing that requires students to reflect upon an opinion other than their own, and assume the role of that person, as they write a support for the opinion may help them appreciate alternative perspectives.

To facilitate classroom discussions that become safe investments for students, the teacher must ensure the emotional safety of students. The following points will help to create an emotionally safe discussion environment to investigate social studies issues.

1. Put limits on how strong emotions can manifest during discussions (e.g., welcome students' opportunities to say anything but limit the ways they state opinions to non-abrasive approaches).

2. Allow highly charged discussions but anticipate them and provide sufficient time for "cool down" afterwards.

3. Recognize that discussions may include initially irrational statements by students as a step in clarifying their actual opinions about some topics.

4. Respond non-judgmentally to students' opinions; teach students to do the same (e.g., address the idea, not the person presenting it).

5. Accept that discussion is a process designed to lead to better, more enriched ideas through democratic input; teach students to accept the messy phase of discussions.

6. Determine your own comfort level with personal disclosure about the issue prior to the discussion.

7. Withhold your views about the issue until students have had sufficient opportunity to express and explore their opinions; this may mean waiting until students show an interest in what you think about the issue.

8. Challenge students to support their ideas with rational argument, examples, and stories.

9. Teach students the difference between examples, definitions, and explanations.

By using these approaches to facilitate classroom discussions, teachers can ensure that discussions do not deteriorate to personal challenges and directionless debate or become a lecture with occasional student comments interjected.

Barton and McCully (2007) present three easily remembered guidelines for teachers to use when managing discussions (see Figure 12.7).

Diversity in perspectives on issues can be addressed by ensuring that students have many opportunities to examine differences of opinion about historical events from the perspective of groups affected by the event. By engaging students in discussions about how history may be relevant today, students also generate a sense of the impact of different perspectives on events.

Students also need exposure to various formats for asking questions to help them open discussion to conflicting views. If they only have exposure to questions with yes/no answers (e.g., "Should Canada continue its military peacekeeping role in. . . .?"), they can fail to develop a view of the subtle differences that influence issues and related resolutions. By learning to pose questions openly to examine all options (e.g., "What role should

Figure 12.7 Examining Differences of Opinion

Approach	Explanation
Deal with emotions	Allow students to express emotions so they can get beyond them to address issues objectively. Respond non-judgmentally.
Mix it up	Expose students to ideological diversity. This will help them to manage conflict in rationales among their peers about the issues that are discussed. Make conflicts in ideology explicit so that students become aware of the degree of consensus and difference around issues. Expose students to ideological differences across groups and within groups, especially within their own social/cultural group. Make explicit the alternative positions within students' own tradition.
Find support	Teachers should be aware of the values and culture of their school, community, and the leadership team of the school. Have confidence in your professional judgment. Respect the unique perspectives and views of the community. Create professional networks to share strategies. Provide opportunities for students to connect historical studies to contemporary and relevant issues. Maintain flexibility in the curriculum to allow time and strategies to address issues of local concern.

Canada play in military peacekeeping in . . . ?"), students learn to withhold quick judgments and examine issues in relation to a full range of criteria.

Teachers cannot assume that students of any age group will automatically transfer thinking patterns learned in relation to the examination of past issues to current situations. They will require teacher support to see the applicability across contexts and feel invited to make use of new thinking patterns before they will start to use and recognize opportunities for transfer.

Finally, teachers will need to remember the power of authority that unequal social standing in a classroom will impart to certain speakers. It becomes the teacher's role to ensure that open discussions of issues do not start with the imposition of the theories of the socially empowered students in the group (Jackson, 2008) so that discussions are fully open to embrace the actual opinions held by group members.

QUESTIONING TO PROMOTE STUDENT INQUIRY THROUGH DISCUSSIONS

In Chapter 9, ideas for asking questions at different levels of Bloom's Taxonomy were explored. As well, we examined ways to encourage young children to learn to ask questions at different levels. The ability to ask questions as an initial step of the inquiry process

Figure 12.8 Example of Learning Expectation References to Students' Questioning Skills

Grade 1	Grade 6
Students will brainstorm and ask simple questions to gain information.	Students will formulate questions with a statement of purpose to develop research plans.

is often cited as an explicit expectation for learning at many grade levels (see Figure 12.8) and in various subject areas. Examination of social studies guidelines shows that questioning is a valued and well-articulated expectation for young learners.

It is evident that growth in the style of students' questions is expected across the Grade 1 to Grade 6 program. While this example promotes asking any type of question at the Grade 1 level, specifically developed questions that lead to research, and therefore call for analysis, synthesis, or evaluation, are required at the Grade 6 level.

To move students from questioning at any level, to questioning for specific purposes, teachers will need to support growth in questioning skills as they develop in students. Teachers should gradually release responsibility for questioning to students. In initial opportunities to formulate questions, students will require examples and support with wording. As question formulation skills develop, students may require support with narrowing the scope of their questions to create manageable guidelines for their research.

What Should the Gradual Release of Responsibility for Questioning Look Like?

Students need to have individual opportunities (see Figure 12.9) to produce questions for a variety of purposes and assess their efficacy as guides for research.

For young students, making the experience of asking questions as concrete as possible will help them to manage large amounts of information and formulate question sentences without getting immersed in writing tasks that may bog down the flow of ideas. This can start in primary grades with students selecting a button from a bin. Each button would have a single question word on it (i.e., Who? Where? When? Why? What? How?). The teacher can then use the student's ideas and write the student's question on the remaining space on their question button, using erasable marker. Students can practise this approach while listening to read-aloud stories each day.

Teachers could also ask students to assemble words from a question word bank to formulate new questions. Question word banks can be designed specifically for a new topic or chosen to be generic and reusable. The example provided in Figure 12.10 is a generic question word bank. Teachers would photocopy this word bank, cut up each cell, and place all words in an envelope. Then, when students are required to create their own questions, they can sort words from the question word bank to make their specific

Figure 12.9 Continuum of Gradual Release of Responsibility

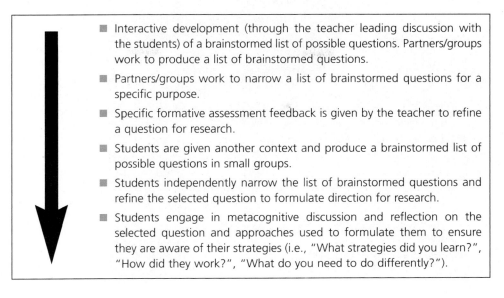

- Interactive development (through the teacher leading discussion with the students) of a brainstormed list of possible questions. Partners/groups work to produce a list of brainstormed questions.
- Partners/groups work to narrow a list of brainstormed questions for a specific purpose.
- Specific formative assessment feedback is given by the teacher to refine a question for research.
- Students are given another context and produce a brainstormed list of possible questions in small groups.
- Students independently narrow the list of brainstormed questions and refine the selected question to formulate direction for research.
- Students engage in metacognitive discussion and reflection on the selected question and approaches used to formulate them to ensure they are aware of their strategies (i.e., "What strategies did you learn?", "How did they work?", "What do you need to do differently?").

questions. This reduces the writing requirement and exposes students to a variety of terms they could use in their questions.

By providing extra cells in an envelope of generic question words, teachers allow students the opportunity to fill in cells with the specific content they need to complete the question words they have chosen. This strategy can be modified by printing individual words on magnetic metal discs and encouraging students to shuffle discs around on a metal cookie tray to form questions.

Encouraging students to ask these probing questions as a part of classroom discussion requires that several conditions for open discussion be established in the classroom. Students will need to feel tacit permission is present for them to get past the established culture of polite interaction to ask probing but politely and sensitively phrased questions. This should be done so that students have opportunities to ask such questions of the teacher first, and

Figure 12.10 Generic Question Word Bank

who	was	the	who	is
the	what	was	the	where
did	this	when	did	this
why	did	this	how	did
how	will	how	should	how
might				

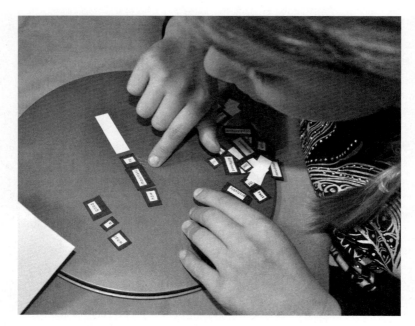

Students can demonstrate their understanding of complex and specific content using this hands-on strategy.

later of each other. Strategies for disagreeing in agreeable ways will need to be modelled by the teacher frequently to maximize students' ability to learn through discussions.

Ultimately, if emotional issues are ignored, then far from learning to deal with difficult issues rationally, students may simply come to see school history as irrelevant to their own concerns. And students are, after all, entitled to their emotions.

—*Barton & McCully, 2007*

Getting students at ask questions from early grades will require creativity and ingenuity on the teacher's part. Some strategies are presented in Figure 12.11. Each of these strategies shares the common characteristic of allowing students to be physically active as they practise a cognitive skill. This will help students engage the task and will support their memory of the strategies they used.

Students should also be taught how to ask guiding questions (see Figure 12.12) that will ensure they focus their research on higher-order thinking (i.e., analysis, synthesis, and evaluation) and creativity. Guiding questions that will serve this purpose have specific characteristics that can be taught and exemplified for students and put on anchor charts for their reference.

Sample guiding questions include:

- What makes a good leader?
- Is Canada a good country?
- Was pioneer life good for everyone?
- Were government settlement policies good for Native people?

Figure 12.11 Strategies for Creating Discussions

- Question Bingo—Read a short historical story to students and provide them with a bingo card of sentence stems. If they can ask questions starting with the stems on their cards, or they can answer questions starting with those stems but posed by others, they can mark that stem on their bingo card.

- Question Hopscotch—Divide students into partners and have them draw a hopscotch pad on pavement (or on a large sheet of paper). Have students ask questions about an historical or geographic topic and record each question on a segment of their hopscotch frame. Then, each pair can partner with another team to play each other's hopscotch game. Instead of throwing a stone or taw onto the hopscotch frame, students must answer each question to skip to the next part of the hopscotch pad.

- Who Am I?—After immersing students in a topic, expose them to questioning skills practice by taping a picture representing some aspect of the topic (e.g., an aerial map of a famous location) onto each student's back. Have students wander around the room and ask each other yes-or-no questions about what is on their back. The student can remove their picture once they have accumulated enough clues to figure out what their picture depicts.

To lead students' development of guiding questions to start the process of their inquiry, teachers can use some or all of the following strategies:

- Lead students to brainstorm every question they can think of about the topic. Then, guide students to sort the questions into two piles. One pile should represent questions that can be easily answered by factual information (e.g., How many women were on the boat?). The second question pile should include all of the questions that require more research, multiple perspectives to be considered, and may be subject to opinion.

- For the questions placed in the second pile, have students work to word them as guiding questions using an anchor chart of the characteristics of guiding questions to support their thinking.

Figure 12.12 Characteristics of Guiding Questions

- The question is open-ended; there is no "right" answer.

- The question focuses upcoming inquiry on a specific and manageable topic.

- The question is stated in a non-judgmental way and may be answered in a variety of ways.

- The question has emotive force and intellectual integrity; it directs true inquiry into the topic—this is often achieved by including the word "good" in front of an object word.

- The question is stated succinctly; it gets to the point of the inquiry.

- The question allows answer(s) that include multiple points of view and connections among ideas.

- Have students sort the guiding questions they have now revised into a priority list with those that interest them most at the top of the list.

- Have students analyze their top priority guiding question to determine if there are embedded supplementary questions that will need to be investigated to help them learn more about the guiding question. To probe for supplementary questions, have students try to frame questions that start with Who? Where? When? Why? What? or How? This can be done in the form of a web so that students' ideas can flow randomly, then get sorted into time priorities later.

The quality of question that is used to focus discussions and inquiry will limit the quality and intensity of the investigation into the topic. The time and effort put into developing useful and clear questions before discussions will be well worth the effort.

SUMMARIZING CLASSROOM DISCUSSIONS: FROM DISCUSSION TO ACTION

The point of engaging students in classroom discussions is to influence their engagement in social action. Passionate beliefs clarified through classroom discussions can translate into passionate commitment and positive actions. In Chapter 6, we examined social justice as a goal for social studies programs. The types of social justice actions that students can engage will be influenced by many factors; teachers will need to consider

- the age of the students;
- previous experience with social justice actions;
- the support of the school staff and administration;
- local culture and community sensitivities to various issues;
- time of the year;
- curriculum priorities;
- safety; and
- short- and long-term impact of actions.

Other criteria specific to your school context may also need to be considered. When considering social justice actions that will support the conclusions of classroom discussions, teachers should ensure that options beyond "giving" are explored. Fundraisers for various charitable actions are a common and valued way of engaging students in social justice action. However, students may find greater satisfaction and personal connection through engagement in more politically active approaches. Letter-writing campaigns and resource sourcing and making projects would require more emotive energy and a greater commitment from students than giving material resources when they may have only vague ideas about potential needs or applications. Non-governmental agencies (NGOs) with missions in other countries of the world may be good sources of information about appropriate social justice actions for classroom foci. For younger students, social action projects that are closer to home may be most suitable.

INNOVATIVE APPROACHES IN YOUR SOCIAL STUDIES CLASSROOM

Students can learn a great deal about analyzing perspectives and ensuring a thorough analysis of a topic from all perspectives by examining news accounts in both written and video format to consider what they present and also what they fail to present in their accounts. Young readers can learn to analyze written accounts by using coloured highlighters to show where each account addresses the questions of who, where, when, why, what, and how. Other articles could be highlighted with two colours to identify areas of the article that address differing perspectives.

If students are learning to analyze the presentation of differing perspectives from video sources, the class can be divided into two groups and directed to examine the video for evidence and ideas that are offered from different perspectives then engage in discussions from the perspective they examined in the video.

Graphic organizers that structure students' reading or viewing will help them sort their thinking in preparation for discussions. Figure 12.13 provides a sample graphic organizer to help students examine sources from differing perspectives.

Using Newspapers in Social Studies

The use of newspapers in the classroom can support students' developing sense of themselves as members of a structured and growing society and students' acquisition of knowledge to support inquiry. Newspapers provide another media literacy venue to support creativity and research skills in students. Positive attitudes and strong abilities support students' growing self-concept and sense of self-efficacy as they engage in using resources that may initially be baffling and very complex for them.

Figure 12.13 Sample Graphic Organizer

Issue:		
Reporters addressed . . .	**Perspective of:**	**Perspective of:**
Who?		
What?		
Where?		
When?		
Why?		
How?		
How much? How long?		

Figure 12.14 Aspects of Creativity

Attitudes	Abilities
Positive self-concept	Originality
Openness to ideas	Fluency
Perceptiveness	Problem solving
Tolerance for ambiguity	Flexibility
Sense of humour	Elaboration
Persistence	Intelligence
Expressiveness	Intuition
Independence	

Source: Adapted from Anne Crabbe, 1986.

Components of newspapers can also support students' use of creative attitudes and abilities (see Figure 12.14) as they search for, apply, and analyze data.

Newspapers can be used as both sources of information in social studies when students are able to manage the reading level of the text, and as formats to emulate in the products that they could produce to demonstrate their learning. Samples of some methodologies for using newspapers in social studies are provided in Figure 12.15.

Figure 12.15 Sample Methodologies to Use with Newspapers

■ After becoming familiar with the questions that are usually addressed in newspaper stories (who? what? where? when? why? how?) students can be asked to present stories about themselves and about life in their family or their community using this format. They might also assume the role of a particular worker in their community and describe that person's working day through the use of the news questions.

■ Students could undertake a word study in their local newspaper by examining word alternatives used to provide variety in a text (e.g., How many ways does the newspaper present the idea of success or defeat using different phrasing on a particular day?).

■ Ask students to find a local news article that relates to a topic of study. Challenge them to design a political cartoon to represent a negative perspective on the topic. Students might also be asked to represent the events of a story in comic strip form.

■ Challenge students to use techniques such as music, dance, poetry, photo journals, storytelling, electronic media, art, or dramatic speech to represent their learning in social studies. The Bloom's Taxonomy wheel (see Chapter 9) provides many examples of alternative products that students could produce. Have those who watch or listen to the presentation write a news report about what they witnessed and address the standard questions of a news report as they write.

Figure 12.15 (*Continued*)

- Students can get a sense of the layout of their local community by examining advertising in the newspaper and plotting the location of businesses on a local map.

- Students can examine local newspapers for issues that revisit historical events and determine the perspective of the writer of the report. They could also look into reasons why particular events are revisited at certain times.

- Students could be given roles to use as filters for examining the local newspaper. They could collect news items that would interest them from their various roles:

  - New resident
  - Police officer
  - Museum curator
  - Reporter for a rival paper
  - Historian
  - Cartographer
  - Explorer
  - Student

- Students can find an article that presents some area for divergence in opinions. They can debate the issue(s) presented in the article.

- Junior students can engage newspapers by learning to read and interpret business reports and stock market listings as they study aspects of Canada's national and international trade relations. Later, junior students could also do some mock investing and stock monitoring related to Canadian natural resources and industries as they study the geography of Canada.

- Have students create a series of pictures for a photo journal news story to depict the pantomimed stages of an historic event. Current computer software allows students to add sound, colour, and special effects to create movies from a series of still photos.

- Have students refine an existing news story to add more human interest detail.

- Have students take two photographs to accompany a local news story. The first photograph should be a simple face shot. Challenge students to add 10 details to the second shot that will give readers more contexts for the story. This can be done in parallel with a classroom study of historical photos from a time period being examined.

- Challenge students to make contact with students in other jurisdictions who are studying the same topic. Students can share news topics about the common topic electronically.

- Have students examine personal ads in the newspapers, especially the lost-and-found section. To practise their questioning skills, have them determine what questions are answered in the ads and list the questions that are still unanswered.

- Use newspaper stories to teach students to discriminate between facts provided by the writer, opinions expressed by the writer, or opinions implied by the writer's tone. Provide photocopies of news articles and three colours of highlighters for this purpose so students can mark each element directly on the photocopies. Teach students to quote text from the articles that support their analysis.

(Continued)

Figure 12.15 (*Continued*)

- Students could collect news articles from the local paper that relate to political action locally, provincially, or nationally. After reading each article they could create a wall web to connect ideas across articles and to consider impacts across actions at different levels of government on people at other levels. They might also consider ways to represent the disclosures of each article by brainstorming a number of alternative headings for the articles.

- Students could collect news articles from the local paper and sort them into categories that relate to a topic being studied (e.g., social news, criminal news, political news, resource news, business news). Students could then select a particular article and continue to follow that story for several days to see how the story develops over time. After locating a story they want to follow, students could anticipate follow-up stories by writing titles for the next four or five days' of coverage of the topic or by writing the next day's story.

- Students can be challenged to create their own "aged" newspaper to report on the events they are learning about in social studies (e.g., the settlement of eastern Canada, the fur trade, the building of the CPR, the fisheries of western Canada, the Winnipeg strike, the Depression, the Klondike gold rush). Aging techniques can be taught by combining art expectations and social studies goals.

- Have students read an historical newspaper account of an event they are studying in history. Have them use this account as background and then take the role of the underdog in the story and write a business letter to their supervisor to explain what went wrong.

- Have students examine an historical artifact and create a human interest news story to introduce this artifact and its significance to classmates. Encourage photography and art to accompany the verbal report.

- Have students use aerial/satellite photography for the local area to examine the location of unused fields or abandoned buildings in the community (e.g., an old hospital site). Have them assume the role of community planner and work with teams to develop lists of options for more productive use of the target land. Have students write a human interest proposal for the local newspaper to introduce their ideas for the land.

CASE STUDIES AND PROFESSIONAL ACTIVITIES FOR INNOVATION IN SOCIAL STUDIES

1. Mr. Masters is interested in introducing discussions into his Grade 5 social studies program. His students have been engaged in inquiry throughout the year but he has done very little work with them that led to any controversial observations or conclusions and he has not addressed any social action with the class. He would like to expand his program now and include discussions, controversy, and social action. Where should he start?

2. As Mr. Masters is preparing to introduce discussions into his social studies program he realizes that it would be wise to include some ground rules for how discussions should progress so that everyone has a fair chance to contribute to discussions if they choose. How should Mr. Masters lead students to create a set of ground rules? How should he go about ensuring that some of the main rules that he thinks are important become part of the classroom list of ground rules?

3. As Mr. Masters is preparing to introduce discussions about treaty rights into his program, he realizes that he is unclear about the difference between treaty rights and Native land claims and that these terms are likely to come up in the discussions because there are several students in the class whose parents are politically active with this issue. How can Mr. Masters ensure that he has these concepts clear in his own mind? How should he teach the differences to his students?

4. During the first discussion about Aboriginal rights in Mr. Masters' classroom, one student made a very offensive remark and angered another student who is of Native ancestry. The two students were visibly upset as they left the classroom and went outside for a nutrition break. The two students continued their discussion on the schoolyard and became very angry with each other. They were heard raising their voices and one student made some further offensive remarks. They both came back in from the break in a very agitated state and were not ready for their next class. What should Mr. Masters do? What might he have done before the break to help ensure that this type of conflict did not become personal?

5. The first opportunities for open classroom discussions in Mr. Masters' classroom went quite smoothly, aside from one instance of personal conflict arising between two students. The students have indicated that they like the discussion opportunities and they feel they are learning a great deal about the issues from them. Mr. Masters wants to continue to use discussions in his next unit about the immigration of new Canadians of Chinese descent into Canada during the building of the national railroad. Mr. Masters would like to address the sexual exploitation of Chinese women during this era. Are there any steps he might consider before introducing this topic for discussion?

CHAPTER REVIEW AND PROFESSIONAL DEVELOPMENT AS A TEACHER

This chapter has examined the following:

- Self-examination leads to differences of opinion.

- Constructive dialogue is a self-examination strategy.

- Classroom discussions can help students develop a sense of their roles as mediators of truth and interpreters of events in a democratic context.

- Discussions promote students' ability to see issues from many perspectives.

- Discussions are a strategy to address controversial issues.

- Students have positive reactions to the opportunity to use discussions to address controversial issues.

- There are many academic and social benefits that accrue from discussion experiences.

- Discussions need to be managed, not controlled, very carefully to be beneficial for all students.

- Immersion in the content of the topic must precede discussions so that discussions are informed by knowledge.

- Some controversial issues matter more than others.

- A teacher's sense of his or her academic freedom may influence choices to engage or avoid discussions of some issues.

- Some classroom ground rules for discussions will support the successful inclusion of all opinions.

- Teachers should not impose their personal views during classroom discussions; neither should they avoid expressing their opinions in the interest of keeping discussions open and honest.

- External factors that impinge on education can put pressure on teachers to avoid or modify classroom discussions.

- Discussions allow students to have experience with forming reasoned judgments, increase their civic efficacy, improve their critical-thinking skills, develop stronger interpersonal skills, provide opportunities to explore their role in political activity, develop tolerance, and create greater interest in current events, social studies, and social issues.

- Students need structured opportunities to clarify their own thinking before they engage in substantive classroom discussions.

- Cooperative learning strategies can be used for pre-discussion preparation.

- Teachers see many barriers to discussions of some current topics.

- Classroom discussions of historical issues may be easier to address than emotionally charged current issues.

- Being aware of their own approach to an issue being introduced for discussion will help teachers expand their use of the strategy.

- There are many persistent social issues that can be discussed in relation to many social studies courses.

- Experiences with classroom discussions in school contexts correlate with desirable citizenship traits in adult life.

- Several strategies can be used to harness the strong emotions elicited by some discussion topics.

- Thorough understanding of the formats of various types of questions will help students open discussions to conflicting views.

- Practice in developing questions that open controversy is necessary for young students.

- Students can be taught to ask guiding questions that will lead to analysis, synthesis, and evaluation during discussions.

- Classroom discussions can lead to social justice actions.

Weblinks

Using Visuals to Create Discussion with Students
This site gives users access to over 65 000 images depicting Canadian events, people, and places throughout history.
www.imagescanada.ca

Using Personal Stories to Instigate Classroom Dialogue
The Memory Project is a living history resource that connects students to the stories of Canadian war veterans.
www.thememoryproject.com

Using a Virtual Museum to Help Create Discussions on Historical Issues
This site provides teachers and students a virtual look into the Canadian history exhibition at the National Museum of Civilization.
www.civilization.ca/cmc/exhibitions/hist/canp1/canp1eng.shtml

Topics for Discussions on Early Civilizations
This site is an excellent resource explaining and depicting the lives of people in early civilizations.
http://ancienthistory.mrdonn.org/indexlife.html

World Cultures: Cultural Profiles Project
This site gives detailed, clear descriptions of various cultures from all over the world. The information includes family life, food, holidays, and sports and recreation.
www.cp-pc.ca/english

Chapter 13

Using Informational Text in the Social Studies Program

Learning Topics

- The Role of Non-Fiction Text in Social Studies
- Structure in Informational Texts
- Using Graphic Organizers
- Note Making and Other Text-Management Skills
- Using Historical Pictures
- Teaching Students to Use Charts, Graphs, and Graphics
- Illustrations and Text Interpretation
- The Role of Fictional Text: Perspective and Bias
- Selecting Text for Use in the Classroom

Historical photos help students picture life in an earlier period.

THE ROLE OF NON-FICTION TEXT IN SOCIAL STUDIES

Non-fiction text is a major source of knowledge in both the historical and geographical components of social studies in early elementary classrooms. However, for the most productive use of these texts to occur, students must be taught how to navigate their unique characteristics successfully. To support text knowledge in children, teachers need to understand the formats of *informational text*, as well as the more commonly used fictional text, and select it purposefully and with full awareness of the adjunctive skills that students will need to learn to use such text successfully. In the early primary grades, as students start to learn to read, the teacher's focus is on the skills related to learning to read. As students acquire these skills and develop increasing facility with reading, they are ready to begin to shift their reading role to that of "reading to learn" (Duke, 2000; Duke & Pearson, 2002; Hall et al., 2005; Williams et al., 2004). The skills of learning to read and reading to learn can progress in parallel once early print concepts are established.

Little comprehension is likely to result if an individual wanders aimlessly through a piece of text. Instead adequate comprehension is the product of a journey guided by a pre-specified destination. Like travelers, successful readers sometimes slow down or even stop, perhaps to think about something of interest. Like travelers, too, they may encounter problems that need to be remedied before their reading proceeds. Throughout all this, the destination—that is, the purpose of the reading—is not forgotten.

—*Durkin, 2004, p. 295*

Some predict that as much as 80 to 90 percent of the reading students do in the future will be informational text (Pike & Mumper, 2004). As greater access to household Internet becomes a reality and mobile sources of Internet become increasing common, we can anticipate a growing need for students to be able to manage informational text venues both in print and electronic form.

Most informational text shares characteristics that are somewhat predictable and can therefore be taught to young readers to help them understand what this type of text is likely to offer.

There are five elements that typically characterize informational text:

1. The author is clear about the purpose of the text.
2. The major ideas that will be provided by the text are outlined early in the introduction.
3. Supporting details are provided to clarify and exemplify the main ideas.
4. Text supports in the form of captions, pictures, charts, sketches, subheadings, and tables are included to support the main text and convey further information.
5. Vocabulary is specific to the topic and sometimes technical to the subject.

To make informational text fully accessible to young students, they will need to be exposed to many examples in different subject areas and have opportunities to see these text elements in operation. But several studies into the use of text types have shown us that teachers appear to avoid the use of informational text in many contexts (Donovan, 2001; Duke, 2003a). These researchers provide several possible reasons for this phenomenon:

- Teachers may lack familiarity with informational text.

- Teachers may be uncertain about how to support students' comprehension when they read informational text.

- Teachers may lack professional methods to teach specific comprehension strategies to students when they use informational text.

- Teachers may believe that students could not handle informational text.

- Teachers may believe that young children don't like informational text.

- Teachers may believe that young children should first learn to read then read to learn at about Grade 4.

Duke (2000) also found that informational text was in scarce supply in school classrooms, on classroom walls and displays, and in the school libraries, with particular scarcity noted in schools with low socio-economic demographics.

[E]lementary readers who understand text organizational structures typically find greater success in identifying important information and relationships between ideas.
—*Marinak & Gambrell, 2008*

Duke also found that the use of informational text in schools could be tracked historically. A school focus on classical literature in the late nineteenth century continued to influence the literature available in classrooms, with small impacts on the trend to the exclusive use of narrative fiction being evident after the First World War and again between 1950 and 1962 when schools focused attention on developmental reading in a wide variety of genres. Recent research (Duke, 2000; Duke & Pearson, 2002; Hall et al., 2005; Williams et al., 2004) suggests that students of all ages should engage in reading all types of text, including informational text. Exposure to all types of text correlates with gains in reading comprehension for both competent and struggling readers; students can learn to use what they know about the structure and formats of informational text in new contexts with new learning tasks, and informational text encourages motivation to read. Students as young as kindergarten age have shown a preference for informational text when choices are available (Pappas, 1993).

However, students are lacking adequate instruction in how to access informational text. At-risk readers are particularly sensitive to text structure and benefit from specific instruction in the characteristics and formats of informational text (Williams et al., 2005). Knowledge of the type of text students are encountering in relation to their social studies inquiries is a critical support to anticipating what the text will present and to surfacing text tackling strategies that the student may have acquired through explicit instruction. Pre-reading knowledge of the text type supports text predictability and comprehension during reading (Williams, 2005) and text structure knowledge does not appear to transfer across

Figure 13.1 Students' Self-Reports About Their Reading Practices

Age Levels of Students	Percentage Who Reported Reading Daily	Percentage Who Reported Reading for Enjoyment Rarely or Never
9 year olds	54%	20%
13 year olds	28%	36%
17 year olds	25%	47%
Source: Adapted from Campbell, Hombo, & Mazzeo, 2000.		

different text structures (Williams et al., 2005). This finding supports the explicit need to teach the structures of informational text in the social studies context.

In the last decade, studies have shown that young children read informational text on average 3.6 minutes a day! Students in low socio-economic contexts are less likely to read informational text, logging only 1.9 minutes of exposure to these formats each day (Duke, 2000).

Students also appear to decline in their enjoyment of reading as they age, even when they have competent reading skills (see Figure 13.1).

To reverse this trend, teachers need to provide explicit text instruction and opportunities to practise accessing informational text in all of its formats. The many benefits of teaching students to use informational text include

- increasing students' interest in learning (Harvey, 2002);
- improvements in literacy development (Duke, Bennett-Armistead, & Roberts, 2003);
- improved interest and skill in writing (Ray, 2004; Kamberelis, 1999; Purcell-Gates, 1988; Purcell-Gates, McIntyre & Freppon, 1995);
- improved text structure knowledge (Dymock, 2005; Moss, 2004);
- improved comprehension skills (Soalt, 2005);
- engagement in literature discussion (Stien & Beed, 2004; Yopp & Yopp, 2004);
- improved writing skills (Kern, Andre, Schilke, Barton, & McGuire, 2003);
- improved vocabulary knowledge (Dreher, 2003);
- transfer of text knowledge to new learning demands (Broer, Aarnoutse, Kievet & van Leeuwe, 2002; Palinscar & Duke, 2004);
- enhanced motivation to read (Pappas, 1993);
- stronger specialized vocabulary development (Duke & Kays, 1998);
- facility with a text format that is read widely in out of school contexts (Venezky, 1982); and
- the ability of young children to reenact nonfiction text as successfully as they do with fiction (Pappas, 1993).

Not all informational text is presented in purely one format. Some text samples may combine forms to change the distinguishing characteristics when text is presented as part narrative, part expository, or a mixture of both. By exposing students to all of the possible combinations of informational text, teachers can make the rich sources of information that are available in each format accessible to young students searching for social studies information. A challenge for teachers is to ensure that classroom reading selections include informational text. Most do not, and have been found to contain mostly story texts (Duke, 2000; Duke & Pearson, 2002; Hall et al., 2005; Williams et al., 2004) despite young students' overwhelming preference for non-fiction (85 percent). Children in classrooms where more informational text is available to them achieve the same levels of reading and writing as other children but are better writers of informational text, have fewer declines than other children in their attitudes toward recreational reading, and have higher reading comprehension (Duke, Martineau, Frank & Bennett-Armistead, 2003). The trend toward a correlation between higher achievement and facility with informational text is evident in older students as well as emerging readers (Bernhardt, Destino, Kamil, & Roderguez-Munoz, 1995).

In the primary/junior classroom, fiction and non-fiction/informational text both have a role in social studies. By knowing how and when to use informational text the teacher can ensure that social studies programs make the best possible use of both genres for students' learning benefit. Recent research into the use and impact of non-fiction in the classroom has highlighted the need to increase the amount of this genre in classrooms and improve the instruction that students receive in relation to the use of non-fiction/ informational text.

Teachers should utilize non-fiction in a sophisticated manner, recognizing the need to use non-fiction in conjunction with a variety of other fiction and non-fiction texts . . . . [and] be encouraged to integrate the use of fiction and non-fiction within a single instructional or content unit.

—Williams, 2009

The most effective teachers use a wide variety of literacy materials and integrate literacy content into all areas of instruction as they plan programs of study (Allington & Johnston, 2002; Pressley, Allington, Wharton-McDonald, Collins Block & Morrow, 2001).

STRUCTURE IN INFORMATIONAL TEXTS

Informational text has unique characteristics that differ significantly from the characteristics of fictional narrative text. Additionally, informational text that is presented in electronic formats has characteristics that are unique to electronic text, whether informational or fictional. We need to ensure that students are taught the skills they need to navigate for meaning when they use both print and electronic sources of informational text.

Students who can navigate for meaning using informational text will demonstrate a(n)

- knowledge of the structures and organization of informational text;
- recognition of the signal words that are used to transition within informational text;
- ability to use and/or create graphic organizers effectively to extract meaning and relationships from informational text;
- ability to understand a variety of graphic organizers used in informational text as support for content;
- understanding of the breadth of variety of forms taken by informational text;
- understanding of the predictable nature of informational text, as derived from the purposes of such text;
- ability to infer as well as extract literal information from text;
- ability to extend the text through inferences, connections, and conclusions;
- awareness of composition techniques and the use of literary devices;
- ability to make critical judgments related to the content of informational text;
- ability to determine how the context of word use influences meaning;
- ability to recall and retell the content of informational text; and
- ability to draw meaning about context from text-based features that occur outside of the main body of the text (e.g., titles, illustrations, graphic organizers, quotes, side bars).

Students' background knowledge will have an influence on how they perceive meaning in any type of text (Reynolds, 2002). The knowledge they acquire from reading an informational text is not totally dependent of what they read, but relies heavily on previous experience and how that experience leads them to interpret what they read and assign primacy to ideas embedded in what they read. The same informational passage may lead different students to different, but equally valid interpretations. Students may interpret different words to have totally different meanings that reflect their prior knowledge rather than the intention of the author. Reynolds explains that this phenomenon supports the interpretation that "reading comprehension is as much about integrating new information into what readers already know (their background knowledge) as it is about properly identifying words." This will be particularly true when an informational passage requires a great deal of inference and when the background experiences of students have been substantially different.

Multiple interpretations of text should be anticipated by teachers when text samples are used in multicultural contexts. Meaning making must be seen as an active process that will require students to construct meaning by applying their background knowledge to interpret new knowledge. When planning the use of informational text in social studies, teachers need to consider all of the possible variations in interpretation that might relate to each of the five features of such text. As well, they will need to remember that the context in which a word occurs will have an impact on how it is comprehended by students (Rayner & Polletsek, 1989) as well as on students' facility with text-based variables such as language conventions, the grammar of the surrounding words, and the meaning of related words.

Teachers' knowledge of the most commonly used structures of informational text will help them to prepare students to manage meaning making from these sources. The organizational logic of texts used in elementary resources commonly follows any of five possibilities: enumeration, time order, compare and contrast, cause and effect, or question and answer (Neufeld, 2005; Richgels, et al., 1987). The purposes of each of these types of texts and key signal words used by authors to provide structure within the text are outlined in Figure 13.2.

Many informational texts available as resources in the elementary context include text structures that combine these most commonly seen types within the treatment of a single topic. It is therefore necessary to teach students to monitor text structure changes within resource samples.

As well, informational text can be presented to the reader in either narrative format, with story qualities that serve to teach through examples that resonate with children, or through expository text that presents facts in more clinical formats, without the use of story to exemplify. By anticipating the type of text structure, and preparing readers with the skills to navigate each structure, teachers can ensure that the text type serves as an optimal resource. Ninety-five percent of websites are expository text (Williams, 2009) so this is a critical structure to teach young students to navigate. The characteristics of both narrative and expository text structures are identified and exemplified in Figure 13.3. (on pages 314–315) Using this chart, teachers can ensure that their classroom libraries contain text resources of both types to optimize students' exposure.

To assist students with the development of reading comprehension strategies to manage informational text, teachers can

- help students learn to decode words quickly and accurately; this will allow them to turn their cognitive attention to meaning making as they read new sources.

- surface prior knowledge about a topic as a pre-reading strategy to help students make connections to the text they are about to read;

- expose students to the use and development of many types of graphic organizers so that they learn to connect, dissect, infer, and exemplify;

- teach text structures so that students can anticipate text and focus greater attention on making meaning when they read;

- teach strategies for analyzing text strategically and critically; changing informational text to another format helps students sort the big ideas from text sources quickly and efficiently (e.g., change the text into a five-part cartoon strip);

Figure 13.2 Structures Within a Text

Text Type	Description of Structure	Key Signal Words Used by Authors to Provide Structure in This Type of Text	
Enumeration	Major ideas are supported by details and examples.	for instance for example to illustrate such as most important(ly)	in addition another furthermore as well first, second, etc.
Time Order/ Place Order	Major ideas are supported by details in a sequence.	at first next then later before after	when finally preceding following to the east (west, north, south) above below
Compare/ Contrast	The supporting details of two or more major ideas indicate how these concepts are similar or different.	but different from same as similar to as opposed to instead of in contrast with although	however compared with as well as both while neither . . . nor either . . . or
Cause and Effect	The supporting details give the causes of a major idea or the supporting details are the results pro-duced by the major idea.	because of as a result of in order to may be due to effects of therefore consequently for this reason	since if . . . then thus hence causing allow(ing) forming resulting from
Question and Answer	The major idea is posed as a question and supporting de-tails are found in the answer to the question.	question answer who? what? where? when? why? how?	Note: Any of these inter-rogative words could be paired with is/are, was/will, should/could/ought to

Source: Adapted from Marinak & Gambrell, 2008

Figure 13.3 Structured Formats of Non-Fictional Instructional Text

Descriptors	Narrative	Expository	Mixed/Hybrid (also referred to as "blended," "dual purpose," or multiple genre")
Definition	Story-like quality Clear beginning and end	Fact based Topic oriented Meant to be accessed in a non-linear manner;may contain some linear elements but these are secondary to the overall text	Has some features of both narrative and expository text Linear, continuous storyline Related information that can be accessed non-linearly Can contain multiple genres and storylines
Purpose	To tell a factual story by describing a sequence of events over time	To inform or describe Exposes ideas through 1. Description 2. Sequence 3. Comparison 4. Causality 5. Problem solving	To present text from multiple genres (e.g., narratives, speech balloons, author's notes, standalone facts)
Value to Students	■ Experience story in a linear, continuous manner ■ Supports instruction in content areas ■ Can provide read-alouds to launch units ■ Provides more depth than many textbooks ■ Familiar structure that is accessible to students ■ Allows a glimpse into another life ■ Exposes students to alternative points of view	Exposes students to four core features of expository text: 1. Introduction of topic 2. Description of topic's attributes 3. Expression of a topic's characteristic processes 4. A summary statement of the topic ■ Can serve as a model for students' writing ■ Offers interaction possibilities through digital text ■ Includes multimedia forms ■ Visually stimulating if in digital formats	■ Has appeal for both capable and struggling readers because it combines novelty and complexity ■ Reduces reading miscues and increases motivation to read ■ May challenge students' ability to differentiate between fiction and non-fiction ■ Exposes students to complexities within genres (e.g., periodicals as narrative non-fiction, exposition, and reference text) ■ Provides good models for student writing (e.g., newspapers) ■ Can increase adult use of newspaper text

Figure 13.3 (*Continued*)

			■ Exposes students to forms of writing that they may encounter regularly outside of school (e.g., posters, calendars, maps, brochures)
Books	Biographies	Procedural or how-to books	Cross-format books or series
	Historical diaries or memoirs	Encyclopedias	
	Informational storybooks	Nature identification books	
		Photography books	
Periodicals	Serial narratives	Almanacs	Magazines
			Newspapers
Other print-based materials		Brochures	Companion websites to print-based materials
		Maps	
		Calendars	
		Posters	
Websites	Blogs	Informational websites	
		Discussion boards	
Digital Books	Digital biographies or informational storybooks	Digital encyclopedia	Digitized cross-format books
Interactive Software		Reference software	Fact-based simulation games
		Interactive map programs	

Source: Adapted from Williams, 2009; Marinak & Gambrell, 2005.

■ teach students to ask questions at all levels of Bloom's Taxonomy and to structure answers that provide effective analysis, synthesis, and evaluation of ideas;

■ teach students to generate relevant criteria for assessing sources of information;

■ teach students to monitor their comprehension as they read, to skim read, and use strategies to re-read when comprehension lags;

■ teach students to generate text maps while reading to reconstruct the logic of text sources;

■ teach summary strategies (e.g., collect all opening sentences; collect key words; use who? where? when? why? what? and how? questions to create summaries);

■ use resources that
  ■ are written with coherence;
  ■ match the comprehension level of the readers;

- provide contextual background so that students' interpretations are accurate;

- provide support characteristics for the information through pictures, headings, captions, tables and graphs, summaries, pre-reading guides, and other graphic supports; and

- use well developed indices to allow students to search for single answers without reading extensively;

■ teach students to create and to deconstruct compound and compound-complex sentences; and

■ teach students to annotate and highlight important ideas in text as they read. (For example: Give students two colours of highlighter and photocopies of a text passage. Guide them to use one colour of highlighter to identify main ideas and the second colour to identify supporting details.)

Proficiency in comprehending informational text will help our students build the enduring skills they need to "read the world" and be successful in school, work, community, and everyday life.

—Marinak & Gambrell, 2008

When using text-structure strategies with students, it is necessary to teach strategies to approach each new structure. Students do not automatically transfer knowledge of how to approach one structure to another structure. A sample text map is shown in Figure 13.4. This requires teachers to analyze each type of text structure carefully to identify the necessary skills for students' instruction prior to reading.

Figure 13.4 Sample Text Map

"People in the Middle Ages were often known by their first name plus the name of the trade they practised. For example, John the butcher, John the blacksmith, and John the fisherman all lived in the same town. In time these names were shortened to John Butcher, John Smith, and John Fisher. Many people today have last names that began in the Middle Ages."

When young students are asked to explain what they have learned from this passage by creating a text map, their resulting text map might look like the sample below.

Names that reflected a person's occupation in the Middle Ages

Middle Ages Occupation	Changes to That Name Today
John the butcher	John Butcher
John the blacksmith	John Smith
John the fisherman	John Fisher

Source: Cruxton, J. Bradley (1998). *Discovering Castle Days*. Oxford University Press Canada. Don Mills, Ontario: 44.

Figure 13.5 Sample Graphic Organizers

Type of Text	Suitable Graphic Organizers
Enumeration	lists
Time Order	timelines (pictorial or numerical)
Place Order	maps
Compare/Contrast	Venn diagrams
	T-charts
	comparison charts
Cause/Effect	if . . . then arrows
Question/Answer	various structures that guide students' attention to the required parts of the answer

USING GRAPHIC ORGANIZERS

Graphic organizers include any type of visual representation of information presented through text. When they are applied to informational text sources, the organizers that will be most useful to young readers are those that mirror the most common text structures experienced in the sources of informational text used by them. Sample connecting words used in each of these types of text are provided in Figure 13.2 (page 313).

Figure 13.5 provides samples of graphic organizers applicable to each of these types of texts.

Question/answer organizers are critical supports for teaching young readers to address the specifics that are asked in a question. Without the support of a graphic organizer to help structure an answer, many students will see one aspect of what a question asks and neglect the second or third parts of the question.

Example

"What types of homes and farm implements were used by early prairie pioneers in Canada?"

Many students will explain the types of homes used by pioneers then move on to the next question or activity. With the support of a graphic organizer that guides the components of their answer, students are able to see the elements that are required in responses.

What types of homes and farm implements were used by early prairie pioneers in Canada?	
Homes	
Farm implements	

Students' perceptions of themselves as readers are positive in early primary grades but decline in higher grades, even when students can read (Chapman & Tunmer, 1997; McKenna et al., 1995; Wigfield et al., 1997). These consistent research findings should direct our attention to teaching students to feel positive and accomplished when they read for information. Strategies that challenge and reward achievement will help students reap the rewards of reading effectively. Students also experience stronger achievement in their reading abilities if they have balanced opportunities to read stories, magazines, and information books (Campbell, Kapinus & Beatty, 1995). We can support their access to these books by teaching students to use a breadth of graphic organizers to support their comprehension and connection making as they tackle new formats of text.

As we increase the amount of informational text used in classrooms, a parallel use of graphic organizers to help students comprehend and connect ideas from information will be needed. Teachers will need to teach students to take gradual responsibility for developing suitable graphic organizers for the text samples they read. This will happen as students experience more informational text as classroom resources but must be structured by the teacher so that students learn the skills involved in creating appropriate organizers for the types of text they use (see Figure 13.6).

Several pre-reading, during-reading, and after-reading strategies can be used in primary and junior classrooms that will support students' manipulation of the content of informational text and their ability to construct and complete appropriate graphic organizers to sort the content they have read.

Graphic organizer use can become part of each of these strategies:

- Build the graphic organizer in teams from concrete material options available to the reading groups.

- Use Reader's Theatre approaches that require students to transfer content to broadcasting prompters (via PowerPoint) that support their radio-style broadcast of the new information.

- Use idea circles that start with each student reading and presenting a graphically organized summary of their resource, and allow students jigsaw opportunities with multiple perspectives.

- Start an inquiry by requiring a resource summary in graphic format.

- Use Internet sources and have students summarize new ideas using computer graphics to create their graphic organizer.

- Expand students' opportunities to use graphic organizers through the expansion of the classroom library to include a broad range of information texts.

Electronic text requires special instructional attention. Electronic text challenges students' understanding because it provides new text formats, with new purposes, and new ways to interact with the information in the text. These three conditions require different skills from young readers and require different classroom instruction to help readers negotiate this text type. Internet searches for information often challenge the student to

Figure 13.6 Teaching Students to Use Graphic Organizers

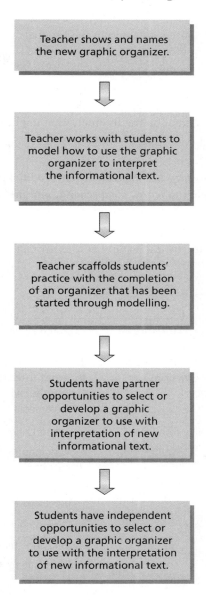

find quick and specific references for precise information requirements. This has been referred to as "snatch and grab" use of text (Sutherland-Smith, 2002). The different comprehension demands of electronic text require that students be taught new text-management skills.

Coiro (2003) suggests that teachers consider four questions when planning to engage students in the use of electronic text:

1. Is the comprehension process different on the Internet?
2. If so, what new thought processes are required beyond those needed to comprehend conventional print?
3. Are these processes extensions of traditional comprehension skills, or do web-based learning environments demand fundamentally different skills?
4. If comprehension is different on the Internet, what implications do these differences have for comprehension instruction and assessment?

Today the definition of literacy has expanded from traditional notions of reading and writing to include the ability to learn, comprehend, and interact with technology in a meaningful way.

—*Coiro, 2003*

Figure 13.7 compares the typical features of Internet text with those of conventional, linear print text:

Figure 13.7 Linear Print vs. Electronic Text

	Characteristics of Conventional Linear Print Text Interactions	Characteristics of Typical Electronic Text Found on the Internet Interactions
Characteristics of Text Features	Linear	■ Includes hypertext and interactive multimedia
Skills Required of the Reader	Ability to create personal meaning from linear information	■ Recognizing new purposes for writing ■ Acquiring new types of background knowledge ■ Using high-level metacognitive processes to evaluate text
Responses to Text	Linear	■ Publishing multimedia projects ■ Verifying credibility of images ■ Participating in online synchronous exchanges
Social Interactions Required	Can complete reading in isolation	■ Includes many collaborative opportunities for sharing and responding to information
Locations	Isolated	■ Can share and respond to information across continents, cultures, and languages

Figure 13.7 (*Continued*)

	Characteristics of Conventional Linear Print Text Interactions	**Characteristics of Typical Electronic Text Found on the Internet Interactions**
Features	Controlled reading level Print and pictures	■ Variety of reading levels ■ Print and two-dimensional graphics including icons, animated symbols, sound, photographs, cartoons, ads, audio and video clips, virtual-reality experiences, and unfamiliar combinations of font size, layout, colour, and positioning ■ May include comments in other languages
Purposes for Reading	Well defined purposes for reading, reading processes (linguistic and semantic processing and monitoring), and activities to respond to the reading	■ May include new social action purposes for the reading and calls for social action in authentic responses required after reading ■ Resource surveying (e.g., web quests, manipulating electronic databases, using multiple search engines, navigating hierarchical subject guides, online dialogue journals, real-time chats, electronic whiteboard exchanges, video conferences) ■ Wide variety of inquiry approaches may be needed to apply site information to tasks
Responses to Reading	Answering literal questions Writing reports	■ High levels of thinking ■ Collaborative problem solving ■ New research roles to detect, investigate, experiment, role-play ■ Creating text for others to respond to ■ Recognizing commercial propaganda and bias ■ Discerning fact from opinion and truth from fiction

Where traditional print text varies in the features of the genres, structures, reading levels, and subject matter, these features are compounded by the non-linear structure of electronic formats. The variety in story formats that are available electronically creates further challenges for the young reader because text types will often be unfamiliar and evolve constantly.

Students can be supported in their exploration and use of both traditional and electronic text by being taught to consider seven habits of mind that can be applied to either print or electronic sources. Habits of mind (Brunner & Tally, 1999) can be taught to young readers as questions that support metacognitive awareness of strategy application. The questions include the following:

1. What perspective of reality is being presented?
2. What explicit or hidden values underlie this text?
3. What media conventions are used in this text?
4. How do the media conventions shape the way the information is interpreted?
5. Who is the intended audience?
6. How might different audiences interpret the text?
7. Who owns the text? Who benefits from it?

Without adequate preparation to use electronic text sources, they can frustrate and confuse readers because so many choices, features, and animations can distract and disorient them (Delaney & Landow, 1991; Eagleton & Guinee, 2002). Electronic experiences in the classroom are further complicated because students do not share common backgrounds in their access and previous experience with electronic media. The rapid expansion of new forms of electronic literacy requires that teachers continue to model the effective use of these technologies. Explicit instruction in the strategies that will help students use these new sources of informational text will be critical to their successful integration into the classroom.

NOTE MAKING AND OTHER TEXT-MANAGEMENT SKILLS

Teaching students to make effective and efficient notes when they use either print or electronic sources of information is an essential role of the social studies teacher. Increasingly, as the range and accessibility of sources of information expands, teaching note making includes the skill of prioritizing information. The proliferation of sources through electronic access requires that students develop their ability to

- narrow the scope of their research through well-defined inquiry questions;
- narrow the sources of information they search;
- be aware of the types of sources most applicable to social studies topics; and
- scan, select, and discard sources quickly and efficiently.

Note-making tasks will be facilitated by clearly defined research tasks. Such tasks may be teacher imposed or reflect the interests of individual students or small groups. Pre-research organization of tasks using graphic organizers will save time, focus attention, and reduce frustration for learners.

When using either print resources or electronic sources, students should be taught a wide variety of note-making strategies. A sample of text from the resource *Medieval Minds: Britain 1066-1500* (Byrom, Counsell, & Riley, 1997) is provided below. Using this text as an example, consider how you might teach students several note making strategies:

FACT 1: POWERFUL TOWNS By the fourteenth century there were about 90 towns in Wales. These towns were very small but very important. Important townsmen (or burgesses) held law courts, made rules, and had all sorts of trading privileges, just as in English towns. Many burgesses were extremely rich. They owned a lot of land in the countryside around the town. They often controlled all the trading activity in the area around the town. The burgesses of Carmarthen controlled all the trade within a 15-mile radius.

FACT 2: POWERFUL TOWNSPEOPLE (WELSH . . . AND ENGLISH!) Welsh towns were not exactly like English towns. Some of the important townspeople were Welsh. Others were English. In some parts of Wales, the towns were more English than in others. Sometimes when the Welsh townspeople were very rich the English townspeople were very jealous. This happened more and more in the late fourteenth century. In some towns, the English tried to strengthen their control by reviving old laws against the Welsh (or by making new ones). In 1393, a new statement was included in the town charter of St. Clears: "No burgess must be judged by any Welshman . . . but only by English burgesses and true Englishmen."

FACT 3: DIFFICULT TIMES FOR TOWNS Taxes were high all over England and Wales. English kings needed a lot of money for all those wars. This was bad enough, but it came at a time when the Black Death had made life very hard. Earlier in the century, lots of people died from the Black Death. This made trading difficult. Sometimes when times are hard, people become more competitive. They try to protect their own privileges and keep others out.

Using the following note-making strategies will help students navigate text types and build a repertoire of strategies that are useful with many text samples:

- Recognizing the text type
- Connecting the titles and subtitles within the text to map the story structure
- Highlighting main ideas and supporting details
- Monitoring opening sentences
- Numbering when a series of ideas is enumerated

- Making margin notes

- Using electronic markup tools

- Looking for standard questions to be answered or not answered (e.g., What's there? What's not there? Who? Where? When? Why? What? How? or the questions of topic elaboration [See Chapter 1])

- Changing the format of the print to another means of communicating (e.g., a poem or picture)

- Using a KWL (Know, Want to Know, and Learned) chart or a modified KWL chart (see Figure 13.8) for older students (e.g., What I think I know, Confirmed, Misconceptions, New Findings, Wondering About)

- Creating an interactive response

The gradual development of these skills through the primary and junior grades supports students' abilities to make notes from all text sources.

USING HISTORICAL PICTURES

Printed and electronic pictures and paintings that are available online and through historical archives and other sources to support learning about social studies concepts and events are prolific. These can be valuable sources of information because they support learning through visual learning styles and can enrich text sources. They provide variety and are a technique for creating interest through stories and personal connections. Pictures and paintings can elicit powerful emotional responses from students and can enliven abstract concepts. They also provide venues for young learners to practise question-asking skills because they provide rich sources of detail in easily accessed formats.

Figure 13.8 Rethinking the KWL Chart: Reading and Analyzing Non-Fiction

Questions	Inquiry Responses
What do I think I know about this topic?	
How sure am I? Why?	
What has my research confirmed about this topic?	
What misconceptions did I have about this topic?	
What new things did I find out about this topic?	
What do I still wonder about/want to find out about this topic?	
Source: Adapted from Stead, 2006.	

Pictures and paintings can be acquired through the following sources:

- ads
- art books
- museum archives
- art collections
- brochures
- calendars
- CD-ROM encyclopedias
- commercial photo sources

- documentaries
- family albums
- governmental agencies
- magazines
- movies
- National Film Board of Canada
- newspapers

- personal photo collections
- posters
- provincial archives
- textbooks
- tourist keepsakes
- videos
- virtual museums
- web quest sites

However, it is important to teach students to use visual resources with knowledge of the conditions and techniques that may have caused any alteration of the message they convey related to the historical and geographic reality.

While photographs may not lie, liars may photograph.

—Hine, as quoted in Everett-Green (1996)

Visual sources of information may be inaccurate because they may be staged to convey a particular message, may depict something that is assumed to be typical of a time or place when the image in fact has captured a unique circumstance, may be altered for an unknown purpose, or may be cropped to exclude some relevant aspects of the context that could cause misinterpretation of events or circumstances (Clark, 1999). Students need to learn that these approaches will have a profound influence on the impressions and overt messages portrayed in visual images. As well, students should come to understand that the state of the technology for creating visual resources in any time period has limitations that may have caused alterations in the overall impact of the resource. For example, early photography required subjects to stay perfectly still so pictures may appear to be unnaturally "stiff" and formal.

The camera can create its own reality.

—Clark, 1999

Once students learn to look for the photographer in the photograph and the painter in the painting, they can become reflective and critical evaluators of these resources and can use them as supplementary sources for text. Visual images can provide a rich source of detail for social studies but must be introduced with both caution and skill. Students need to be taught to interrogate the representation of reality that each presents. Some sources of visual images may be accompanied by captions and it is important to question the role of the caption in the creation of the overall impression of the image and to ask *why* creators chose *that* caption. Students must also come to understand the historical practices of access to having your picture taken. They should learn to question what is excluded from paintings and photographs in the historical context of times when women and minorities were underrepresented in accounts of momentous historical occasions.

Students will also need instruction in how to look closely for detail in historical visual representations. They can be taught to use small frames and ruler edges to narrow the parts of larger pictures and paintings they are examining so that they can focus on small but significant details. Movies and videos provide valuable resources to allow students to imagine realistic action in historical context. Opportunities to recreate such actions in drama, tableaux, or diorama format help students to process and attend to the details they observe in visual resources. Magnifying glasses and zoom features of computers allow students to investigate closely and look for symbols and patterns.

Clark (1999) provides valuable guidance about the characteristics for visual artifacts that should be examined by students when they use these resources to reconstruct evidence. Clark suggests that students be taught to consider the photographer's or painter's treatment of the subject, the lighting, the framing of the subject, and the focus of a picture to determine aspects of the context that may not be evident through casual inspection of the picture.

When video sources are used to exemplify historical or geographical concepts, Clark suggests a thorough examination of the aspects of production to determine the bias and perspective of the creator(s) (see Figure 13.9).

Figure 13.9 Determining Bias and Perspective

Criteria Used to Determine the Message of a Visual Resource	Questions/Ideas that Should Be Asked/Focused to Interrogate the Message under the Surface of the Visual Resource
Dialogue	Identify use and reuse of value-laden words.
Actors	Identify stereotypical representations of characters.
	Identify racial generalizations or misrepresentations (by inclusion or absence).
Character development	Identify generalizations and stereotypical portrayals.
Colour and lighting	Identify how lighting is used to affect impressions and the viewer's mood.
Music	Identify how music adds to overall impressions.
	Identify how volume is used for effect.
Camera angle and choice of shot	How is perspective created? Whose view is behind the camera? Does this change within the piece of work?
Selection and arrangement of scenes	Whose viewpoint is represented? How and when does that change? Which view is dominant?
Overall impression	What message is being presented by the developer of the resource?

Source: Adapted from Clark, 1999.

Historical images are often used in "before–after" approaches to examine what has happened to a particular location over time. This approach can provide comparative data that reveals a great deal about the development of communities and their histories.

Kirman (2008; adapted) provides a series of questions that can be adapted to different age groups to guide their examination of visual resources for comparative purposes (see below). These general questions can guide discussion and inquiry using photographs and digital images.

- How has the scene changed?
- Is the scene better or worse? How?
- What common elements appear in both photographs?
- What elements appear in the "now" photograph that could not have been present in the "then" photograph?
- What might have been done differently over time to develop this area more effectively? Why?
- What lifestyle does each photograph represent? What evidence is there?
- What environmental considerations are evident in each photograph?

Using historical photos allows students to analyze existing landforms critically.

- What machinery/technology is evident in each photograph?
- What cultural sensitivities are evident in each photograph (i.e., things that would not happen today or in the historical photo)?
- What trends are evident in comparing the photos?

The careful use of visual resources can help students learn that visual sources may lead to misinterpretations of historical information because of the preparation and presentation techniques used by developers. This tension between text and visual artifacts presents unique interpretive challenges for historical inquiry.

Computer technology allows us to use visual images in the classroom as both artifacts for analysis and as student-created products that can represent students' understanding of historical and geographical concepts. Capture technology for video and photo on modern computers makes access to visual images to demonstrate ideas readily available for teacher or student use.

TEACHING STUDENTS TO USE CHARTS, GRAPHS, AND GRAPHICS

Visual representations that can be achieved through the use of charts, graphs, and graphics support many learning-style preferences and provide variations on text information. In inquiry, charts, graphs, and graphics support what students have found, and allow them to present their findings in unique and visually appealing and accessible ways. Students need to be taught how to read and interpret these displays and how to create them to demonstrate their own learning.

Students at all grades can be taught to use the computer as a learning tool to create products quickly and easily. A broad range of programs is available in many formats to support the creation of computer-generated charts, graphs, and graphics. Young students should have many opportunities to explore the capacity of these programs to supplement their understanding of data management in social studies. Reading comprehension skills need to expand to include new literacies that engage the capacity of powerful software programs that can represent data management and manipulation for analysis.

As well, students will need to be taught to read and interpret information presented in traditional print text in chart, graph, or graphic formats. By teaching these skills to students, we expand their capacity to make connections, look for patterns, and determine correlations and causality.

Teachers should take opportunities to integrate mathematics concepts in social studies so that the study and use of charts, graphs, and graphics is integrated and applications of mathematics concepts can be seen in social studies topics.

In primary grades, tally charts in either picture or symbol format can be the starting point for learning about graphing in simple bar graph formats. As children's skills with graphic concepts evolve through exposure and practice, graphing in complex formats can be used. Students can learn to apply double and triple bar graphs to comparative data, generate line graphs to demonstrate change over time, and develop pie graphs to represent proportions. Many provincial and territorial guidelines provide direction for the gradual evolution and introduction of different types of charts, graphs, and graphics in different grades.

Children need to be taught the skills of charting and graphing by moving from the initial exposure and naming of the visual format to

- reading the data in charts, tables, and graphs;
- interpreting overall meaning from charts, tables, and graphs;
- practising collecting data and charting it;
- creating tables to relate data;
- creating simple bar graphs;
- creating more complete charts and graphs to compare and proportion data; and
- identifying misleading data presented in charts, tables, graphs, and graphics.

Through early and progressive practice with data displays through charts, graphs, and graphics, young students can learn to use this form of communication with competence and ease. Software programs make it particularly appealing and easy to develop charts, graphs, and graphics.

ILLUSTRATIONS AND TEXT INTERPRETATION

Illustrations have two roles in a social studies context. They can support text meaning in sources being used by students during inquiry and they can be used by students to demonstrate their understanding of a topic or idea they have been investigating. Whether illustrations are used for exploration or expressive purposes, students will need to be taught techniques for using illustrations fruitfully.

Illustrations that support text ideas will usually be either historical interpretations or caricatures. Students will need opportunities to study the techniques of both genres. The subtleties of caricature may be very difficult for young children to understand but assistance with examining several examples and noting trends and techniques will support their growing awareness.

Students will need to be taught how to understand and contextualize the captions that will appear with either historical or caricature illustrations. The concept of speech bubbles may be new to some groups so exposure to using them by reading cartoons or using electronic cartoon-making software will help to develop their awareness of how speech bubbles work. When captions are cryptic comments below an illustration, students will need to consider questions such as

- Why did the author choose this illustration to support this text?
- What does it add to the overall message in the text?
- What bias or point of view is presented in the caption? In the illustration?

- What does the author of this illustration and caption want me to believe? Do I agree? Why? Why not?
- What background information do I need to understand this?

Understanding illustrations that support instructional text will help students construct meaning from this type of text.

When illustrations are used to help students demonstrate their understanding of informational text, their developing awareness of this approach can be supported by many opportunities to make books in various formats including flip books, comic strips, film sequences through electronic means, and big book creations. The creation of captions that capture the meaning of illustrations in pithy and concise ways will need to be modelled and practised as students are exposed to increasingly sophisticated contexts.

THE ROLE OF FICTIONAL TEXT: PERSPECTIVE AND BIAS

Fictional text has a role in teaching social studies concepts to young children. Fictional sources help them to imagine situations and experiences that they can relate to through parallel experiences and through structured contrasts. The challenge for users of fictional text is to ensure that students understand such text is fictional. Textbooks, expository writing, historical documents, and graphic information in various forms will also present challenges related to perspective and bias that should be detected by the reader. While fictional text may illustrate possibilities that can enliven the study of social studies and create empathy and connections through story, it may also contain many inaccurate depictions that are softened deliberately to make the text palatable for the intended age group.

By understanding the role of both fiction and non-fiction text (see Figure 13.10) in the contributions that can be made to a thorough social studies program, teachers can help students benefit from the richness of both forms of text, whether samples are accessed in print or electronic formats. Many samples of fictional text that can support social studies for young students are provided in Chapter 9.

Historical fiction sources should always be examined by the teacher to uncover the perspective and hidden bias attendant in the text. These features should then be taught to students so they learn to be critical consumers of fictional sources and to understand the impact and intent of both fictional and informational text.

Figure 13.10 Comparison of the Value of Non-Fiction and Fiction Text Sources Used in Social Studies

Value of Non-Fiction (Informational) Text	Value of Fictional Text
Can be used as read-aloud material.	Can be used as read-aloud material.
Can launch a unit of study by creating interest in uncovering further facts about the topic.	Can launch a unit of study by creating empathy for fictional characters and sympathy for their predicaments.
Provides deeper treatment of topics than is typically available in textbooks.	Provides intense and emotionally based treatment of topics, which is another way of connecting than is typically available in most textbooks.
The language of narrative non-fiction/informational text is familiar and comfortable for students.	Students enjoy stories and can access the books independently if the reading level is targeted for their skills.
Biographies appeal to students' sense of curiosity but may be written outside of their reading level for instructional independence.	Fictional characters can be involved in circumstances that are somewhat recognizable for students; the familiar context of the story allows students to stretch beyond their usual instructional level with informational text because the motivational power of story is engaging.
Provides opportunities to examine historical events through alternative points of view.	May soften historical events to create less graphic detail for the consumption of young readers.

SELECTING TEXT FOR USE IN THE CLASSROOM

When planning units of social studies, teachers will need to examine the resources that are available for the topic, both in the many forms of print text and in electronic forms. Text should be considered at two levels:

1. Instructional level—What level and type of print can students learn to use now with full support to help them decode text, understand format, and make meaning?

2. Independent level—What level and type of print can students use independently with decoding success, an understanding of format features, and the ability to make meaning?

Teachers should investigate strategies to determine the instructional levels of texts. Primary students are often taught the "five finger rule." This strategy allows young students to count, using five fingers, the words on a page that cause recognition or comprehension problems and to abandon text as too difficult if they encounter more than five unfamiliar words on a page.

Instructional-level text will be more difficult for students to use and will require ongoing guidance to enable students to use it successfully. The features of each level of text sources should be examined carefully to determine what prior teaching might be needed to ensure success when students access each resource. Some jurisdictions will require that teachers receive approval from school authorities to use some text sources. Teachers will need to investigate related local policies.

Teachers can also support text use by homogenous grouping of students. This will help students get to know the strategies used by successful readers and provide peer support for their initial attempts at research. When using Internet text sources, teachers can narrow the accessible sites to make available only those sites that have been vetted for their readability. Additionally, teachers can provide access to the widening range of text-reading software available to schools. This software is becoming easier to use and can readily provide students with oral reading in a range of voices to give them auditory support as they read print or online text.

Each strategy benefits from being interactive and encouraging students to work on ideas as they read.

INNOVATIVE APPROACHES IN YOUR SOCIAL STUDIES CLASSROOM

Processing ideas that are presented in informational text can be challenging for young students. By providing students with interactive strategies to support text processing, teachers can help students build their confidence and their ability to synthesize ideas.

Samples of strategies for achieving student comfort with processing ideas from informational text include

- limiting responses;
- inside-outside circles;

- newspaper headlines; and
- "steal one."

While many other approaches may also support these abilities, these four approaches will be explained as examples.

Limiting Responses When we ask students to make notes about something they have read, many students are challenged to determine what to include and what to leave out. It is helpful to students if they are limited to a certain number of points (three, for example) about the selection's message. This forces the students to synthesize information and to relate ideas to each other. Typically, students will formulate compound and complex sentences that connect ideas because they want to include more thoughts than the allowed number of points.

Inside-Outside Circles Inside-outside circles is a cooperative learning structure that can be used at all phases of reading—pre-reading, during reading, and after reading. Students form two circles with one outside of the other. The inside circle faces out and the outside circle faces inward. At a signal, the students facing each other start to discuss what they are about to read, are in the middle of reading, or have finished reading. Then, after a signal, one circle rotates to face a new partner and they continue discussion. This continues until enough discussion has taken place to reach the teacher's goal. Students return to their seats and reflect on new ideas they have discovered through discussion.

Newspaper Headlines Once students have completed a selection of reading, they are challenged to write a one-line headline to capture the main ideas of what they have read. They find a partner (or work in an inside-outside circle) to share the meaning of their headline with other students.

"Steal One" This strategy can be used between students or between the teacher and the student. While reading a text, students (and the teacher) can record main ideas from the text on individual sticky notes. After reading, give students a brief period of time to circulate and record ideas they observe in other students' (or the teacher's) sticky notes and "steal" ideas to record on their own sticky notes. After a set period of time (one minute, for example) all students return to their desks and continue developing main idea notes on their stickies, newly energized by their excursion and interactions with other students. A discussion about the accuracy or comparison of details could follow students' excursions.

CASE STUDIES AND PROFESSIONAL ACTIVITIES FOR INNOVATION IN SOCIAL STUDIES

1. Ms. Richards is examining textbook possibilities for the coming school year. Brainstorm a list of criteria she should consider for making this decision.

2. Create a web quest that could be used to have students explore at least three Internet sites to investigate a topic. Provide guidance that will help students start by narrowing a question for their research.

3. Examine an Internet site that will provide promising support for students' research of a topic. Deconstruct the site requirements in terms of students' informational text skills and identify all of the text management skills that you will need to teach your students before they can use this site effectively.

4. Create a collection of photographs that can be used to support the study of a topic. Write the main ideas you want students to learn from the artifact on the back of each photograph. Continue this archiving of historical photos as a professional collection to support your social studies reference collection.

5. Start a collection of examples of graphic organizers you have used or seen other teachers use in social studies. For each example, show how you might adapt the organizer to improve its usefulness to students.

CHAPTER REVIEW AND PROFESSIONAL DEVELOPMENT AS A TEACHER

This chapter has examined the following:

- Informational text comes in many different formats that must be taught to students.

- Text becomes a source of learning when students can read to construct meaning.

- Eighty to ninety percent of the reading students will do in the future will involve informational text.

- Informational text is in both print and electronic formats. Students must be taught to use both formats.

- Informational text in any format shares some characteristics related to its purpose, sequencing of ideas, the support characteristics of its presentation, and vocabulary characteristics.

- There are many reasons why teachers may avoid the appropriate use of informational text in the classroom.

- Informational text sources are relatively scarce in classrooms and school libraries.

- Exposure to informational texts of all types correlates with gains in reading comprehension.

- Students prefer informational text when choice is given.

- Students benefit from instruction about the structure of informational text, to support comprehension while reading.

- There are many motivational and learning advantages to having students engage in explicit instruction about accessing informational text.

- Informational text can be presented in many combinations of narrative and expository text so exposure to the possible combinations will be valuable to learners.
- Children who are exposed to instruction about informational text are better writers of informational text and otherwise match their peers in reading and writing achievement.
- Informational text has unique and distinct characteristics. Some characteristics typify electronic sources.
- Previous experience influences how students perceive meaning in texts. Meaning making is an active, constructive process.
- There are five most commonly used informational text structures in elementary contexts: enumeration, time/place order, compare and contrast, cause and effect, and question/answer.
- Students should be taught to monitor text structure changes as they read.
- The characteristics of narrative, expository, and hybrid/mixed text structures are identifiable.
- Several reading comprehension strategies can help students to manage informational text productively.
- Students will not automatically transfer knowledge of one text structure to their use of another text structure. Each text structure variation must be explicitly taught.
- Graphic organizers support text structure comprehension.
- Question and answer structures require clear guidance from teachers to help students learn to organize clear responses.
- The use of graphic organizers to reconstruct meaning needs to be taught explicitly and practised frequently.
- Accessing informational text through electronic sources requires special instructional attention because of the non-linear nature of electronic text.
- Seven "habits of mind" questions can be used by students to interrogate their comprehension of informational text in both print and electronic formats.
- Note-making skills need to be taught explicitly.
- Historical pictures support informational text and provide valuable additional information and opportunities to make connections and meaning.
- Visual images must be examined critically and in the context of the time they were created.
- Photographs have unique compositions that can both reveal and conceal messages consistent with the photographer's intentions.
- Hand-produced and computer-generated charts, graphs, and graphics should be explicitly taught to students and their interpretation and development practised in both contexts.

- Illustrations can support social studies learning as both artifacts to explore and as a means of expressing learning and understanding.

- Captioning should be taught when examining visual resources within text.

- Fictional text can help students relate to historical or geographical contexts but must be taught with sensitivity to its perspectives and biases.

- Several criteria should be considered by the teacher to guide the selection of text sources for student use.

Professional Development Opportunities

1. Work in a small group to identify three or four new strategies you could use to motivate students to use informational text sources effectively. Be ready to demonstrate your strategy to your colleagues.

2. Examine a randomly selected paragraph from a social studies text resource. In that sample paragraph, analyze the text features that may cause comprehension challenges for some students (e.g., unfamiliar concepts, polysyllabic words, complex sentence constructions, interrelated ideas). Rewrite that paragraph so that the same ideas are more readily accessible to students who would struggle with the reading level of the original text.

3. Examine sources of software to read printed text to students. Consider ways you might use this software in your social studies program to make some resources more readily available to weaker readers in your classroom.

Weblinks

Ideas Dealing with Photography in Lessons
This site provides plans and ideas for teachers who want to include the use of photography in their classes.
www.kodak.com/global/en/consumer/education/lessonPlans/indices/art.shtml

Ideas for Teaching Media Literacy
This site promotes critical thinking and information literacy through media.
www.mediaawareness.ca

Let's Book It with Tech'Knowledge'y—Making Books with Children
These sites provide a variety of templates for bookmaking to promote literacy.
www.vickiblackwell.com/makingbooks.html
www.makingbooks.com/freeprojects.shtml

The Official Flat Stanley project
Flat Stanley is a symbol of a male person who has been flattened to be able to go into an envelope, enabling him to travel around the world and have many unique experiences.
www.flatstanleyproject.com

Webquest
This site provides current information about creating inquiry-oriented lessons.
wwwww.webquest.org

Chapter 14
Working with Maps in an Inquiry Context

Learning Topics:

- The Role of Map and Globe Skills
- Problem-Based Learning Using Maps
- Teaching Map and Globe Skills
- Electronic Mapping Systems
- Mapping Symbols for Classroom Display

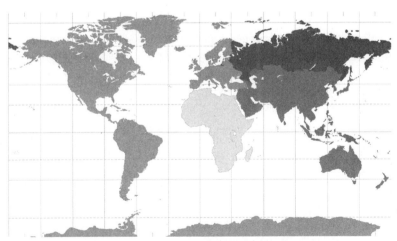

Maps are an important resource for inquiry in social studies.

The problem-based learning environment transcends disciplinary boundaries by placing the problem (rather than the discipline) at the center of the learning environment.

—*Drennon, 2005*

THE ROLE OF MAP AND GLOBE SKILLS

Chapter 4 examined several approaches to teaching map making to young children when investigating the topic elaboration question, *What are its interesting characteristics?* This chapter will provide a framework for considering types of map and globe skills that should be taught in the primary and junior grades.

Many teachers in elementary classrooms have had very little exposure and training in the use of maps and globes in their own background. Some jurisdictions in Canada do not require geography qualifications beyond early secondary grades for graduation so recent exposure may be limited to use of maps for historical purposes. This makes having some broad conceptions about the role of maps and globes in elementary social studies instruction critical for teachers so that they can make appropriate and informed choices about map and globe work to support their social studies courses in the primary and junior grades.

Often, classroom uses of maps and globes in social studies have failed to extend students' thinking to examine the assumptions, perspectives, biases, and beliefs inherent in these representations of reality. Alan Morantz (2002) explains that maps "are windows on worldviews, assumptions, and dreams . . . mirrors of the best and worst in human nature." He points out that maps have been made and used to show vested interests as history has evolved.

Maps can be used in both the historical and geographical aspects of social studies programs to promote inquiry when they are subjected to the same scrutiny and critical stance as other resources. They can help learners understand differing perspectives, make connections between people and places and past and present, consider future possibilities, think critically, situate themselves geographically and socially, and consider our societal identity in relation to where we are geographically and in relation to other places that influence our location.

Ideally, maps should support the inquiry-focused approach to classroom investigations in social studies. Teachers should examine maps critically and interrogate what they present as granted. They should consider how maps create opportunities to mislead viewers, or misrepresent reality for the map creator's purposes. Learning about maps should include opportunities to examine historical misuses of maps for power or monetary gain. Teachers can support students' developing analytical skills in relation to maps by using these approaches.

The concept of *carto-controversy* guides teachers to include examination of the use of maps in historical contexts to ensure that part of our social studies courses consider the purposes of historical and contemporary maps. Many early maps of Canada were made for economic purposes to name and claim territory related to the fur trade. These purposes made the perspective on maps slanted to the potential of the land to yield furs. Naming territories with little European settlement in them also provided a way for explorers to attempt to legitimize their claims to spaces. This approach has had far-reaching consequences that still influence Canada's development today as Native land claims are established where early map makers created claims across traditional lands.

Maps represent the elements of space and time in relation to human development. These elements change and shift as society evolves. Hurren (2004) says, "[N]either space nor identity is seen as a static entity. Each is always in process: space changes over time (who uses the space, how it is used) and identity changes over time (often as a result of the particular spaces we inhabit or frequent)." These are elements that students should have opportunities to examine and consider as they work with maps.

As we expose students to working with maps that have been created for different purposes, we also need to expose them to examining the tendency of maps used in isolation to make issues and conflicts represented by the completed maps seem like sanitized and finalized entities. Students should have opportunities to use maps in conjunction with other sources that would allow them to consider how the map evolved, what social issues influenced the vision of reality the map represents, and what the map is *not* showing about how boundaries and affiliations are represented by the map. The evolution of maps is an area of study that will connect the visual with the historical aspects of social studies.

To teach map making and map interpretation to young children, they need opportunities and practice

- understanding a model;
- following a map's directions;
- developing their conception of point of view and perspective;
- determining alternatives and rotations to points of view;
- interpreting map symbols;
- understanding scaling; and
- understanding rotations of a whole map.

As children's conceptions related to mapping develop, they can begin to be exposed to various types of maps and the differing purposes of maps. Graphic organizers to relate types and purposes of maps will help to build their understanding of the diversity of maps.

Interrogating the purposes, perspectives, biases, inclusions, and exclusions of map samples is another strategy that teachers can use to teach critical questioning skills to students. As students develop increasing skills with maps, they are building their repertoire of geoscience concepts, which in turn will enable them to understand increasingly complex maps.

The concept of one-to-one correspondence between a spot on earth and a corresponding spot on a globe or on a flat map is very abstract and will require considerable exposure for students to make the connection that a map is another type of model. The wide variety of maps, including those that are surface, subsurface, satellite, solar, and stellar, create an even more complex variety of possibilities for initial instruction. Technology has enabled, and made readily available, increasingly sophisticated maps that can be used for a wide range of purposes. Map types that may be useful in elementary contexts are outlined in Figure 14.1.

By developing students' knowledge of maps and providing opportunities to work with different types of maps, we are able to use these valuable resources within the classroom as another source of information for students as they engage inquiry.

Figure 14.1 Types of Maps

Map Types	Focus of Map Type
Landforms/topographic	Information about the surface features of the earth and the elevations of features (e.g., mountains, rivers, lakes, etc.)
Physical regions	Characteristics of the surface features of the earth
Climatic	Features of earth caused by the winds, ocean currents, and latitude, as they interrelate to create climate patterns
Vegetation	Information about natural growth in various regions
Political	Information about country and inner-country boundaries
Socio-demographic	Information about social issues and impacts by country or region
Environmental impact	Information about natural disaster areas and their progress or about pollution trajectories
Stellar	Information about star and satellite locations and paths
Oceanic	Information about the ocean floor contours and related resources

PROBLEM-BASED LEARNING USING MAPS

Problem-based learning is a type of inquiry. In social studies, problem-based learning can be used to integrate concepts from social studies with those ideas studied in other program areas. Integrated conceptions are applied to real-life problems without overly stressing the artificial boundaries of any one subject area. The problem, rather than the discipline, becomes the focus of study and students employ strategies and analytical techniques from all disciplines to address the problem. Maps are one resource that can be used to identify aspects of the problem and seek resolutions.

In problem-based learning approaches, the students wrestle with elements of the problem and their need to know creates the theatre for teaching the skills that will support their problem-based inquiry. The teacher takes on the roles of both catalyst and strategic supporter.

In a problem-based learning environment, evaluation of the result, and learning process should meet four criteria (Engel, 1991):

- Learning is cumulative with the basic problem being revisited frequently over time so that skills can develop along with analysis of the problem.

- Learning is integrated rather than discipline centred and all perspectives are brought to bear on the problem, as are all resources.

- Progress is made in the learning as students grapple with various aspects of the problem. As learning progress is made, elements of the problem and criteria that surface in relation to possible solutions become more evident. The ways of knowing that are discipline bound (e.g., mapping) become tangled with ways of knowing from other disciplines.

- There is a direct link between how the learning is happening and how the assessment takes place. Students participate in the assessment of their own learning in relation to solutions to the problem. Assessment modes suit the problem.

In the primary/junior context, teachers would guide students' analysis of age-relevant problems and support students' breakdown of the larger complex problem into a series of smaller problems. The students' growing ability to ask the right questions to sort out the embedded elements of the problem support this breakdown. Maps may be an integral resource in helping students to conceptualize the elements of the problem. Geographic Information Systems (GIS) technology can be used to create fast and easy access to information to highlight patterns and visual aids such as maps so that problem elements can be examined readily.

To support the analysis of problems for use in this approach, students can gradually develop a conception of the commonality of all topics by using and reusing the questions of topic elaboration (see Chapter 1). The problem that students are addressing will define the scope and iteration of the questions and the resulting GIS resources that are used to frame and investigate the problem.

Problem-based learning must gradually become a self-directed, reiterative, recursive, and reflective process. However, early primary learners will rely on considerable support and direction from the teacher as they interrogate problems to determine their elements, consider and investigate possible solutions. A scenario is outlined below to provide an example of a problem-based learning situation that might become a primary/junior social studies project.

Example

The local school board has provided funds for improvement of the playground area of the school, which currently is a small, fenced area, with about one-third of the space covered in pavement and two-thirds of the space gravelled. There are no trees, playground elements, or sitting areas in the playground. Teachers want to ensure that students get a say in how their new playground is designed. A total of $50 000 has been budgeted for this project. How should the money be spent?

The problem is one that can draw in skills that students are developing from many disciplines. Map making can be a focus as students develop, scale, and propose possibilities. Map-making software can be used to situate students' proposals in scaled drawings. The sense of engagement and empowerment that result from students' immersion in such tasks will carry their interest forward as they look for new tools to conceptualize their proposals. The ties of such a project to the primary/junior social studies curriculum, and many other curriculum guidelines are evident in the selected nature of the problem-based learning task.

TEACHING MAP AND GLOBE SKILLS

Map and globe skills can be taught in fascinating and sometimes awe-inspiring ways because of the power of software available to schools. The use and availability of SMARTboards make projection and manipulation of map elements easy and understandable. Teachers would benefit from an overview of the options for use of electronic teaching aids (e.g., GIS) to understand their power and potential as program development resources. Drennon (2005) proposes five perspectives on software that can be used to manipulate geographic data, including maps:

1. GIS tools are used in combination with other approaches to automate common geography tasks such as mapping.
2. GIS tools are taught separately from the need for their use (similarly to how initial computer introductions in schools were achieved in the 1980s).
3. GIS tools are taught in isolation, then course content is applied.
4. GIS skills are taught as a separate science focusing on the capture, storage, analysis, and visual representation of data.
5. GIS is integrated into the geography field as a tool for understanding data as needs arise.

It is the fifth approach of these possibilities that is essential to problem-based inquiry curriculum in social studies.

Chen (2007) promotes the use of map-based problem-solving strategies as part of the curriculum for very young children. In his microgenic approach to studying learning about mapping with young children, Chen highlights the need to ensure students develop mapping strategies through both instruction and discovery. The use of symbolic representations for mapping require direct instruction and exposure to shift students' strategies from less developed initial ones to more sophisticated approaches. Chen defines strategy discovery as "acquiring a new rule or novel problem-solving approach with experience" (p. 386). The discovery approach to learning requires that young children

- recognize an unproductive strategy (encoding);
- choose to abandon it (analogizing); and
- construct new ways to map spaces mentally (corresponding).

Provincial and territorial guidelines and commercially prepared resources typically approach mapping and other geographic skills in one of three ways (Hurren, 2004). First, they may be presented as a set of tools needed by the educated person to help their efforts to manage their world. Second, an approach that emphasizes the separation of human and physical geography systems may be prevalent. Third, an approach that focuses on exclusively physical elements of geography may be used in documents. It is advantageous for the teacher to examine guidelines and resources at the outset of course planning to determine which of these approaches local resources seem to espouse.

Analysis of one provincial guideline's identified map and globe skills for the primary and junior students is outlined in Figure 14.2.

Figure 14.2 Map and Globe Skills Commonly Taught in Primary and Junior Grades

- Read maps of familiar areas in their local community
- Use non-standard units to measure distance on a map
- Demonstrate an understanding of scale
- Use their own symbols on a map
- Recognize that different colours represent different things on a map
- Use appropriate words to describe relative locations
- Map and use maps of urban and rural communities containing the necessary map elements of title, scale, symbols, legend, and cardinal directions
- Consult map legends when looking for selected features
- Locate boundaries
- Label maps
- Use a variety of maps to locate and label Canada's physical regions
- Use cardinal and intermediate directions, pictorial and non-pictorial symbols, scale, and colour to locate and display information on maps

- Use number and letter grids to locate places on base maps, road maps, and atlases
- Create and use a variety of thematic maps
- Construct maps of transportation routes, cities, railways, and capitals
- Prepare various forms of maps
- Use familiar units of scale to measure distance on maps
- Construct and read a variety of maps, graphs, diagrams, and models to display and interpret information
- Use base maps and other information sources to sketch relative positions of places
- Use information about time zones
- Use special purpose maps to find specific geographic information
- Use latitude and longitude to locate specific areas
- Compare various map projections and analyze their differences to determine the bias of each

This analysis certainly yields a workable list of map and globe skills but the focal purpose of learning the skills, as implied by how they are stated, seems to be inconsistent across the grades, with a problem-based approach being introduced only at the end of the list, which corresponds to expectations for the later junior grades. Prior to that, the focus seems to be on the isolated acquisition of skills.

Map projections that are different from what students commonly experience can cause some unique opportunities to question perspectives. There are many active learning strategies that can be used to expose students in early grades to various types, characteristics, and uses of maps. Active approaches to the use of maps are listed in Figure 14.3.

Map projections are mathematical functions that attempt to display the Earth's surface as portions. These portions allow for easy location by isolating spots through the cross-referencing of coordinates. The horizontal functions are called parallels or lines of latitude. The meridians, or lines of longitude, run in opposite directions, starting opposite to lines of latitude at the equator. This creates global coordinates of two lines, often referred to as

Figure 14.3 Active Approaches to Mapping

- Solving practical problems with maps (e.g., How long will this trip be?)
- Using stories that relate to places and trips
- Field trips using maps to navigate to exhibits
- Field work (e.g., students work in an open space with several geographical features and navigate the space by using maps)
- Creating map models (e.g., using salt and flour, plasticine, beach balls, or software)
- Mapping from memory; students sketch and compare to see other peoples' perceptions of places
- Internet global studies (e.g., web quests, virtual tours, using Google Maps to compare most direct approaches to locations, etc.)
- Simulations that relate to learning directions (e.g., battleship)
- Scavenger hunts and orienteering
- Directional games (e.g., "Simon says . . . ")
- Using GPS systems for schoolyard tasks
- Trip planning
- Imaginary car rallies (i.e., combined with scavenger hunts to have students "pick up" items as they travel [e.g., collect a basket of apples from the Okanagan Valley])

a polar two-coordinate system. However, ways of displaying lines of latitude and longitude are prolific, with over 95 possible map projections being developed between the time of Leonardo da Vinci and modern-day projections. Typically in elementary social studies, students are introduced to some of the most common map projections (see Figure 14.4), including

- Mercator;
- Peters;
- Mollweide;
- Atlantic-centred; and
- Pacific-centred.

Teaching the abstract concepts of latitude and longitude to young children can be challenging. As with any abstract concept, the teaching needs to be made concrete so that students can grasp these big ideas. One strategy that works well with young students is also easy to use in the classroom. Tape an area of the classroom floor with lines of tape about two meters long running perpendicular to each other. Space will dictate how large you can make this grid but try for at least six lines of tape running in either direction. Label the ends of each line of tape so that lines running in one direction are labeled with alphabet letters (A, B, C, D, E, F) and those running perpendicular with numbers (1, 2, 3, 4, 5, 6). Each student can be given a soft item such as an eraser to toss onto the grid. Then they can reclaim the item by naming its closest location using the two coordinates (e.g., "My eraser is close to C5."). Once students have done this, they can be introduced to the globe and lines of latitude and longitude.

Figure 14.4 Common Map Projection Types

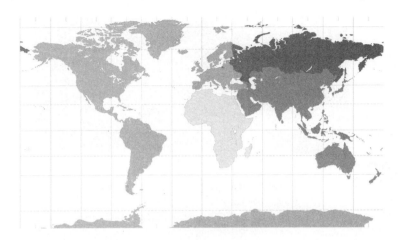

Mercator

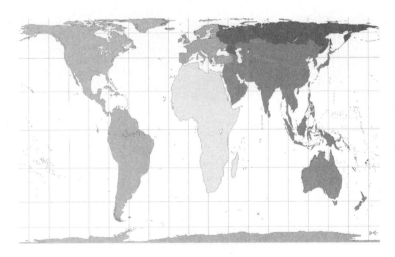

Peters

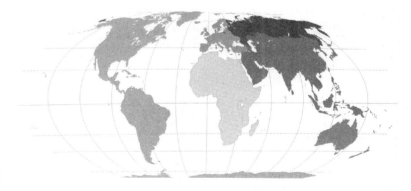

Mollweide

Figure 14.4 Common Map Projection Types

Atlantic-centred

Pacific-centred

Sand tables or sand platforms made of a sheet of plywood bordered by 2 x 4 edging, can be very useful in the classroom for teaching mapping concepts. Sterilized sand can be used in the table/platform and can be purchased from educational supply companies. Cheaper forms of kitty litter can also be used. Students can investigate mapping concepts in easy-to-erase forms and investigate community layout, transportation routes, urban expansion, waterway use, and even erosion concepts through experimentation in the sand table/platform followed by discussion.

Many school boards have centralized sets of resources for orienteering and may have personnel within the board with responsibility for teaching orienteering to school groups. Orienteering can be both motivating and initiating for students, giving them their first exposure to mapping for a practical purpose. In many urban jurisdictions, local police forces also manage and instruct students about urban safety by engaging students in a "Safety Village" simulation where students learn about street layout and signage while driving sit-in cars on the streets of a village that can be laid out in the school gym.

Mapping and Web Quest Ideas for the Classroom

Internet resources have allowed teachers to use current and dynamic maps to make mapping and globe skills available to students. The use of satellite maps makes the study of local communities more interesting because of the unique perspective and special use and relative location that are available in these views.

We must remember, however, that students will require some prerequisite mapping skills to be able to engage more complex maps productively. Recent brain research highlights the essential need to engage students holistically through mind–body connections to ensure that they connect abstract concepts. A holistic approach to mapping skills would have students making connections to maps using all of their senses and through as many learning styles or modalities as possible.

An organizer to help teachers consider ways of introducing and practising mapping concepts with young students can help to conceptualize the possibilities. An example, using the mapping skill of recognizing the role of lines of latitude and lines of longitude in the process of reading maps is outlined below. Each of these approaches to learning this concept using multiple intelligences (Gardner, 1983) is supported by brain research that promotes the essential elements of multiple intelligences approaches.

- Every person has some degree of intelligence or learning style preference from each way of knowing.
- Any intelligence or learning style can be nurtured and strengthened through exposure and practice.
- Everyone learns different things, at different rates, for different reasons.
- All ways of learning and knowing should be equally valued.
- Ways of learning and knowing may manifest in different ways.
- Assessments used in schools should reflect the question "How are you smart?" rather than "How smart are you?"

Brain research suggests that ability is not static and connections among ideas can be made using different ways of knowing (see Figure 14.5) to support neuron development.

Figure 14.5 Multiple Intelligence and Its Role in Understanding Latitude and Longitude

Expectation: Students will be able to recognize the role of lines of latitude and longitude in the process of reading maps.		
Multiple Intelligence	**Meaning**	**An Approach to Understanding Latitude and Longitude**
Intrapersonal	Learns best by introspection; focus on self	Students use an orange and string to tack lines of latitude and longitude on the sphere and figure out what problematic issues may arise for whatever way they determine to do this.
Visual-spatial	Learns best through pictures and visual support	Students will create lines of latitude and longitude on a flat map to indicate one way of examining their intersection and naming locations based on the resulting grid.
		(Continued)

Figure 14.5 (*Continued*)

Musical-rhythmic	Learns best by making musical connections	Students will create a musical rhyme to help them remember the role of lines of longitude and latitude in map reading.
Logical-mathematical	Learns best through numbers	Students will examine the most commonly used map projections (e.g., Mercator, Peters, Mollweide, Atlantic-centred, Pacific-centred) and compare the impact of the different degree systems used to develop each map.
Verbal-linguistic	Learns best through words read	Students will read a description about how lines of longitude and latitude work on maps and write brief summaries of each.
		Students write a letter to a randomly selected latitude and longitude and post their letter to a school in that area, enclosing a Flat Stanley in their letter.
Interpersonal	Learns best by interacting with people	Students work in pairs or small groups to teach each other how to use lines of latitude and longitude.
Spiritual	Learns best through making connections with personal spiritual beliefs	Students use visualization techniques to imagine the lines of latitude and longitude and identify locations through visualizing intersections.
Naturalist	Learns best by making connections with nature	Students use satellite maps to locate positions of natural beauty on the earth's surface then compare those images to surface maps showing lines of latitude and longitude for each spot they viewed by satellite image.
Kinesthetic	Learns best through movement and physical contact with objects	Students play a game of tag based on being able to move only within points of intersection that represent lines of latitude and longitude. Following the game, they move an object across a wall map to indicate locating their object using the intersecting lines.

Web quests should be designed by teachers to ensure access through many ways of knowing and learning styles. To do this, teachers must design web quests with care and detail, responding to the learning characteristics of the group of students and of individuals within the group. While it may be tempting to use web quests that are available commercially or through Internet sources, these may fail to address the needs of the class and should be modified for those needs.

Figure 14.6 Web Quests in the Elementary Classroom

Pioneer Lifestyle Web Quest: Pioneer Days in Canada by Elyse Malick

Attention all students: A science experiment has gone very wrong! You have been transported back in time to the Canada of the early 1800s. It will take your teacher one week to fix the machine and return you to our time. During that week you must live among the people. You must try to fit in so you do not upset the inhabitants of that time. They should not notice you are different.

Keep a journal recording what you have learned about the people who lived in Canada in the early 1800s. You should write one page about each of the following topics:

- Food
- Clothing
- Housing
- Transportation
- Occupations
- Agriculture

Include pictures you have taken with your hidden camera during your week-long stay. They should illustrate the life of people who lived in the 1800s. When you return you will have two days to complete a report on the following topics using information you gathered in your journal:

- mapped location of your travels
- location of various settlements around you are shown on a map
- sketches of people in the clothing worn at this time
- a diary description to show what you did each day

Since you will be missing the exams, your teacher will use this report for your mark.

Visit the following site to complete this web quest on pioneer life:
www.swlauriersb.qc.ca/english/edservices/pedresources/webquest/pioneer/index.html

---

Well-designed web quests should have the following characteristics:

- Learning expectations for the web quest are clearly articulated by the teacher and understood by the students.
- The reading level of quest directions is targeted to the specific group of students.
- Directions are provided in easy-to-follow steps.
- Screen captures guide students' searches.
- Expected products from the quest are explained in detail and supported by examples.

An example of a web quest for an elementary classroom is given in Figure 14.6 to illustrate these characteristics.

Students can produce web quest products of high quality when their research is supported by well-designed web quests.

ELECTRONIC MAPPING SYSTEMS

Online mapping systems have made mapping in the classroom context much more sophisticated than in the past. Students are able to make and manipulate representational and satellite maps with ease through commonly available classroom hardware.

Students can also be taught to use land and marine global positioning systems (GPS) to identify features on the land's surface and below water. Many school jurisdictions have GPS labs available for loan to students. Some students may even have these features available through cell phone technology. High technology maps will become increasingly common and available to students through their classrooms and through personal convenience devices such as phones. The challenge for teachers will be to help students interpret and contextualize the resources they have available.

Additional software can help students generate and modify maps for specific purposes. The teacher will need to provide guidance for students about the cartography standards for the various applications of maps. Students can be guided to customize electronically available maps through Google using programs that allow them to add custom icons to support the purpose of their maps (http://mashable.com/2007/09/20/custom-google-map-icons). Sophisticated software to help students produce specific map features from data is increasingly available for classroom use.

Since 1982, global positioning systems have been available to help commercial and private users to track the location of vehicles, people, and assets in real time or after the fact. The recorded location data can be stored within the tracking unit, or it may be transmitted to a central location database, or Internet-connected computer. The capabilities of such GPS units make classroom simulations and applications of concepts to their everyday use more accessible within social studies. Because many students have exposure to everyday applications of these devices as they become more common, their need to know how to use them motivates increased interest. The websites available through GPS TRACK expose teachers and students to the broad range of current uses of this technology.

MAPPING SYMBOLS FOR CLASSROOM DISPLAY

Map symbols allow us to represent map abstractions in symbolic form to present natural and human-made features of the Earth's surface. Map symbols can be used to represent three types of surface features: points, lines, and areas. These symbols can be applied to many types of maps for the purposes of travel, tourism, orientation, navigation, and entertainment, or social activities. Well-designed map symbols will have two main features: they will allow the map viewer to have an intuitive recognition of the feature represented by the symbol and they will help map makers as well as map readers, by reducing the clutter or footprint on the surface of the map.

The earliest maps were made over 5000 years ago and made use of many materials and simple symbols that reflected the materials available. Early maps were made of sand drawings, wood, clay, bone, and stone. The symbols featured in these maps are relatively simple compared to those we can generate using computer and space technology. However, both early and modern maps include symbols that are integral to the representation of larger surfaces. In order to understand the symbols used in maps, some assumptions about the purposes of the maps and the nature of the culture in which the maps were used are needed. Map keys are used to identify the meaning of map symbols on modern maps with consistency. However, much earlier maps also had keys that represented the priorities of trade and exploration in earlier societies. Ptolemy, a Roman citizen of Greek or Egyptian ancestry, published the first geographical encyclopedia—called the "Geographia"—of map keys and symbols in the second century A.D. He brought together his mixed skills from mathematics, astronomy, geography, and astrology to create the first symbols used to represent latitude and longitude on maps.

Modern cartographers use the principles of minimal clutter and intuitive recognition to create symbols for modern maps for many applications. Students can be taught the symbolic nature of map symbols using cutouts or by engaging in easy-to-use electronic tutorials to learn this concept. National Geographic hosts a simulation site where very young students can learn map symbol use and design, and they can time the improvement in their ability to recognize symbols on an island map. The terms *symbols* and *keys* are the main concepts addressed in this easy-to-use simulation (www.mywonderfulworld. org/toolsforadventure/games/adventure.html).

Cartographers create map symbols for many uses. These map symbols should be learned by students over time as their use of maps expands. Steven Gordon (2008) has created a databank of intuitively recognizable and light footprint map symbols that can be manipulated for size and display in classrooms (see Figure 14.8). Teachers can modify and add to these symbols as needs arise. The map symbols created by Gordon are provided here in summary. They can be accessed online for refinement and manipulation at www.map-symbol.com.

Teachers can make an interesting activity centre to help students learn to recognize common map symbols by following the directions in Figure 14.7.

Figure 14.7 Teaching Young Students to Recognize Map and Globe Symbols

---

Students can be taught to match map symbols to locations using simple circuits to turn on a light or ring a bell when a symbol and its map feature are matched. To make this classroom resource follow the directions below.

1. Draw a map to scale on a large piece of poster board using a grid system. Leave room on one edge to place appropriate names. Colour the map.
2. Print appropriate names. Tape the names to the map's edge.

(Continued)

Figure 14.7 (*Continued*)

3. Laminate the entire map. After lamination, poke solid brass fasteners through the map next to the place names on the edge of the map and on the countries, oceans, capitals, or other features that students are to learn.

4. Bend over solid brass fasteners on the back of the map and connect pieces of wire to them by using solder and a soldering gun. Wire should be connected between the place name on the edge of the map and to its appropriate country, ocean, capital, or other feature.

5. Connect an electric doorbell, phone bell, or small light bulb to a 6 volt battery. Allow two insulated wires (about 45 cm each) to extend out from the bell or bulb. By touching one end of the wire to one solid brass fastener and the other end of the wire to the appropriate name on the edge of the map the electrical circuit is closed and the bell will ring (or the light bulb will glow), indicating a right answer.

INNOVATIVE APPROACHES IN YOUR SOCIAL STUDIES CLASSROOM

1. Create your own web quest using Webquest.org. This site provides a complete and current source of information that will guide you step by step in the process of creating engaging online activities for your students.

A web quest is an inquiry-oriented approach to learning. Web quests use lessons in which most or all the information that learners work with comes from the web. Using web quests, students are able to create their own understanding and take control of where their interests take them.

Creating your own web quest is not as challenging as some might think. If you can develop a simple document with hyperlinks you are well on your way to creating a web quest. You can use almost any word-processing software (e.g., Word or PowerPoint) to create a web quest.

In order for your document to be considered an authentic web quest, WebQuest.org suggests that it must meet several criteria. The web quest should

- be wrapped around a doable and interesting task, ideally a scaled-down version of things that adults do as citizens or workers;

- require higher-level thinking, not simply summarizing. This includes synthesis, analysis, problem solving, creativity, and judgment;

- make good use of the web. A web quest that is not based on real resources from the web is probably just a traditional lesson in disguise. Books and other media can be used within a web quest, but if the web is not at the heart of the lesson it is not a true web quest;

- not be a research report or a step-by-step science or math procedure;

- not be just a series of web-based experiences; and

- be designed to promote higher-level thinking.

Figure 14.8 Map Symbols for Classroom Display

Source: Adapted from www.map-symbol.com.

2. Chapter 4 presented a summary of many map and globe skills for early primary students. Review these strategies as a starting point for teaching map and globe skills in your classroom.

It is often difficult to determine a starting point for teaching map and globe skills until you have a clear understanding of the background your students have with map making and map interpretation skills. To determine a starting point, you can develop a class analysis checklist that allows you to synthesize and analyze students' map-related skills and thereby determine where to start your teaching of these concepts.

A class analysis checklist for map and globe skills is presented in Figure 14.9.

Figure 14.9 Class Analysis Checklist: A Diagnostic Look at Map and Globe Skills

Map and Globe Skill	None of the students knows this	Many of the students know this	All of the students are aware of this	All of the students are confident users of this	I need to teach
Use one-to-one correspondence between maps and actual locations					
Use colour coding on maps					
Use map scale					
Use the mathematical nature of map projection variations					
Identify map types					
Separate maps into critical, cultural, and feminist categories					
Use a variety of map projections					
Identify types of maps that address particular inquiry problems					
Separate map uses into physical and cultural					
Use mapping symbols and map keys					

(Continued)

Figure 14.9 *(Continued)*

Map and Globe Skill	None of the students knows this	Many of the students know this	All of the students are aware of this	All of the students are confident users of this	I need to teach
Use concepts of latitude and longitude					
Identify features of Mercator, Peters, Mollweide, Atlantic-centred, and Pacific-centred maps					
Use GIS technology					
Use a GPS system					
Use map-based web quests					

CASE STUDIES AND PROFESSIONAL ACTIVITIES FOR INNOVATION IN SOCIAL STUDIES

1. Mr. Areas has used many types of maps in his classroom throughout his social studies course. However, he finds that his students do not understand that there are many different kinds of maps. Create a game he can use with his Grade 4 students to help them identify different types of maps.

2. Create a schoolyard scavenger hunt that requires the use of handheld GPS units to complete mapping and location tasks.

3. Examine a variety of space age maps available on the Canadian Social Studies Super Site (www.ualberta.ca/~jkirman). Identify the characteristics of these maps that you would want to teach to your students. For any one characteristic, explain an interactive strategy you could use to teach that concept to young students.

4. Create a card game that you could use with young students to teach them map-making and map-interpretation concepts.

CHAPTER REVIEW AND PROFESSIONAL DEVELOPMENT AS A TEACHER

This chapter has examined the following:

■ Maps have inherent assumptions, perspectives, biases, and beliefs built into them.

■ Maps must be exposed to critical use in both historical and geographical inquiry contexts.

■ Map study should include opportunities to examine historical misuses of maps for power or monetary gain (carto-controversy).

■ Early maps of Canada still have societal impacts for our Canadian culture.

■ Maps represent elements of space and time.

■ Using maps in conjunction with other sources allows optimal use of maps in problem-solving contexts.

■ Students need many opportunities to practise map-making and map-interpretation skills.

■ Critical map studies consider the map's purposes, historical context, biases, and perspectives.

■ Increasing students' repertoire of geosciences concepts helps to build their ability to understand increasingly complex maps.

■ One-to-one correspondence is a critical skill needed by students to help them understand maps as a representation of reality.

■ There are many different types of maps that have different foci.

■ Problem-based learning is a type of inquiry where maps can be used as one source of information to conceptualize and resolve problems.

■ In problem-based learning, maps are a resource, not an end product, for learning.

■ GIS technology can be used to help students grapple with the elements of a complex problem.

■ Problem-based learning approaches can help teachers to integrate curriculum.

■ GIS technology can be used in many different ways to develop understanding of geographical concepts.

■ Strategy discovery using maps can promote young students' ability to encode, analogize, and correspond effectively when using maps.

■ Guidelines from provincial and territorial sources should be examined to determine how mapping and other geographical skills are presented.

■ Guidelines can identify all of the skills students are required to learn in relation to map and globe competencies.

■ Active learning approaches can be applied to the study of maps and globes so that skills are not just learned in isolation.

- Students should be taught to understand maps as mathematical projections with inherent assumptions that result in a particular projection.

- The most commonly used map projections include the Mercator, Peters, Mollweide, Atlantic-centred, and Pacific-centred.

- Using active and physical strategies to teach young students abstract concepts such as latitude and longitude can help them understand these ideas at a young age.

- Orienteering and Safety Village experiences can help young children develop understanding of abstract mapping concepts.

- Multiple intelligences and brain-research based approaches to teaching can support students' understanding of abstract mapping concepts.

- By consciously considering multiple intelligences, teachers can generate many appealing strategies to help students learn abstract mapping concepts.

- Web quests are appealing to students because they draw on many forms of intelligence and engage students holistically.

- Well-designed web quests have clear expectations, understandable directions, screen capture supports, and clearly explained product details.

- Electronic mapping systems, including GIS software, make sophisticated mapping products possible for very young students.

- GPS systems can support classroom mapping projects.

- Well-designed mapping symbols allow for intuitive recognition by the map reader and reduce map clutter.

- Map keys can highlight the purposes of particular maps.

- Simulations and strategies that help students make mind–body connections support students' learning of map symbol correspondence.

- Teachers might consider a class analysis of map and globe skills prior to instruction to diagnose current skill levels in relation to major mapping concepts.

References for Further Reading

David, D. W. (1990). Big maps—little people. *Journal of Geography*, 89:58–62.

Gregg, M. (1997). Seven Journeys to Map Symbols: Multiple intelligences applied to map learning. *Journal of Geography*, 96,146–152.

Keiper, T.A. (1999). GIS for elementary students: An inquiry into a new approach to learning geography. *Journal of Geography*, 98 (2), 47–59.

Kirman, J.M. (1996). Urban map tag: An elementary geography game. *Journal of Geography*, 95, 211–212.

Weblinks

The Canadian Social Studies Super Site

This site provides resources that relate to geography, map skills, and space age maps; indexed and annotated collection of sites useful to social studies.

www.ualberta.ca/~jkirman

World Wide Web Virtual Library

This site allows teachers to consider criteria for evaluating websites.

www.vuw.ac.nz/~agsmith/evaln/evaln.htm

Hammond Geography Corner

This site teaches skills and concepts related to latitude and longitude.

www.hammondmap.com/catalog/classroom_activities/latlong1.html

The National Atlas of Canada

This site teaches map skills at many levels.

www.atlas.gc.ca

Maps and Travel Information: Canadian Geographic

This site provides geographic information and maps of Canada.

http://canadiangeographic.com

Educational Resources

This site provides links to various educational geographic websites.

www.geoworld.ca

Lesson Planning and Activities

This site provides directions and lesson plans related to map and globe skills are provided.

www.canteach.ca

Environmental Systems Research Institute (ESRI) Canada Schools and Libraries Program

This site provides GIS software access for comparisons and manipulation.

http://k12.esricanada.com

GIS Software:

This site provides GIS software access for comparisons and manipulation.

www.geocomm.com

Chapter 15
Using the Community as a Resource

Students gain a deeper understanding of the sacrifices of war veterans by visiting a local war museum.

FIELD TRIPS TO PROMOTE INQUIRY

Field trips are one of the many community-based learning opportunities available to teachers to help them enrich their social studies programs. The community can provide supportive program experiences in many forms, including

- areas that can be investigated for rich information;

- speakers to talk about their personal experiences and interests, whether on-site or in the classroom;

- materials to share that reflect the business, concerns, or interests of groups within the community; and

- field experiences that simulate adult experiences and provide intense ways of connecting to learning in the classroom.

Careful preparation is the key to making the most of such resources.

—Clark, 1999

If the community is used for any of these purposes, learning can be both rich and memorable for students. When community experiences are well conceived and well planned, they expand the learning of students through holistic connections the learners are able to make more meaning of abstract concepts experienced in the classroom. The community provides venues where students can see and participate in democratic and social action learning in meaningful ways.

Field trips are unique opportunities to engage learning in the community. They allow students to see classroom concepts in action and engage learning through preferred learning styles by seeing, doing, manipulating, and interacting. Field trips have the power of simulations; they allow students to use imagination to engage ideas that let them be part of the experience. Experiencing aids memory so field trips have longevity as learning experiences.

Careful planning is essential to making successful use of the community as a learning resource. Teachers must consider the time needed to plan community trips, the safety issues for every child in the group, accessibility issues for any challenged children, background learning required for students to benefit from a community experience, readability of resources related to the experience, costs, and time away from other possible learning in the classroom.

Teachers should consider these questions before deciding on the inclusion of a field trip in their programs:

- Is this the best way for my students to learn about this idea?

- Are there safely issues that would make this field trip problematic?

- Is this experience affordable?

- Is this experience accessible for every child, both physically and cognitively?

- Is the expenditure of time and money worth the learning available through the experience?

In considering these questions, teachers need to remember that field trips are not just experiences. They are learning experiences. To maintain an emphasis on the learning part of the field trip, teachers must first prepare students in the classroom so that they can anticipate what they will see and do and prepare for what will happen in the classroom following the experience. The field trip alone will not ensure learning. Preparation can maximize the learning available from the trip.

Field trips for young children will generally be one of four types. They may be designed to

- create a common base of experience on which to build future learning;
- have students discover new learning in a structured way;
- allow students to practise new learning in context; or
- provide opportunities for students to apply and solidify new learning through experiences not available in the classroom (e.g., community action).

Each of these four purposes for field trips is exemplified in Figure 15.1.

Each of these purposes for a field trip requires a different type of preparation from the teacher and different levels of pre-trip knowledge in the students. Prior to arranging a field trip, the teacher needs to be very familiar with the facilities at the site and know what learning can be uniquely provided by this experience that is not possible in the classroom. Often, the teacher will need to visit the trip site ahead of time. Some facilities provide teacher kits that describe all programs at the site and may include videos of the site so that the teacher can do a virtual trip before the class visits.

Most school boards have policies that govern the types of trips that teachers may plan for their classrooms. School board insurance policies may identify some opportunities as high risk, and therefore school boards may not allow these trips for their students. In some jurisdictions, school boards may require special levels of permission (e.g., from the superintendent or director). For all trips, the teacher should discuss the idea with the school administrator early in their planning. This will allow the teacher to ensure support for the idea, as well as provide an opportunity for guidance about travel arrangements, financing, and safety provisions for the trip.

For every field trip that is arranged under the auspices of the school, the teacher should plan for all arrangements that are required before, during, and after the trip. While many of these arrangements will be pragmatic and relate to the physical movement of a large group under safe circumstances, some arrangements will relate to ensuring that the intended learning actually happens. Figure 15.2 provides a generic list of areas the teacher will need to attend to in planning an effective field trip.

After the Trip

After field trips, students should engage in activities that help them consolidate and assess the information they have learned. Without follow-up, a field trip is just an event, not a learning event. Students should be engaged in examining the value of

Figure 15.1 The Value of Field Trips

Type of Field Trip	Example of How This Would Differ by Purpose with a Trip to a Farm
To create a common base of experience	A group of Grade 3 students from an urban school visit a mixed produce farm to explore ways that the farm serves the local urban community. Two thirds of the students in the class have never been on a farm, so this trip is planned primarily to strengthen their common understanding of what a farm is and how a farm is worked to produce food items.
To discover new learning in a structured way	Students from a rural environment are learning about irrigation systems used in local farms. One local farm has a new automated overhead irrigation system. The students are visiting this farm to see how this system works and to compare its advantages and disadvantages to more usual ditch or underground irrigation approaches. They have a comparison chart to complete while they are on this trip and they have generated a list of questions to ask the farmers about their choice of this irrigation system.
To provide opportunities for students to practise new learning in context	Students have been learning about planting and harvesting cycles on farms. They understand that different crops are ready for harvesting at different times and farmers are able to test crops to determine the best time to start harvesting. However, this is an abstract concept. This field trip will allow young students to walk through cornfields with the farmer and witness and participate in the testing being done to determine when harvesting should begin.
To provide opportunities for students to solidify learning through experiences not available in the classroom	This field trip is designed to allow students to track the process of preparing fields for planting, rotating crops, tending fields during growth, harvesting, and marketing crops. The students will visit the manager of a large cooperative mixed farm. Through a combination of formal presentation and visits to the various buildings on the farm, students will be able to see the complex interaction of people who manage the different aspects of the farm. Students are divided into cooperative groups; each group is responsible for creating a photo-journal of one aspect of the farming operation and presenting that to classmates after their trip.

Figure 15.2 Planning Field Trips

Before the Trip

- Identify grade, date of trip, time, and location
- Determine the expectations of the trip and state for your planning purposes exactly what learning goals will be met/enriched by the trip
- Plan to teach skills that will be needed by students during the trip
- Ensure that the trip is allowed under board policy
- Preview any site-based resources that will help you with planning for this trip
- Plan and teach pre-trip activities and skills
- Determine risks and follow recommendations for safety
- Get permission from school principal, superintendent, or director (if necessary) in a timely way; application timelines may apply under school board policy
- Book the venue
- Book transportation
- Calculate the individual cost per student
- Consider if fundraising will be involved or if requests for funding are being made (from school funds, school council, etc.)
- Anticipate any students who may be unable to pay for their trip and have a plan for addressing this
- Acquire volunteers to supervise the trip; be aware of supervision ratios required by the school board
- Determine if the board requires volunteers to have a criminal reference check for vulnerable sector screening
- Determine how meals or snacks will be arranged

- Roll and count funds for submission to the main office; complete fund submission forms as required
- Confirm the venue a few days prior to the trip
- Get a cheque from the school to pay door fees and/or get a bill from the venue to be paid after the trip
- Discuss, teach, and anchor social skills and behaviours you expect to see during the trip
- For younger students, consider a "uniform" for the trip so that students are readily visible in crowds (e.g., red baseball caps that can be used by a whole division and shared after laundering)
- Have a plan for how you will address unacceptable behaviour during the trip (for example, the principal will be available by phone and will come and get any student who is not managing the responsibilities of the trip well); ensure that students know the plan well ahead of the trip date; follow the plan!
- Discuss bus safety (or other transportation) rules well before the trip; use key phrases (e.g., "nothing that distracts the driver")
- Create a quick (30 seconds) attendance check technique so that you can ensure all students are present several times during the day (e.g., number off or buddies)
- Ensure that volunteers understand the academic tasks and the behaviour expectations for your trip well beforehand; it's a good idea to have this reviewed with volunteers in front

(Continued)

Figure 15.2 (*Continued*)

- Consider physical needs that are responsive to the length of the trip (e.g., meals, sun block, medications, sunglasses, clothing)
- Determine on-site accessibility for every student
- Determine how parents/guardians could contact you during the trip if an emergency arises
- Visit the trip site if possible
- Develop a permission letter for parents/guardians
- Set a due date for return of all permission forms and any health forms you may require
- Provide a copy of the permission letter to the main office/principal (so that office personnel can answer questions about the trip if/when you are not available)
- Check students' school records for any medical conditions that may be affected by the trip (e.g., anaphylactic reactions); note any medications that need to be taken along
- Collect permission forms and fees at least a week before the trip (Note: Train your students to be responsible for response well ahead of the trip date to avoid last-minute phone calls home because of lack of permission)
- Create a class list record of fees and permission forms collected.

During the Trip

- Take a cell phone with a speed dial to the school's phone number
- Take a secure portfolio of the students' medical data with you; keep it with

of students so that they don't consider "trying it on" with volunteers
- Photocopy medical record pages for each student; take this copy with you in a confidential file you keep securely in your possession
- Know how to contact a school administrator on the day of the trip should the need arise
- Divide students into workable groups for supervision during the trip
- Ensure that students have some time for team building and socializing as a group before the trip; teach the social skills that may be needed for productive interaction
- Create workable academic tasks for the trip so that students are responsible for some product following the trip
- Develop a communication phone tree so that students' parents/guardians can be contacted readily if buses are late or there is some unanticipated disruption in the plans for the day

- Remind students of expectations for the trip (e.g., academic learning, social behaviour)

Figure 15.2 *(Continued)*

you throughout the trip and ensure that all volunteers know that this is with you

- Take an emergency medical kit with you; consider feminine hygiene products as well (can also be used as compression bandages)
- Take any students' medications that may be required during the day
- Have students bring a healthy packed lunch in a hard-sided container with their name clearly printed on the outside; insist on at least one bottle of water per student
- Adhere to school guidelines about food cautions while on the trip
- Take a clean recycling bin (or two) onto the buses to store students' lunches for later on the trip

After the Trip

- Send appropriate thank-you letters to hosts and volunteers
- Review students' academic tasks and provide immediate feedback about the work
- Review social skills that you found students may have needed and were not prepared for prior to the trip; teach these skills and create opportunities to practise them
- Pay bills
- Destroy or store confidential medical record portfolio in an appropriately secure location (Note: Be sure these are reviewed and refreshed before using them again)

- Don't give second chances on social behaviour; if you have prepared students well, they will need to see you being firm and fair in your expectations
- Have a predetermined and commonly understood method for having students complete the tasks that you have required during the trip
- Check up regularly on students' completion of the tasks required
- Bring pencils, markers, clipboards, etc., as required; store them safely near you during transportation and collect them again at the end of the day before getting back on transportation
- Collect completed academic work before boarding transportation for home

- Report any concerns about students' safety to the school office
- Make records of what you would do to improve the trip
- Return medications to the school office if necessary
- Adjust academic assignments if/as needed
- Create a display of the tasks students completed as a result of the trip; invite parents to see the display or incorporate it into some other aspect of a class celebration; focus on demonstrating to parents that the trip was the best way for students to acquire the knowledge or skills that were the focus of the trip

(Continued)

Figure 15.2 (*Continued*)

> - Teach follow-up lessons to ensure that the learning from the trip connects to the learning from the classroom
> - Make, date, and sign any records of accidents, injury, or severe incidents experienced during the trip
>
> - Connect what was learned from this trip to the next new learning in the classroom
>
> Note: This planning checklist should be updated from time to time as local policies and classroom conditions change regularly.

the trip in terms of the learning it offered as well. Follow-up activities should be known to students beforehand so that they have specific reasons for focusing on certain types of information during the trip. Follow-up will often involve students sharing what they learned with classmates but may also include more personal responses to the learning through some form of authentic assessment. (See Chapters 7, 8, and 9 to review the possible products students could produce in response to their trip experience.)

RESOURCES FOR LEARNING IN THE LOCAL COMMUNITY

Depending on the age of the students involved, school board policy may limit the types of trips and field experiences that students may take for safety reasons. It is common for primary students to be limited to day trips in the local community. Some jurisdictions may approve one-night overnight trips for students in junior grades, while out-of-province, multi-day trips may be acceptable for intermediate students. Knowledge of these policies is critical for teachers planning to use field trips as community resources to enrich social studies programs. If a field trip is not possible, teachers may have the option of bringing resources into the classroom that may provide the same type of learning without leaving the classroom.

Many topics in the curriculum may be enriched through a community resource (Clark, 1999) in either print or artifact form. The quality, accuracy, timeliness, and practicality of information available through community resources will support social studies program goals. Topics that may be enriched through interactions with community sources are outlined in Figure 15.3

While this list is extensive, it is not exhaustive. The potential for community resource use by schools fluctuates and often reflects the successes community organizations have had with previous school groups. Teachers should always consider approaching representatives to access community contacts if the potential learning for the students is anticipated to be beneficial.

Figure 15.3 Community Resource Topics

■ Roles of people within the community	■ Cultural activities in the community
■ Economic structure of the community	■ Industry in the community
■ Community labour action	■ Waste management in the community
■ Community services	■ Water treatment
■ Local rules and laws	■ Commerce and business incentives
■ Local signage	■ Architecture and historical preservation initiatives
■ Community transportation routes	
■ Natural resources in the community	■ Zoning and the bylaw development process
■ Green space preservation	
■ Land use issues	■ Recreation
■ Erosion and pollution issues	■ Governance
■ Accessibility issues	■ Special interest groups

MUSEUMS

Most communities have a local museum. Communication with the local curator can help teachers understand what services are offered locally. The museum may be available to support social studies programs in one of five ways:

1. In-house museum tours
2. In-class lectures and presentations on a specific topic by museum personnel
3. Loans of museum kits on specific topics
4. Professional development for teachers
5. Support partnerships with school-based history clubs.

In-house museum tours can be arranged directly with museum personnel. This is an opportunity for the teacher to discuss specific learning expectations for a museum visit with museum personnel and to arrange for pre- and post-visit teaching so that the visit to the museum results in optimal learning. When arranging an in-house museum visit, be sure to negotiate who will provide the main teaching role while on-site at the museum. Curators do not typically have teacher training so personnel often want to work in a co-teaching role with the classroom teacher to share the tasks related to managing a large group of children. In-house museum trips are often popular at different times of the school year so it is wise to book an in-house trip many months ahead of the intended time.

In-class lectures and presentations can often be arranged with museums large enough to have more than one full-time staff member. Museum staff can bring artifacts to the classroom. These artifacts are often collection extras so the students are allowed to touch the items, which can be more interesting than viewing static displays in-house. Teachers can also arrange to use some of the artifacts for an activity that relates to the study (e.g., candle making, butter churning) and this can be done with the support of the museum personnel to give historical background during the activity.

Many larger museums have school outreach programs whereby they loan artifact kits to schools. These kits are organized by themes of curriculum study (e.g., early settlement, pioneer cooking, early schools) and can be booked for the duration of a unit of study. Teacher requests can often influence the availability and development of such kits for classroom use so it is advisable to speak to the local curator if you see possible needs. Some kits may incur small costs for the kit delivery, maintenance, or the use of disposables from the kit.

Museum personnel provide a valuable and up-to-date resource for historical data and interpretation for teachers. They are often willing to participate in professional development opportunities to speak to teachers about a topic from curriculum guidelines and teach them the information needed to enrich learning in their classrooms. Many museums have a specialty focus (e.g., early railway transportation, seafaring, fur trade) and can provide access to both knowledge and examples that enable teachers to enliven the subject in their teaching practice. Museum personnel may have a special interest in one aspect of the community (e.g., cemeteries) and may be willing and able to provide support during a field trip to help the class investigate their area of interest.

Finally, many museums welcome partnerships with in-school history clubs. Even young students can engage in supporting their local museum through events such as fundraising to help acquire a particular artifact, participation in special ceremonies at the museum (e.g., opening a new gallery), or helping to make decorations for special displays and events (e.g., Remembrance Day, Christmas, Hanukah).

Increasingly, museums are developing interactive displays so that students can be more engaged when they visit museums. By determining the best ways for the local

At the Royal Ontario Museum students are invited to touch and experience the history of the dinosaurs using interactive displays.

museum to be part of your social studies program, teachers can be sure to make the most of this valuable and irreplaceable community resource. Many museums also welcome teacher involvement on their museum board of directors. These boards are usually responsible to the local or regional government of the area and teachers can contact these governments directly to learn more about this avenue of engagement.

VIRTUAL MUSEUMS

Virtual museums are available for many topics and provide unprecedented access to artifacts through high-quality photography. The use of virtual museums provides a time- and cost-effective alternative to some field trips and appeals to many learning styles because of the relatively low verbal needs of this resource. Some virtual museums even provide a virtual walk through the space so that the architecture of the actual museum becomes part of the simulated experience. Maneuvering within a virtual museum requires some practice and will need to be modelled for young students.

When using virtual museums, teachers will need to use the same criteria as for any community-based resource. It is critical that the museum experience has specific and achievable learning goals. Web quest approaches (see Chapter 14) can support students' examination of virtual museums.

Some virtual museum sites that will complement the primary and junior social studies program include those from the McCord Museum, which offers rich inquiry-based activities. Students can compare historical photos with photos of today using interactive tools. They are also able to select from a wide variety of skill-building challenges. These virtual museums are highly motivational in nature and allow students to choose which experiences they would like to discover.

ARCHEOLOGY SITES: REAL AND SIMULATED

Archeological studies can provide a wealth of historical and geographical information for students of any age. *Archaeology* is a term that began being used early in the seventeenth century. The word comes from two Greek words, *archaios* meaning old or ancient and *logos* meaning word or speech. Archeology is the discussion or study of ancient things. The opportunity to be involved in an archeological dig would provide rich learning for students. However, most classrooms will not have access to an authentic archeological dig site. If there is a university in the local community, teachers could contact the chair of the history department of the university to find out about what sites might be active locally.

When an actual archeological site is not available for a field trip, teachers can simulate archeological digs with their students in many ways. Young students will benefit from early exposure to archeological techniques from using the classroom or division sandbox (indoors for sanitary reasons) to uncover items that are buried beneath the sand. In this context, grid work, accurate recording, artifact preservation, photography, archiving, and restoration can be taught.

Visits to archeological or historical sites teach children about the richness of the past.

As students mature, more authentic opportunities for archeological simulation will be desirable. This may be achieved through computer-based simulations or by "planting" an archeological dig. Teachers have planted archeological digs for older students on local beaches, with the advantage that sand is easily excavated to uncover artifacts. Another simulated archeological dig involved students at four grade levels "planting" and excavating a dig in a donated unused and isolated section of a local graveyard. In this instance, three levels of a dig (e.g., native village, pioneer kitchen, and modern car garage) were systematically buried one spring by two classes of students then excavated the following fall by two other classes. All four classes of students learned about the archeological skills of gridding, contextualizing, accurate recording, artifact preservation, photography, interpreting, archiving, and restoration through their experience.

Archeology skills and concepts can also be learned through online simulations. A growing number of sites offer archeological simulations for students of all ages. As with any online site, teachers need to examine the site for security, appropriate images, and accessibility of the reading level. Laser scanning as an archeological tool has made it possible for students to view site artifacts from some digs in detail and many of these laser images are embedded in modern archeology simulations. Simulations and resources about archeology can be found at the end of this chapter.

CEMETERY STUDIES

Cemetery studies can provide a fascinating source of data about the history of the local community. Graves in early times in Canadian history were not as organized around church and municipal sites as is the case today. Many graves and even small graveyards can be found in obscure and unlikely places in both small and larger cities. Graveyards on small islands, behind car dealerships in major cities, or below paving stones in town squares are all part of Canada's graveyard history. Most graveyards are always open to the public. This has changed somewhat in recent years because of incidents of vandalism. Local funeral homes can be a source of information about access to cemeteries for study if the local cemetery does not have an office that is easily accessible for information.

When planning a cemetery study for young students, start by ensuring that you are clear about what you want students to learn from the study. The teacher's prior knowledge about the history of the graveyard can ensure the optimal use of time during students' visits.

If a goal of the study is to examine gravestones for symbols, teachers need to be cautious about not over-generalizing meaning in some engraving or encased photographs. Generally, gravestone symbols will be indicative of

- the person's attitude toward death and the hereafter;
- membership in a fraternal or social organization;
- an individual's trade or occupation;
- interests of the deceased; and/or
- ethnic identity of the deceased.

However, sometimes gravestones will include symbols that have no particular significance for the deceased or their family and were chosen merely because they are attractive. Historical times also have an impact on the popularity of some symbols used on gravestones.

The following pages provide examples of several activities that could be undertaken in a graveyard for historical study. Use professional caution in selecting and timing some of the activities. Their suitability for study will depend on many factors, including the age of the students, the culture of the local community, the recent experiences of students with death, and the curriculum expectations for the grade level.

Before you plan cemetery studies in your area, be sure to contact the appropriate authority to receive permission. This is often a responsibility of the local parks and recreation department. A call to your community town or city hall should help clarify whom you should speak to about access to a local cemetery for this purpose.

Be aware that some areas of the cemetery are likely to be off limits during your visit because of funeral services. Clarify expectations about this with the cemetery caretaker before you plan your visit date and activities. As part of your planning, explain the following to students:

- There may be traditional funeral routines for observers (i.e., quiet, stay still as the funeral procession passes, hats off, heads bowed).
- Explain the purpose of special vehicles in a funeral procession (e.g., hearse, family car, flagged cars).
- If possible, check on the morning of your trip to be sure you are aware of possible funeral activities before leaving the school.

As students are likely to produce several large pieces of paper during a thorough graveyard study, collect and provide mailing tubes for on-site storage of these sheets for each student or small group.

Cemetery Activities

1. Working in small groups, have students plot the location of gravestones in a particular area and show a top view of these stones on a large sheet of paper that can be taped together to show the entire area once students are back in the classroom.

2. Have students create a map of an area in the cemetery showing gates, roadways, public monuments, gravestones, trees, bushes, maintenance sheds, cardinal directions, unused areas, and chapel(s). Have students use keys to identify area elements and colour the map to help distinguish special areas.

3. Have students select one monument to study in detail. Using sketch paper, have the students write the message that is on the stone and sketch other details in proportion to the size of the stone.

4. Prepare students to do a gravestone rubbing by having them shade over the surface of many types of coins while working in the classroom. This will help students to get a feeling for how much pressure is needed on the paper to produce an even but clear rubbing.

5. Teach students how to do a gravestone rubbing using the edge of a pencil against a sheet of paper. Several sharpened pencils will be needed for each rubbing. Stress to students that they need to be very careful not to leave any marks from their pencils on the gravestones.

6. Direct students to do a study of gravestone symbols. The class could be divided into small groups to study symbols of the following types:

   a) religious
   b) military
   c) personal interest (e.g., motorcycles, planes)
   d) photo insets
   e) anti-culture (e.g., drug symbols)

   Provide each group with any of the following to support their records of the symbols they find:

   - disposable or digital cameras
   - sketch paper
   - gravestone rubbing paper (heavy white bond) and several sharp pencils

7. If available, have students examine the military area of the graveyard. Study the style of grave markers (typically plain white crosses) used in military areas of the graveyard. Brainstorm reasons why crosses for this purpose were created in this style (i.e., cost, labour shortages, relatively high number of graves needed in a relatively small time period, paid for by government so one style was used for everyone).

8. Have students study the dates and changes of dates in the areas of the graveyard devoted to military graves. Relate dates to the military conflicts that caused these deaths (e.g., WWI, WWII, Korean War, Afghanistan War).

9. Have students identify the largest monuments in the graveyard. Record the names on the stones. If possible, have a laptop computer and mobile Internet available, so that students can research these names to see if there is a record of who these people were and why their monuments are larger than average. If a laptop is not available, you could

   ■ prepare in advance a folder of information about the person buried at each site;

   ■ record names and do computer research when back at the school; or

   ■ study in advance selected deceased local historical personalities and direct students to study those stones when you are at the cemetery.

10. Discuss and examine the number of baby graves (i.e., deaths before three years old) in particular areas of the cemetery (e.g., oldest part of the cemetery contrasted to the newest).

11. Before going to the cemetery, study areas of the continent/country/community that may have different styles of gravestones. See Figure 15.4 for examples.

Figure 15.4 Styles of Gravestones

Area	Type of Gravestone/ Marker	Reason
New Orleans	Aboveground crypts covered in concrete	High water levels make burial impractical because water will surge into ground holes quickly. These areas typically do not have basements either. Relate this to how water fills a hole on the beach.
England	In church, floor graves; mold of the person on the top of the graves	These were a form of recognition for wealthier land owners, knights, and nobles. The symbols meant that certain things were characteristic of the person's life or death (e.g., if the raised symbols had a dog at the person's feet, this symbolized that the person died at home; a lion at the person's feet meant that the person died in battle).
Densely populated areas	Above-grade markers are not used; head markers are small and flat to the ground	Can reflect many changes in belief: ■ less focus on religion so religious symbols are not prevalent ■ high land costs, so land is used very carefully ■ plots are very expensive so people buy the land and put less money into a stone *(Continued)*

Figure 15.4 *(Continued)*

Area	Type of Gravestone/Marker	Reason
		<ul><li>owners of high-end houses in the area may prefer a less intrusive view, which flat markers can provide</li></ul>(i.e., look like a park from a distance)
Military graveyards	Flanders, France	When there were many deaths in short period of time, people were buried close to where they died to save transportation costs. Iinternational cooperation was required to determine symbols for grave markers. Often temporary markers were used until after the conflict was over so markers were added all at once, allowing for a common style.
Modern markers in local areas of the province	Cities in each province/territory	Many stones are made of granite. Thick, polished stones are possible because of the use of powered stone-cutting tools. Some markers may be made of inexpensive, modern materials such as ABS plastic pipes.
Areas of cemeteries that date around 1880	Older sections of urban and rural cemeteries	Many stones are made of thin slabs of limestone. This porous stone allows lichens and mosses to grow on the stones, discolouring the surfaces.
Vaults	Some urban and many rural areas	Varying beliefs about death and afterlife allow for different treatments of corpses. Cremation is becoming a common option. Crematoriums are more easily available to more people. International agreements allow for bodies to be moved across borders for cremation. In some areas, same-day cremation is available and this may suit the family's wishes to have the formal and public part of the grieving over with as soon as possible.

12. Divining rods are used in many areas where graveyards were established and were commonly used before systematic records of burials were kept. Divining is an easy way to get an indication of the increased water count in the ground around areas where a body is buried (the human body is 80 percent water!). Often, you will be able to arrange for the use of divining rods used in the local cemetery. Alternatively, two straightened clothes hangers can be used for divining. This is an interesting experience for students to see divining rods being used or even to have them work when they try it! They don't work for everyone.

13. In some cultures (e.g., Mexico), special days are set aside where families go to visit the graves of ancestors and picnic at the spot, often leaving behind some parts of the picnic as a tribute or "offering" to the ancestor. Have students find out more about these celebrations of the dead.

14. Record books (e.g., Guinness World Records) contain references to the oldest living people in the world. In some places in Mexico, grave dates indicate that the people lived for 120 years or more. Have students study longevity statistics for many cultures and prepare a PowerPoint presentation of their findings. GIS software can correlate statistical data. Have them consider the ways that increased longevity of whole populations affects the way cultures operate. Have them consider reasons why some of the oldest marked graves in some locations may not be the same as the oldest recorded dates in record books such as Guinness World Records.

15. Graveyard decorations are fairly common in Canadian graveyards. Family and friends use flowers, bushes, trees, benches, wreathes, enclosed candles, and other decorations to mark graves at certain times of the year (e.g., birthdays, Christmas, Easter). Have students look for decorations on the graves they are examining. List what celebrations are being marked by these decorations. Create tally charts to identify the frequency of the decorations.

16. Undertake a mathematical study of dates of death to determine statistics such as

   - average age of death;
   - age of the different areas of the graveyard; and
   - possible cause of large numbers of deaths in any one time period.

17. Have students undertake a sketching or clay art project to design a gravestone, based on their observations of traditions for design that reflect different areas and eras (not horror movie or Halloween style).

18. Gravestones often display partial quotes from famous poems or scripts. Have students select one such quote from a gravestone and do some research to find its source and the remaining script. Have them word process the script in Kidpix slides and present the full piece of literature to the class. Discuss the imagery and allusions/references in the quote.

19. In small groups, have students work together to plan the layout of a new town, showing where they would locate graveyard(s) for the new settlement. Have them make decisions about the potential number of gravesites needed, best location, size of land required, and style of graveyard. Results can be displayed as a 3-D model or as a topographic layout.

20. Have students consider what symbols they think should mark a person's life interests as found on an English-style knight's tomb. Using plasticine, have students create a tomb covering using symbols that represent the imaginary person's life and death.

21. Laws for grave depths vary based on the type of burial. For example, coffins must be buried 6 feet (2 meters) below ground, while cremation containers may be buried 1 foot (30 cm) below ground, even on top of another coffin. Have students perform research to find the reasons for each of these laws.

22. Have students find out why modern coffins are often buried inside of concrete boxes.

23. Certain types of flowers (e.g., lilies) are traditionally representative of funerals. Often these are flowers with very strong scents. Have students perform research to find out about why such traditions developed.

24. In some types of funerals, flags are used to drape coffins. Have students do research to find out why this is done. Have them also find out how and why flags are often folded in a formal ritual, into a triangular pattern, and presented to the family in the burial ceremony. What is this process intended to symbolize/create?

25. The gun salute (3, 7, or 21 guns) is a military method of honouring soldiers, dignitaries, or police officers who have died on duty. Have students research where this tradition started and how the number of "salutes" from guns is determined for each person.

26. For large funerals, honour guards or attendants are used to carry a coffin or walk along the sides of a coffin as it is moved. Have students research why this is done to find the origin of this tradition.

27. Some societies bury their dead with materials and items that person used in life. Have students research this practice in ancient cultures (e.g., Egypt) and discover the beliefs behind these rituals. Determine if/where similar practices may still be used.

28. The practice of burying riches with the dead led to common grave robbing in ancient times. Have students find out more about this practice.

29. Have students research the purpose and history of "pauper's graves."

30. Some jails and penitentiaries had burial sites on their own grounds for the placement of prisoners' bodies after death. This also happened near some ports in early Canadian settlements (e.g., the graves of several people who were hanged in the

early days of settlement can be found around what is now downtown Victoria in British Columbia). Have students complete research to find out how these sites developed, and how they have been handled in modern times (e.g., removals, monuments, archeological excavations, historical recreations, tourist management).

31. Have students create a "graveyard dictionary" to list and explain all of the vocabulary that they have learned that relates to deaths and graveyards. Many of our casual expressions relate to death and "black humour." Many of these expressions mean something much different from what the actual words portray. (For example, "You slay me" really means "You're really funny." "You'll be the death of me" really means "You're trying my patience" or "You're bothering me.") Have students add to a class chart of these expressions. Explain "colloquialisms" to the students.

As you promote graveyard studies as an authentic historical inquiry practice with young students, it will be necessary to ensure that parents are aware of your learning goals and that each activity directly addresses these goals. It is unwise to get committed to graveyard studies without careful consideration of the age of the students, family histories, and religious sensitivities in the school community. With these aspects considered, graveyard study can be fascinating for classroom investigations and for the focus of history club events.

GUEST SPEAKERS IN THE CLASSROOM

It can be very difficult to connect with suitable guest speakers for the primary and junior social studies classroom. In this context, guest speakers need a unique variety of skills in order to provide a learning experience that is more valuable that what can be provided by the day-to-day classroom experience. A passionate and detailed knowledge of their topic is critical to ensuring the effective use of learning time guided by a guest speaker. As well, it is critical that the guest speaker has had previous successful interaction with young children, who can be a ruthlessly critical audience when their interest is not engaged. With these criteria in place, a guest speaker can engage and encourage young learners to examine ideas from new perspectives and through new ways of knowing.

Preparing for the visit of a guest speaker in the classroom is a key to ensuring the success of the learning opportunity. Ideally, the guest speaker will need to know and understand the learning expectation(s) that should result from their visit. They should have opportunities to plan with the classroom teacher and to adjust their presentation and resources to the special needs of the class.

Students should also understand exactly what they are to learn from the guest speaker. To engage the speaker in discussion, a presentation by a guest speaker should include a warm-up activity that introduces the speaker to the students and opens up communication by creating comfortable interaction. An introductory activity can be planned by the classroom teacher but the guest speaker needs to know and understand its purpose. At the end of an effective introductory activity, a level of trust and comfort should be established that will allow students to participate in questioning and open discussion.

To prepare to discuss a topic with the guest speaker, students should have a clearly defined task to complete during the time period and should have several questions about the topic in hand before the speaker arrives. An effective guest speaker will be able to weave the students' questions into their presentation if they are given access to the questions before they visit the classroom. Guest speakers may also come to the classroom to be interviewed by students rather than to present to them. If this is the case, students will benefit from having a graphic organizer that allows them to relate interview questions and the responses of the speaker (see Figure 15.5 for an example).

After the guest speaker's presentation, students can be engaged in helping to write a thank-you letter to the speaker. This will help students be more aware of what they learned from the speaker and will support students' metacognitive development.

Figure 15.5 Preparing for Classroom Visitors

INTERVIEW ORGANIZER

Our Guest _____ will talk about _____

I know these things about this topic:

Our guest speaker knows about this topic because:

I want to find out about these things:

I will ask the guest speaker:

Question _____?

Answer _____

Question _____?

Answer _____

A guest speaker can provide a rich learning experience, if the teacher gives both the class and the visitor adequate preparation.

INNOVATIVE APPROACHES IN YOUR SOCIAL STUDIES CLASSROOM

Project work will inevitably bring students into contact with the school or Internet community as they gather resources, learn strategies, or invite other people to celebrate their learning. The following ideas present four sample strategies for dealing with students' project work:

1. Work with a small group of colleagues to identify all of the field-trip possibilities in your local area that would support specific social studies curriculum for a grade of your choice. Collect all of the trip sites identified by your colleagues and create a data bank that identifies the site name, a contact person, contact details (phone, email, web pages, etc.) and information about the destination that would be useful for trip planning (hours of operation, distance, costs, program flexibility, etc.).

2. Choose a topic for which you might invite a guest speaker into the classroom. Create a question bank for the guest speaker that anticipates questions that your students might ask during the speaker's presentation.

3. Create a warm-up activity that you might use to acquaint a guest speaker and a group of young students before the guest speaker starts a presentation in your class. Be sure that the activity serves the dual purpose of acquainting and relaxing the students so that they can focus on learning from the presenter.

4. Create an activity centre for your classroom that will allow students to practise the skills needed to produce effective gravestone rubbings before they do this in a cemetery visit.

CASE STUDIES AND PROFESSIONAL ACTIVITIES FOR INNOVATION IN SOCIAL STUDIES

1. Ms. Tangent was very disappointed by the behaviour of her students during their first class trip of the school year. She is not sure what went wrong but she is certain it was not a good learning experience for her students. What questions would you ask of Ms. Tangent to help her determine what she needs to do differently to make the next field trip more effective?

2. You have just had a guest speaker talk to your class about the need for more tourism in the local area. Identify what you will have your students do after the guest speaker leaves to help them assess, synthesize, and evaluate the information they learned from the guest speaker.

3. Tour a local graveyard in preparation for planning a unit that includes a graveyard study. Identify the learning expectations you would want students to achieve through the study of this graveyard. Also, create a small booklet of activities that your class can use to achieve the intended expectations during their trip to the graveyard.

CHAPTER REVIEW AND PROFESSIONAL DEVELOPMENT AS A TEACHER

This chapter has examined the following:

- The community can provide supports for social studies through many experiences that include area investigations, field trips, speakers, and resources in print forms that can supplement the normal classroom resources.

- Community-based experiences must be well conceived and well planned so that they provide enriched learning experiences.

- Before deciding to use community resources such as field trips, the teacher must consider the benefits of learning in comparison to the effort, time, cost, and safety aspects of alternative experiences.

- Field trips can be designed for four purposes; each purpose requires different preparation prior to the field trip.

- School board policies may influence the types of trips that are options for local students.

- There are many details to be planned before, during, and after an effective field trip.

- Field trips need to be followed up in the classroom to ensure that learning is solidified.

- Community resources in print or artifact form may help teachers bring current community information into the classroom.
- Many social studies topics may be enriched through the use of community resources that can be brought into the classroom for reference.
- Museums can support classroom programs in many ways.
- Museums are becoming increasingly interactive in their display approaches.
- Virtual museums provide a cost- and time-effective option to field trips to examine some topics.
- Real and simulated archeology experiences can create interest in historical details.
- Many archeological skills can be used in the classroom, on the beach, or in a small area of land to examine "planted" digs.
- Online simulations teach students many archeology skills and concepts effectively.
- Cemetery studies provide unique sources of information about the local community.
- Teachers need to be well acquainted with students' prior experiences and sensitivities before introducing cemetery studies as part of their program.
- Many activities can be planned for cemetery studies to complement the other aspects of the program in social studies.
- Guest speakers who are passionate, knowledgeable, and aware of the learning needs of young students can provide valuable learning experiences.
- Students need to know what they are to learn from a guest speaker.
- Students need opportunities to plan what they want to learn from a guest speaker before their visit to the classroom.

Weblinks

Encourage your students to create their own historical photo comparison activity using the classroom computer. Use photos from your local museum or students' family collections. Take pictures of the same locations for a "today" photo. Scan both photos into separate document files. Open up both files on the desktop. Have students click on each file to change the size of the open file. This will allow them to compare both photos at the same time.

Many of the 2400 Canadian museums offer online activities. Visit www.virtualmuseum.ca to link to Canada's museum treasures!

Virtual Museum: General
This site provides links to online exhibits from various Canadian museums.
www.museevirtuel-virtualmuseum.ca

Canadian War Museum

On this site there are primary source materials, educational resources, and virtual exhibits.

www.warmuseum.ca

Virtual Museum: Métis History and Culture

This site has virtual exhibits on the subject of Métis culture and heritage.

www.metismuseum.ca/main.php

Virtual Museum: Canadian Museum of Civilization—New France

This site has a variety of virtual exhibits depicting the history and culture of New France.

www.civilization.ca/cmc/explore/virtual-museum-of-new-france

Chapter 16
Projects in the Social Studies Classroom

Learning Topics

- The Role of Projects
- Defining a Topic for Inquiry
- Inquiry Models and Project Work in the Classroom
- Selecting Resources for Effective Inquiry
- Creation, Application, and Communication of Independent Project Work
- The Role of Heritage Fairs in Your Program

Heritage fairs offer students the opportunity to share their inquiry-focused research with their peers and community.

When students become truly engaged in a project they take off in unexpected directions, producing work that is vastly superior to their customary levels of achievement.

—Sears, 1999

THE ROLE OF PROJECTS

Projects are a common occurrence in primary and junior classrooms. They vary in size, scope, and style, but all projects serve essentially the same purposes. Projects provide opportunities for students to work with ideas they have encountered to sort information and consider deeper understanding. Projects are constructivist in approach as they allow room for students to grapple with ideas to look for personal meaning. The teacher's role is to ensure that projects assigned in the classroom have the substantive content to allow manipulation and interpretation by students in an effort to make meaning.

As students develop increasing facility with word meanings, projects can become more sophisticated and provide opportunities for students to use the histographer's skills to learn from different text sources. Case (1999) identifies three ways that students can work with text to create personal meaning as they engage in project work (see Figure 16.1).

Figure 16.1 Working with Texts to Create Personal Meanings in Project Work

Ways to Engage Project Text	Details
Interrogating (analyzing) the text	■ Examine competing accounts of an event
	■ Examine a single account of an event that is problematic in details that are included or excluded
	■ Consider the credibility of the text source
Reframing the text to work with the ideas presented	■ Look at the text from a different perspective
	■ Present personal understanding of the text in another genre (to display the reader's synthesis of ideas)
	■ Apply the information from the text in a new situation
	■ Apply an analytical framework (e.g., a series of analysis questions) to examination of the text account
Solving the problem	■ Guide the project so that it focuses on learning about the big ideas or enduring understandings rather than bogging down in minute details
	■ Facilitate students' increasing understanding of the social world and conceptual understanding of its complexities

By focusing project work in the classroom on these three main types of text interaction we can ensure that projects do not deteriorate to time spent learning and memorizing facts. Students should have many opportunities to engage in project work to question, understand, consider relationships in time and place, and use relevant facts and concepts.

Using project approaches can allow students opportunities to become discriminating users of historical sources of information. They can be "armed" with a number of analytical questions that gradually become habits of mind as they interrogate new text. Students can learn to consider questions such as

- Whose account is this?
- Why would this person write about this event? What is their motivation?
- Is this a firsthand or secondhand account of these events?
- What details might differ between first- and secondhand accounts of the same event?
- Does the account include bias?
- Is the event well described? Does the author appear to be well informed?
- Is there evidence of inaccurate or unexplored details in the account?
- What does the author appear to want a reader to believe about the people depicted in this account?

When opportunities for projects are presented in the classroom, their timing in the learning sequence is critical. Students should have been immersed in the topic and able to gather many details about the era and significant events. They should have had opportunities for guided discovery of personal areas of interest and opportunities to identify personal choices about areas they would like to examine further. Chapter 2 discussed phases of instruction. Project work should be offered as a way to consolidate and apply developing conceptual knowledge to support students' deepening understanding of these concepts and relationships among them. Projects also give students many contextualized opportunities to consolidate and apply the skills of research, allowing them to analyze, synthesize, and evaluate data from a variety of sources.

Before engaging in project work, students require significant understanding of process skills to ensure successful investigation of the resources. They also need to be taught many ways that ideas can be presented and displayed in project format so they can make informed decisions about the most effective methods of presenting their findings. With these process and product skills, students can then address new content through time spent interrogating text, reframing ideas, and looking for solutions.

There are many types of projects that students can engage in the primary and junior social studies context. The type of project chosen (see Figure 16.2) should have clear and close ties to articulated learning expectations and should support constructivist (meaning making) learning. Project foci will become more sophisticated and inquiry focused as students expand their skills and reading abilities.

Teachers can develop further the students' examples of each type of project by considering projects that 1) interrogate the text, 2) reframe the text, and 3) solve the problem.

Figure 16.2 Types of Projects in the Primary and Junior Social Studies Classroom

Types of Projects	Example
Telling Stories	Grade 1 students may explain what a day in their community involves through photo journals and drawings.
Understanding Events over Time and Place	Grade 2 students may explain how traditions and celebrations in their community vary each season and reflect the religious and cultural beliefs of people in their community.
Understanding Technology	Grade 3 students may study farm technology changes over time and offer some conclusions about how the size of farms and cooperative farming practices have changed the types of technology used on Canadian farms.
Uncovering Patterns	Grade 4 students may study aerial maps of farms along the St. Lawrence River and identify patterns in their layout and relate these patterns to historical information about early transportation.
Identifying Problems	Grade 4 students may examine accounts of the same current event from different news sources and propose reasons why different details were highlighted in different accounts.
Offering Solutions	Grade 5 students may study transportation challenges in the far north and experiment to consider other options and examine the potential impact of their proposals on the environment.
Making Connections	Grade 5 students may examine immigration patterns across Canada and consider strategies to determine the needs of new immigrants in various areas and propose ways to monitor the changing needs and their differences across communities and groups of origin.
Making Predictions	Grade 6 students may examine the stories of Canadian soldiers in previous wars and in current conflicts from both primary and secondary sources and make some predictions about the types of post-conflict supports that may be needed by veterans.

When projects are introduced to young children, the learning goal of the project should be clear to both the teacher and the students. Parents often play an important role in supporting project work that is done in the classroom by providing encouragement, and often supplies for project completion. Parents can become supportive partners in the classroom's project work if they are informed of the goals of the project.

As students develop enough language and conceptual understanding to engage in reflection about their learning, rubrics become a critical support to guide project work. A rubric can identify the criteria being considered by the teacher for project work completion and can help students consider the aspects of the work that will be under scrutiny by the teacher to provide evidence of their learning. When used in the latter way, rubrics become the standards that students can aspire to and identify specific, criterion-based growth schemes for students to use as a reference point. Rubrics help parents understand how they can support and encourage their child's project work.

In order to develop project rubrics that can serve all of these purposes, teachers must have an understanding that rubrics display both the *criteria* and the *standards* for evaluation. (See Chapters 17 and 18 for further details about developing assessment criteria and standards.) As rubrics are developed, careful consideration needs to be given to specific descriptors within a rubric so that these descriptors provide clear and definitive pictures of the likely differences that can be observed in students' project work. The rubric template provided in Figure 16.3 can be used as a starting point and standards can be inserted and adapted to the specific project.

Teachers can work with older students to complete the rubrics by inserting statements of standards for a specific project. This practice will help students understand what is expected and encourage high standards of achievement. More details about rubrics and their use in assessment are developed in Chapter 18.

Figure 16.3 Displaying Criteria and Standards within Rubrics

Topic: _____

Expectation(s): _____

Name(s): _____

Cooperative Rubrics					
	Achievement Categories	Level 1	Level 2	Level 3	Level 4
Content	Knowledge and understanding				
Process	Thinking and Inquiry				
	Communication				
Product	Application				

When students engage in learning and demonstrating their learning through projects, they should have examples of the expected outcomes of their work available to examine and guide them. This is especially important for initial attempts at projects with young children. To provide this guidance and support, the teacher should provide an *exemplar*. An exemplar is a sample of the expected product that students have structured opportunities to examine and analyze in relation to both criteria and standards. As well, a rubric to guide growth toward the expected achievement is always useful at the outset of project work.

Sources of information to support students' project work must be carefully considered by teachers. Students should have many opportunities to work with historical and geographical information in raw forms and to engage reports of current events. These materials allow students to use source documents through interaction with people, exhibits, objects and artifacts, reports of events or phenomena. Source kits such as Jackdaw or the Canadian Scrapbook Series allow students to work with copies of original documents. These can provide motivation for students because they have a sense of touching history when they are exposed to these sources. When students have original sources or secondary or even tertiary sources to work with, they can engage the skills of historians to investigate and interrogate these sources.

There are many advantages of using primary, secondary, and tertiary sources in classroom projects with young students (Dhand, 1999). Source approaches use the raw materials of history and current events to

- support inquiry;
- provide easy-to-access sources (e.g., through topical kits of primary and secondary sources);
- provide insights into events and personalities;
- allow examination of different points of view;
- support skill building as students try to determine bias; establish authenticity, validity, reliability, and frame of reference; draw inferences; generalize; interpret; compile; and conclude;
- apply historiography approaches to help students learn to seek truth;
- promote connections between events, their causes, and their impacts over time and space;
- help students develop higher-order thinking skills;
- learn to relate reports of events to the reporter's frame of reference and context;
- understand the impact of changes in attitudes, beliefs, and values on interpretations of events over time;
- create students' desire to engage history as active and critical participants; and
- allow students to reflect on the balance and comprehensiveness of their own sources of information and the approach they apply to interpreting them.

Source approaches must include opportunities for students who are pursuing projects to consider the frame of reference of the source, its authenticity or validity, its accuracy, and its objectivity. See Figure 16.4 for a breakdown of primary, secondary, and tertiary sources and their characteristics.

Figure 16.4 Types of Sources

Primary Sources	Secondary Sources	Tertiary Sources
■ Include many forms of documents that have survived over time	■ Include some documents that have been interpreted over time	■ May demonstrate considerable distortion because accounts have passed through more hands
■ May reflect the emotional reactions of a recent event to allow for greater empathetic response from readers	■ Advantage of emotional distance	■ Degree of removal in time and space from the original event adds potential for further distortion
■ From the time of the event so language conventions will be authentic and may reflect subtleties	■ Disadvantage of a lack of social context for interpreting accounts	■ Context clues become harder to interpret
■ May not reflect much processing of the impact of the event on later events	■ Language may incorporate modern idiom that can distort the original event and its significance	■ May misrepresent both primary and secondary sources
■ Are likely to present a single perspective on events	■ May misinterpret a primary source	■ May be developed for the sole purpose of presenting balanced perspectives

If primary sources are made available to students for project work, the teacher will need to use instructional strategies to bridge the gap between script styles and to support reading and comprehension of concepts.

When projects are chosen as a way for students to represent their learning, they should have clear links to the main threads of the appropriate provincial or territorial guideline. Typically, guidelines share many common foci (Gibson, 2009). Guidelines usually

- ■ present a view of social studies as an interdisciplinary subject;

- ■ give primacy to historical and geographical concepts;

- ■ require students to engage topics about relationships within their community, between communities, and with the environment;

- ■ present the past as a vehicle to help form understanding of the present and consider aspects of the future and impacts on it;

- ■ present social studies as a vehicle to help students understand the local and global contexts of their lives and experiences; and

- ■ promote supporting students' development of the skills needed for active citizenship in a democracy.

Projects that are carefully designed can help to enrich each of these foci by engaging students through the portals of their interests in various subtopics within themes being studied.

Interviews are special sources of information for projects. These sources of information are readily available to young learners without the need to navigate text sources to acquire rich information. People in the community can be invited to the classroom to engage the students in interviews about current topics of study. Interviews will need careful preparation so that students benefit from the time spent interviewing people. Clear expectations for the outcome of interviews will help to direct students' questions of the interviewee. In community studies or career-related topics, visitors can be questioned about their job description, work history, long-term goals, responsibilities, hours, wages, benefits, advantages and disadvantages of their job, connections with other industries in the community, and working conditions. If the interview relates more to the community history and generational experiences, interviews may focus on the visitor's childhood experiences, school days, family structure, memories of key events, hard times in the family or community, or personal interests such as crafts, hobbies, pastimes, family traditions, religious practices and celebrations, or foods and music memories.

To prepare for visitor interviews, students should be taught to plan two types of interview interactions. The first is a list of specific questions related to the reason that the visitor is coming to the classroom. Different groups of students may have vastly different lists of questions and may take turns addressing their specific interests. The number of questions should reflect the goals of the visit and the amount of time that will be allotted to the interview. The second type of interaction that students need to be taught is the use of probes and prompts to encourage more detail about an interview question. This type of interview interaction would include comments such as

- "Can you give us an example of . . . ?"
- "What would cause this?"
- "Can you explain the details?"
- "What do you think . . . ?"

Older students may be taught to generate interview questions using an organizer that will allow them to prepare questions ahead of a visitor interview but also allow them to generate additional questions as they listen to interactions during the interview. An organizer such as Figure 16.5 may provide support for this purpose.

Sears (1999) identified several benefits to students from engaging in interviews with classroom visitors. In addition to providing rich data for the students to digest, synthesize, and apply to a task, interviews also provide

- strong motivation;
- opportunities for self-discovery as students view incidents through the impressions of another person;

Figure 16.5 Preparing for Visitor Interviews

Interviewee: Purpose(s) of This Interview: Date:	
Types of Interview Questions	**Interviewee's Responses/Notes**
Facts (What is/was . . . ?)	
Emotions (How does/did this feel . . . ?)	
Impacts (How did this affect . . . ?)	
Probes (Examples and expansions)	

- opportunities to appreciate the value of storytelling;
- exposure to the language of another person who can connect students' studies to life outside the classroom;
- data without the risk of plagiarism;
- information that can be collected systematically (if pre-interview preparation is done thoroughly);
- opportunities for purposeful talk;
- increased independence in the quest for specific information from alternative sources;
- flexibility and accessibility to all age groups of students;
- opportunities to make community connections that may influence future interactions in the community;
- opportunities to build intergenerational relationships in the community; and
- exposure to active, integrative learning.

After visitor interviews, students should have opportunities to process and present what they have learned from the interview. This will help them to synthesize and evaluate the ideas they heard and allow processing that will support deeper understanding. Every classroom visitor interview should have three phases that the students engage: preparation for the visit, conducting the interview during the visit, and working to synthesize, evaluate, and present the information after the visit.

Older students can also be given guidelines for preparing for effective interviews that they can study and self-monitor as preparation for the actual interview process (see Figure 16.6). Sears (1999) suggests that students work in triad teams to prepare for the interview with one member of the team conducting the interview, one simulating the responses of the interviewee, and the third being the active observer, providing input to improve the quality of the interview.

Figure 16.6 Strategies for Preparing Effective Interviews

- Create triad teams to conduct mock interviews.
- Have the team work together to find out background information about the interviewee.
- Have the team generate potential interview questions using a framework to align questions for facts, emotions, impacts, and probes, with spaces for interview notes.
- Plan for recording during the interview. This will help students listen as well as probe so they do not have to take all notes on the spot. Video or tape recording must be approved by the interviewee before their arrival.

- Check all interview questions for sensitivity, careful wording, and potential misunderstanding.
- Be prepared to follow the story as the interview progresses and jot down new questions as the interviewee uncovers anything unexpected but interesting.
- Consider how individuals or the class will thank the interviewee for their time and sharing at the end of the interview and more formally after the interviewee leaves.
- Revise plans for how to work with the data and present it after the interview.

Students may collect a considerable amount of print, photographic, and audio data from classroom interviews. They will need guidance in how to sort, classify, and isolate main ideas after interviews.

DEFINING A TOPIC FOR INQUIRY

As students engage in project-based learning to consolidate and apply ideas they have been learning, there will be growing opportunities for them to delineate the focus and scope of their projects. This flexibility to encourage personal interests and opportunities to explore ideas within a common topic will motivate students. The students will need practice with defining project topics initially and with following projects through from conception to completion.

Teachers will have goals for learning when assigning a project in social studies. In age-appropriate ways these goals should be shared with the students so that they start to learn to focus their project choices within parameters that will encourage their interests and still meet the required learning. The initial challenge in doing this in early primary classrooms is that students lack the background knowledge to determine what fits and what does not. Therefore, initial forays into project work with young children may benefit from framing choices in a limited set so that students have a few options but not a wide-open field within the topic. As students acquire experience with completing projects, they will need the teacher's guidance to develop inquiry questions to frame the scope of their project. Topic elaboration questions can serve as a generic set of starters to help students adapt to their interests. Topic elaboration was introduced in Chapter 1 and developed in subsequent chapters. The generic questions of topic elaboration include

- What is it?
- How does it work?
- What are its interesting characteristics?
- How do those characteristics change over time? Space?
- What are those changes related to?
- What would happen if . . . ?
- What should/could/might/will be done about this?

By analyzing the types of projects presented in Figure 16.2, it will be evident that the topic elaboration list can be applied to all of them. Ideally, older students should be taught to incorporate all elements of these types of projects into a super project that addresses all of these aspects of their chosen topic. This expansive treatment of the topic will provide powerful evidence of students' sophisticated understanding of the topic and related issues. Teachers will need to help students define topics that are not so narrow in scope that resources will be unavailable.

INQUIRY MODELS AND PROJECT WORK IN THE CLASSROOM

Throughout this book, the theme of inquiry as an essential social studies process skill has been revisited. Re-examine the models and inquiry components that have been presented. While there are many ways to approach inquiry, students will benefit from having some consistency in the model they are using throughout the early grades. Variations can be introduced as confidence increases.

When students engage in sustained inquiry projects they can be supported by having teacher-planned check-in points as their work progresses. A check-in point allows the teacher and student to have regular planned conferences to examine the student's progress, redirect if needed, and support with emerging resources. Check-in points also provide opportunities for the teacher to provide guidance about the type of presentation of the final project work that will best fit the student's study and findings (see Figure 16.7 for an example).

Teachers can formalize the check-in process by making it a student's responsibility to have each part of their project "signed off" as it progresses. A check-in record sheet can be maintained by the student and also serves to remind them of the expected steps of their inquiry.

Teachers can adapt any of the check-in steps to reflect the specific project that students are pursuing.

By supporting students through the stages of a sustained inquiry with regular check-in points teachers can help students meet with success in their early experiences with inquiry projects.

Figure 16.7 Project Completion Check-In

Inquiry Topic: Student's Name: Inquiry Focus:				
Inquiry Model Steps	**Check-In Date for Conference**	**Directions for Next Steps**	**Student's Initials**	**Teacher's Initials**
Has identified an inquiry question or series of questions.				
Has identified initial resources.				
Has started to read, observe, interview, collect samples, and/or view.				
Has formed a hypothesis to guide further research.				
Has written records of research.				
Has planned a way to present ideas.				
Has prepared a bibliography of references and resources.				
Has planned a visual display to represent their findings.				
Has completed a visual display to represent their findings.				
Has planned a verbal- and media-supported presentation to present findings to the selected audience (e.g., classmates, school fair, student-led parent–teacher conference).				

SELECTING RESOURCES FOR EFFECTIVE INQUIRY

Finding resources of appropriate reading levels can pose a substantial challenge for inquiry projects in elementary classrooms. Students will need help to acquire a wide range of resources and will need support as they use informational text, photographs, documents and records, artifacts, and other sources for the first time. They will need to have support identifying sources of resources and, initially, may benefit from having specific numbers and types of resources available for their use. Too many possibilities may overwhelm the emerging reader and subvert the purpose of the use of a variety of resources.

As students mature in their inquiry and project skills and reading levels develop so that more types of resources are readily accessible for research, students should be taught to consider and monitor the types of resources they are using. By monitoring what they do use, students can also consider what they have not yet used and can engage in searches for those resources. Students can monitor their resource selections on a framework that exposes them to all of the possibilities and teaches them to keep accurate records about their research sources (see Figure 16.8).

Resources may need to be selected to meet specific provincial or territorial guidelines. Teachers must be aware of these local requirements as they consider the resources that are to be made available to students.

Variations of this resource-recording list (see Figure 16.8) can be prepared to be suitable for younger grades. Such a list will provide direction for students' searches.

Earlier chapters addressed ways to teach young students how to ask "fat" or significant questions to guide inquiry. As well, the Bloom's Taxonomy Wheel (see Chapter 9) can guide some of the products students could produce to demonstrate learning from their inquiry. Strategies for instruction in the use of informational text were provided in Chapter 13. When students address new sources of text, a text walk-through will help them to refresh their knowledge of text features (see Figure 16.9 on page 397). A text walk-through can happen in cooperative learning groups and will help to draw students' attention to the unique features of text they may encounter during research. A text walk-through will also help to reinforce students' developing concept vocabulary as they learn to name text features. A review of the use of graphic organizers to sort and relate information (see Chapter 13) will also support students' research work.

A text walk-through in scavenger hunt format could be structured so that students work with a team but compete against other student teams to find many features of their text or visual source. This sample could also be adapted for a walk-through of electronic sources.

As students start work on projects in social studies they should be introduced to the role of other people in the school who may be able to support them. The school's teacher-librarian may be available to visit the classroom and talk about accessing resources from the library. Students should also know how to go about accessing community resources that may support their research.

The types of supports that students may need for each project will reflect the origin of the project ideas. Projects may be teacher directed, student directed, or be negotiated between students and teacher (co-directed).

In teacher-directed project work the teacher typically determines the content, process, and required product from the inquiry. All students are likely to learn the same content, following the same process, with the same resources, and may be required to produce identical products to demonstrate their learning.

Figure 16.8 Project Research Sources

Sources	Primary Source	Secondary Source	Tertiary Source
Almanacs			
Business directories			
Business files			
Cartoons			
Cemetery records			
Census records			
Charters			
Chronicles			
Deeds			
Diaries			
Electronic media			
Family bibles			
Genealogies			
Harvest records			
Journals			
Lecture notes or tapes			
Magazines			
Maps			
Newspapers			
Oral histories			
Pamphlets			
Photographs and/or paintings			
Poems			
Real estate abstracts			
Reminiscences			
Statistical data			
Telephone directories			
Treaties			
Websites			

In student-directed projects, the students may have a wide range of choice about the specific content within the overall topic that they wish to study. They may use very different research resources and processes to arrive at the product and may elect to produce products that are varied and reflect their specialized focus.

Figure 16.9 Documenting a Text Walk-Through

Text Feature	Found on Page . . .
Introduction	
Main Headings/Titles	
Subheadings/Subtitles	
Table of Contents	
Credits	
Chapter Overviews	
Chapter Summaries/Reviews	
Vocabulary (Bold or Italicized)	
Charts, Tables, Graphs, Timelines, Graphic Organizers	
Fictional Text Inserted into Informational Text to Illustrate a Point	
Personal Stories	
Profiles	
Diagrams	
Captions	
Quotations	
Photos and Illustrations	
Maps	
Cartoons	
Websites	
Bibliography	
References/Footnotes	

In co-directed research, the teacher and students work together to determine the best focus to take on the wide range of content that may be available. The teacher and student work together to develop a plan for gathering resources, planning a process, and laying out a product that demonstrates the unique learning of the student or small group. When research projects are unique and varied within a common area of study, students often have opportunities to share their research with the class so that they can learn to consolidate what they have found and relate it to others.

Web-based inquiry projects present unique challenges for students. The text scavenger hunt approach can be modified to introduce unique text from websites at the outset of web-based inquiry. Whether web-based resources are interactive or passive sources of information, they can provide valuable up-to-date research information in appealing formats that motivate researchers.

CREATION, APPLICATION, AND COMMUNICATION OF INDEPENDENT PROJECT WORK

The creation, application, and communication of projects should be a celebration of the student's work. To make the opportunities a successful learning experience for all students, each student should be taught communication skills that support presentations to a group. Prior opportunities to engage in drama activities and to use Readers' Theatre approaches will support students' confidence as they present individually. Readers' Theatre allows students to prepare scripts to present ideas from their research and to assign reading roles to other students so that active engagement in a classmate's presentation is possible. The use of strategies such as Readers' Theatre in social studies allows the teacher to integrate learning and provides students with opportunities to connect ideas across subjects. Integration has the added advantage of saving learning time when the strategies of one subject area are practised in another subject area.

Provincial and territorial social studies guidelines outline creation (process), communication, and application skills among the expectations for the various topics of each grade level. These skills are outlined in Figure 16.10.

These skills may be incorporated into the guidelines and identify the grade-appropriate variation of each skill. If not, this will be a task that the classroom teacher will need to undertake. The resource book *Curriculum Speak* (Meyers, 2006) provides many ideas for

Figure 16.10 Creation, Communication, and Application Skills

- Analyzing
- Asking questions
- Brainstorming
- Building models
- Comparing
- Connecting
- Contrasting opinions
- Considering change over time and space
- Considering implications
- Creating simulations to model concepts
- Drawing and labelling
- Drawing conclusions
- Evaluating
- Explaining
- Expressing personal viewpoints
- Formulating
- Identifying
- Identifying examples
- Justifying
- Locating
- Modifying
- Monitoring
- Planning
- Reading and interpreting maps
- Re-creating
- Representing another point of view
- Responding through imaginative works
- Revising
- Suggesting problems and potential solutions

(Continued)

Figure 16.10 *(Continued)*

■ Sequencing	■ Using scale
■ Using bibliographic conventions	■ Using sources to locate information
■ Using graphic organizers to show relationships	■ Using specialized vocabulary
■ Using illustrations, key words, and writing	■ Using symbols
■ Using media	■ Weighing options
	■ Writing reports

strategies students could incorporate in their presentations of project work to ensure the active engagement of listeners.

THE ROLE OF HERITAGE FAIRS IN YOUR PROGRAM

In 2009, the Historica Foundation of Canada and the Dominion Institute merged to create the Historica-Dominion Institute. This national program's mission is to encourage students to engage in celebrating and learning about Canadian history. School and regional heritage fairs are held all over the country, especially during early springtime. In late April or early May, many jurisdictions hold a regional heritage fair (also known as Historica Fair) to allow representatives from each school fair to come together and share their research. The strongest projects from the regional fairs may be selected to go on to represent the region at the various provincial fairs.

The fair's program brings together students who enjoy history and have chosen to delve deeply into a particular Canadian history topic. Typically, heritage fairs involve students from Grades 4 to 9, but school fairs may include students from any grade. Parents are often invited to visit the fairs at the school level and many regional fairs welcome visitors from the local community.

During the fairs, students usually have further opportunities to delve into Canadian history. In addition to having time to visit the displays of research done by other students, many school and regional fairs hold history-focused workshops during the day(s) of their fair. Students may have opportunities to learn about Native traditions, watch an historical play, learn how to set up full-sized teepees, cook foods using methods available in the 1700s, or engage in a wide variety of other history-based experiences.

Heritage fair displays are usually three-dimensional and mounted on backboards, comparable to the style used for science fairs. There are no size restrictions for heritage displays. However, entries may also be history-based plays that are presented to all fair participants. Students who are presenting their research in a three-dimensional display are encouraged to add interactive components to their displays so that visitors and fellow historians can see, touch, and even taste some of their research. Many participants develop and wear a costume that matches the theme of their display. Pioneers, Native people in traditional dress, soldiers, and early firefighters can be seen at a typical fair. Heritage fairs are indeed a celebration of Canadian history!

The list of types of projects presented earlier in this chapter (Figure 16.2) can support exploration of a wide range of heritage fair approaches and help students avoid trivial or inconsequential studies.

INNOVATIVE APPROACHES IN YOUR SOCIAL STUDIES CLASSROOM

Project work represents a unique opportunity for students to offer their ideas to the scrutiny of others. Public displays, celebrations, and electronically formatted presentations such as PowerPoint or Keynote provide opportunities for students to examine their work with awareness of the perspective of potential viewers. Some ideas to help students benefit from project work in your classroom include the following:

1. Projects are often completed in display style and students from the same grade or from other classes have an opportunity to visit the displays. Develop a project scavenger hunt ("Find a project that . . . ") that could be used for an in-class or school-wide project-display event so that the visitors get the most out of their time viewing the displays.

2. Hold a seniors' tea (Sears, 1999) in your classroom to allow students opportunities to interview a variety of seniors about topics of interest in the lives of an earlier generation. Help students generate lists of specific and prompting questions that they can ask during an interview. Provide students with a framework to record answers and help them analyze and draw conclusions from their interview responses. Support them in writing thank-you letters to the seniors after the tea.

3. Create a PowerPoint presentation to teach your students about heritage fairs. Include some sample photographs of heritage projects from the many photos available on the national Historica-Dominion Institute website (www.historica-dominion.ca). Find out about heritage fairs in your region. Most heritage fair committees welcome teachers to participate in hosting the regional fair.

CASE STUDIES AND PROFESSIONAL ACTIVITIES FOR INNOVATION IN SOCIAL STUDIES

1. Develop detailed plans, including planning check-in pages, for your students to encourage them to create a heritage fair project.

2. Select a topic from the curriculum for any grade. Work with a group of other teacher candidates to compile a resource kit that could be used by a small group of students to study that topic. Include both primary and secondary resources in your kit. Create an index and a storage system for the resource kit.

3. Introduce a text scavenger hunt to your students on your next practicum. After the hunt, reflect on what students learned from it and what they enjoyed about doing it. Also consider things you might do differently in the future to have students benefit from this experience even more.

4. There are several virtual and interactive websites identified in the Weblinks section at the end of this chapter. Surf these sites to determine where each one might be used in your social studies program.

5. Lists of resources for project and inquiry work are provided in this chapter. Examine these lists. With a group of colleagues, brainstorm ideas for how you will teach students to consider the limitations and benefits of using these resources and of using a wide range of resources.

CHAPTER REVIEW AND PROFESSIONAL DEVELOPMENT AS A TEACHER

This chapter has examined the following:

■ Projects provide opportunities for students to work with ideas and synthesize and evaluate information to develop deeper understanding.

■ During projects, students can engage text by analyzing/interrogating it, reframing it to examine perspectives and display understanding, and by solving a problem presented through research.

■ Analytical questions can be used to guide project work to ensure its validity.

■ Immersion in a topic must precede project work so that the topics of projects have substance.

■ Projects should provide opportunities to consolidate and apply learning.

■ Students need process skills and understanding of product options before engaging in beneficial project work.

■ Project types include telling stories, understanding events over time and place, understanding technology, uncovering patterns, identifying problems, offering solutions, making connections, and making predictions.

■ Parents should be informed of the goals of a project so they can support the project as valid learning and in practical ways.

■ Rubrics can provide direction for students about goals for producing high-quality projects.

■ Specific project rubrics can be co-developed by teacher and students to help students conceptualize the characteristics of high-quality projects.

- Exemplars provide targets for students' project work.

- Source kits provide excellent resource materials for students to use for projects.

- Source approaches to project work have many advantages.

- Primary, secondary, and tertiary resources have unique characteristics and unique advantages.

- Primary sources may present unique vocabulary and script challenges for young students.

- Project work can support many guideline goals for student learning.

- Interviews are special types of projects that require unique skills from students before, during, and after the interview.

- Students need support in preparing valid and viable questions for interviews.

- Projects provide unique opportunities for students to pursue personal interests related to a topic.

- Topic elaboration questions can be used to guide the scope of a project.

- Check-in points during project work provide a useful way to help students stay on track and to provide timely support for their work.

- The reading level of project resources can create challenges in primary/junior project work.

- Providing a list of potential sources of information for projects can help students in their quest for resources.

- Text walk-throughs can help prepare students to navigate texts for project work.

- Web sources may require additional support as students navigate this unique text style.

- Projects provide opportunities for students to develop many of the process and product skills targeted in provincial and territorial guidelines.

- Heritage Fairs provide motivating venues for the display and presentation of students' project work.

Weblinks

Online Pen Pals
Opportunities for teachers to connect their students with computer-based pen pals.
http://epals.com

Web Inquiry
Examples of web-inquiry projects
http://cnx.org/content/m18042/latest/

Online Interactive Game: WWII Tank Crews
The Canadian War Museum website "Armoured Warrior" allows students to simulate the experience of tank crews in WWII.
www.warmuseum.ca

Online Interactive Game: WWII Trench Life

The Canadian War Museum website "Over the Top" allows students to simulate life in the trenches in WWI.
www.warmuseum.ca

Online Simulation: Early Canadian Explorer

This simulation allows students to simulate the experience of an early Canadian explorer.
www.civilization.ca/cmc/explore/virtual-museum-of-new-france/pierre-boucher/pierre-boucher

Online Simulation: Canadian Arctic

This simulation allows students to simulate a trip in the Canadian Arctic through "Journey to Kitigaaryuk."
http://www.civilization.ca/cmc/exhibitions/kids/kitigaaryuk/index.shtml

Online Simulation: Upper Canada Settlers

This simulation allows students to simulate life as a settler in Upper Canada using "Great Upper Canada Adventure."
www.sydenhamdiscovery.ca/english/game.asp

Online Interactive Game: Early Civilizations

In this interactive game students investigate life in other early cultures (e.g., Roman, Viking, Tudor England, and Victorian England).
www.bbc.co.uk/history/walk/games_index.shtml

Online Interactive Game: Canadian Clothing History

This site allows students to explore changes in clothing over Canada's history.
www.pc.gc.ca/apprendre-learn/jeunes-youths/index_e.asp

Online Interactive Game: Samuel Champlain

This game allows students to learn about the adventures of Samuel Champlain in "Budding Explorer."
www.pc.gc.ca/apprendre-learn/jeunes-youths/index_e.asp

Online Interactive game: Women in Canadian History

On this site students will learn about women's roles in Canadian history in "Women in Canadian History."
www.pc.gc.ca/apprendre-learn/jeunes-youths/index_e.asp

Online Lesson: Plate Tectonics

Students are introduced to a tour that explains the concept of plate tectonics in "Plate Tectonics: Our World in Motion."
www.uen.org/utahlink/tours/tourFames.cgi?tour_id=13380

Virtual World Tours

Students can take virtual tours to many countries.
www.northvalley.net/kids/cities.shtml

Virtual Tours: Northwest Territories

Students can take virtual tours through Canada's Northwest Territories.
www.lessonsfromtheland.ca

Chapter 17

Improving Student Achievement in Social Studies

Learning Topics

- Approaches to Authentic Assessment and Respectful Tasks

- Assessment Strategies that Engage Students

- Designing Culminating Tasks to Show Evidence of Learning

- Using Rubrics to Ensure Success: Rubrics as Growth Schemes

- Creating and Using Exemplars for Social Studies Tasks

- Moving from Assessment to Evaluation

- Testing and Rich Performance Tasks: Choosing the Right Medium

- Creating Social Studies Portfolios: The Road to Motivation

A student demonstrates her understanding using an authentic assessment using an interactive white board. These strategies measure the real evidence of students' learning. This concept is juxtaposed to traditional assessment, which tends to measure the acquisition of memorized facts and processes.

What is counted counts!

—*Author Unknown*

APPROACHES TO AUTHENTIC ASSESSMENT AND RESPECTFUL TASKS

The purpose of any form of assessment is to provide the teacher with information to improve learning experiences for students. The most effective assessment provides students with respectful tasks that give them an opportunity to demonstrate what they really know about a topic. Assessment can be done prior to learning to determine what students already know or what misconceptions they may have about a topic. This type of assessment is called *diagnostic assessment*. Assessment that is done during the learning to determine what changes in instruction may be needed for individuals is called *formative assessment*. When assessment is used to measure the learning that has taken place, we call this *summative assessment*. Whether assessment is used for diagnostic, formative, or summative purposes, it should be authentic in nature, unless there is a need to assess the memorization of facts, which traditional assessments such as tests and quizzes do well.

The purpose of any assessment is to support students' growth. Teachers and students should work together to support this growth using a breadth of strategies. Criteria and standards guide growth. Exemplars provide examples to support growth. Non-examples help students understand the relevance of criteria and standards. Criteria and standards are displayed in relation to each other in rubrics that show levels of growth. Portfolios provide evidence of growth over time. Culminating activities may provide significant evidence of growth for a student's portfolio. All of these aspects of assessment are used to develop a comprehensive approach to social studies assessment and create an authentic learning environment.

Authentic assessment is a concept that has evolved from many prior efforts to connect learning and assessment into an integrated learning experience for students. Other terms that preceded the more inclusive concept of authentic assessment include performance assessment (Boykoff Baron, 1989), alternative assessment (Maeroff, 1991), performance-based assessment (Boykoff Baron, Forgione & Rindone, 1991), whole assessment (Nickell, 1992), and naturalistic assessment (Reithaug, 1992). Many provincial and territorial curriculum guidelines are unclear about the types of assessments that should apply in classrooms, but many support documents from the same governmental sources via Ministries of Education are very specific about philosophies and approaches to assessment.

Today, our conception of authentic assessment has come to be understood as strategies to measure the real evidence of students' learning. This concept is juxtaposed to traditional assessment, which tends to measure the acquisition of memorized facts and processes. Authentic assessment is a strong approach because it

■ has greater authenticity—the goals for learning match the approach to assessing the learning;

- supports learning—the approaches to authentic assessment are non-intrusive, inclusive (in that they support peer- and self-assessment as well as teacher assessment), and are designed to measure understanding rather than memorizing; and

- is fair to students—authentic assessment approaches consider the question, "What will I accept as evidence that students know or are able to do this?"; authentic approaches include choices that students can make about how they demonstrate their learning and provide many alternatives to traditional paper-and-pencil testing.

The spirit of authentic assessment is one of support and encouragement for the learning. Assessment is engaged *for* and *as* learning, not only *of* learning. In overvaluing memorization, traditional assessments such as paper-and-pencil testing may inhibit genuine learning related to inquiry.

Case (1999) identifies four principles of authentic assessment (see Figure 17.1).

Figure 17.1 Case's Four Principles of Authentic Assessment

Assessment focuses on measuring what really matters.	■ By ensuring that clear criteria for assessment are evident to students ■ By measuring the big ideas in the learning ■ By reflecting measurement attention to the elements of content, process, and product in a carefully considered balance
Assessments must provide valid indications of student competence.	■ By ensuring that the assessment strategy assesses what it purports to assess ■ By including realistic elements in the assessment and making them problem embedded ■ By ensuring that testing and assessment are comfortable for all students ■ By using assessment strategies that promote the use of knowledge in real-life contexts
Assessments should encourage and guide further learning.	■ By developing assessments that span the full range of learning expectations ■ By clearly communicating learning expectations to students ■ By using techniques that clearly analyze the results of learning episodes ■ By including students in the assessments of their work through peer- and self-assessment

Figure 17.1 *(Continued)*

	■ By ensuring that assessment is used for formative purposes as well as summative ones
	■ By structuring self-assessment opportunities that teach students how to respond to criteria for assessment and recognize standards for assessment
	■ By setting standards through exposure to exemplars
	■ By discussing assessment criteria with students before each task to guide their growth
	■ By using rubrics as growth schemes to help guide students to produce work at the next level of achievement
	■ By clarifying standards to reduce inconsistencies and arbitrariness in assessments
Assessments must be efficient.	■ By using detailed descriptors of expected performance criteria and standards in rubrics; these provide clear visions of the targeted performance, give clear and consistent feedback in detail, and save the teacher marking time

Source: Adapted from *Principles of Authentic Assessment* (Case, 2008).

Authentic assessment is rich in feedback. The students are provided with details that support redirection for improvement. By using a wide variety of authentic assessment techniques, teachers can ensure that they have several rich ways to assess the desired learning expectation(s) and can vary the assessment as needed to respond to the students' learning style preferences. Authentic assessment approaches include extensive and detailed feedback so the assessment itself becomes part of the learning, where students gather more information about the topic through the nature of the feedback.

Authentic assessment also changes the relationship between the teacher and the learner in the assessment process (see Figure 17.2). Traditional assessment has the learner receiving assessment from the teacher. In authentic assessment, the teacher and learner become partners in assessing the student's efforts, and the focus of the assessment shifts from measuring what *was* done to support what *could be done*.

Assessment language is very specific. Effective assessment techniques require that the teacher has a clear understanding of how criteria, standards, and exemplars work together to help the student see the requirements of assessment tasks.

In the sample exemplar shown in Figure 17.3, students can see that the required elements of transportation, housing, population density, and vegetation are displayed in three-dimensional forms, in both urban and rural environments. The exemplar shows the qualities required in the students' work and the high degree to which those qualities are displayed in the sample.

Figure 17.2 Shifting from Traditional to Authentic Assessment

Shifting from Teacher Assessment to Authentic Assessment	How the Assessment Shifts in This Process
Teacher Assessment	■ Teacher generates and applies assessment criteria and standards. ■ Teacher or student applies the criteria to a teacher- prepared exemplar that displays the standards for achievement.
Self-Assessment	■ Students apply the criteria for assessment to personal learning tasks. ■ Students apply criteria to an anonymous exemplar to standardize their understanding of requirements.
Self- and Peer-Assessment	■ Students have opportunities to work with anonymous exemplars to identify specific areas for improvement. ■ Students have specific opportunities to identify ways to improve an anonymous exemplar.
Co-Assessment between Students and Teacher	■ Students have opportunities to work with known sources of work, including their own, to identify specific areas for improvement. ■ Students have specific opportunities to identify ways to improve their own work. ■ Student-teacher conferencing supports growth.

Criteria: The qualities and aspects/parts we consider in students' work
Standards: The degree to which specific criteria are met
Exemplars: Examples and non-examples that demonstrate applied criteria set at a high standard

Figure 17.3 Exemplar Showing a Comparison of Urban and Rural
Communities

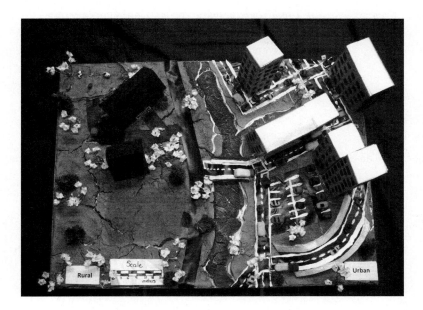

When authentic assessment with criteria, standards, and exemplars is not used
to measure learning and promote growth, factual accuracy becomes the most common criterion for student assessment (Goodland, 1984). Conversely, authentic
assessment approaches use a relevant, comprehensive, and clearly articulated set of
criteria and standards that address the content, processes, and products being
learned (see Figure 17.4).

Standards help teachers to translate assessments into evaluation. Evaluations require
that the teacher consider all of the collected evidence about the student's work performance and make a professional judgment about the level to which it approaches the
required standards.

Rubrics are useful to display both criteria and standards in an economical way.
Although rubrics can be developed as holistic scales with all criteria grouped together to
describe the expected outcome at each level, more useful examples apply analytical scales
where each criterion is separated to help students see exactly what is expected. Rubrics are
most useful to guide students if they are provided when the assignment is given so that students can determine precisely how they can achieve at the expected level. Analytical scales
can also help to focus students' attention of the specific things that require improvement
and support self-assessment when students can focus on examining one criterion at a time.

A rubric can be developed using a common template that teachers adapt to specific
tasks. Figure 17.5 expands on the details of achievement categories provided in the sample in Chapter 10 (Figure 10.3 on page 250).

Figure 17.4 Characteristics of Assessment Criteria in Authentic Assessment

Relevant Criteria	■ Criteria are based on the learning purpose of the assignment.
	■ The criteria reflect the main goals of the subject area (e.g., content knowledge, critical thinking, information gathering and reporting, personal and social values, and individual and collective action).
Comprehensive Set of Criteria	■ Criteria reflect the elements/qualities of content, process, and product.
Clearly Articulated Criteria	■ Criteria are expressed in a way that is understood by the age group of students.
	■ Criteria are specific enough to reflect the importance of the task.
	■ Criteria are descriptive of what is required.
	■ Criteria are separated so that the required qualities can be identified; the teacher (or teacher and student together) can use the criteria to determine if the qualities are present in the product (e.g., What should this look like? Sound like? Qualities it should reflect?)

Rubrics can outline any number of levels that the teacher requires and should include, in a way that is clear to both teachers and students, a clear description or explanation of how each level relates to the expected standard. To help teachers develop specific descriptors of achievement for each level, a list of potential qualifiers that can be applied to each criterion-based standard can be used (see Figure 17.6 on pages 412 and 413).

ASSESSMENT STRATEGIES THAT ENGAGE STUDENTS

Traditional assessment strategies can be very demanding for students whose reading and reading comprehension skills are weak. Traditional assessment strategies such as tests, quizzes, exams, and essays are very heavily reliant on the student's ability to read and write fluently. For those students who can provide better representation of their learning through other forms of assessment, traditional forms represent a disadvantage and may be measuring reading and writing skills more than the intended social studies expectations.

Whether the form of assessment being used is traditional or authentic, it needs to be characterized by some common features that help to ensure that the approach is doing what it was designed to do. Assessment approaches always need to

Figure 17.5 Rubric Design

	Achievement Categories	Criteria	Level 1	Level 2	Level 3	Level 4
Content	Knowledge and understanding Specific Topic Knowledge Concepts Relationships Map and Globe Skills					
Process	Thinking and Inquiry Comparing Analyzing Locating Formulating Identifying Explaining Classifying Connecting					
	Communication Using Specific Vocabulary Explaining Drawing Labelling Constructing					
Product	Application Investigating Preparing Using Describing					

Topic: _____

Expectation(s): _____

Name(s): _____

Overall Comments:

Summative Assessment Comments:

Figure 17.6 Level Descriptors for Use in Rubric Development

Level 1—Well Below Provincial/ Territorial Standard	Level 2—Slightly Below Provincial/ Territorial Standard	Level 3—At Provincial/ Territorial Standard	Level 4—Above Provincial/ Territorial Standard
■ a few simple ideas	■ a variety of simple and related ideas	■ a few minor errors	■ all/almost all
■ basic	■ accurately	■ accurately	■ almost always
■ constant major errors	■ basic	■ analyzes and interprets	■ analyses
■ few	■ familiar contexts	■ appropriate	■ complete
■ for a limited range of simple purposes	■ for a variety of simple purposes	■ appropriately	■ complex
■ imprecisely	■ frequently	■ complete	■ complex ideas
■ inappropriately	■ in a mechanical and sequential way	■ consistent	■ confidently
■ incomplete	■ incomplete	■ consistently	■ congruent/ coherent
■ introductory	■ limited	■ correctly	■ consistently
■ limited range of strategies	■ misconceptions	■ for specific purposes	■ consistently complete
■ limited understanding	■ occasionally	■ generally good understanding	■ consistently with clarity
■ little awareness	■ partial	■ ideas of some complexity	■ consistently with precision
■ major errors	■ several	■ independently	■ creates new forms
■ only with assistance	■ simple/related	■ logically	■ for a wide variety of purposes
■ rarely accurate	■ some	■ nearly complete	■ in a complex and logical way
■ rarely complete	■ some accuracy	■ precision/precise	■ in a wide variety of contexts
■ rarely with precision	■ some clarity	■ sufficiently	■ independently
■ unclearly	■ sometimes	■ usually	■ justify
■ with several major errors	■ sometimes complete	■ usually complete	■ modifies
■ with several major omissions	■ with frequent assistance	■ usually with clarity	■ no misconceptions
	■ with limited assistance	■ usually with precision	■ refined
	■ with several different forms	■ with a few minor omissions	■ significant
		■ with a variety of forms	
		■ with clarity	

Figure 17.6 *(Continued)*

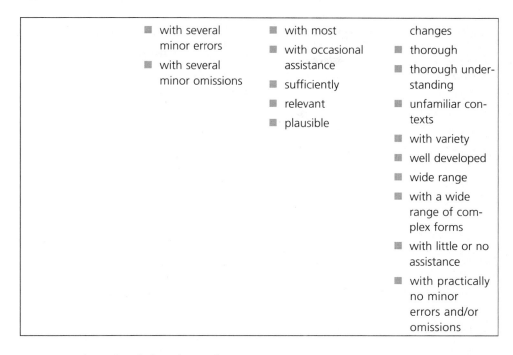

- with several minor errors
- with several minor omissions

- with most
- with occasional assistance
- sufficiently
- relevant
- plausible

changes
- thorough
- thorough under-standing
- unfamiliar con-texts
- with variety
- well developed
- wide range
- with a wide range of com-plex forms
- with little or no assistance
- with practically no minor errors and/or omissions

- use explicit, detailed, and unambiguous instructions;
- provide frameworks for student responses;
- measure students' understanding of big ideas, supported by evidence/reasons;
- be grounded in foci on students' understanding of critical thinking as it relates to their courses; and
- break components of the expected responses into related pieces that provide both structure and direction for the responses.

An overview of the types of assessments that are considered to be traditional and authentic is provided in Figure 17.7.

Traditional assessment approaches may be useful to establish students' knowledge base before they engage more demanding authentic assessment tasks. Such tasks will provide evidence of learning embedded within the task and therefore serve the dual purpose of providing a venue for learning and a product to help teachers measure the learning. If traditional approaches such as quizzes are used by the teacher, it must first be determined what is being measured. To plan for effective tests and quizzes, teachers can use a test-planning framework (see Figure 17.8) that matches questions to two criteria:

1. The format of the question
2. The level of thinking required in the question (Bloom's Taxonomy)

Figure 17.7 Samples of Traditional and Authentic Assessment Practices

Traditional Assessment Approaches	Authentic Assessment Approaches
■ Tests	■ Performance tasks
■ Quizzes	■ Interviews
■ Exams	■ Portfolio exhibition
■ Cloze answers	■ Learning logs
■ Essays	■ Conferences
■ Selected response (e.g., matching)	■ Question and answer (oral)
	■ Observation
	■ Response journal
	■ Self-assessment
	■ Peer assessment

Figure 17.8 Using Bloom's Taxonomy to Plan for Tests

Unit: _____   Grade: _____

Testing Date: _____

Teacher: _____

Question Format	Knowledge	Comprehension	Application	Analysis	Synthesis/ Creativity	Evaluation
■ Fill in the Blank						
■ Short Answer						
■ Long Answer						
■ Matching						
■ Essay						
■ Sketch/Draw						
■ Create/Make						
■ Circle Correct Answer						
■ Multiple Choice						
■ Cloze						
■ Label Diagram						
■ True and False						

By using this framework to plan test, quiz, and exam questions, teachers can ensure that the test is doing precisely what they intend it to do. This knowledge will then allow the teacher to supplement traditional assessment with authentic approaches that can provide evidence of students' deeper understanding and internalization of ideas.

With young children, teachers must also be aware of their need to be supported by answer frameworks when they are exposed to questions in evaluative contexts. Consider the example, "What were the causes of the Red River Rebellion? What were the short-term effects and long-term effects of the Red River Rebellion on the people of Manitoba?" For many students this is a difficult question for the wrong reasons. They may know the causes and short- and long-term effects of the Red River Rebellion but, without support, they cannot sort out that they are being asked three different questions. A graphic organizer following the question would make the requirements easier to understand and would help students know exactly what to address in their answer. As well, a more definitive wording of the question could provide better direction about the level of detail expected in an answer. Consider the differences between the first question and this example.

Identify the main cause of the Red River Rebellion. What were three short-term, and three long-term effects of the Red River Rebellion on the people of Manitoba?

Answer:

Main cause of the Red River Rebellion: _____

Short-term effects of the Red River Rebellion	Long-term effects of the Red River Rebellion
1.	1.
2.	2.
3.	3.

By providing definitive requirements for the number of causes, and the number of effects required in the student's answer, and by providing a graphic organizer to delineate the space provided for the response about effects, the teacher reduces the short-term memory demands on the student, supports weaker readers, and gets a better opportunity to measure what the students know about the topic.

In the group of authentic assessment tasks, performance tasks are the most inclusive of many types of projects and products that students could produce to demonstrate their learning. Review the Bloom's Taxonomy Wheel provided in Chapter 9 (Figure 9.3). This wheel identifies many types of performance tasks that could be required to demonstrate students' learning of both lower-order and higher-order thinking. The most vibrant performance tasks will require students to analyze, synthesize, create, and evaluate ideas to produce a single product. Performance tasks should engage students' interest because they require students to use their knowledge in the production of an age-appropriate realistic inquiry. Such a task should further the students' understanding of the topic and allow the teacher to measure that learning. Performance tasks can be weighty because they have the potential to blend students' competencies with content, process, and product. They are contextualized opportunities to integrate learning from many areas of the program to demonstrate understanding in social studies.

Performance tasks have many important characteristics (Borich, 2008):

- They ask learners to demonstrate understanding and skills learned through modelling and after practice opportunities have been provided.

- They require learners to use what they have learned in realistic contexts so that they demonstrate mastery of the learning.

- They involve higher-order thinking when analysis, synthesis, creativity, and evaluation are required.

- They "test" the learner's internalization of the learning, going beyond factual recall.

- They have clearly articulated standards for achievement.

- They illustrate graphically what some end products of schooling are for the student's metacognitive awareness and for the parents' interest.

- They value real application of understood ideas above book learning.

A portfolio is one example of a performance task. With a portfolio, students are asked to collect work over time to provide a purposeful sample of evidence of their understanding of key ideas in a unit or course. Portfolios can be flexible to assess a wide range of objectives and allow the teacher to monitor and support growth over time. Portfolios also allow students to engage in significant self-assessment as they select and prepare artifacts for their portfolio. This opportunity generates greater ownership of personal growth for each student and can support conferencing between students and teachers to discuss and guide growth. By combining opportunities to determine criteria and standards for artifacts that are included in the portfolio, monitoring patterns of growth, highlighting students' strengths, allowing for identification of specific and personal areas for growth, and, through conferencing, planning for that growth, portfolios can support authentic assessment opportunities in the social studies program.

Strong portfolios will

- provide criteria and standards for students so that they can determine which artifacts from their work should be included in their portfolio;

- provide a portfolio checklist (which students can help to generate) that identifies specific artifacts or categories of artifacts that should be included in the portfolio (e.g., Provide evidence that you understand food preservation techniques used by early settlers).

- provide a structure to guide students' self-assessment of their portfolio;

Figure 17.9 Portfolio Tracking Sheet

Artifact List	This artifact provides evidence that I . . .					
	Have met this criteria for this unit	Have met this standard for this unit	Have improved in . . .	Have shown my personal strengths in . . .	Have plans for personal growth in . . .	Will improve by . . .
1.						
2.						
3.						
4.						
5.						

■ increase students' accountability by ensuring that they examine their work critically; and

■ structure the feedback that teachers provide as portfolios develop (formative) and after completion (summative).

When teachers use portfolios for assessment, the contents that are included in the final portfolio should be tracked so that contents represent students' best work. As students become more familiar with tracking portfolio contents, they should take control of managing record keeping related to tracking what they include in the final portfolio (see Figure 17.9).

Effective assessment in the classroom should have many characteristics that make it fit the classroom climate and sustain assessment's role as a supportive aspect of learning. Teachers can ensure that assessment meets their needs and those of the learners by using assessment approaches that are largely formative in purpose, not intrusive in the learning, happen along with the learning not as an event after the learning, include data from many sources and learning opportunities, and allow for triangulation of information about learning so that single sources of learning data are not overvalued in the process of measuring the learning.

DESIGNING CULMINATING TASKS TO SHOW EVIDENCE OF LEARNING

Culminating tasks are opportunities to celebrate a body of learning that has taken place throughout a unit or a course of study. Culminating tasks are designed specifically to allow students opportunities to pull all of the big ideas from recent learning together into one task that demonstrates their learning. The format of that task should reflect students' skills with the task required and their accumulated understanding and processing skills that can be applied to a new product.

Culminating tasks can be structured to allow students further opportunities to work together and to draw on the strengths of members of a group. They should include as much choice as possible to encourage students to use their learning style strengths. As a culmination of a study, these tasks should be big and students should see them as opportunities for reflection on their own growth.

To develop ideas for culminating tasks, teachers need to identify the big ideas of the unit or course. Sometimes provincial and territorial guidelines will do this in the layout of the units for a grade. However, teachers may have to do considerable interpretation and extrapolation from some guideline sources to identify these ideas.

Example

Examples of the big ideas of a unit that are separated for teacher use in a guideline include the following expectations for the culmination of a Grade 3 unit:

- Students will identify and compare the distinguishing features of urban and rural communities.
- Students will use a variety of resources and tools to gather, process, and communicate geographic information about urban and rural communities.
- Students will explain how communities interact with each other and the environment to meet human needs.

To culminate this unit, the teacher has asked students to form a Chamber of Commerce for an imaginary region that is laid out geographically on a map. The map includes both urban and rural areas and the features of each are shown through satellite imagery. Students elect a caucus for the Chamber of Commerce then organize into committees to address improvement proposals for the area. Each committee will select an improvement project they would like to propose to the Chamber caucus. To do this, they study the area and develop a budget and a display booth to pitch their proposal. Time is set aside for the public to view display booths and hear students' persuasive arguments. The views of the public are solicited on each proposal. Following the display day, the caucus meets with each committee to identify the public's and the committee's perception of their proposals. The caucus then decides which proposals will be funded and the extent of the funding. Students then revisit original proposals to determine any of the following: If they did get some funding but not all they asked for, how will they adjust their proposal to reflect this? If they received no funding, will they abandon, adjust, or postpone their proposal? What are the impacts on the community of each of these options? If they received full funding for their proposal, how will they move into implementation?

This example may seem very complex for Grade 3 students, but they can address these complex issues if they are provided with appropriate structures and supports along the way. If teachers deconstruct the elements of the culminating task into parts that need to be taught as students progress, they can achieve amazing results.

Culminating tasks should be framed at the early stages of planning a unit or course (backwards design). That way, teachers can assure that the necessary knowledge and skills to support success with the culminating task can be built up throughout the progress of the unit(s).

Culminating tasks are complex by nature. To assess them, teachers will require well-developed rubrics that sort out the many elements of the task that will be brought together to achieve success with the culminating task. Students should see and understand the assessment rubric prior to starting on the culminating task.

USING RUBRICS TO ENSURE SUCCESS: RUBRICS AS GROWTH SCHEMES

The success of a rubric to develop and assess students' work depends largely on the quality of the rubric. To ensure that rubrics are used successfully to do what they are intended to do, they need to be developed with care. Teachers also need to determine which combination of possible uses of a rubric is to be used for a task. Rubrics can be used to

- assess students' work;
- guide students to achieve at a higher level;
- support self-assessment; and
- target new learning goals for individuals or the class.

  To develop effective rubrics

- identify the expectation(s) that are to be assessed;
- develop a blank template for the rubric that separates descriptors for each of the possible levels of achievement;
- generate criteria for the assessment; criteria can be sub-divided by content, process, and product;
- identify social skills that should also be evaluated in conjunction with the criteria;
- set the number of levels of performance that may be observed to reflect common assessment levels proposed in provincial/territorial guidelines;
- develop a full descriptor for each criterion that identifies the expected level of performance and place it on the template under the level that best describes the provincial/territorial guideline directions;
- generate full descriptors for each of the other levels;
- examine all descriptors to ensure that there is sufficient separation to provide clearly observable differences in learning;
- insert an "overall comments" box at the bottom of the rubric to provide specific direction for student growth;
- refine the draft based on clarity and clear delineation across descriptors for each criterion;
- determine a weight to be assigned to each criterion based on the relative importance of content, process, or product for the specific evaluation;

- determine how the rubric-based assessment will be evaluated to assign a mark or grade;

- use the rubric to assess a sample and adjust any descriptors to reflect the best possible discrimination among levels of achievement; and

- provide the revised rubric to students when assigning a task to be evaluated.

Rubrics are most powerful when students have frequent exposure to them and learn to use them to picture the next level of achievement. A clearly articulated and thorough rubric will tell the student what they need to do to earn top marks and achieve the best understanding. Students can be taught to use the rubric to contract for a specific level of achievement by showing them how to highlight what they want to achieve. Some students may feel confident that they could achieve top marks in the area of content but may choose to aim for a lower level of process and product for a particular task. By keeping these components separated, teachers can help students plan for their growth and be fully invested in achieving their targets.

CREATING AND USING EXEMPLARS FOR SOCIAL STUDIES TASKS

Exemplars are like targets: they provide something concrete and specific to aim for when students undertake a task. They are clear and they can be submitted to detailed examination against specific criteria. They show students what their efforts should look like at the end of their work. Non-examples are also useful exemplars if students have structured opportunities to examine them carefully in relation to criteria and standards.

Whether tasks are written or based on models or multidimensional tasks, young students will need to see examples of the expected product in order to achieve parity with the expectations. However, simple viewing is not enough guidance to ensure equal quality in students' work. They will need many opportunities to examine, question, consider, and pull apart in order to connect the exemplar with stated criteria for achievement. Instructionally, this is time well spent. Once students understand the concepts of criteria and standards, they can take a more active role in their own learning by engaging in self-and peer assessment.

To help students examine exemplars productively, teachers can provide individual or small-group observation record sheets to guide observations (see Figure 17.10).

This observation sheet is heavily laden with instructional concepts (e.g., criteria, standards, strengths, weaknesses) but these can be supported to full development over time and many exposures to examining exemplars led by the teacher, in cooperation with the teacher, in small heterogeneous groups, and individually.

One concern about providing exemplars must be considered. Students can become too closely attached to the exemplar and may try to reconstruct it rather than seeing it as a starting point that can be used to guide but springboard their efforts. Ensuring a balanced assessment of the exemplar by the students and supporting them to generate a broad range of responses to task challenges will help to ensure diversity and expansion beyond the exemplar.

Figure 17.10 Using Exemplars for Improvement

This exemplar was used to show that the students understood . . .

This exemplar addresses these criteria:

This exemplar addresses these standards:

This exemplar is good because it:

This exemplar could be improved by:

MOVING FROM ASSESSMENT TO EVALUATION

Assessment is the collection of data about a student's achievement. Evaluation is the professional judgment of the teacher applied to that data to assign a mark that relates the quality of the student's work to the criteria and standards sought for the work. Data should be collected from the widest possible range of traditional and authentic sources given the time and resources available.

Teachers need many ways to examine the data that attests to students' achievement and devices for recording their observation so that accumulated data can be assessed. This can be done using several recording devices that will help the teacher examine a summary of all sources of information when it is time to create a summative mark or comment that evaluates the student's work. Five main types of recording devices can support the transition from assessment to evaluation: anecdotal records, checklists, rubrics, rating scales, and learning logs.

Anecdotal records can be useful for recording on-the-spot observations related to a specific task. In a primary/junior classroom, file folders can be used to keep on-the-spot records and separate observations by expectations. A single file folder can be used for the entire class with each student's name written inside, separated widely enough to allow sticky notes to be inserted below names. As the teacher observes students at work, anecdotal observations can be added to the student's sticky note and dated. Additional notes can be added on top of previous ones to identify observed changes over time. The note that is on top of the stack will always represent the student's most recent performance in relation to the specific expectation.

Checklists are commonly used to record observations and other forms of traditional or authentic assessment in many subject areas. They have the advantage of being quick and efficient to use and can be recorded in a way that allows quick comparisons across time and among classmates. Checklists can be used with checkmarks, level numbers (e.g., 1 to 4), graded numbers (e.g., 8/10), or symbols (e.g., Y for yes; N for no). A single checkmark sheet can be used to record many assessments for several key expectations within a unit (see Figure 17.11).

Rubrics provide both assessment and evaluation data in one economical display. They present both criteria and standards and can be formatted to display on a single sheet. Rubrics provide detailed feedback and can reduce the need for extensive writing if the feedback in the rubric is detailed enough to be informative for the students. Rubrics are especially effective when the assessment they are applied to is a multi-criterion assessment, combining elements of content, process, and product.

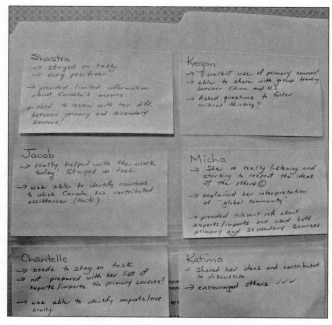

Up-to-date anecdotal records can be recorded efficiently on a file folder then transferred to a more permanent file at the end of a unit.

Rating scales can be effective for recording assessments if the assessment relates to a single criterion demonstration of learning. For example, if students are required to memorize the names of Canada's provinces and territories, they will demonstrate that they know none of them, know all of them, or know some of them. Since there are 13 possibilities, a rating scale from 0 to 13 can be set up and a strategy to assess students' memory of the names can be used

Figure 17.11 Teacher's Evaluation Records

Unit Title:								
Unit Expectations and Evaluation Value:								
Name	Observation sheet from museum visit /10	Photo-journal research /20	Pioneer artifact display /10					
Joey	8	18	7					
Anna	8	17	9					
Yussef	7	19	10					
Michel	9	16	9					

(see example below). The student's score can be recorded on the rating scale. Rating scales can be used in conjunction with checklists to record students' scores after they are rated.

Expectation: Students will be able to name Canada's provinces and territories.

Student's Name:_____

0---1---2---3---4---5---6---7---8---9---10---11---12---13

Learning logs can be used by students to record their awareness of their own growth as a unit of study progresses. Students are asked to record what they learn in a course or unit each day and their observations and metacognitive awareness is assessed by the teacher after examining the log. Learning logs can be part of the student's notebook or can be used as a separate learning diary.

By using anecdotal records, checklists, rating scales, rubrics, and learning logs for recording assessments, teachers can examine growth over time during a unit or course and apply their professional judgment to the assessment records to determine an appropriate evaluation for the student's work.

TESTING AND RICH PERFORMANCE TASKS: CHOOSING THE RIGHT MEDIUM

The way that we assess what students do in our social studies program will reflect what we value in the program. If disproportionate value is placed on tests, the learning that cannot be measured through testing is undervalued. Tests do some things very well. Their main strength is in providing opportunities to demonstrate students' lower-level learning through well-structured questions that measure factual knowledge, comprehension, or the simple application of ideas. Test questions that are well designed can also measure analysis, synthesis (including creativity), and evaluation of knowledge but there are many other more effective strategies for evaluating those outcomes. Effective assessment is about making the best choices of how to assess students' learning using the best methods available.

If tests are overused as a way to measure learning of higher-order thinking skills, the students' ability to expand on their knowledge is limited by the test structure and often by the time allowed to write a test. Additionally, tests are intrusive and stop learning in order to measure learning. This can create high levels of anxiety for some students and the end result is the test, no matter how well designed, can measure test-taking skills rather than providing a valid measurement of the students' learning. If teachers attempt to use tests to measure higher-level thinking, they often elicit isolated bits of information that may be overvalued as evidence of higher-order thinking because they are limited by the structure of the test question itself (Borich, 2008).

If, however, teachers balance their assessment strategies and use tests to do what they do well, measure lower-level thinking, and use authentic assessment techniques to measure higher-level thinking, students will have more effective ways to demonstrate the real learning that has taken place. Real learning at higher levels is best measured through various types of performance assessments (Resnick & Resnick, 1991). Performance assessment approaches balance the traditional importance of memorized knowledge with opportunities for intense and prolonged engagement with a topic through problem solving, inquiry, critical thinking, and social justice action.

When authentic assessment strategies are used and performance tasks are highlighted as an assessment strategy, the teacher has sustained opportunities to observe students as they engage in a guided process to produce a product that demonstrates their applied learning. In authentic assessment, both process and product are held to high standards. Both process and product may vary from student to student as they engage in inquiries that interest them individually, within the scope of the broader topic. When examining the learning, the teacher considers assessment criteria related to both process and product (see Figure 17.12).

Figure 17.12 Assessment Criteria for Process and Products

Process	Products
■ Use of primary, secondary, and tertiary sources	■ Organization
■ Ability to articulate ideas	■ Validity of conclusions
■ Problem identification	■ Thoroughness of research
■ Questioning skills	■ Technical quality
■ Interviewing skills	■ Accuracy
■ Record keeping	■ Ability to consider strengths and weaknesses of all viable options
■ Linking ideas	■ Problem solutions
■ Using graphic organizers	■ Sense of audience
■ Interrogating and navigating text	■ Presentation skills (relevance, sufficiency, plausibility, accuracy, logic flow, support/evidence)
■ Determining bias and perspective	
■ Presentation skills (sense of audience, clarity of voice, animation, use of visual supports, rapport)	

Teachers can develop assessment plans as a component of their unit plans to ensure that they make balanced use of both traditional assessment approaches and authentic assessment approaches. This will support the deliberate emphasis on authentic assessment and ensure that the goals of social studies are extended to the assessment of learning.

CREATING SOCIAL STUDIES PORTFOLIOS: THE ROAD TO MOTIVATION

Choice is a powerful motivator for students of all ages. As students choose, they begin to get a sense of themselves as empowered learners. They have opportunities to exercise their choices with guidance and support and to develop connections with other students with similar interests.

Providing choices in social studies is often dependent on the teacher's ability to anticipate student needs for a topic and collect a breadth of accessible resources that can be used to investigate a topic. Resource kits can help teachers amass related resources over time. Teachers can use plastic bins or banker's boxes to sort resources by subtopic and manage resources for a topic to keep references up to date. Internet skills can also be taught to students so that they can search for accessible and appropriate resources.

As students investigate topics of personal interest, they can start to produce products that attest to their individual learning about a chosen subtopic. Each of these products can become an artifact in the student's expanding portfolio of evidence of their learning. To determine what should become part of the student's portfolio, the teacher must ask, "What will I accept as evidence that students know or can do this?" As students develop increasing capabilities with self-assessment and become competent portfolio managers for themselves they need to keep the question, "Is this good evidence that I have learned something?" in mind to guide their portfolio development.

In the process of developing portfolio management skills in young students, peer feedback can provide guidance. Students can be required to get specific feedback from other students who may be studying different aspects of the same topic. Based on peer feedback, the validity of each artifact as portfolio evidence of learning can be determined. Even very young students can be taught to provide criterion-based feedback without overly intense language demands. Figure 17.13 provides an example of a peer feedback form that could be used in early grades.

Figure 17.13 Peer Feedback for a Portfolio Artifact

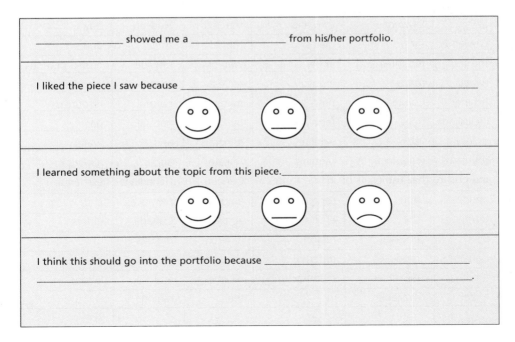

_____ showed me a _____ from his/her portfolio.

I liked the piece I saw because _____

I learned something about the topic from this piece._____

I think this should go into the portfolio because _____
_____.

INNOVATIVE APPROACHES IN YOUR SOCIAL STUDIES CLASSROOM

Students who are preparing for taking a test often have no starting point because they have never been taught how to review for a test. A pre-test review can be done in cooperative learning groups by showing students how to relate ideas within the unit. To prepare this type of review, teachers should create a grid or table. Each box on the table has one word written into it that relates to sentences created to review main ideas within the unit. No capitalization is used, except on proper nouns. No punctuation is used. The number of boxes reflects the age level of the students. For the youngest students, words can be printed separately on magnetic discs and moved around on a metal cookie sheet.

Figure 17.14 provides an example of such a framework for a Grade 4 unit about Canada's provinces, territories, and regions.

Figure 17.14 Preparing Students for Testing and Unit Review

a	region	is	an	area	that
is	similar	throughout	its	extent	and
different	from	the	places	around	it
Canada	has	many	physical	regions	including
the	Canadian	Shield	the	Great	lakes
St.	Lawrence	Lowland	the	Hudson	Bay
Lowlands	the	plains	the	Arctic	and
the	mountains	large	waterways	provide	transportation
water	for	industry	recreation	and	commercial
fishing	Canada	has	many	natural	resources
including	trees	farmlands	oil	natural	gas
uranium	fish	wildlife	minerals	and	water
tourism	manufacturing	farming	forestry	and	mining
are	industries	in	Canada	Canadians	exchange
goods	and	services	among	provinces	and
territories	the	environment	across	Canada	differs
by	physical	region	different	regions	of
Canada	produce	different	products	based	on
the	resources	manufacturing	facilities	and	labour
force	available	in	the	region	

Once the framework is created, leaving a few blank squares at the end, the teacher photocopies and cuts it up so that a set of the resulting word cards is available for each small group of students (two to four in a group). These cards are then put in an envelope. The unit title is recorded on the outside of the envelope.

Students are then given the following directions:

- Create as many sentences as possible, using the word cards.
- Sentences must be true and grammatically correct.
- Use the blank cards to print any necessary words that weren't provided.
- Add, in pencil, an "s," "ed," or "ing" to any word as required.

Teachers can model this using a magnetized blackboard set of word cards. Students will not create the same sentences that the teacher wrote on the original word framework. However, by creating the framework, the teacher has ensured that there are several connecting words and verbs available to help students form their own sentences. The word cards that are available will help students to remember concepts and relationships from the unit.

This activity can encourage even stronger participation if the teams of students compete against each other and the activity is timed. If each used word is awarded a point, students are motivated to use every word possible in each sentence. Doing this will cause students to start to create compound and compound-complex sentences and create relationships among ideas. This will move the level of thinking from comprehension to analysis and synthesis.

This approach could even become the unit test. Students could be asked to glue word cards onto a sheet of paper when they have created all of the sentences possible for their group. Once students understand this strategy, they can create unit review envelopes for each other and for personal study. The approach also provides valuable review of existing knowledge that can support upcoming inquiry into the topic.

CASE STUDIES AND PROFESSIONAL ACTIVITIES FOR INNOVATION IN SOCIAL STUDIES

1. Examine the expectations for a single social studies unit in your jurisdiction. Brainstorm in a small group to identify at least three culminating tasks that could be used to pull together students' understanding of the big ideas of the unit. Discuss each idea in detail to determine which of the three would be the best way to address the students' understanding.

2. Use a Bloom's test-planning framework to examine several samples of tests for social studies units. Collect sample tests for a variety of grades. Using the framework,

determine the number and format of questions used in several tests. Calculate the value of marks assigned to parts of the test to determine any patterns related to marks given to each level of thinking required by the questions. Discuss the effectiveness of the test for assessment of the overall learning of a unit.

3. Students should be well prepared before taking tests. List some test-taking skills that would need to be taught for a selected grade level. For each skill, identify one way you would teach that test-taking skill to your students.

4. Examine the requirements of a unit of study in a local guideline. Determine what products you will accept as evidence of the students' learning for that unit. Identify how many of the products are traditional assessment items and how many are authentic assessment items. Create a sample test for the traditional assessment items. Create a sample rubric for an authentic assessment item.

5. Create a portfolio inventory monitoring page that can be used by students to index artifacts they are choosing to include in a portfolio to provide evidence of their learning. On the inventory monitoring page provide space so that students have a spot to explain what each artifact shows about their learning.

CHAPTER REVIEW AND PROFESSIONAL DEVELOPMENT AS A TEACHER

This chapter has examined the following:

- Purposeful tasks give students opportunities to demonstrate what they really know about a topic.

- Diagnostic assessment determines what students already know about a topic or what misconceptions they may have prior to the study of a unit.

- Formative assessment is done during learning to determine changes to instruction that may be needed.

- Summative assessment is used to measure learning that results from instruction.

- Authentic assessment connects the learning and the assessment into an integrated whole, and measures real evidence of the students' learning.

- Traditional assessment approaches tend to measure the acquisition of facts and memorization of processes.

- Authentic assessment aligns the goals of learning and the approach used to assess those goals.

- Authentic assessment is non-intrusive, inclusive, and designed to measure deep understanding.

- Authentic assessment considers the question, "What will I accept as evidence that students know or are able to do this?"

- Authentic assessment is assessment used *for* and *as* learning rather than just providing data related to the assessment of learning.

- Authentic assessment focuses on what really matters, provides valid indications of student competence, encourages and guides further learning, is rich in feedback, and is efficient.

- Authentic assessment includes feedback focused on improvement.

- The relationship between the teacher and the student shifts toward a more cooperative one as authentic approaches are used.

- Teachers must understand the assessment criteria, assessment standards, and exemplar characteristics when they plan for effective assessment.

- Assessment criteria used in authentic assessment should be relevant, comprehensive, and clearly articulated.

- Standards support the use of assessment data to formulate evaluations.

- Rubrics display both assessment criteria and standards in an economical way.

- Analytical scales can be applied in rubrics to separate assessment criteria.

- Traditional assessment approaches (i.e., quizzes, tests, and exams) are heavily reliant on students' ability to read and write fluently.

- Assessment approaches need to be explicit, provide frameworks for students' responses, measure understanding of big ideas, be grounded in critical thinking, and provide support when multi-component responses are required.

- A test-planning framework will help teachers plan tests effectively and know exactly what each question is measuring.

- Response organizers on tests support students' understanding and recall of what is being asked by each question.

- Performance tasks are a form of authentic assessment that require students to analyze, synthesize, and apply ideas to produce a product.

- Performance tasks blend content, process, and product.

- A portfolio is one type of performance task that requires students to collect samples of their work over time to provide evidence of their learning.

- Students need support to identify criteria and standards to help them decide what work samples should or should not become part of their portfolios.

- Rubrics can be used as growth schemes to help students envision the actions needed to achieve the next level of performance.

- Culminating tasks provide opportunities for students to demonstrate their learning by pulling together big ideas from the unit into one final task.

- Culminating tasks should be planned in detail before a unit begins so that teachers can determine what skills need to be taught throughout the unit to ensure success with the culminating task.

- Systematic development of rubrics strengthens their use in assessment contexts.

- Exemplars provide targets for student aspirations for achievement.

- Assessment is a collection of data about a student's achievement.

- Evaluation is the professional judgment the teacher applies to the collected data.

- Recording devices help teachers remember and sort all of the assessment data they collect.

- Recording devices include anecdotal records, checklists, rubrics, rating scales, and learning logs.

- How we assess reflects what we value in students' learning.

- Assessment strategies should be balanced between authentic assessment and traditional assessment and should be selected purposefully to do what each does best.

- Portfolios are motivating strategies for assessment because they allow students to choose artifacts that best represent their learning.

Weblinks

These websites may help you introduce authentic assessment techniques into your social studies program.

Parent–Teacher Interview
Guidance about improving the parent–teacher interview experience
www.canadianliving.com/family/parenting/ask_an_expert_improving_parent_teacher_interviews.php

Research Projects
Guidance for students about how to do a research project
www.doug-johnson.com/dougwri/designing-research-projects.html

Graphic Organizers
Creating graphic organizers with Word Techtorial
www.education-world.com/a_tech/techtorial/techtorial095.pdf

Rubrics
Rubistar is a free online tool to help teachers create quality rubrics
http://rubistar.4teachers.org
This site has a wide range of examples and templates of rubrics. They are categorized by subject and grade level.
www.rubrics4teachers.com

Chapter 18

Program Planning and Achievement Measures in the Social Studies Classroom

Learning Topics

- Provincial Guidelines: An Analysis
- Dynamic Planning for Social Studies
- Integrating Social Studies in an Inquiry-Based Program
- Engaging Culminating Tasks: A Transformative Perspective
- Authentic Assessments: Adding New Approaches to an Assessment Plan
- Year-at-a-Glance: Long-Range Planning for the Primary and Junior Classroom
- Templates for Planning Social Studies Programs

By using a wide variety of assessment strategies, teachers can ensure that students receive meaningful, timely, and detailed feedback to support their growth toward the criteria and standards of assessment.

Making the right choices as a teacher depends on knowing the kinds of errors or mistakes students are likely to make, being able to identify such mistakes students are likely to make, being able to identify such mistakes when they occur, and being prepared to address the sources of students' errors in ways that will result in student learning.

—*Darling-Hammond & Bransford, 2005*

PROVINCIAL GUIDELINES: AN ANALYSIS

The previous chapter considered the relationship between assessment, evaluation, and learning. Provincial and territorial guidelines across jurisdictions and over time vary in the effectiveness of the guidance they provide for teachers in relation to assessment. Assessment at the classroom level is challenging for teachers because there may be some misalignments among messages about assessment from the various sources of information that teachers use to plan programs. Standards for assessment are typically provided in statements of expectations in provincial or territorial guidelines and may be mandated by provincial bodies or within boards of education at the local level. Instructional approaches are usually developed by individual teachers. Even though teachers must make the final decisions about the quality of students' achievement, the task is compounded when the standards, assessments, and instruction are determined by different levels of educational governance and enacted by different groups (Martone & Sireci, 2009).

To bridge the gap among the mandates provided by different levels of educational authority and structure, the classroom teacher must be able to analyze the alignment of the messages. The valued assessments should reflect the standards that are determined to be central to the aligned ideas from all sources. When the tasks that we ask students to do to demonstrate their learning are in alignment with the criteria and standards that are identified in provincial/territorial guidelines and provide clarity of direction for students, the alignment is complete in range and depth. Shepard (2003) refers to this as *embodiment of assessment.*

To create clearly embodied assessment strategies in the social studies program, teachers must be well informed about the image of the learner that is envisioned in provincial/territorial mandates. This vision is often reflected in preamble components of guidelines. Teachers need to examine these components and address the question, "What is the student who is well educated in social studies to know, value, and be able to do?" Identifying these characteristics provides the vision of the learner that is the starting point of good planning. Next, the effective teacher needs to examine the overall and specific expectations or objectives within a specific unit of study. From these statements, the big ideas or enduring understandings need to be identified, after which the teacher will use backwards design principles (design down) to determine how to assess these big ideas.

[D]evising assessments that embody the standards and goals of instruction is central to good teaching, not just a matter of measuring outcomes.

—*Shepard et al., 2005*

Once the vision of the social studies learner is aligned to the big ideas of the guidelines and assessment techniques are determined, the teacher can begin the process of planning for strong instruction. By using this sequence of processes to begin planning, teachers will ensure that assessment is both aligned and embodied in their program and that the full value of assessment as a gateway to strengthen instruction is reflected in every instructional decision they make as they plan their program. By ensuring that program planning is aligned and assessment is embodied in the program, teachers meet the main goals of assessment through multiple means.

The wide variety of assessment formats helps to ensure that the assessment captures the important learning. Assessment can be integrated and unobtrusive if the widest possible range of strategies is used. The bias inherent in single forms of assessment is avoided when multiple forms are used throughout the program. The teacher has opportunities to look for convergence or triangulation of assessment results if data is collected from many sources to provide different views of the learner's progress toward the stated criteria and standards. Convergence and triangulation of assessment evidence allows the teacher to change his/her mind about the level of student performance over time.

Embodied assessment is only possible when students receive meaningful, timely, and detailed feedback to support their growth toward the criteria and standards of assessment. Formative feedback is growth focused and relies on students receiving information that relates their work to stated criteria, provides exemplars, identifies strengths and specific areas that need improvement, and allows for both time and support for improvement. When assessment is embodied in program planning, teachers will observe growth on an ongoing basis and will have the time and criteria to revise assessment decisions as they observe evidence of learning from many sources.

[N]ot everything that is listed in the standards [guidelines] can or should be assessed.

—*Martone & Sireci, 2009*

By analyzing guidelines carefully, teachers can separate learning goals into those that are easiest to learn and those that represent the big ideas, enduring understandings, social justice values, and habits of mind of the effective social studies learner. This will help teachers to determine what is worth measuring in their assessment of students' learning.

DYNAMIC PLANNING FOR SOCIAL STUDIES

A common saying among those who teach new teachers to plan is, "If you fail to plan, you plan to fail." To be sure that planning is effective for the delivery of a dynamic social studies program, teachers must ensure an understanding of their own curriculum conceptions and of how these conceptions grow with experience and professional development. Once teachers understand that program expectations or objectives, instructional strategies, and assessments must be mutually supportive to guide learning, they can begin to consider the parameters that influence the intended curriculum, the taught curriculum, and the learned curriculum. The *intended curriculum* is the curriculum mandated by provincial/territorial guidelines in the form of units, and specified expectations or learning objectives within each unit. The *taught curriculum* is reflective of these guidelines but operates within the realities of the specific classroom. The taught curriculum reflects the background knowledge and skills of the students, their interests, and their readiness to learn, as well as external realities such as resource and time limitations. The *learned curriculum* represents what students actually demonstrate that they know after instruction. The learned curriculum is the enduring understandings that students acquire through a unit of study, which is influenced by their interests, attention, attendance, values, and efforts. The strongest programs will seek to ensure the smallest possible difference among the intended, taught, and learned curriculum (see Figure 18.1).

Well-aligned and embodied social studies plans will ensure that the consequences of assessment (i.e., how assessment data is used) are reflective of the activity that represents the students' opportunities to learn in the classroom. Some assessment consequences may have low stakes, such as giving the student further instruction, while others have higher stakes, such as withholding promotion.

When students have a clear understanding of learning goals, the goals are more attainable and allow the student to develop a clearer understanding of the nature of the discipline itself (Shepard et al., 2005). When goals are understood by students the

Figure 18.1 What We Assess Indicates What Is Valued in the Curriculum

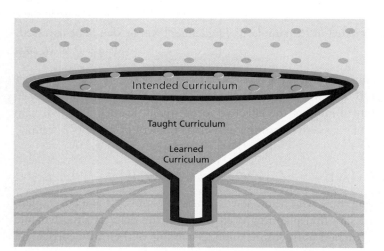
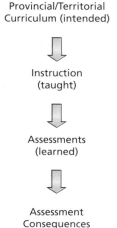

students take on a partnership role in their learning and can use formative assessment to self-correct to reach toward both criteria and standards for a task. Formative assessment (see Figure 18.2) becomes a form of insurance for learning and the summative assessment becomes a celebration of learning success.

When planning social studies programs, teachers must develop alignment within the program so that we *measure what we teach and teach what we intend to teach.* Assessment strategies must have content validity. *Content validity* is the degree to which the assessment approach represents a valid measurement of what it is intended to measure. Poorly structured assignments or poorly framed summative assessment questions can give wrong messages about what is valued in the classroom and undermine the learning by teaching students not to trust that teachers are invested in their best interests.

Consider the two assessment questions provided below:

Name aspects of the local community that you use and explain why these are of value to you.

This question is difficult for students to respond to accurately for several reasons. First, it does not identify the numbers of aspects of the community that are required in the response to meet the standard required. Second, the word "aspects" is vague and may be unfamiliar to students, causing them to misinterpret the question. Third, there are two imbedded questions in the stem: one asks students to "name" and the second asks them to "explain." Finally, a response structure is not provided so the question is actually measuring some elements of students' test-taking strategies as well as their knowledge.

Contrast this with the wording of second sample question, which is designed to measure the same content but supports students in the four areas that are problematic in the previous question.

<u>Name</u> and <u>explain</u> **any three services available in your community. Tell how each service benefits you. Use the chart to organize your response.**

Samples of Community Services	Explanation of How Each Service Benefits Me
1.	
2.	
3.	

In the second sample, underlining shows students the two required elements of their response. The number of examples required in their answer is provided. The word "aspect" is replaced by the more specific word "service" and a response structure is provided to guide students to complete all elements of the question.

Teachers must plan to avoid the usual shortcomings of testing. Effective planning will allow teachers to use testing to its best advantage and use authentic assessment approaches strategically to support program goals for learning. When testing is mandated from other

Students can assess their evidence against exemplar evidence to make specific criterion- and standards-based plans for improvement.

Students can provide specific evidence that aspects of their work meet criteria and standards.

Students can use the criteria and standards for assessment, described on a continuum of growth, to plan for their personal improvement toward highest standards.

Teachers can use the criteria and standards for assessment, described on a continuum of growth, to plan formative assessment feedback to guide students' improvement.

Teacher and students are equally aware of the criteria and standards for assessment, developed on a continuum, to describe students' growth.

Teacher is aware of criteria for assessing big ideas and is able to use them to develop a continuum of standards to envision students' growth.

Teacher is aware of criteria for big ideas in the learning and is able to use them to develop a single set of standards.

Teacher uses criteria that reflect specific knowledge but neglects assessment of big ideas in the learning; no standards are developed.

Teacher is unaware of standards or criteria for assessment.

Figure 18.2
Generating
Formative
Feedback

levels in the educational spectrum (e.g., provincial/territorial, national, or international assessments) it may have several impacts on the program. Such testing may

■ reduce teaching time because test preparation and administration requires classroom time;

■ narrow the curriculum to overemphasize elements that are anticipated to be the focus of external assessment;

■ limit opportunities to assess higher-order thinking such as analysis, synthesis, and evaluation because of the test structure and the limitations of this form of assessment; and

■ decrease morale among students and teachers when control of what is learned is reduced.

(Roach, Niebling & Kurz, 2008; Smith & Rottenberg, 1991).

Overcoming the limitations of traditional assessment in their daily practice and planning for assessment that is integrated with instruction is particularly challenging for many teachers because they may have experienced few, if any, models of effective assessments in their background as students. If they teach as they were taught and assess as they were assessed, teachers are unlikely to provide their students with a full range of opportunities to pursue and later demonstrate their learning. Effective professional development in understanding and using authentic assessment is essential for teachers.

While grade-appropriate testing may be part of the assessments that are planned for later primary and junior grades in social studies, a balanced approach to modifying the impact of assessments through formal tests is advisable to allow students opportunities to display the full range of their personal growth during and following instruction. Testing may have some benefits (see Figure 18.3), but used as a sole arbitrator of evidence for a student's learning, the disadvantages and shortcomings of formal testing may outweigh the advantages. Generally, students seem to learn more if they expect to be tested (Crooks, 1988) but these findings may reflect other factors related to testing rather than the acquisition of knowledge.

When planning effective social studies programs, teachers must consider what and how they will assess learning early in the planning process. By aligning and embodying

Figure 18.3 The Benefits of Testing

■ Testing provides further exposure to the content and engages students in review and relearning.

■ Testing requires students to act on information and address it through mental processing.

■ Testing may direct students' attention to key ideas within a topic, which in turn may direct further study.

■ Testing may help students understand the criteria and standards for assessment and create mutual understanding of them (i.e., both the teacher and the students have the same understanding of requirements).

Source: Adapted from Shepard et al., 2005.

their assessment practices into their program planning (see Figure 18.9), using backward design principles, teachers can ensure that the most appropriate approaches to assessment enrich their program and help them to measure what they intend for students to learn.

INTEGRATING SOCIAL STUDIES IN AN INQUIRY-BASED PROGRAM

Determining what we will teach, how we will teach it, and how we will assess what we have taught are the central considerations of effective program planning. These align with the three key elements of instructional pedagogy: content, process, and product. These elements of pedagogy are shared by all subject areas in the curriculum. In the primary and junior grades, it is common and often valuable to use integrated approaches to curriculum planning. *Curriculum integration* means that teachers plan learning experiences to develop learning expectations for more than one subject area. It is often advantageous to start such planning with the social studies topic as a central theme because the strong story elements that are integral to these themes give structure to the integrated study.

There are many advantages to integrating other subjects with social studies:

- Instructional time can be optimized.
- Students can see connections among topics.
- Processes that are common across subject areas (e.g., reading graphs and tables) can be taught once and practised many times in different applications.
- Products can be designed to be more sophisticated and can draw from real-world knowledge that is not separated along academic lines.
- Greater depth of understanding is possible if students can see several uses of new learning.
- Rich, multidimensional resources can be used.
- Social justice applications can be more realistic because they draw knowledge from many subject backgrounds.
- Skill transfer is facilitated when students see new opportunities to use what they have learned.

As teachers plan for integration, it is critical to keep the standards of each subject area in mind and strive to use teaching and learning strategies to achieve learning outcomes through inquiry. Some subject areas or individual units within a subject area will lend themselves to easy and expansive integration while other efforts to integrate topics may seem more artificial and forced. It may be wise to use natural and easy topics in early efforts to integrate and build on those successes with later efforts.

To teach social studies effectively, through integration or as a separate subject area, teachers need strong pedagogical content knowledge (Shulman, 1987). *Pedagogical content knowledge* is a strong understanding of the subject matter for the purpose of teaching it to others. Strong pedagogical content knowledge allows teachers to see opportunities for meaningful integration and supports teachers' analysis of students' learning. Through integration teachers can provide rich opportunities for students to "delve deeply into a field of study and to understand how questions are generated and pursued within a field" (Grossman, Schoenfeld, & Lee, 2005).

Integration that maintains the critical processes of each subject area allows teachers to model strategies for students to support future investigations. This approach starts the gradual shift of responsibility for the approach to learning from the teacher to the learner. To do this effectively, the teacher must have facility with a wide range of teaching strategies so that he/she can select the strategy with care and sensitivity to the students, and with professional knowledge of which strategies are likely to provide the strongest learning return in relation to the integrated goals. Successful integration starts with clear conceptions of the criteria and standards of learning that are essential to each of the disciplines. The goals for learning, and the processes for learning them, should be bonded in direct and intentional ways and be realistic to create meaningful connections to the lives of the students.

ENGAGING CULMINATING TASKS: A TRANSFORMATIVE PERSPECTIVE

In Chapter 17, we examined ways to design culminating tasks and their role in unit design. Culminating tasks are designed to provide students with encompassing opportunities to demonstrate their learning of the big ideas or enduring understandings from a unit of study. Culminating tasks should be designed to take account of the students' age, interests, literacy levels, readiness, and strengths. These tasks are designed to highlight what the student does know about the topic, not to pinpoint what the student does not know. Identifying areas of weakness should be done prior to assigning or helping students to design a culminating task. Culminating tasks are designed for summative assessment and follow many opportunities for formative assessment, correction, strengthening, and re-teaching.

Choice is an essential element of well-designed culminating tasks. By offering choice, teachers build in strategies for differentiation, improve their own diagnostic skills, and prepare to support learning styles within the group of students (Grossman, Schoenfeld & Lee, 2005). These abilities help teachers become better teachers of all students.

Teachers need to be fully involved in students' selection, design, and completion of culminating tasks. During these processes, teachers have several complementary roles:

- They intervene when students need support.
- They monitor progress and guide changes of direction, looking for problems, misconceptions, resource needs, and stalls in progress.

- They support revisions of the product to guide students to deeper understanding.
- They ensure safety as students pursue plans.

Through these roles, the teacher ensures that the culminating tasks become successful celebrations and markers of the students' learning and remain responsive to both what and how students are learning. The teacher's involvement in all phases of culminating tasks ensures responsiveness to the spirit of the program requirements and opportunities to guide students' reflections on the big ideas and enduring understandings of the program. Culminating tasks provide opportunities for inclusive, sustained engagement with an aspect of the topic, and may include sustained opportunities for social skill practice and development through cooperative projects.

Well-designed culminating tasks allow students to continue to learn as they reflect on big ideas and provide a venue for ongoing learning as needs for new knowledge or skills develop. By their nature, culminating tasks have a metacognitive, self-assessment component. Teachers can build in structures to help students articulate what they know and compare their efforts to the criteria and standards for the specific task and the discipline of social studies. By building flexible choices and opportunities for divergence into a culminating task, teachers can ensure the potential for accommodations and modifications, and allow time for strategic instruction throughout the task time.

Ultimately, the culminating task should be designed with transformative goals of the discipline in mind. Tasks should allow students latitude to become aware of their personal assumptions about a topic, to challenge their assumptions and those of other students, and move forward with their age-appropriate role related to social justice issues. Culminating tasks should be big classroom events, and given the time and attention they need to serve as recognition of students' learning over time.

AUTHENTIC ASSESSMENTS: ADDING NEW APPROACHES TO AN ASSESSMENT PLAN

Assessment should not be separate from learning. Rather, the learning purpose of assessment should help to guide the teacher's selection of assessment approaches. Historically, 95 percent of assessment data obtained through tests has provided information about students' knowledge, understanding, and ability to apply ideas (Madeus, West, Harmon, Lomax & Viator, 1992). This tendency has excluded opportunities for students to represent deeper understanding at the analysis, synthesis, creation, and evaluation levels.

The educational psychologist Maslow once said, "If you only have a hammer, you tend to see every problem as a nail." This quote can also apply to teachers' breadth of understanding and skill with the use of a wide range of assessment techniques. If the teacher only knows how to use tests to determine students' level of understanding, they will tend to see all learning as testable. By expanding their range of ways to assess learning, teachers can assess the breadth and depth of students' learning relative to many learning expectations that may not be readily measured through testing.

In Chapter 17, methods of traditional assessment and methods of alternative assessment were identified. In the following pages, more detailed descriptions of these forms of assessment are provided to support the journey toward developing greater familiarity with these strategies (see Figure 18.4).

Teachers can support their growing awareness of these strategies by gradually adding new approaches to their repertoire and by assessing the value of each approach to provide them with useful information for problem spotting where re-teaching may be required, to provide the most complete picture of the student's developing awareness of the new topic, or to inform future instructional decisions. Many of these strategies taken together can provide triangulated data to support summative assessment and the

Figure 18.4 Methods of Assessment

Assessment Strategy	Explanation	Potential to Assess These Levels of Bloom's Taxonomy
Tests	Questions are formally posed in pencil-and-paper format, usually with a preset response time	Particularly lower-order questions (knowledge, comprehension, application) but well-formed questions that anticipate misunderstandings and potential responses are also valid to assess analysis, synthesis/creativity, and evaluation
Quizzes	Questions are posed in pencil-and-paper format, usually with fewer questions isolated to a few main ideas	Particularly lower-order questions (knowledge, comprehension, application)
Cloze Questions	Sentences that are designed for students to complete by filling in words that are chosen from a limited set and may include a word bank	Knowledge
Exams	Very formally posed questions are designed to assess many units of study; may be used at the end of a course rather than at the end of a unit; may	Particularly lower-order questions (knowledge, comprehension, application) but well-formed questions that anticipate misunderstandings *(Continued)*

Figure 18.4 (*Continued*)

Assessment Strategy	Explanation	Potential to Assess These Levels of Bloom's Taxonomy
	be selected by the teacher or mandated locally, provincially/ territorially, nationally, or internationally; the broader the sampling of people being tested the more likely the exam is to employ items that can be marked quickly through electronic means, thereby limiting the types of questions that can be asked	and potential responses are also valid to assess analysis, synthesis/creativity, and evaluation
Essays	Formal writing opportunities allow students to start with a thesis or statement that is then supported through narration, description, correlation, comparison, or defense of a decision	Analysis, synthesis, evaluation
Selected Response (e.g., matching)	Prompts are matched to responses from a limited set	Knowledge, comprehension
Performance Tasks	A wide range of products is offered as a method of demonstrating new learning	Knowledge, understanding, application, analysis, synthesis/ creativity, evaluation
Portfolios	Students and/or teachers select a range of work produced by the student to demonstrate their developing awareness of a topic.	Knowledge, understanding, application, analysis, synthesis/ creativity, evaluation
Learning Logs	Students write ongoing journal entries that reflect their growing awareness of a topic of study. Learning logs focus on the question, "What do I now know about this topic?"	All levels but particularly analysis, synthesis/creativity, and evaluation
Conferences	Students engage in a discussion with the teacher about what they have learned about a topic of study. Conferences	Knowledge, understanding, application, analysis, synthesis/ creativity, evaluation

Figure 18.4 *(Continued)*

Assessment Strategy	Explanation	Potential to Assess These Levels of Bloom's Taxonomy
	may include others (e.g., parent). The teacher probes students' learning by asking questions designed to attest to the students' awareness of the big ideas and enduring understandings of the topic. Questions may evolve from students' responses and reflect students' special areas of interest in the topic.	
Question and Answer (oral)	Students engage in a discussion with the teacher about what they have learned about a topic of study. The teacher probes students' learning by asking questions designed to attest to the students' awareness of the big ideas and enduring understandings of the topic. The questions may be asked of individuals or small cooperative groups. Responses may be used for formative redirection or summative assessment	Knowledge, understanding, application, analysis, synthesis/ creativity, evaluation
Exhibition	Students prepare a static or interactive display that demonstrates new learning about a topic undertaken within the framework of a larger unit of study. The exhibit usually represents what students have studied independently that has branched off the main topic and represents a special area of interest for the student	Analysis, synthesis/creativity, evaluation

(Continued)

Figure 18.4 (*Continued*)

Assessment Strategy	Explanation	Potential to Assess These Levels of Bloom's Taxonomy
Interview	The teacher meets with the student and asks specific preset questions to assess the level of the student's awareness of the topic. Data may be used for formative redirection or summative evaluation. Interviews are usually one-on-one between the student and teacher	Analysis, synthesis/ creativity, evaluation
Observation	The teacher systematically observes and records evidence that a student is developing awareness of the topic as they address specific tasks. Results of observations may be used for formative redirection, re-teaching, or for summative evaluation	Knowledge, understanding, application, analysis, synthesis/ creativity, evaluation
Response Journal	A written or recorded entry that asks students to respond to limited prompts requiring them to analyze, synthesize, create, or make judgments and/or decisions about a topic. Response journals may be records of social action	Application, analysis, synthesis/ creativity, evaluation
Self-Assessment	Structured analysis of personal work in relation to pre-identified criteria and standards is undertaken by the student, usually for formative use (i.e., What do I still need to learn about this topic? How will I do that?)	Knowledge, understanding, application, analysis, synthesis/ creativity, evaluation

decisions that follow summative assessments. As authentic assessments become the norm in the classroom, teachers will see the benefits of increased student interest, students' involvement in their own assessment, ongoing support for achievement, stronger scaffolding through strategic teaching, and increased ownership of the learning as students learn new strategies for self-monitoring (Shepard et al., 2005). Through experience, teachers will learn to set high standards and provide optimal support for high achievement within a classroom where a broad range of culminating tasks is being pursued simultaneously. Converging sources of evidence about students' learning will help teachers improve their instruction and support the diversity of learners' needs in their classrooms.

YEAR-AT-A-GLANCE: LONG-RANGE PLANNING FOR THE PRIMARY AND JUNIOR CLASSROOM

Long-range planning is the first step in effective course design, followed by unit planning and lesson planning. Long-range planning is essential to help teachers manage time, resources, and learning expectations in a busy and productive learning environment. These plans provide a rough but flexible and responsive outline of the units to be taught for the entire year. They provide a roadmap over time.

In most elementary contexts, primary and junior teachers will teach many subjects. A year-at-a-glance long-range planning process helps primary and junior teachers search for points of intersection and connection among topics from different curriculum mandates. Although students' interests may cause a variation from the plan, its design is an essential element of anticipating needs prior to detailed unit planning.

Year-at-a-glance planning can be done readily with chart paper, markers, and sticky notes of the smallest size. To start, lay out a piece of chart paper in landscape on a table top. Across the top of the paper record the months of the school year separated by the width of a sticky note. Down the left side, record all of the subject areas that you will be responsible for teaching. See Figure 18.5 for an example.

Now, gather the provincial/territorial guidelines that govern what is taught at the grade level for each subject area you are assigned to teach. Review each guideline and write the topics or unit titles on separate sticky notes. Place the notes under the month in which you intend to start teaching that topic. Adjust the position of the notes as you add subject areas to take advantage of opportunities for integration. Draw pencil arrows across the chart to extend into the months when you anticipate completion of a unit of study. Once all of the sticky notes are added, you are able to see how the full year will evolve and what units need to be fully developed first, and which resources will need to be acquired immediately.

Teachers should be aware that some school jurisdictions require specific formats for long-range planning to help more detailed transitions between year-at-a-glance plans and unit plans. Regardless, year-at-a-glance planning is an effective first step in the planning process and will support the next level of planning.

Figure 18.5 Long-Range Planning Using Year-at-a-Glance

Subjects	Sept.	Oct.	Nov.	Dec.	Jan.	Feb.	Mar.	Apr.	May	June
Language										
Math										
Social Studies										
Science										
Art										
Physical Education										
Health										

TEMPLATES FOR PLANNING SOCIAL STUDIES PROGRAMS

The following pages provide sample templates that teachers can use and adapt to support effective planning in primary and junior social studies programs (see Figures 18.6, 18.7, 18.8, and 18.9). Included are templates for

- rubric development;
- independent inquiry planning by students;
- long-range year-at-a-glance planning; and
- assessment and evaluation planning for a unit.

Teachers can use the concepts presented in this text to develop further templates to support effective planning.

Figure 18.6 Rubric Development Template

Criteria		Standards			
		Level 1	Level 2	Level 3	Level 4
Program Elements	Category of Expectations				
Content	Knowledge and Understanding				
Process	Thinking Inquiry				
Product	Communication Application				

Figure 18.7 Independent Inquiry Planning Template

Topic:_____

Name(s):_____

Questions I/We have considered:
_____

Questions I/We plan to investigate:
_____

Resources I/We have:

Resources I/We need:

Where I/We will look for them:

Proposal for a product to show you what I/We have learned:
_____

Our timeline plan:

Today | Day 2 | Day 3 | Day 4 | Day 5 | Day 6 | Day 7 | Day 8 | Day 9 | Day 10 | Day 11 | Day 12

Figure 18.8 Long-Range Year-at-a-Glance Planning Template

Teacher:_____ Year: _____ Grade:_____

	Sept.	Oct.	Nov.	Dec.	Jan.	Feb.	Mar.	Apr.	May	June
Social Studies Units										
Integrated Units * *										

Figure 18.9 Assessment and Evaluation Planning Template

Social Studies Unit: _____

Integrated Units/Goals: _____

Big Ideas/Main Expectations for the Unit:

*

*

*

*

To identify students' ability to:	Diagnostic Approaches	Formative Approaches	Summative Approaches

INNOVATIVE APPROACHES IN YOUR SOCIAL STUDIES CLASSROOM

Student-led parent-teacher conferences are not new to education but they are not widely used in some jurisdictions. These conferences can be very valuable sources of communication with parents and help students take ownership for their learning and monitor their progress more specifically. Both students and parents report enjoying such opportunities to talk to each other about the student's work and to do this in a structured environment where the student is responsible for presenting their work in detail and justifying their summative grades.

Successful student-led parent-teacher conferences rely on careful preparation. Both the teacher and the student have roles in the preparation. The teacher must explain the purpose and process of these interviews to school administration, parents, and students. Students must be taught to start, monitor, and contribute to a developing portfolio that represents their work over time. Parents must be told about how these interviews will function and how the student will be involved. Parents need to be told about the interviews well in advance and provided with reminders of specific times and dates.

Student-led parent-teacher interviews work best if the whole school is implementing this approach simultaneously. However, with the approval of the school administration, they can also be initiated on a divisional or classroom basis. Preplanning for the development, storage, monitoring, and maintenance of the portfolio is critical to the success of these interviews. The student must be able to provide a clear explanation of what each piece of work in the portfolio demonstrates about their learning. When portfolios are used for many subject areas, teachers will need to determine a way to help students separate work artifacts from each subject area to maintain order during their interviews. This can be done by using a three-ring binder or by creating a set of coil-bound file folders for each student with a separate file for each subject. Students can decorate and label each folder or divider as an art project.

Once the teacher has determined that student-led parent-teacher interviews will be used for the reporting process, schedules will need to be developed. The teacher will lay out a schedule that allows rotation to a different set of student and parent(s) approximately every 10 minutes. This is most readily accomplished by setting up a schedule that has three sets of student and parent(s) being engaged over the same half hour. The teacher meets with Set A during the first 10 minutes; then the student and parent(s) review the student's portfolio for the next 20 minutes. After approximately 10 minutes, the teacher moves on to see the student and parent(s) of Set B, who have already had 10 minutes to look at the portfolio and will follow the teacher's conversation with another 10 minutes to look at the portfolio. Finally, the teacher moves to Set C where the students and parent(s) have fully reviewed the student's portfolio in the first twenty minutes. Each half hour, three new sets of students and parents start the interview process. See Figure 18.10 for an example.

Student-led parent-teacher interviews have the added advantages of dramatically increasing students' awareness of their own learning and their progress over time and of creating and sustaining parents' attendance at parent-teacher interviews.

Details about strategies for developing social studies portfolios are provided in Chapter 17.

Figure 18.10 Planning Student-Led Parent-Teacher Interviews

Time	Set A	Set B	Set C
4:00-4:10	Meet with teacher	Student walks parent(s) through portfolio	Student walks parent(s) through portfolio
4:10-4:20	Student walks parent(s) through portfolio	Meet with teacher	Student walks parent(s) through portfolio
4:20-4:30	Student walks parent(s) through portfolio	Student walks parent(s) through remainder of portfolio	Meet with teacher

CASE STUDIES AND PROFESSIONAL ACTIVITIES FOR INNOVATION IN SOCIAL STUDIES

1. Mr. Weiler is required to submit an assessment plan for his Grade 2 social studies course. This is part of the school's improvement planning process and each teacher's assessment plan will be scrutinized by the school improvement team to provide assistance for teachers to help make their assessments more authentic and responsive to diverse student needs. Select one unit of the Grade 2 social studies program in your jurisdiction and lay out a unit assessment plan for the unit you have chosen. Provide details about the diagnostic, formative, and summative approaches you would use.

2. Acquire two or three examples of classroom tests that were designed by social studies teachers. Develop a recording instrument to help you determine the following about each of these test samples:

   ■ To what extent does the test provide opportunities to measure the students' acquisition of the big ideas in the unit?

   ■ To what extent does the test reflect the criteria for achievement expressed in the guideline for this unit?

   ■ To what extent does the test reflect the standards of performance evident in the guideline for this unit?

3. Using what you have learned about assessing guidelines for the unit's big ideas, and the criteria and standards within guidelines, develop a revised framework that will help you determine these elements of a guideline prior to planning for unit assessments in the future. Be prepared to share your framework and demonstrate its use to colleagues.

CHAPTER REVIEW AND PROFESSIONAL DEVELOPMENT AS A TEACHER

This chapter has examined the following:

■ Guidelines provide varying amounts of support and direction in the use of classroom assessment.

■ Standards for assessment are usually provided in guideline assessment statements.

■ Standards, assessments, and instructional decisions may be made at different levels of educational governance, creating some alignment disparities.

■ Assessment is embodied when the expectation criteria, standards, and strategies for assessment match.

- Start planning for embodied assessment by aligning the vision of the learner with the learning expectations to identify the big ideas or enduring understandings to be learned.

- There are many research-based reasons for using a wide range of embodied assessment techniques.

- Meaningful, timely, and detailed feedback are critical to effective formative assessment.

- Formative feedback must reflect the learning criteria and standards identified in expectations.

- Not all expectations provided in guidelines support understanding of big ideas nor are worth measuring.

- Sound planning closes the gaps among the intended, taught, and learned curriculum.

- Content validity is the degree to which the assessment approach represents a valid measurement of what it is intended to measure.

- The structure of test questions is critical to their successful use in assessment.

- Testing should be used cautiously and represents only one of many assessment strategies.

- Testing that is mandated from agencies outside of the classroom may have impacts on teaching time, topic coverage, levels of understanding, and classroom morale.

- Students' expectation that they will be tested may result in students learning more about the topic.

- A balance of assessment approaches creates a bank of evidence from many sources that testifies to students' learning.

- Units are often integrated across subject areas in primary and junior grades, providing many curriculum advantages.

- When social studies is integrated an inquiry approach must be central to the strategies used to maintain a focus on a central way of knowing within the discipline.

- Pedagogical content knowledge allows teachers to access a broad range of strategies to ensure the best approach is used to achieve each learning expectation.

- Culminating tasks allow students to demonstrate their understanding of big ideas.

- Culminating task products are a form of summative assessment.

- Teachers shift across many supportive roles as students engage in the completion of culminating tasks.

- Culminating tasks should be designed to extend the learning, not intrude into it.

- Various forms of assessment address different levels of learning.

- Time engaged in completing culminating tasks is time when teachers can do strategic teaching to individuals or small groups.

- Year-at-a-glance planning promotes effective course design.

- Standard templates for some aspects of planning support program development that maintains a focus on the criteria and standards of the discipline.

- Student-led parent-teacher conferences support authentic assessment principles.

Weblinks

Parent-Teacher Conferences
These sites give information on student-led parent-teacher conferences.
www.cbe.ab.ca/faqs/par_st_t.pdf
www.educationworld.com/a_admin/admin/admin112.shtml

Assessments
These sites give information on authentic assessment.
www.ed.gov/pubs/OR/ConsumerGuides/classuse.html
www.712educators.about.com/od/portfolios/a/portfolio_list.htm

Culminating Tasks
This magazine (*Our Canada*) may provide some examples for culminating tasks for students' work and perhaps a venue for publication of some of their work.
www.education-world.com/a_tech/techtorial/techtorial095.pdf

Glossary

accommodation The learner changes his/her existing schema to apply new information.

activity centres Areas of the classroom where students engage in structured activity to consolidate or apply new learning.

anchors Samples or procedures that students can refer to as they attempt a task with increasing independence.

assimilation The learner adds to his/her existing schema to acquire new understanding.

authentic instruction Instruction that includes opportunities for the learner to construct meaning and produce knowledge, use disciplined inquiry, and work toward producing discourse, products, and performances that have value or meaning beyond success in school.

Bloom's cognitive taxonomy The six levels of thinking—including knowledge, comprehension, application, analysis, synthesis, and evaluation—that can be used to analyze and teach ways of thinking.

caring curriculum Using curriculum studies to teach students to demonstrate care, respect, and understanding of diversity in the human condition.

change and continuity The cluster of concepts that relate to differences and similarities over time and space.

character education A way of nurturing the development of desirable social attitudes and behaviours by promoting, modelling, teaching, expecting, celebrating, and practising them in everyday life.

cognitive dissonance A sense that what one previously believed does not fit with what one is experiencing in a new learning situation.

concept clarification The cognitive ability to define and explain a term through connections among defining elements.

constructivism The educational philosophy or view that learning involves the constant reorganization and reconstructing of experiences; the learner must individually discover and transform complex information to create personal understanding.

cooperative learning Approaches that can be used within a lesson to support and facilitate students' interaction and to promote social learning contexts.

creative thinking The habit of mind that allows teachers to present curriculum ideas in ways that engage, excite, and challenge students' thinking.

criteria Common elements or fields for comparison.

critical inquiry pedagogy Inquiry that focuses on approaches from equity pedagogy, transformative pedagogy, engaged pedagogy, inquiry pedagogy, and critical theory.

critical thinking The habits of mind that cause a learner to systematically consider, analyze, question, investigate, and promote action in a safe, productive, and socially responsible manner.

culture Expressions and manifestations of humanity that are learned and shared within a specific population.

curriculum goals Statements that guide instruction by identifying what students are to know, value, or do at the end of instruction (may also be called aims, competencies, ends, expectations, objectives, outcomes, or purposes).

data-based decision making Evidence collected to support decisions and inform subsequent actions.

deconstruction Pulling apart learning activities to identify and then teach all of the component skills and knowledge that will ensure success with the larger learning tasks.

differentiated instruction Alterations to the content, process, and/or products of instruction to meet the needs of learners.

direct instruction A teaching approach that uses teacher modelling and scaffolded practice for consolidation, followed by increasingly independent opportunities, to apply new learning until learning becomes internalized.

discipline standard The set of criteria and approaches that are identified with a way of knowing and learning in a particular subject area.

environment All of the natural and constructed elements of the earth and its atmosphere in dynamic interaction with each other

essential question A multi-dimensional question that that can be examined from the perspectives of many disciplines; examines the boundary between the known and the unknown and challenges the imagination to support the construction of new knowledge.

explicit curriculum The curriculum mandated by provincial or territorial governments.

"fat" questions Open-ended, higher-order questions that are open to discussion and investigation from many perspectives.

globalization Connections among the world's geography and its peoples in relation to economics, labour, conflict, peace keeping, resource and waste management, common territories, political interfacing, technology, humanitarian interaction, immigration, and space exploration.

governance The laws and rules supported by a society.

gradual release of responsibility The process through which the teacher gradually removes scaffolded support as students show appropriate success with new learning, to allow them to practise with increasing independence.

guiding questions Student-developed questions that guide inquiry of a topic by promoting analysis, synthesis, or evaluation throughout a study.

habits of mind Unique perspectives brought to an inquiry from the discipline being studied.

holistic learning approaches Students engage in learning actions that help them construct relevant knowledge.

implicit curriculum The unstated and unconsciously implemented set of values, standards, and priorities that appear to have value in the day-to-day operation of a classroom or school.

inclusiveness Attitudes and practices that respect the racial, ethical, and democratic pluralism of a country.

inclusivity The welcoming and encouragement of all perspectives; actively seeking out non-dominant perspectives .

inquiry The systematic investigation and engagement of knowledge to examine, query, explore, and make plans and decisions as a strategy for learning.

instructional intelligence The teacher's ability to match what is taught to how it is taught.

interactions and interdependence The cluster of concepts that relates to how people assimilate, accommodate, or come into conflict with other people, groups, or the environment.

lesson planning The set of experiences designed to promote learning of a stated expectation or group of expectations.

metacognition The awareness of what you know.

meta-language Language that allows the learner to name what they know and can do (skills).

models Graphic or physical representations of how things work.

moral reasoning Making judgments and informing actions based on our personal stage of moral development and reflective of a universal concern for justice, reciprocity, or equality in relation to others.

power and governance The structures and means by which laws and rules are enforced in a societal context.

praxis Professional practice that is informed by theory.

prior knowledge Information students already know, or think they know, about a topic they are going to study.

productive pedagogies A systematic way of considering the instructional choices for classrooms that focuses on increased effective and equitable learning for all students.

reflection-in-action Activity the learner engages in during learning to adjust strategies to improve opportunities for success.

reflection-on-action Activity the learner engages in after learning to improve learning for the next opportunity.

restorative justice Social problem-solving strategies that help an offender recognize the personal human impact of their actions by requiring restitution to the harmed.

rubric A multi-criterion recording device used by teachers or students to record detailed assessments of achievement; can also be used to plan growth (growth scheme).

scaffolding Providing support for the learner and gradually removing it as the learner achieves increasing independence.

schema Cognitive structures through which learners build their understanding by either adding to (assimilating) or changing (accommodating) their existing understanding.

simulation A gaming approach that helps students understand complex concepts or experience emotional responses to situations to deepen their understanding.

situated learning A teaching approach that uses social constructivism to develop students' knowledge, through interaction with other learners and with key content.

situational constructivism The philosophy of learning that promotes the appropriate and selective application of a teaching approach to reflect the intent of the learning goal or expectation.

social action A culminating act after thorough inquiry, which engages students in positive change as responsible citizens; the commitment to do something to create change toward a more equitable distribution of resources.

social action continuum The variety of direct or indirect actions taken to create a more equitable distribution of resources.

social justice The belief that society should afford individuals and groups fair treatment and an impartial share of the benefits of society, including its advantages and disadvantages.

social literacy Understanding the law and social norms and values that allow people to coexist productively.

springboards Examples, vignettes, or stories that relate to a topic being studied and that allow students to connect to the topic through an emotive response.

story model A holistic model to guide the examination of personal values and goals.

strands The big ideas or central concepts around which a discipline is organized.

systems and structures The cluster of concepts that relates to patterns in our environment and in our society.

"thin" questions Questions that are closed and have a specific answer; they are lower-order questions and usually open to a single perspective.

topic elaboration The sequential application of a series of questions that require connected inquiries to develop a topic.

transaction Arrangement of new learning by providing learning skills instruction.

transformation Arrangement of learning experiences that immerse the student in actively investigating ideas to guide them to expand (assimilate) or revise (accommodate) existing schema.

transmission The delivery of curriculum knowledge by the teacher as teller of knowledge.

universal design for instruction A design for effective classroom instruction that respects the needs of all learners, including those with special needs.

References

Allington, R.L., & Johnston, P.H. (2002). *Reading to learn: Lessons from exemplary fourth-grade classrooms*. New York: The Guilford Press.

Angelo, T.A. (1995). Beginning the dialogue: Thoughts on promoting critical thinking: Classroom assessment for critical thinking. *Teaching of Psychology*, 22(1), 6–7.

Auger, W. & Rich, S. (2007). Curriculum theory and methods. Mississauga: Wiley and Sons Ltd.

Balaban, N. (1995). Seeing the child, knowing the person. In Ayers, W. *To become a teacher*. New York: Teachers College Press.

Banks, J.A., Banks, C.A.M., Cortés, C.E., Hahn, C.L., Merryfield, M.M., Moodley, K.A., et al. (2005). *Democracy and diversity: Principles and concepts for educating citizens in a global age*. Seattle: Center for Multicultural Education, University of Washington.

Barton, K. & McCully, A. (2007). Teaching controversial issues: Where controversial issues really matter. *Teaching History*, 127. Ireland: The Historical Association.

Bennett, B., & Rolheiser, C. (2001). *Beyond Monet: The artful science of instructional integration*. Toronto, Ontario: Bookation, Inc.

Bernhardt, E., Destino, T., Kamil, M. & Rodriguez-Munoz, M. (1995). Assessing science knowledge in an English/Spanish bilingual elementary school. *Cognosos*, 4, 4–6.

Bernstein, B. (1972). A critique of the concept of "compensatory education." In C.B. Caxden, V. John, and D. Hymes (Eds.), *Functions of language in the classroom*. New York: Teachers College Press.

Beyer, B.K. (1995). *Critical thinking*. Bloomington, IN: Phi Delta Kappa Educational Foundation.

Biskup, P. (Ed.). (1974). *Australian law*. Australia: McGraw Hill.

Boler, M. (1994). All speech is not free: The ethics of "affirmative action pedagogy." In M. Boler (Ed.), *Democratic dialogues in education: Troubling speech, disturbing silence* (p. 19). New York: Peter Lang.

Borich, G. (2008). *Observation skills for effective teaching* (5th ed.). New Jersey: Pearson Education Inc.

Boykoff Baron, J. (1989). Whole assessment: Moving toward assessing thinking in situ. Paper presented at the Second National Conference on Assessing Thinking, Baltimore.

Boykoff Baron, J., Forgione, P.D. & Rindone, D. (1991, March). Performance-based assessment at the state level: Developing and implementing high school mathematics and science assessments. Paper presented at the American Educational Research Association Annual Meeting, Chicago.

Brandt, R.S. & Tyler, R.W. (2003). Goals and objectives. In A.C. Ornstein, L.S. Behar-Horenstein, & E.F. Pajak (Eds.), *Contemporary issues in curriculum* (3rd ed.) (pp. 10–19). Boston, MA: Pearson Education, Inc.

Breaux, A. & Whitaker, T. (2006). *Seven simple secrets: What the best teachers know and do*. New York: Eye on Education.

Broer, N., Aarnoutse, C. Kieviet, F., & Van Leeuwe, J. (2002). The effects of instructing the structural aspects of text. *Educational Studies*, 28 (3), 213–238.

Bruner, J. (1960). *The process of education*. Cambridge, Mass.: Harvard University Press.

Bruner, J. (1966). *Toward a theory of instruction*. Cambridge, Mass.: Belkapp Press.

Bruner, J. (1996). *The culture of education*. Cambridge, Mass.: Harvard University Press.

Brunner, C.B. & Tally, W. (1999). *The new media literacy handbook: An educator's guide to bringing new media into the classroom*. New York: Anchor Books.

Byrom, J., Counsell, C., & Riley, M. (1997). *Medieval minds: Britain 1066–1500*. England: Pearson Education Limited.

Campbell, C., Comper, J., & Winton, S. (2007). Successful and sustainable practices for raising student achievement in literacy and numeracy. *Changing Perspectives*, 31–35.

Campbell, J. R., Kapinus, B.A., & Beatty, A.S. (1995). Interviewing children about their literacy experiences: Data from NAEP's Integrated Reading Performance Record (IRPR) at Grade 4. Washington, DC: National Center for Educational Statistics.

Campbell, J.R., Hombo, C.M. & Mazzeo, J. (2000). *NAEP 1999 trends in academic progress*. Washington, DC: National Center for Education Statistics.

Campione, J. (1981). Learning, academic achievement, and instruction. Paper delivered at the second annual conference on Reading Research of Center for the Study of Testing, Evaluation, and Educational Policy, Boston College.

Case, R. (2008). Four principles of authentic assessment. In R. Case, & P. Clark (Eds.) *The Canadian anthology of social studies* (pp. 319–328). Vancouver: Pacific Educational Press.

Case, R., & Clark, P. (Eds.). (1999). *The Canadian anthology of social studies*. Vancouver: Pacific Educational Press.

Case, R., & Clark, P. (2004). Four purposes of citizenship education. In R. Case, & P. Clark (Eds.), *The Canadian anthology of social studies* (pp. 17–28). Vancouver: Pacific Educational Press.

Cassidy, W. (2004). Law and social studies: Preparing students for citizenship. In A. Sears, & I. Wright (Eds.), *Challenges and prospects for Canadian social studies* (pp. 126–137). Vancouver: Pacific Educational Press.

Center for Critical Thinking (1996). Three definitions of critical thinking. Available **www.criticalthinking.org/University/univlibrary/library.nclk.**

Chamberlin, C., & Glassford, L. (1999). Activism in social studies: The Chamberlin/Glassford exchange. In R. Case, & P. Clark (Eds.), *The Canadian anthology of social studies* (pp. 255–264). Vancouver: Pacific Educational Press.

Chapman, J.W. & Tunmer, W.E. (1997). A longitudinal study of beginning reading achievement and reading self-concept. *British Journal of Educational Psychology, 67,* 279–291.

Chen, Z. (2007). Learning to map: Strategy discovery and strategy change in young children. *Developmental Psychology. 43* (2): 386–403.

Chiodo, J.J., & Byford, J. (2004). Do they really dislike social studies? A study of middle school and high school students. *Journal of Social Studies Research, 28*(1), 16–26.

Clark, P. (1999). Between the covers: Exposing images in social studies textbooks. In R. Case, & P. Clark (Eds.) *The Canadian anthology of social studies: Issues and strategies for teachers.* Vancouver: Pacific Educational Press. 339–348.

Clark, P. (2004). The historical context of social studies in English Canada. In A. Sears, & I. Wright (Eds.), *Challenges and prospects for Canadian social studies (pp. 17–37).* Vancouver: Pacific Educational Press.

Clifford, P., & Friesen, S. (2007). Creating essential questions. **www.galileo.org/tips/essential_questions.html.** Retrieved February 15, 2007.

Coiro, J. (2003). Exploring literacy on the internet: Reading comprehension on the internet: Expanding our understanding of reading comprehension to encompass new literacies. *The Reading Teacher, 56,* 458–464.

Crooks, T.J. (1988). The impact of classroom evaluation practices on students. *Review of Educational Research, 58,* 438–481.

Crossa, V. (2005). Converting the "small stories" into "big" ones: A response to Susan Smith's "States, markets and an ethic of care." *Political Geography, 24,* 29–34.

Cruxton, J.B. (1998). *Discovering castle days.* Don Mills, ON: Oxford University Press.

Curtis, C.K. & Shaver, J.P. (1980). Slow learners as the study of contemporary problems. *Social Education, 44,* 302–309.

Darling-Hammond, L. & Bransford, J. (Eds.) (2005). *Preparing teachers for a changing world: What teachers should learn and be able to do.* San Francisco: Jossey-Bass, John Wiley and Sons.

Delany, P. & Landow, G.P. (Eds.). (1991). *Hypermedia and literacy studies.* Cambridge, MA: MIT Press.

Dewey, J. (1928). Freedom in workers' education. In *The later works of John Dewey, 1925–1953* (v. 5). Carbondale, IL: South Illinois University Press.

Dhand, H. (1999). The source method to teach social studies.. In R. Case, & P. Clark (Eds.), *The Canadian anthology of social studies.* Vancouver: Pacific Educational Press.

Donohue, G. Creating SMART Goals. June 25, 2006. **www.topachievement.com/smart.html**. Accessed August 3, 2010.

Donovan, C. (2001). Children's development and control of written story and informational genres: Insights from one elementary school. *Research in the Teaching of English*, 35,394–447.

Drake, S.M., Bebbington, J., Laksman, S., Mackie, P., Maynes, N., & Wayne, L. (1992) *Developing an integrated curriculum using the story model*. Toronto: University of Toronto Press.

Dreher, M.J. (2003). Motivating struggling readers by tapping the potential of information books. *Reading & Writing Quarterly*, 19, 25–38.

Drennon, C., (2005) Teaching geographic information systems in a problem-based learning environment. *Journal of Geography in Higher Education*, 29, 3, 385–402.

Duke, N. & Pearson, N. (2002). Effective practices for developing reading comprehension. In A. Farstrup & S. Samuels (Eds.), *What research has to say about reading instruction* (3rd ed., pp 2-5-252). Newark, DE: International Reading Association.

Duke, N. (2000). 3.6 minutes per day. The scarcity of informational text in first grade. *Reading Research Quarterly*, 35, 202–224.

Duke, N.K., Bennett-Armistead,V.S., & Roberts, E.G. (2003). *Filling the great void: Why we should bring non-fiction into the early-grade classroom*. Washington, DC: American Educator.

Duke, N.K. and Kayes, J. (1998). "Can I say "once upon a time?"; Kindergarten children developing knowledge of information book language. *Early Childhood Research Quarterly*, 13, 295–318.

Duke, N.K., Martineau, J.A., Frank, K.A., Bennett-Armistead, V.S. (2003). 33.6 minutes a day: The impact of including more informational text in first grade. Michigan State. Unpublished manuscript.

Durkin, D. (2004). *Teaching them to read*, (6th ed.) Boston, MA: Pearson Education.

Dymock, S. (2005). Teaching expository text structure awareness. *The Reading Teacher*, 59, 177–181.

Eagleton, M.B. & Guinee, K. (2002). *Strategies for supporting student inquiry*. New England Reading Association, 38(2).

Egan, K. (1989). Layers of historical understanding. *Theory and Research in Social Education*, 17(4), 280–294.

Eisenberg M., & Berkowitz, R.E. (1997). The big six and electronic resources: A natural fit. *Book Report*, 16 (2), 15, 22. (EJ 550 884).

Eisenberg, M.B., & Berkowitz, R.E. (1999). *Teaching information and technology skills: The big 6 in elementary schools*. Worthington, OH: Linworth Publishing.

Elbow, P. (1973). Appendix essay. The doubting game and the believing game: An analysis of the intellectual process (pp. 147–191). In P. Elbow (Ed.) *Writing without teachers*. New York: Oxford University Press.

Engel, C. (1991). Not just a method but a way of learning. In D. Bond & G. Feletti (Eds), *The challenge of problem-based learning* (pp. 23–33). New York: St. Martin's Press.

Evans, M., & Hundley, I. (2004). Instructional approaches in social studies education: From "what to teach" to "how to teach" (pp. 218–235). In A. Sears, & I. Wright (Eds.), *Challenges and prospects for Canadian social studies*. Vancouver: Pacific Educational Press.

Evans, R.M. & Passe, J. (2007). *Dare we make peace: A dialogue on the social studies wars*. Philadelphia: Heldref Publications.

Friesen, J.W. (1999). Establishing objectives for a multicultural program. In Case R. and Clark, P. (Eds.), *The Canadian anthology of social studies*. Vancouver: Pacific Educational Press.

Fullan, M., Hill, P., & Crevola, C. (2006). *Breakthrough*. Thousand Oaks, CA: Corwin Press.

Gagnon, C.W.J. & Colley, M. (2001). *Designing for learning: Six elements in constructivist classrooms*. Thousand Oaks, CA: Corwin Press.

Gardner, H. (1983). *Frames of mind: The theory of multiple intelligences*. New York: Basic Books.

Garrett, M. (2004). *Orienteering and map games for teachers*. U.S. Orienteering Federation.

Gibson, S. (2009). *Teaching social studies in elementary schools: A social constructivist approach*. Toronto: Nelson Education.

Goldenson, D.R. (1978). An alternative view about the role of secondary school in political socialization: A field experimental study of the development of civil liberties attitudes. *Theory and Research in Social Education*, 6, 44–72.

Goodland, J.I. (1984). *A place called school*. New York: McGraw-Hill.

Gordon, S. (2008). Digital wisdom inc. Cartographic map symbols. **www.map-symbol.com/?gclid=CL6hmeyrjZ4CFdx05Qodn2cVog**, accessed November 15, 2009.

Goulet, L. (2001). Two teachers of Aboriginal students: Effective practice in sociohistorical realities. *Canadian Journal of Native Education*, 25, 68–81.

Grossman, P., Schoenfeld, A., & Lee, C. (2005). Teaching subject matter. In Darling-Hammond, L. & Bransford, J. (Eds.), *Preparing teachers for a changing world* (201–231). San Francisco: Jossey-Bass.

Hall, K., Sabey, B., & McClellan, M. (2005). Expository text comprehension: Helping primary-grade teachers use expository text to full advantage. *Reading Psychology*, 26, 211–234.

Hargraves, S. (1999). Peace education: Politics in the classroom. In R. Case, & P. Clark (Eds.), *The Canadian anthology of social studies*. Vancouver: Pacific Educational Press.

Harvey, S. (2002). Non-fiction inquiry: Using real reading and writing to explore the world. *Language Arts*, 80, 12–22.

Harwood, A.M. & Hahn, C.L. (1990). *Controversial issues in the classroom*. (Report No. ED 327 453). Washington, D.C.: Office of Educational Research and Improvement.

Hein, L., & Selden, M. (2000). *Censoring history: Citizenship and memory in Japan, Germany and the United States*. Armonk, NY: M.E. Sharpe.

Henry, L. (2010) **http://lorihenry.ca/http:/lorihenry.ca/08/wikwemikong-cultural-festival-pow-wow-ontario/**, accessed August 3, 2010.

Hess, D. & Posselt, J. (2002). How high school students experience and learn from the discussion of controversial public issues. *Journal of Curriculum and Supervision*, 17 (4), 283–314.

Hine, L. (1999). **www.spartacus.schoolnet.co.uk/IRhine.htm**, accessed August 3, 2010.

Horton, T. (1999). Forms of dimension-based strands. In R. Case, & P. Clark (Eds.), *The Canadian anthology of social studies*. Vancouver: Pacific Educational Press.

Hughes., & Sears, A. (2004). Situated learning and anchored instruction as vehicles for social education (pp. 259–273). In A. Sears, & I. Wright (Eds.), *Challenges and prospects for Canadian social studies*. Vancouver: Pacific Educational Press.

Hurren, Wanda (2004). *School geography and academic geography: Spaces of possibility for teaching and learning*. Pacific Educational Press, Vancouver.

Jackson, L. (2008). Dialogic pedagogy for social justice: A critical examination. **www.springerlink.com/content/a81012v2316n1628/**, accessed January 29, 2008.

Jansen, B. (2009). Differentiating instruction in the primary grades with the big 6. *Library Media Connection*. January/February.

Johnson, D.W. & Johnson, R.T. (2009). An educational psychology success story: Social interdependence theory and cooperative learning. *Educational Researcher*, 38 (5), 365–379.

Kagan, M., & Kagan, S. **www.teach.nology.com/currenttrends/cooperativelearning/kagan**, accessed August 3, 2010.

Kagan, M., & Kagan, S. **www.kaganonline.com**, accessed August 4, 2010.

Kagan, S. (1994). Cooperative learning. San Clemente: Kagan Publishing & Professional Development.

Kelly, T.E. (1986) Discussing controversial issues: Four perspectives on the teacher's role. *Theory and Research in Social Education*, v14 n2 p113–38

Kern, D., Andre,W., Schilke, R., Barton, J., & McGuire, M.C. (2003). Less is more: Preparing students for state writing assessments. *The Reading Teacher*, 56, 816–827.

Kirman, J.M. (2008). *Elementary social studies: Creative classroom ideas*. Toronto: Pearson Education Canada.

Kober, N. (2001). *It takes more than testing: Closing the achievement gap*. Washington, DC: Center on Education Policy.

Kohn, A. (1990). *The brighter side of human nature*. New York: Houghton Mifflin Company.

Latz, A., Spiers-Neumeister, K.L., Adams, C. & Pierce, R. (2009). *Peer coaching to improve differentiation: Perspectives from project CLUE*. Roeper Review, Routledge Taylor & Francis Group, 31:27–39.

Levesque, S. (2004). History and social studies in Quebec: An historical perspective (Chapter 3). In A. Sears, & I. Wright (Eds.), *Challenges and prospects for Canadian social studies*. Vancouver: Pacific Educational Press.

Lingard, B;, Ladwig, J., & Luke, A. (1998). School effects in postmodern conditions (pp. 84–100). In Slee, R., Tomlinson, S. & Weiner, G. *Effective for whom? School effectiveness and the school improvement movement*. London: Falmer Press.

Madaus, G.F., West, M.M., Harmon, M.C., Lomax, R.G., & Viator, K.A. (1992). *The influence of testing on teaching math and science in grades 4–12: Executive summary*. Chestnut Hill, MA: Boston College Press.

Maeroff, G.I. (1991). *Assessing authentic assessment*. Phi Delta Kappan, 72, 273–281.

Mager, R. F. (1962). *Preparing instructional objectives*. Belmont, California: Lear Siegler, Ltd.

Marinak, B., & Gambrell, L. (2008). Elementary informational text structure: A research review. *The International Journal of Reading*, 15 (9), 75–83.

Martone, A. & Sireci, S. (2009). Evaluating alignment between curriculum, assessment, and instruction. *Review of Educational Research*, 79:4. 1332–1361.

McKay, R., & Gibson, S. (1999). *Reshaping the future of social studies*. Edmonton: Alberta Learning.

McCall, A. (2006). Supporting exemplary social studies teaching in elementary schools. *Social Studies*, 97(4), 161–167.

McKenna, M.C., Ellsworth, R.A., & Kear, D.J. (1995). Children's attitudes towards reading: A national survey. *Reading Research Quarterly*, 30, 934–956.

Meyers, M. (2006). *Curriculum speak*. Toronto: Mainstream Publications.

Miller, J.P. (1983). *The educational spectrum: Orientations to curriculum*. New York: Longman.

Misco, T. & Patterson, N. (2007). The study of pre-service teachers' conceptualizations of academic freedom and controversial issues. *Theory and Research in Social Education*. 35 (4), 520–550.

Morantz, A. (2002). *Where is here? Canada's maps and the stories they tell*. Toronto: Penguin.

Mortimore, P. and Whitty, G. (1997). Can school improvement overcome the effects of disadvantage? London, Institute of Education, Occasional Paper.

Moss, B. (2004). Teaching expository text structures through information trade book retellings. *The Reading Teacher*, 57, 710–718.

Neufeld, P. (2005). Comprehension instruction in content area classes. *The Reading Teacher*, 59(4), 302–312.

Newmann, F.M. & Wehlage, G.G. (1993). Five standards of authentic instruction. *Educational Leadership*, 50, 8–12.

Nickell, P. (1992). Doing the stuff of social studies: A conversation with Grant Wiggins. *Social Education*, 56(2), 91–94.

Noddings, N. (2003). *Caring: A feminine approach to ethics and moral education* (2nd ed.) Berkeley: University of California Press.

Obenchain, K. & Morris, R. (2007). *50 social studies strategies for K-8 classrooms*. New Jersey: Pearson Education Inc.

Ontario. Ministry of Education. (2005). Education for all: The report of the expert panel on literacy and numeracy instruction for students with special education needs, kindergarten to grade 6. Toronto: Author.

Ontario. Ministry of Education. (2009). Learning for all K-12 Draft. Toronto: Author.

Ornstein et al. (2003). *Curriculum: Foundations, principles, and issues*. Massachusetts: Allyn & Bacon.

Orr, J. (2004). Teaching social studies for understanding first nations issues. In Sears, A. & Wright, I. (Eds.) *Challenges and prospects for Canadian social studies*. Vancouver: Pacific Educational Press.

Ozel, A. (2009). The practice of information processing model in the teaching of cognitive strategies. *Journal of Instructional Psychology*, 36(1): 59–68.

Palinscar, A. & Duke, N. (2004). The role of text and text-reader interactions in young children's reading development and achievement. *The Elementary School Journal*, 105(2), 183–197.

Pappas, C. (1993). Is narrative 'primary"? Some insights from kindergarteners' pretend readings of stories and information books. *Journal of Reading Behaviour*, 25, 97–129.

Parker, W. (1989) How students learn history and geography. *Educational Leadership*, 47(3) 39–43.

Pearson, P.D., & Gallagher, M.C. (1983). The instruction of reading comprehension. *Contemporary Educational Psychology*, 8(3), 317–44.

Pike, K., & Mumper, J. (2004). *Making nonfiction and other informational texts come alive*. New York: Pearson Education Inc.

Pressley, M., Allington, R.L., Wharton-McDonald, R., Collins Block, C., & Morrow, L.M. (2001). *Learning to read: Lessons from exemplary first-grade classrooms*. New York: The Guilford Press.

Purcell-Gates, V. (1988). Lexical and syntactic knowledge of written narrative held by well-read-to kindergarten and second graders. *Research in the Teaching of English, 22,* 128–160.

Purcell-Gates, V., McIntyre, E., & Freppon, P. (1995). Learning written storybook language in school: A comparison of low-SES children in skills-based and whole language classrooms. *American Educational Research Journal, 32,* 659–685.

Ray, K.W. (2004). Why Cauley writes well: A close look at what a difference good teaching can make. *Language Arts, 82,* 100–109.

Rayner, R. & Pollatsek, A. (1989). *The psychology of reading*. Englewood Cliffs, New Jersey: Prentice-Hall.

Reithaug, D. (1992). Naturalistic assessment: Capturing success in reading. *Research Forum, 9,* 46–50.

Remy, R.C. (1972). High school seniors' attitudes toward their civics and government instruction. *Social Education, 36,* 590–597.

Resnick, L.B. & Resnick, D.P. (1991). Assessing the thinking curriculum: New tools for educational reform (pp. 37–75). In B.R. Gifford and M.C. O'Connor (Eds.), *Future assessments: Changing views of aptitude, achievement, and instruction*. Boston: Kluwer Academic.

Reynolds, R. Understanding the nature of reading comprehension, basic research and instructional implications. **www.sprakaloss.se/reinolds_englich.htm**, accessed August 3, 2010.

Richgels, D., Megee, L., Lomax, R., & Sheard, C. (1987). Awareness of four text structures: Effects on recall of expository text. *Reading Research Quarterly, 22,* 97–129.

Roach, A.T., Niebling, B.C. & Kurz, A. (2008). Evaluating the alignment among curriculum, instruction, and assessments: Implications and applications for research and practice. *Psychology in the Schools, 45,*158–176.

Rosenshine, B. (1997). *The case for explicit, teacher-led, cognitive strategy instruction*. Chicago: American Educational Research Association.

Scriven, M. (1996). Types of evaluation and types of evaluator. *Evaluation Practice, 17*(2), 367–382.

Sears, A. (1999). Using interviews in social studies. In Case R. and Clark, P. (Eds.) *The Canadian anthology of social studies*. Vancouver: Pacific Educational Press.

Sears, A. (2004). In search of good citizens: Citizenship education and social studies in Canada. In A. Sears, & I. Wright (Eds.), *Challenges and prospects for Canadian social studies* (pp. 90–106). Vancouver: Pacific Educational Press.

Seixas, P. (1999). Making sense of the past in a multi-cultural classroom. In Case R. and Clark, P. (Eds.) *The Canadian anthology of social studies*. Vancouver: Pacific Educational Press.

Shepard, L.A. (2003). Reconsidering large-scale assessment to heighten its relevance to learning. In J.M. Atkin, J. Coffey, and National Science Teachers' Association (Eds.), *Everyday assessment in the science classroom* (pp. 121–146). Arlington: NSTA Press.

Shepard, L.A. et al (2005). Assessment. In L. Darling-Hammond, J. Bransford (Eds.), *Preparing teachers for a changing world* (pp. 275–326). San Francisco, CA: Jossey-Bass.

Shields, P.N., & Ramsay, D. (2004). Social studies across English Canada (pp. 38–54). In A. Sears, & I. Wright (Eds.), *Challenges and prospects for Canadian social studies*. Vancouver: Pacific Educational Press.

Shulman, L.S. (1987). Knowledge and teaching: Foundations of the new reform. *Harvard Educational Review, 57* (1), 1–22.

Slavin, R. (2000). *Educational psychology: Theory and practice* (6th ed.). Englewood Cliffs, New Jersey: Allyn and Bacon.

Smeets, E. & Moojt, T. (2001). Pupil-centred learning, ICT, and teacher behaviour: Observations in educational practice. *British Journal of Educational Technology, 32*(4): 403–417.

Smith, I. (1981). Educational differentiation and curricular guidance: A review. *Educational Studies, 7*(2), 87–94.

Smith, M.K. (1999). "Learning theory," the encyclopedia of informal education. **www.infed.org/biblio/b-learn.htm**, accessed August 4, 2010.

Smith, M.L. & Rottenberg, C. (1991). Unintended consequences of external testing in elementary schools. *Educational Measurement: Issues and Practice*, 10(4), 7–11.

Soalt, J. (2005). Bringing together fictional and informational texts to improve comprehension. *The Reading Teacher*, 58, 680–683.

Statement of Academic Freedom from the U.S. National Council for Social Studies, 2007 **www.socialstudies.org/positions/academicfreedom**, accessed August 3, 2010.

Stead, T. (2006) Reality checks: Teaching reading comprehension with nonfiction K-6. Portland, ME: Stenhouse Publishers.

Stien, D,, & Beed, P.L. (2004). Bridging the gap between fiction and nonfiction in the literature circle setting. *The Reading Teacher*, 57, 510–518.

Sutherland-Smith, W. (2002). Weaving the literacy web: Changes in reading from page to screen. *The Reading Teacher*, 55, 662–669.

Thornton, S.J. (2005). *Teaching social studies that matters*. New York: Teachers College Press.

Torney-Purta, J., Lahman, R., Oswald, H. & Schulz, W. (2002). Citizenship and education in twenty-eight countries. Amsterdam International Association for the Evaluation of Education Achievement. **www.wam.umd.edu.iea**, accessed August 3, 2010.

Tyler, R. (1949). *Basic principles of curriculum and instruction*. Toronto: OISE, University of Toronto.

Venezky, R.L. (1982). The origins of the present day chasm between adult literacy needs and school literacy instruction. *Visible Language*, 16, 112–128.

Vygotsky, L.S. (1929). The problem of the cultural development of the child II. *Journal of Genetic Psychology*, 36, 415–32.

Wigfield, A., Eccles, J.S., Yoon, K.S., Harold, R.D., Arbreton, A. Freedman-Doan, C. &

Blumenfled, P.B. (1997). Changes in children's competence beliefs and subjective task values across the elementary school years: A three-year study. *Journal of Educational Psychology*, 89, 451–469.

Wiggins, G. (1990). *The case for authentic assessment*. Washington, DC: Office of Educational Research and Improvement (Ed.).

Wiggins, G.P. & McTighe, J. (1998). *Understanding by design*. Upper Saddle River, NJ: Prentice Hall.

Williams, J., Hall, K., & Lauer, K. (2004). Teaching expository text structure to young at-risk readers: Building the basics of comprehension instruction. *Exceptionality*, 12 (3), 129–144.

Williams, J., Hall, K., Lauer, K., Stafford, B., DeSisco, L., & DeCani, J. (2005). Expository text comprehension in the primary classroom. *Journal of Educational Psychology*, (97) 4, 538–550.

Williams, T.L. (2009). A framework for nonfiction in the elementary grades. *Literacy Research and Instruction*, 48: 247–263.

Willms, J.D. (2006). Learning divides: Ten policy questions about the performance and equity of schools and schooling systems. Report prepared for UNESCO Institute for Statistics.

www.ammsa.com/publications/windspeaker

Woods, B. (2001). Viscount School Cluster. Inquiry Learning.doc **http://eastnet.wikispaces.com/file/view/inquiry_learning.doc**.

Yeager, E., & Patterson, M. (Eds.). (1996). Teacher-directed social action in a middle school classroom. *Social Studies and the Young Learner*. 8 (4), 29–31.

Yopp, R.H., & Yopp, H.K. (2004). Preview-predict-confirm: Thinking about the language and content of informational text. *The Reading Teacher*, 58, 79–83.

Index